RECONFIGURING FAMILIES
IN CONTEMPORARY VIETNAM

A Series Sponsored by the East-West Center

CONTEMPORARY ISSUES IN ASIA AND THE PACIFIC

John T. Sidel and Geoffrey M. White, Series Co-Editors

A collaborative effort by Stanford University Press and the East-West Center, this series focuses on issues of contemporary significance in the Asia Pacific region, most notably political, social, cultural, and economic change. The series seeks books that focus on topics of regional importance, on problems that cross disciplinary boundaries, and that have the capacity to reach academic and other interested audiences.

The East-West Center is an education and research organization established by the U.S. Congress in 1960 to strengthen relations and understanding among the peoples and nations of Asia, the Pacific, and the United States. The Center contributes to a peaceful, prosperous, and just Asia Pacific community by serving as a vigorous hub for cooperative research, education, and dialogue on critical issues of common concern to the Asia Pacific region and the United States. Funding for the Center comes from the U.S. government, with additional support provided by private agencies, individuals, foundations, corporations, and the governments of the region.

EDITED BY MAGALI BARBIERI
AND DANIÈLE BÉLANGER

Reconfiguring Families
in Contemporary Vietnam

Stanford University Press · *Stanford, California*

Stanford University Press
Stanford, California

Printed in the United States of America on acid-free, archival-quality paper

Library of Congress Cataloging-in-Publication Data
Reconfiguring families in contemporary Vietnam / edited by Magali
Barbieri and Danièle Bélanger.
    p. cm. — (Contemporary issues in Asia and the Pacific)
  Includes bibliographical references and index.
  ISBN 978-0-8047-6057-7 (cloth : alk. paper) — ISBN 978-0-8047-6058-4
(pbk : alk. paper)
    1. Family—Economic aspects—Vietnam—Congresses.   2. Vietnam—
Economic policy—1975—Congresses.   3. Family policy—Vietnam—
Congresses.   4. Social change—Vietnam—Congresses.   I. Barbieri,
Magali.   II. Bélanger, Danièle.   III. Series.
  HQ674.5.R43 2009
  306.8509597′09045—dc22
                                    2008042352

Typeset by Thompson Type in 9.75/13.5 Janson

Contents

Acknowledgments

This volume brings together some of the presentations given at a conference titled "Post-transitional Vietnamese Families: Exploring the Legacy of *Doi Moi*," held in Paris, France, October 21–23, 2004. Generous financial support for the conference was provided by the *Institut National d'Études Démographiques*, France, by the University of Western Ontario (Research Services and the Faculty of Social Science), Canada, and by the French Consulate in Hanoi. Subsequent funding for editorial expenses was provided by the *Institut National d'Études Démographiques* and by the University of Western Ontario.

We wish to take this opportunity to thank all the conference participants, including those whose presentations are absent from this volume. We extend our gratitude to the discussants of the conference sessions, namely Isabelle Attané, Elizabeth Croll, Dang Nguyen Anh, John Kleinen, and Cécile Lefèvre, for their insightful and intellectually stimulating contributions. We are particularly grateful to the authors of this volume who patiently revised their chapters through the multiple-round review process. Remarkable editorial work was carried out by Gale Cassidy and Catriona Dutreuilh, whose behind-the-scene edits and recommendations helped stitch the chapters into a seamless whole. We extend our thanks to Belinda Hammoud who helped with the preparation of the final manuscript. Finally, we greatly benefited from the careful reading and thoughtful and constructive criticism of two anonymous readers during the several stages of revision.

In addition, we wish to express here our gratitude to George Alter for his unfailing encouragement and support during the early stages of this project. We also thank the three Vietnamese artists who exhibited paintings and drawings about families and women at the conference and who helped to make the initial scientific meeting a memorable event. The exhibition of works by these three internationally known Vietnamese artists, Pham Cam Thuong, Dinh Thi Tham, and Le Quoc Viet, was made possible by the unconditional support and dedicated work of Susan Lecht, Director of Art Vietnam, a beautiful art gallery located in Hanoi. Susan Lecht brought their works to Paris herself and gave a presentation on Vietnamese contemporary art to our conference participants. The author and journalist Dana Sachs also contributed her perspective on Vietnamese families by reading significant excerpts from her book *The House on Dream Street: Memoir of an American Woman in Vietnam*, which recounts her experience of living with Vietnamese families in the early 1990s in Hanoi.

Last but not least, we are indebted to the editorial committees at the East-West Center and at Stanford University Press who made the production of this book a smooth process, and we have been fortunate to work with Elisa Johnston, Jessica Walsh, and Stacy Wagner.

Contributors

Magali Barbieri is a researcher for the *Institut national d'études démographiques* in Paris, France. She is the head of the Population and Development Division there. Her Vietnamese experience began in 1993 when she worked as an expert on a number of projects in Hanoi for the United Nations. She is the author of numerous publications on the demographic situation in Vietnam.

Danièle Bélanger is Associate Professor and Canada Research Chair in Population, Gender and Development at the University of Western Ontario, London, Canada. Her research focuses on population, migration, gender, development, family, and reproductive health in Vietnam and other Asian countries. After coediting the book *Gender, Household, State: Doi Moi in Viet Nam*, published by Cornell University in 2002, she is currently working on a manuscript titled *Building Happy Families. Son Preference and Fertility Decline in Vietnam.*

Anil Deolalikar is Professor of Economics and Director of the Public Policy Initiative at the University of California, Riverside. His area of research specialization is economic development. He has published more than fifty articles and three books in the areas of poverty, health, education, and social protection in developing countries. He is coeditor of the *Journal of Asian and African Studies* and the *Journal of Developing Societies,* and is an elected Fellow of the American Association for the Advancement of Science (AAAS).

Rukmalie Jayakody is Associate Professor of Human Development and Family Studies, Sociology, and Demography at Pennsylvania State University. Dr. Jayakody's international research focuses on Vietnam. She is affiliated with the Institute of Sociology in Hanoi, where she currently collaborates with colleagues on a survey of Vietnamese families in the north and south to examine how recent social changes have affected family life.

Le Thi Minh Chau is employed in the Education Division of UNICEF in Hanoi, Vietnam.

Myriam de Loenzien is a researcher for the French *Institut de recherche pour le développement*. From 2002 to 2008, she was based at the Institute for Population and Social Studies (IPSS) of the National Economic University in Hanoi, Vietnam. She has been working on issues of reproductive health and HIV/ AIDS in Sub-Saharan Africa and Southeast Asia since the early 1990s. She has co-edited a book about qualitative approaches in population studies, published in 2006.

Hy Van Luong is Professor of Anthropology at the University of Toronto, Canada. He has published several books on Vietnam, the most recent of which are *Postwar Vietnam: Dynamics of a Transforming Society* (edited volume, 2003); *Tradition, Revolution, and Market Economy in a North Vietnamese Village, 1925–2006* (2009); and *Urbanization, Migration, and Poverty in a Vietnamese Metropolis: Ho Chi Minh City in Comparative Perspectives* (edited volume, 2009). He has been conducting fieldwork on gender, social organization, discourse, political economy, and social capital in Vietnam since 1987.

Nguyen Dinh Chung is a research expert in the General Statistics Office in Hanoi, Vietnam.

Nguyen Duy Khe is the Director of the Department of Reproductive Health in the Ministry of Health in Hanoi, Vietnam.

Nguyen Huu Minh is the Director of the Institute of Family and Gender in Hanoi, Vietnam.

Xavier Oudin is a researcher at the French *Institut de recherche pour le développement*. He is an economist and has conducted extensive research on the informal economic sector and changes in labor markets in developing economies, especially Vietnam and Thailand. He is currently assigned to the

Chiang Mai University in Chiang Mai, Thailand, contributing to a Thai–French project on labor and skills.

Katherine Pendakis is a doctoral candidate in sociology at York University, Toronto, Canada. Her areas of interest include gender, sociological theory, collective memory, oral history, and labor.

Catherine Scornet is Assistant Professor at the Université de Provence, France. Most of her research focuses on the Vietnamese society and, more specifically, on the links between political change and sociodemographic transformations. She lived in Vietnam for more than four years during the 1990s while working on her dissertation, which dealt with the issue of reproductive health and behavior in a rapidly developing Vietnam in collaboration with the National Committee for Human and Social Sciences, Hanoi, Vietnam.

Margaret Sheehan was a Technical Adviser at the World Health Organization office in Hanoi, Vietnam. She is currently at the UNICEF office in Bangkok, Thailand.

Bussarawan Teerawichitchainan is Assistant Professor of Sociology, School of Social Sciences, Singapore Management University. Her areas of interests include poverty, family, gender, health, and human development in Southeast Asia. Her most recent publications are featured in *Social Science and Medicine*, *Population and Development Review*, and the *Journal of Population and Social Studies*.

Truong Huyen Chi is an independent researcher based in Hanoi, Vietnam. She received her Ph.D. in Anthropology from the University of Toronto in 2001 with a dissertation titled "Changing Processes of Social Reproduction in the Northern Vietnamese Countryside: An Ethnographic Study of Dong Vang Village (Red River Delta)." Her current research interests include societies in transition, transnational narratives and memories, and education among the minorities.

Hung Cam Thai is Associate Professor of Sociology and Asian American Studies at Pomona College, Claremont, California. He completed his Ph.D. in Sociology at the University of California at Berkeley. He has conducted research in Vietnam and in the United States, with a special focus on Vietnamese transpacific marriages. His most recent book, *For Better or For Worse: Marriage and Migration in the New Global Economy*, has been published by Rutgers University Press (2008).

Vu Manh Loi is a research expert at the Institute of Sociology in Hanoi, Vietnam.

Vu Tuan Huy, trained as a sociologist, is now the Head of the Family Section in the Institute of Sociology, Vietnam Academy of Social Sciences in Hanoi. His research focuses on family change, gender, marriage, and reproductive behavior. Throughout his career, Vu Tuan Huy has collaborated on multiple scientific projects involving national and international organizations. Most of his publications are in Vietnamese.

Peter Xenos is a Senior Fellow at the East-West Center in Honolulu, Hawaii. He focuses on demographic and social change in Southeast Asia, particularly Vietnam, the Philippines, and Thailand. His recent work has included the design of sample surveys of youth in a number of countries, including Vietnam. He is currently involved in the design of a second Survey and Assessment of Vietnamese Youth (SAVY) for Vietnam.

RECONFIGURING FAMILIES

IN CONTEMPORARY VIETNAM

Chapter One

Introduction

State, Families, and the Making of Transitions in Vietnam

DANIÈLE BÉLANGER AND MAGALI BARBIERI

Vietnamese families have experienced dramatic and transformative events through the country's social, political, and economic history between the colonial period and current times. Indeed, historical benchmarks, such as colonization, independence, socialism, collectivization, the American War, the end of the Cold War, and the transition to a market economy have all resulted in far-reaching changes for family life. At the same time, families, through their agency and the deployment of myriad strategies, have also given shape and direction to these major historical events and social mutations. Among the numerous important events in Vietnam's contemporary history, two dates stand out as particularly significant for Vietnamese families: first, the formation of an independent socialist state in the North in 1954 and, second, the official adoption of a market-oriented economic system in 1986. The respective institutional and moral environments brought about by these two "transitions" meant that families had to adjust, adapt, negotiate, and accommodate to new settings and imperatives of daily life. Several significant events are comingled in these two major transformations. These include the 1945–54 Colonial War, followed by independence and the partition between North and South in 1954, which separated entire families for two decades; the wars fought in Cambodia, against the United States, and at the Chinese border that took millions of men and women away from home either temporarily or permanently; and the end of the American War, followed by reunification in 1975, which opened the internal border and reinvigorated exchanges and migration between the North and the South. This book focuses on the most recent and significant change for families in Vietnam's recent past—the transition to a market economy, referred to as *Doi Moi* in Vietnamese and generally translated as the "renovation." Over two decades have passed since a wide range of institutions were transformed, which reconfigured the ways families produce and reproduce.

The impetus for this book lies in the argument that much of the renovation's accomplishment as an economic transition is attributable to families' strategies in adapting to the new institutional and economic setting. The new economic and political bargain between the state and families prompted families to take a central role in making the Vietnamese transition a success. Put simply, the downsizing of the socialist welfare system and the return of the household as the unit of production and consumption redefined the boundaries between the public and the private. Some other edited collections have examined the widespread implications of the transition to a market economy for Vietnamese society (see Luong 2003; McCargo 2004; Taylor 2004). This volume, however, is the first to utilize a multidisciplinary perspective and to focus exclusively on processes at work in the everyday lives of families and on the implications for gender and intergenerational relations. By focusing on families, this book shifts the spotlight from macrotransformations of the renovation era, orchestrated by those in power, to microlevel transformations, experienced daily in households between husbands and wives, parents and children, and grandparents and other family members. In addition, it is our contention that while a rich body of scholarly work on Vietnamese contemporary society exists, a focus on families can contribute to a better understanding of postsocialist or late socialist capitalism, a shift also experienced by several countries of the world in the aftermath of the Cold War. For this reason, throughout this book, we refer to the renovation as a broad term encompassing not only economic changes but also a wide range of transformations experienced by Vietnamese society and, more particularly, families in many aspects of daily life. It is our hope that the accounts provided in this book will bring to life the significance of *Doi Moi* for families and of families for *Doi Moi*.

Through a multidisciplinary lens, authors of this book constructed their chapters around the following questions: What is the significance of the economic and institutional restructuring for families? How has the elimination of entitlement programs and fully subsidized social services impacted families' modes of organization? Have gender and intergenerational relations been reconfigured by the new institutional setting? What is the significance of increased socioeconomic differentiation and geographic mobility on family relations? How have life-cycle transitions, such as marriage, home leaving, school leaving, and entry into the workforce, changed? How have state-family relations been redefined? Examining these issues from the standpoints of sociology, anthropology, demography, and economics, and using a variety of theoretical and methodological perspectives, authors of this book examine the renovation from the family's viewpoint to take stock of two decades of family life in late socialism.[1] In sum, this book brings together chapters with a common focus on "families" and transcends disciplinary boundaries in order to shed light on fundamental social processes that define contemporary Vietnamese society.

This introductory chapter summarizes the contributions of this book to the recent literature on contemporary Vietnam. First, we discuss the "transition" period from socialism to capitalism that this book focuses on. Second, we introduce the conceptual and theoretical perspectives that bring the chapters together. Third, we examine family changes in presocialist and prerenovation times. Fourth, we place families in the context of *Doi Moi* and present the major themes emerging from this book. Our readership includes those who share an interest in families in developing Asia, in postsocialist societies, and in Vietnam.

The Contested Terrains of "Transition" and "Renovation"

One danger of dissecting Vietnam's history using the disputed concept of "transition" as a departure point for examining society lies in the perils of making recent history "begin" with capitalism in the late socialist era. The collapse of communist regimes in Europe and Russia generated a new research area in the social sciences—postsocialism or postcommunism—that is concerned with the causes and implications of the "transition" to new social, political, and economic structures (Bonker, Muller, and Pickel 2002; Pickles and Smith 1998). Some critics have called the transition concept "a construct of the West" (Bersegian 2000), implying a "rescue scenario" from the economic failure and political oppression of communism to the promises of the market economy and freedom of liberal democracies (Berdahl 2000). In short, evolutionary assumptions often impregnate the language and discussion around the "transition." Several authors have scrutinized the assumption that the renovation was the turning point for families. Scholarly work on Asian states that abandoned the socialist soviet-style economy reached Western audiences after the end of the Cold War and thus heavily emphasized the transition. In the 1990s, international collaboration and funding allowed the development of a new wave of research in Vietnam, including projects and surveys on family issues. In the bulk of firsthand research on Vietnam conducted since the early 1990s, the transition has prompted much research and been conceived as necessarily entailing change.[2] While this departure point is generally taken for granted in scholarly work on Vietnam,[3] one of our objectives is to step back and view families in their historical context to situate "change" in a wider perspective.

In this respect, we consider that the so-called "transition" is far from being an entirely abrupt transformation in all arenas of social life. In fact, the renovation partly legitimized processes under way for some years: the state had no choice but to legalize and accelerate a de facto situation. In other words, to conceptualize that political leaders and international actors essentially concocted and imposed the transition on the country is to ignore the power of local and daily politics to redefine and redirect national objectives (Kerkvliet 2005). In nations that experienced open, or even revolutionary, processes, this fact is perhaps evident. In the cases of China and Vietnam, where limited public contestation took place before the official dismantling of the communist economy, it is less so. Kerkvliet's look at agriculture has vividly brought to light the importance of local contestation and adaptation that preceded the abandonment of the socialist economic system (Kerkvliet 2005). His examination of the role played by local-level politics in the abandonment of collective agriculture powerfully illustrates how at least a decade of resistance and local initiatives undermined and weakened collectives to the point that they were no longer viable in the early 1980s. We echo this argument in the sphere of families. The state's approach to family matters had to adapt to processes of resistance and negotiation in which families actively engaged. Family practices antedating the official renovation of the economy included a vibrant underground private petty trade; families' contestations of state involvement in marriage, divorce, and reproduction; and the maintenance of presocialist worldviews and rituals in family daily life. Part of the difficulty here, nonetheless, lies in the dearth of research examining family strategies and practices prior to the abandonment of the socialist planned economy.

While maintaining our awareness of the complex meaning of the renovation and sharing a desire to avoid preconceived "impacts" and "consequences" of this process on families, the chapters of this book, together, indicate that, on the one hand, the late 1980s and 1990s did encompass fundamental changes that have altered family relations, practices, and behaviors. Based on firsthand fieldwork and the analysis of existing data, the authors document and discuss how the transformation of the institutional and economic settings affected family relations. For instance, a new organization of work, both in the urban and agricultural areas, assigned new roles to households and families, entailing new modes of sharing and collaborating (see Danièle Bélanger and Katherine Pendakis, Truong Huyen Chi, Hy Van Luong, and Xavier Oudin, this volume). On the other hand, this book shows how families are both core and stable institutions, that retained and reinvented old ways in an attempt to mediate and attenuate the speed of change imposed, in part, by internal and international forces. As leading family historian Tamara Hareven contends, families are both agents of change and custodians of tradition (Hareven 2000). Research on Vietnam has documented the revival and adaptation of presocialist rituals and symbolism, since the early 1990s, and shows how families never really abandoned these practices during the decades in which they were discouraged, if not prohibited (Luong 1993; Malarney 2002). Thus, families—as the guardians of practices and symbols—can actively contest change and retain values. Through processes of contestation, adaptation, resistance, and negotiation, families turned the transition into a daily reality (Perry and Selden 2000). Together, chapters of this book provide compelling evidence that the reforms have had a far-reaching impact on families. At the same time, they vividly illustrate how families propelled and made possible the transition, while living in continuity with the past. One observation emerging from this volume is that Vietnamese families are complex and connected entities that reflect actively and strategically.

In addition to being cautious about the meaning of the economic transformations for families, we apprehend the reforms of 1986 in a broad sense. Indeed, the political shift that accompanied the economic transition, and the changes in daily lives that were brought about by this political change, have often been neglected in research (An and Tréglodé 2003). Since the 1980s, the Communist Party has abandoned many mechanisms previously devoted to the promotion of the socialist ideology and to the close surveillance of its citizens. The nation's insertion into the global economy and the maintenance of a political status quo within the country are examples of how resources have been mobilized to other ends. In family daily life, these changes have translated into a reduced need to comply with norms, including family norms, imposed by Communist Party lines. Outdoor speakers that used to educate peasants in villages about socialist ideology practice and imperatives are still utilized today, but for other purposes. In rural communities, for instance, private recruitment agencies enter villages to enroll peasants as international migrant workers bound for Japan, South Korea, Malaysia, or Taiwan and "advertise" their need for (cheap) labor using the community speakers. The public speakers (*loa*), which are emblematic of Vietnam's communist history, are found in many localities of the country (particularly in the North) and now serve a capitalist order. While the country has not experienced a collapse of its communist regime, like the former Union of Soviet Socialist Republics (USSR) and countries in Eastern Europe, the development of capitalist modes of production and consumption has profoundly altered the political state-family relations in Vietnam. This shift in political relations between the state and its citizens constitutes a central element of recent social change in Vietnamese society (Kerkvliet 2003).

Theoretical Lines of Inquiry and Contributions

FAMILY AGENCY

Another objective of this collection is to move family theory forward using Vietnam, taken here as a developing country of Southeast Asia and as an example of a socialist country that experienced a recent transition to capitalism and became an increasingly globalized and connected nation. In this regard, we conceive of families primarily as active agents of social change. The concept of agency is central to contemporary sociology; however, the focus is primarily on individual agency. Edgar argues that we need to shift our attention to families because "it is not the individual that acts reflexively; it is the family which mediates the impact of globalization, community resources and government action for and with individuals acting as part of a sharing, interactive unit" (Edgar 2004, 4). Thus, he puts forward the concept of family agency as being the driving force behind social change, particularly in developing societies "where life chances are largely constrained by family background, networks and values" (Edgar 2004, 3). For family theory to become relevant to non-Western societies, Edgar contends that a reassessment of family theory, a theoretical body fraught with a Western bias, is required. A critique of existing family theory that considers the individual above the family and the call for reversing this order is particularly relevant in the case of Vietnam. The conceptualization of families as central, mediating agents of social change and globalization informs this introduction as well as the analyses presented in this book. Indeed, the following chapters point to the centrality of agency, resilience, and adaptation in understanding Vietnamese families. This agency, however, manifests itself in a context that shapes the space in which families have to adjust, negotiate, and strategize.

FAMILY IDEALIZED MORALITY

In an attempt to develop family theory relevant for the study of Asian societies, family theorist Peter McDonald has put forward the concept of a "family idealized morality." A "family idealized morality is embedded within the belief structure of what is proper family behavior and "this belief structure will have developed over a long period of the society's history" (McDonald 1994, 22). Furthermore, McDonald postulates that an idealized family morality exists within all societies but with large variations in the "degree to which deviation from that ideal is considered permissible" (McDonald 1994, 22). He further argues that, in societies where the idealized family morality is strictly enforced and little deviation is allowed, those in power can transform the prevailing idealized morality only through a redefinition of formal institutions.

In this argument, McDonald draws our attention to the fundamental importance of ideologies and belief systems in capturing the intensity and direction of family change. His theoretical proposition emerges from the failure of convergence and modernization theories to predict family change in the developing world, and, more specifically, in Southeast and East Asia. Indeed, modernization theory typically examines changes in the characteristics of individuals to infer changes in the family and broader society. This approach, however, has failed to predict many features of contemporary families in Asian societies (Vervoorn 1998, 180). For instance, family theory predicted the nuclearization of Asian families with socioeconomic development;

however, the most recent data indicate that, of all continents, Asia has the smallest proportion of elderly living alone (below 7 percent) and the highest proportion of elderly living with an adult child (70 percent) (United Nations 2005). Such trends refute the idea that all societies will necessarily follow a Western model. In this example, the dominant idealized family morality of children being responsible for their elderly parents continues to be the norm. This is the case in Vietnam (see Magali Barbieri, this volume), as in the other Asian countries (Cho and Yada 1994; Mason, Tsuya, and Choe 1998). Nevertheless, individual preferences alone cannot explain this phenomenon. This idealized morality of the intergenerational contract is, in part, created by the absence, or the weakness, of a public welfare system that takes responsibility for the elderly segment of the population.[4] Japan, where women's difficulties in reconciling work and motherhood lead to very low fertility, is a case in point that illustrates the tension created by a certain family's idealized morality. Unless political leaders put forward a different family model through discourse and policies, the current idealized family morality—including a very clear-cut gender division of labor in families—is likely to survive.

Fertility is a good example of recent theoretical development in family-related behaviors and practices. In contrast to most approaches that focus on individual level "factors" and "determinants," recent anthropological and sociological work has called for a consideration of the global, national, and local politics of power and gender relations in the shaping of reproductive behavior in families (Ginsburg and Rapp 1991, 1995; Greenhalgh 1995). The role of the state in shaping family behavior and norms with respect to reproduction has been the thrust of Greenhalgh's work on China. Through a political economy analysis of China's population policy, Greenhalgh has brought to light how state policy has transformed norms with respect to family size and reinforced gendered constructions of children through the daughter-only exception of the one-child policy. This provision allows families who have a daughter first to have a second child in order to produce a son (Greenhalgh 1988, 1994; Greenhalgh and Li 1995). Other recent accounts of China's families also argue that the largest victory of the one-child policy and its campaigns have been the transformation of the "family idealized morality" (Yan 2003). Indeed, families in China do recognize the advantages of having one child, or possibly two children, and they no longer need a coercive policy to enforce such an idea. In Vietnam, this shift became apparent through the recent termination of the 1989 one-or-two-child policy, a milder version of

China's one-child policy (Goodkind 1995b; Population and Development Review 1989). In 2003, Vietnam adopted a population ordinance stipulating that families are free to have as many children as they wish, as long as they can economically support their offspring (see Catherine Scornet, this volume).

FAMILY AND FAMILIALISM

Other scholars have pushed forward the centrality of institutions for family theory under the banner of "familialism" (Haney and Pollard 2003). Familialism examines how states' discourses and institutions use and redefine family images and ideals to pursue political and economic objectives. As a theoretical standpoint, it conceives family behaviors as being the "counterpart, or by-product, of the practices of States of all sorts at different stages of development" (Haney and Pollard 2003, 1). Haney and Pollard argue:

> States have attempted to mobilize families and deploy familial images for a
> variety of political ends. Sometimes the family has been deployed as a meta-
> phor for imagining the state; at other times, the family has been used in more
> concrete terms as a model for state-building. At still other times, the family
> has been used to move state policies in new directions or as a vehicle for state
> goals. (2003, 1)

Familialism does not focus on individual behaviors extricated from the larger institutional frameworks in which families live and proceed through their life course. Instead, this approach puts the role of institutions squarely on the shoulders of family theory across disciplines. The state's active and prominent role in constructing idealized family moralities and in reformulating them is particularly evident in socialist countries of Asia and Eastern Europe. Socialism entailed the reconfiguration of family relations as the basis for the revolutionary project. To this end, socialist states have explicitly reconstructed family forms, relations, and practices in their attempt to transform society. Regarding familialism in socialist states, Haney and Pollard further argue that:

> early state socialist regimes in Eastern Europe often distinguished themselves
> from their capitalist predecessors through campaigns to redefine family behav-
> iour. These states are known for their deployment of kinship–familial meta-
> phors. In socialist rhetoric, society became a family . . . composed of individual

nuclear families embedded in a broader familial organization headed by the father-state. As a family head, the state made the key allocative and redistributive decisions, thus positioning the populace as recipients of state kindness and benevolence. (2003, 7)

Indeed, socialist powers often reproduced the vocabulary of families to articulate their ideas. By making a parallel between the Vietnamese family and the socialist ideology, leaders hoped to gain their citizens' confidence in the process of building a new society. Vietnam's attempts to reconfigure families, both through discourse and policies, illustrate "familialism" under socialism. Before examining Vietnamese families in the early socialist era, we turn to a brief consideration of the construction of the "traditional" Vietnamese family.

Unpacking the "Traditional" Vietnamese Family

Writings about Vietnamese society are replete with references to the "traditional" Vietnamese family. Scientific and popular accounts frequently gauge contemporary observations against constructions of the traditional family to assess the magnitude and direction of change, or lack thereof. The traditional family typically refers to family forms prevailing during the pre-socialist period, so mostly prior to the 1950s. One common thread in these accounts is the assertion that the family is the fundamental unit of Vietnamese society.[5] Indeed, research examining Vietnamese society from the colonial period to the present consistently stresses family institutions and kinship networks as being central to individuals' lives and the foundations for the entire society. For instance, Cadière wrote: "The essential feature of this civilization lies in the dominance of the family in all domains: religious, cultural, social. Since the fundamental institution of this society could not be politics or the economy, it is the family" (1930, 66).[6]

   In addition, many depictions of the traditional family are couched in terms of the Confucian precepts of family relations. In these writings, it is rarely observations of families in day-to-day life that nourish accounts, but often the Confucian idealized family. Here, principles of hierarchy between genders and generations are central; throughout the life course, fathers, husbands, and sons have authority over women. Children owe filial piety to their parents until their death and beyond, through ancestor cult rituals. Sons hold a considerably higher value than daughters do because they are the only ones who can continue the family line and inherit the parental estate. In this Confucian vision, patriarchy, virilocality, and patrilinearity, all elements of a patrifocal kinship pattern, are the thrusts of the Vietnamese traditional family. Some research specifies that the degree of adherence to this ideal varied socially; it was more strictly observed in educated and ruling classes than in peasant and uneducated classes.

Research points to three features of the Vietnamese family and kinship system highlighting its specificities. First, closer examinations of the traditional presocialist Vietnamese family and its proximity to this "traditional-Confucian" model have revealed a more complex picture (Bui 2003). Some observers of the colonial period discuss this gap between theory and practice, particularly with reference to the power of women in the households, which departs from the totally submissive version of the law and of the idealized Confucian ideal (Lustéguy 1935). This "gap" is also present in the kinship system of Vietnam in the presocialist period, which was far from being strictly "patrifocal" (Krowolski and Tung 2005, 155). Research on the colonial period reveals practices that depart from this model, such as daughters being able to receive inheritance in the form of agricultural land and other assets (Papin 2003). In addition, in the absence of a son, daughters could practice ancestor worship and continue their fathers' family line (mostly through uxorilocal marriage) (Bélanger 1997b; Papin 2003). There were variations in practices, and such variations still exist today. The legal code in effect when the French took power in Vietnam and the day-to-day practices that puzzled the French colonial power who had difficulties legislating family affairs, reflect the gap between the idealized family and the reality.[7] The Vietnamese family that the French found in the 1800s was a mix of pre-Confucian and Confucian influences, based on analyses of the Le Code of Vietnam and other sources, as argued by some (Tai 1981; Yu 1978). In fact, the Vietnamese family and kinship system seemed much more flexible than a Confucian model suggests—one in which women and young people had more autonomy than prescribed (Yu 1978). Commonly reiterated historical constructions of Vietnamese families, however, are being revisited by historians. For instance, Vietnamese daughters' supposedly favorable status, based on provisions of the Le Code giving them the right to inheritance, has been questioned by Tran (2006). Based on local historical evidence from the eighteenth century, she argues that women's good position in Vietnamese society—or better at least than that of Chinese women—relies on flawed constructions and assumptions. She claims that the idea of gender equality in indigenous Vietnamese culture, based on interpretations of the Le Code, is a myth. Recent revisions of Vietnam's history thus further lead us to question the notion of Vietnam's traditional family. Second, the problem with generalizing about the traditional Vietnamese family stems from the risk of overlooking important regional differences within Vietnam. Research on postnuptial co-residence patterns is emblematic of attempts to attribute either East or Southeast Asian influence to the Vietnamese family (Hirschman and Vu 1996). Contrary to families of Confucian Asia, Southeast Asian families are viewed as being more egalitarian and more favorable to women, since both the maternal and paternal sides matter. As a result, virilocality and uxorilocality are two possible scenarios for newlywed couples after marriage. These features are geographically more often situated in the South of Vietnam than in the North (Bélanger 1997b, 2000).

A third difficulty with the notion of a stable traditional family that preceded the socialist era is the failure to recognize the far-reaching impact of the colonial period on Vietnamese society. In his seminal book titled *Vietnamese Tradition on Trial, 1920–1945*, David Marr offers compelling evidence of the crisis of identity experienced by Vietnamese society after its encounter with Western-French ideologies and in response to the exploitation suffered by its people under colonial power (Marr 1981). As Marr eloquently argues, in order to understand the socialist revolution of Vietnam, we must take into account "fundamental changes in political and social consciousness among a significant segment of the Vietnamese populace in the period 1920–45" (Marr 1981, 2). This change in outlook on life and on the established moral order fostered questions about family relations and the position of women. On the eve of the 1945 revolution, the foundations of the "traditional" family had already been severely shaken by more than two decades of fierce discussion on equality, women's role, parent-children relations, and marriage, to name a few. While these debates often took place among the Vietnamese intelligentsia, they reached the larger population through popular newspapers and lively discussions in public places, mostly in urban areas where literacy was more common.

Despite ample evidence offering a historically situated and dynamic vision of traditional Vietnamese families, the "traditional family" tends to be used as a fixed form from which to gauge change, particularly in contemporary sociological works by Vietnamese and non-Vietnamese scholars. This static vision of the traditional and the modern suggests that external forces, such as colonialism, socialism, and capitalism, are essentially shaping families. In contrast, we conceive families as active agents in the making of Vietnam's history. Marr's account of presocialist Vietnamese society powerfully illustrates that change was primarily propelled from within, even if external events and influences contributed to the process. The same argument could be made about the renovation and the significance of family change for this process.

The Making of Socialist Families

The revolutionary government of Vietnam that took power in North Vietnam in 1954, following a decade of colonial war against the French, created a new institutional environment for families. Moreover, the promotion of the socialist ideology and practice, orchestrated by the Communist Party and its mass organizations, explicitly aimed to transform, and even replace, families. Vietnamese families, though glorified by Ho Chi Minh as the "cells of society" and the barometer of the well-being of the nation, also received the stamp of "feudal" and "backward." These negative labels designated the so-called "traditional" Vietnamese family as being an obstacle for the building of a socialist society. Thus, in state discourse, the family became an emblematic site for the construction of idealized social relations prescribed by Marxism as the cornerstone of an egalitarian and socialist nation (Pettus 2003). In the politics of daily life, families were subject to tensions and questions through their struggles to redefine their place and role in the new institutional setting. With the collectivization of agricultural land and the nationalization of production, the near elimination of private property and enterprises severely challenged the very bases of families and kinship modes of organization. Local power structures crumbled under land reforms and the attacks on former landowners, bourgeoisie, and intellectual classes. Families had to negotiate their spiritual meaning and self-representation in the midst of attempts to reform and simplify rituals of marriage, funerals, and ancestor worship (Malarney 2002). Theoretically, the revolution aimed at sweeping away the very core of family functions, relations, and symbolic reproduction. Socialism would be achieved primarily through a family revolution; from these reformed families a new society was to flourish.

The 1959 Law of Marriage and the Family laid out the Vietnamese version of a socialist new family morality (Wisensale 1999). In this law, the egalitarian, nuclear, and monogamous family, as described in Engels's writings, constitutes the new "legal" framework and prescribes different aspects of family life and family relations. In this text, gender equality between spouses is affirmed, and child marriage, forced marriage, and polygamy become illegal. The law also calls for equality between sons and daughters and an equal right to parental inheritance. In addition to legal reforms, social campaigns educated and glorified the new family and its virtues.[8] In practice, the law proved difficult to enforce, and remains so today. This legal document and its subsequent revisions, discussed by Catherine Scornet in her chapter, represent one of the main building blocks in the attempt to alter the existing family hierarchy and order. Unlike many laws that tend to legalize de facto practices, socialist laws like this one were, in fact, instruments created to foster revolutionary social change.

Presocialist Legacy and Socialist Ideals

The phoenix-like rebirth of families envisioned by the leaders and thinkers of the socialist revolution was hampered by entrenched patriarchal thinking, in spite of the questioning that had emerged during the colonial period. It is well-known that patriarchal societies established communist regimes, and patriarchal order did not vanish from daily lives and social relations after the revolutions (Salecl 1994). As argued by Weigersma, Vietnamese socialist institutions themselves often reproduced patriarchal structures and gender hierarchies, thus undermining and counteracting egalitarian and reformist discourse (Wiegersma 1988). Wiegersma contends that "the patriarchal system is so entrenched as to be invisible to many practitioners of Vietnamese socialism" (Wiegersma 1988, 242). She also states that "patriarchal interests are so established that they interact with, interconnect with, and support socialism as well as subverting ultimate socialist goals" (Wiegersma 1988, 242). Her arguments rely partly on an analysis of the agricultural point system, which attributed more value to men's labor than to women's work, and partly on the structure of small-scale industry, which, Wiegersma contends, gave limited scope to women. She also notes that kinship membership determined access to leadership positions, thus reinforcing patriarchy as a structural principle of society. In Hanoi, for instance, she observed that production teams in industrial and handicraft collectives in the late 1970s and early 1980s were run by families, not collectives. In a similar argument, Stacey contends that in China the revolutionary family was a "democratic partiarchal" family, indicating the juxtaposition of egalitarian principles and patriarchal culture (Stacey 1983). In addition, Parish and Whyte have argued that in China family changes took place, but these changes "occurred primarily through indirect responses of peasants to the structural transformations of rural life rather than through direct change efforts by the government" (Parish and Whyte 1978, 154). Regarding gender in Vietnam, Goodkind has shown that inequalities increased in the 1970s and 1980s (Goodkind 1995a). Leshkowich (2005) provides an illuminating analysis of the state's construction of Ho Chi Minh City's female petty traders in the 1970s and 1980s as primarily inferior women in need of being reformed into cooperative members. According to these arguments, the family and kinship system in Vietnam partly shaped the nature of socialism and, in many ways, limited the possibilities of transforming gender and family relations (White Pelzer 1989).

Ethnographic work on this period of Vietnam's history documents how the state's desires to transform families met with strong resistance at the local level. Families engaged in diverse and elaborate processes of negotiations and accommodations with local Communist Party units and organizations that were orchestrating ideological campaigns and monitoring adherence to the new morality. Malarney's work on communities' response to the reform of cult and other family and community rituals offers compelling evidence of the clash between existing practices and the state's agenda. Households continued to maintain, often secretly, rituals qualified as feudal, and they never abandoned their conceptions of the symbolism attached to the family line, as expressed in cult, funeral, and wedding rituals (Malarney 2002, 2003).[9] The issue of internal migration offers another telling account of families' resistance to new policies. Between the 1960s and the 1980s, the socialist state discouraged and even forbade spontaneous migration and organized migration programs (Desbarats 1987; Jones 1982). One objective of these programs was to avoid massive rural to urban migration perceived in Marxist terms as being an obstacle to socioeconomic development. A second objective was to "vietnamize" provinces populated by "backward" and underdeveloped ethnic minorities. In stark contrast with earlier accounts on the repressive nature of this migration policy (Desbarats 1987), Hardy's ethnography of migration throughout the twentieth century very convincingly demonstrates that families continued to migrate spontaneously, in spite of such policies, and, through processes of resistance and negotiation, eventually prompted policy change toward freer mobility (Hardy 2003). Another example comes from Danièle Bélanger's research on the politics of reproduction, which indicates how leaders' noncompliance with provisions of the Law of Marriage and the Family hampered family reforms among peasants. Community leaders married second wives in order to produce male heirs throughout the 1960s, 1970s, and 1980s. Such behavior undermined the state's attempts to promote monogamy and reinforced the idea that having male children would bring status, eventually leading to the local legitimization of polygamy and the supremacy of male children (Bélanger 2001). Ultimately, kinship corporate power remained vital, as expressed by the annual competition for the number of male births each year in some communities (Bélanger 2002). This is one illustration of the continuity of gendered and hierarchical notions of children in families and communities, and it demonstrates local resistance to the diffusion of new norms and morality with respect to gender equality. As these few examples and other research indicate, prerevolutionary practices and conceptions were enmeshed in the communist revolution, as in any type of revolution. The hope of a social movement that would allow for a tabula rasa of society's history and collective memory ignored inevitable processes of social reproduction and family resilience. These examples illustrate how the family reform was, to some extent, hampered by existing cultural norms and behaviors and by the reproduction of patriarchal structures and dynamics in the new institutions created in the name of socialism.

In addition, the state reinforced the subordination of the individual to the family by creating institutions enabling leaders to use the family as a gauge for judging any individual's worth and actions. One such institution was an official document (*ly lich*), which contained the political, personal, and familial history (going back three generations). Antedating the revolution, this document became a powerful tool of political hegemony under communism. After the communist government took power, these documents were interpreted in a new political light, mostly in terms of adherence to or contestation of revolutionary ideals. For instance, a grandfather who had been a landowner or a father who had worked for the French public service under colonial rule, circumscribed and limited all his descendents' education, employment, and marriage prospects. In sum, political authorities created a new social stratification between families who supported the revolution and families labeled as real or potential detractors. Family membership remained an individual's most fundamental social affiliation, and one's reputation and future depended on actions and behaviors of his or her entire family and kin group.

The political history of a family mattered for marriage as well. Those with a poor or suspicious family past were unable to marry individuals with impeccable pasts (Bélanger and Khuat 2001). As a result, a political homogamy existed, monitored by Communist Party units who had the responsibility for delivering marriage licences after examination of the marriage candidates' respective political genealogy. Divorce was another area in which the state interfered by offering counseling to couples in difficulties. While making divorce legal, the state strongly discouraged it, and divorcees and their children suffered social discrimination and even stigmatization. Hareven, in commenting on the difficulty of obtaining a divorce in a Chinese court, makes a parallel between the People's Republic of China's powerful role in setting a strong family morality and intervening in family affairs, and the Puritan elders of Victorian England who subordinated the individual to the larger community (Hareven 2000, 297). As in China, Vietnam rather forcefully imposed the idealized morality. Sexuality, too, became the object of state control, through the repression of extramarital and premarital sexual relationships (Khuat 1998). Thus, the new "idealized morality" that promoted the free, nuclear, and egalitarian family was juxtaposed to collectivist principles subordinating individuals to kin groups. Such collectivist principles, however, often found their rationale in a moral order antedating the revolution.

While an individual's actions could instantly spoil the lives and futures of his or her relatives, people found ways to maneuver through the system. Friendships and connections made prior to independence, during the war, or in school formed extremely efficient networks and sources of social capital. With a good "connection," one could achieve much in terms of silencing an event or making one possible. Besides personal networks that provided benefits to one's relatives and friends, there were other mechanisms to circumvent the apparent rigidity of the system. A family could improve its life chances by demonstrating devotion to the revolutionary cause. For instance, one family member becoming a war volunteer greatly improved the entire kin group's situation. Thus, in this respect, the Vietnamese communist regime offered some room for political mobility, the key to social mobility. Therefore, families often came up with strategies and maneuvered to protect and negotiate their positions within the new political and institutional setting. This emphasis on family agency and innovative strategies shifts the focus from the apparent authority of the communist regime to the relative flexibility of its rules.

Socialist Ideals and the Transformation of Gender and Intergenerational Relations

Despite evidence that patriarchy persisted in socialist institutions and families resisted the new proposed morality, the revolutionary process partly succeeded in amending the existing family moral order and legitimizing new behaviors, norms, and conceptions previously deemed socially unacceptable. The meeting of the Vietnamese and Marxist family order created an opportunity for family change. The dissolution of hierarchies, control, and inequalities was central to the new rhetoric about families, and this discourse, communicated through propaganda campaigns, laws, and policy, sparked questions regarding existing family practices and relations. Campaigns aimed at putting forward the "new culture family" (*gia dinh van hoa*) might have had limited success (Kleinen 1999) because they questioned assumptions about family relations and hierarchy. Malarney's above-cited work on communities' responses to the state's attempts to reform marriage and funeral rituals shows family and community resistance, and it also convincingly illustrates processes of negotiation and accommodation through which norms and practices were deeply altered. Eisen's account of family change after Vietnam's independence highlights the diminution of polygamy, access to divorce, and women's recognition of equality with their husbands as signs that Vietnamese families had endorsed revolutionary ideals (Eisen 1984, 199). In contrast with Weigerma's above-cited argument, Werner has shown how setting up cooperatives in agricultural production served to empower women and transformed the family in many respects (Werner 1981, 1993). Werner also discusses how the combination of collective agriculture and war (with men being away) led to a "women's economy." She contends that "a new type or model of family emerged during the war, which should be seen as a 'socialist' family, and this is attributable as much to State policy as to the peasant basis of society" (Werner 1993, 92). In addition to collective agriculture, the development of the Vietnamese socialist welfare state offered alternatives to previous ways of functioning and relating within families. In spite of meager resources, the Vietnamese state stepped in to offer free education to all; it also opened daycare centers in many villages; and it created village health centers throughout the country. Free and general access to education and health were the cornerstones of the Vietnamese socialist revolution. For families, these policy initiatives meant a reliance on the state for basic welfare needs. These social policies and programs did not mean, however, that family and kin networks lost their importance. Instead, their purpose and usefulness were moved to other spheres of daily life, such as the crucial maintenance of networks and friendships.

Despite the relative incompleteness of "the promissory notes" of socialism in the realm of gender equality, the position of women in society was definitely altered (Kruks, Rapp, and Blatt 1989; Quinn-Judge 1983; Werner 1981). Indeed, policies and institutions aimed at increasing women's position in society modified the realm of possibilities. Women's massive entry in the wage labor force in cities, while not necessarily changing women's position in the domestic sphere, transformed the public place. In rural areas, the point system for agricultural work, in spite of its imperfections, officially rewarded and acknowledged women's work in the fields in an unprecedented way (Werner 1981). The development of childcare facilities to facilitate women's entry into the workforce contrasted with previous modes of organization that relied exclusively on kin to care for children. Rapid advancements in girls' access to primary and secondary schools made Vietnam a pioneer in narrowing the gender gap in education (Bélanger and Liu 2004; Fraser 1993; Knodel and Jones 1996).

The socialist perspective on families as egalitarian units also led to some changes in the hierarchical relationship between generations. A consensus between parents and children regarding the choice of a mate replaced the dominance of arranged marriage by the parental generation (Bélanger 1997a, 1997b; Bélanger and Khuat 2001). At the village level, the new leadership structures reduced the corporate power of lineage (Kleinen 1999). The family, as the prime political target for social change, became the site of interrogations and negotiations. In spite of the intrinsic cultural structures hampering a total family revolution from hierarchy to equality and from feudalism to modernism, the socialist ideology and policies led to a questioning of existing and dominant moralities and helped propel Vietnam into a different age. Only emphasizing the failures of family reform envisioned by the socialist government would not render justice to the complexity of processes that took place in families' lives, particularly since 1945 in the North. In this respect, we firmly believe that the changes typically associated with the renovation, in terms of family forms, strategies, and relations, were initiated, for the most part, prior to the renovation. However, before discussing the main themes associated with family change in renovated Vietnam, we next review the characteristics of renovation and the particular role assigned to the family since the mid-1980s. As with other periods of Vietnamese history, the family in the renovation period remains central to state narratives, although the revised contents of this narrative serve new economic and political objectives.

The Family as the Cornerstone of the Renovation Process

In the 1980s, simultaneously prompted by international events in the former USSR and other countries of the Eastern Bloc and by the aforementioned internal grassroots resistance and discontent, the Vietnamese state made significant leaps toward the transition to a "market economy with a socialist direction" (Turley 1993, 2). The immediate cause of the dramatic ideological shift, exemplified by the reforms, was the acute crisis suffered by the Vietnamese economy throughout the 1980s. The lack of funds and the accompanying shortage of goods led to dramatic inflation—2000 percent—of the price of basic foodstuffs between 1976 and 1986, a rapid decline in the level of salaries, and a general loss of faith in the dominant ideology at all levels of society (Dang 2004; Turley 1993). Given a choice between its own survival as a political system and a major reorientation of its socioeconomic strategy, the Vietnam Communist Party—following the lead taken by other former communist nations—reformed its entire economic and social system (Marr and White 1988). The Sixth Congress of the Communist Party voted in the core elements of the shift from a soviet-style to a market-oriented economic system in December 1986.

The change was not a brutal one as a few experimental measures had paved the way to the 1986 Declaration. Among the most significant of these, an ordinance in 1980 first authorized a number of provinces to experiment with the contract system in paddy cultivation, and its implementation was generalized in 1981. Under the contract system, cooperatives could divide farmland into small plots and allocate them to contract households, even though this weakened their own economic and social roles (Le 2001). Early steps were also taken in the 1980s to liberalize domestic and foreign trade within narrow limits. However, we agree with Beresford that "The 1986 Congress [. . .] became a turning point for the reform process in the sense that it took a conscious decision to build a market economy in Vietnam" (Beresford 2003, 61).

The most significant measure following the 1986 Declaration was to officially authorize the development of a private sector, dismantled in 1958 in the North and soon after reunification in the South.[10] In addition, legal and material resources were provided to the household sector in order to reinstate the family as the basic unit of production. Families rapidly embraced their new role in the midst of the dismantlement of collectives. In the private sector, the contract system was first generalized, and then relaxed, in terms of the obligations of farmers in dealing with the cooperatives. State monopoly on the produce market was abolished.[11] Farmers could "manage their entire production process, decide what to produce, what to invest and to sell all their output at market prices" (Dang 2004, 37). A few years later (in 1993), property rights were reformed as well, so that even though land ownership remained a privilege of the state, households' land use rights to inherit, sell, lease, or mortgage were reinstated, creating a whole new range of possibilities for capital accumulation at the household level (Tran 2004).

In the manufacturing and service sectors, in contrast to other transition economies, the family stood as the prime candidate to take over the activities formerly controlled by public institutions. As underlined by Turley, "whereas China began reform with a large public industrial sector, help from a strong entrepreneurial tradition and a receptive international environment, Vietnam began with very little industry and relatively weaker entrepreneurial traditions while isolated from the West and Japan" (Turley 1993, 4). In Vietnam, the family was initially the strongest institution with the position, the means, and the motivation to take advantage of the new economic opportunities created by the reforms. A series of policy measures specifically intended to accelerate the household's ability to reinvest its productive role, making the family instrumental in the implementation of the reforms, further reinforced this phenomenon (see Dang, Tacoli, and Hoang 2004, for a monographic example). Werner clearly emphasizes this point when she states:

> A major component of the renovation agenda of the *Doi Moi* state is the development of the household economy (*phat trien kinh te gia dinh*). State organizations on the national and local levels are directly charged with encouraging and assisting households to develop their family economy and find new ways to bring in income. In the countryside, Party leaders and representatives from the mass or-

ganizations give advice to peasant households on how to diversify their sources of income, integrate their farm, livestock, gardening, and fishing activities, practice thrift and husband their resources, and invest in home-based income-generating activities. (2002, 32)

Werner's analysis underlines how the family was an inherent part of the state strategy to achieve its political agenda, and her work shows how an implicit family reform is embedded within official economic reforms.

The strategy proved highly effective, as demonstrated by the overwhelming economic success achieved over the past two decades. The reforms had a dramatic impact on economic growth, with an increase in per capita gross domestic product (GDP) of between 5 and 10 percent a year from the early 1990s to the early 2000s (Kokko 2004, 70), which translated into a parallel increase in household wealth. According to a recent estimate by the World Bank, per capita GDP more than doubled in less than fifteen years (from 228 current U.S. dollars in 1991 to 540 in 2004 [World Bank 2006, 20]). All sectors benefited from this increase as income rose both in rural and urban areas. Farmers' gains were particularly important in the early 1990s, as the price of agricultural produce increased by 10 to 15 times, compared to previous levels when 80 percent of the labor force worked in agriculture (Kokko 2004). Consequently, returns on investment in this sector also increased, leading to a steep rise in productivity and resulting in a surplus of rural labor. Workers were then free to seize new opportunities created by other economic sectors and liberate the forces behind a fundamental transformation of Vietnamese society (for some vivid descriptions of these changes at the village level, see Le 2001). Most of the new economic opportunities were concentrated within a few provinces and, more particularly, in the largest cities. One of the most visible effects of the transition was a rapid shift in the nature and allocation of labor among sectors and geographic areas through a massive reorganization of the production system that is still taking place twenty years later (Dang, Tacoli, and Thanh 2003; Oudin 1999). The increasing monetization of the economy that accompanied the transition, as well as the parallel growth of household income, had major influences on the control of resources within and among families. The central position of families and households in the new economic system, explicitly recognized by the state, profoundly reformed social organization as a whole. The downsizing of the welfare system further imposed a redefinition of the social contract.

Redefining State Social Responsibilities

Starting in the 1950s in the North and in the mid-1970s to a lesser extent in the South, the communist regime had introduced a number of social policies leading to an actual welfare system, with the explicit purpose of protecting all individuals and satisfying their basic needs (in particular, housing, food, health, and education). In the 1980s, however, it became clear that the government did not have the means to support its policy. Following the financial crisis, the state was compelled to cut expenditures, and a marked degradation of already fragile and basic social services resulted. By the end of the 1980s, the Vietnamese government had abdicated the greater part of its previous social obligations. The phasing out, or substantial reduction, of most entitlement programs and universal benefits was followed by the introduction of user fees and the replacement of universal subsidies by poverty allowances for the neediest. Two sets of social policy reforms that hit families particularly hard were in the areas of health and education. A private sector for health and education services progressively expanded throughout the 1990s, which resulted in an increasing shift of the cost to households (Haughton 1999). As noted by London:

> The distinguishing feature of mass education and health during the market period was the State's withdrawal from its historic commitment to the principles of universalism in education and health policies, symbolized by the modification of the 1980 constitution in 1989, and the adoption of a new constitution in 1992 in which guarantees for access to education and health were conspicuous by their absence. (2004, 131)

The unilateral reshuffling of social responsibilities by the government led to the progressive redefinition of the boundaries between the private and public realms. Starting in the 1980s, state withdrawal reinstated the family as the de facto locus of social security and welfare. The official position on public services within the new system further manifested itself in the 1989 Law on Marriage and the Family, which clearly states that "the family, far more than the State, is responsible for the care and well-being of its members" (Wisensale 1999, 608). This law, and others along the same lines, such as the 1994 Decree on Marriage and the Family, became major policy tools in shaping and structuring a new social order and morality in which families had the primary responsibility for most of the welfare functions formerly held by the state.

The downsizing of the welfare state and the increasing reliance of nation-states on families has taken place in all postsocialist and late socialist countries, but in Vietnam, the changes have been particularly abrupt. The promise of reform in Eastern Europe and the former Soviet Union did not meet early expectations, while China and Vietnam, which did not undergo political upheavals, yielded better results in terms of economic growth (Kerkvliet, Chan, and Unger 1999). Russia, which experienced a decline in life expectancy in the early 1990s, following the fall of the communist regime, sadly reflects the tragedy of a painful transition (Meslé and Vallin 2002; Shkolnikov 1995). In Vietnam, socioeconomic development and overall wealth have increased steadily since the 1990s, in the midst of deepening inequality. In the realm of education, for instance, Vietnam offered free and universal education at primary and lower secondary schools until the late 1980s (Fraser 1993; London 2004). Following the introduction of school fees in 1989, households were eventually responsible for more than half the education expenditures for primary and secondary schooling (Bélanger and Liu 2004; Bray 1996). In spite of this strong financial pressure on households, enrollment rates have been increasing since the mid 1990s (Bélanger and Liu 2004; Desai 2000). While inequalities stand as the challenge to reforms (Taylor 2004), families' resourcefulness has also allowed for remarkable adaptation. Therefore, as this book shows, families' responses to new opportunities and the difficulties posed by the retrenchment of the socialist welfare state were instrumental in the renovation's success, as measured by the country's rapid economic expansion and increased productivity (Fforde and Vylder 1996).

Themes and Chapters of the Book

This collection explores the impact of the economic transition in five inter-related areas of family life and practices. Each of these areas corresponds to a section in the book and investigates a separate set of social relations. The book begins with Part One, an exploration of what the new social contract means for family forms and organization in the two areas of reproduction (Catherine Scornet's chapter) and health (Anil Deolalikar's chapter). Part Two continues the studies of the previous chapters by looking at the redeployment of family solidarities to compensate for the collapse of the socialist welfare state (with a chapter by Myriam de Loenzien and another by Magali Barbieri). Increasing variations in the transition to adulthood, with marriage as a focal point, is the object of Part Three (with three chapters by Peter Xenos et al., Rukmalie Jayakody and Vu Tuan Huy, and Hung Cam Thai). Part Four focuses on a more gendered understanding of family practices. While two chapters more specifically question whether the growing economic opportunities and earning potentials of women are threatening the traditional balance of power within the family (those by Danièle Bélanger and Katherine Pendakis and by Truong Huyen Chi), a third contribution (Puk Bussarawan Teerawichitchainan's) more specifically warns against stereotypical views of women's improved status. Part Five examines how families have adapted their livelihood strategies to the new context by diversifying their activities (with chapters by Xavier Oudin on employment and by Hy Van Luong on migration). Though most of the contributions simultaneously address several of the five main issues, they have been organized to maximize proximities in terms of the questions raised by their authors rather than for their methodological similarities in order to engage the reader in a lively exchange among different disciplines resorting to different sources of information. The overall background and approach of each of the five major themes are successively reviewed below, with a brief summary of the relevant chapter's contents.

A NEW SOCIAL CONTRACT

The family plays a central role in the transition to a market system as it has been endorsed with major productive, reproductive, and welfare functions. However, the state has not relegated its power in all areas. With respect to reproduction, it has even reinforced its control on families and the behavior of individual couples. Catherine Scornet's chapter in this volume shows that, during the first fifteen years after the onset of *Doi Moi*, the major and inherent reproductive role of the family remained as strong as it had during the previous period; it also remained the object of state intervention, as in China, though in a less coercive manner. Vietnam's one-or-two child policy, implemented in the late 1980s and early 1990s in most parts of the country, was launched three years after the onset of renovation. The "Prosperous, Egalitarian, Progressive and Happy Family" campaign launched in 1994 was a major instrument of the birth control policy. In line with Catherine Scornet, Gammeltoft identified state campaigns promoting "happy families" as a tool to convince women to endorse the use of modern contraceptive methods (Gammeltoft 1999). In analyses of state discourse on gender and health, feminist scholars argued that the construction of the wife as being responsible for "family happiness and family health" is also leading to a representation of women as mainly belonging to the domestic sphere (Nguyen-vo 2002; Pettus 2003). Through the description of national propaganda campaigns, the activities of local family planning cadres, and local responses to and adaptations of the policy, Catherine Scornet illustrates both the proeminent role of the state apparatus in shaping family norms and ideals, and the continued ability of individual families to pursue their own agenda beyond government imposed targets. But, as underlined by Anagnost for China, while the state has been tightening its control on the family and reproduction, it has been loosening it in other social fields (Anagnost 1995).

The explicit transfer of roles that had been fulfilled by public institutions, such as the collectives, cooperatives, and local communities as well as by the government of Vietnam itself in the production of goods and services during socialism, provides direct evidence of the particularly important place allocated to the family in the renovation process. An examination of health care and changes in the health system is particularly enlightening in this respect. In his chapter, Anil Deolalikar provides strong evidence of the consequences of state retrenchment for the health of the population before and after *Doi Moi*. He finds that after a general deterioration of the services provided by the public sector at the end of the 1980s and early 1990s, the situation improved during the subsequent period. The improvement was due to the rapid development of a private health sector, rather than to the still embryonic public health programs and insurance schemes. As a result, changes in the structure of the health system have mainly benefited those able to afford its cost, and socioeconomic inequalities in terms of both access to the services and quality of care have increased. In this context, family support can be critical when someone is unable to provide for his or her own care.

THE REDEPLOYMENT OF FAMILY SOLIDARITIES

Studies in other transitional economies have emphasized the role of families to compensate for increased vulnerability resulting from economic fluctuations and the state's disengagement from its former welfare responsibilities.

In Russia, for instance, a recent survey by Rousselet found that the family operated as a buffer to lessen the impact of the economic crisis on individual household members. Intergenerational transfers among kin have intensified in recent years, and co-residence between married children and their parents has increased (Rousselet 2005). Rousselet also shows that other forms of support have developed within family networks in response to particular events, such as kin helping family members financially, logistically, and psychologically when their relatives are in need (Rousselet 2005). In Vietnam too, one might wonder to what extent state policies reconfigured the family institution by strengthening ties of individuals to their relatives.

Intrafamily strategies to provide for the neediest are the subject of two chapters in this book. In her contribution on the role of relatives in the support for HIV/AIDS patients, Myriam de Loenzien discusses how the government strategy to fight the disease has squarely put the task of negotiating, funding, and monitoring patients' treatment on the shoulders of family members from the very beginning to compensate for its own initial lack of resources in this area. Her research supports the view that *Doi Moi* has had mixed influences on the family's traditional role of supervision and control, and it provides a vivid example of the tensions generated between individuals and their kin in a context in which the relations between state and society are being redefined. Though her study focuses on the specific context of the HIV/AIDS epidemic, her findings apply to many situations where individuals are compelled by sheer necessity to rely on family support, a support that, in spite of the many pressures and obstacles of modern Vietnam, remains very strong as further shown by another chapter in this volume.

Concentrating on the consequences of increased migration flows of young adults on their older parents, Magali Barbieri demonstrates that, though residential arrangements remain the preferential strategy for elderly support, alternative forms of solidarity have emerged in the wake of economic development. In her research on the patterns of exchange between adult children and their ageing parents, she found that cultural norms remain powerful, and geographic distance does not represent a retreat from the traditional support of the older generation by the younger generation. She also found that other means of support, primarily financial remittances, have developed in parallel with the decline in co-residence, a finding also emphasized by Danièle Bélanger and Katherine Pendakis. One might wonder however, whether over time, the departure of adult children from their parents' community will mark the loss of full contributors to the household income for most families and will promote a scarcity of preferential caretakers for the elderly (Eng and Blake 1998). Depending on the future volume and pattern of migration (whether permanent or temporary, long distance or short distance, individual or collective), the social consequences of separation for the migrants as well as for those left behind (children, spouses, and older parents) pointed out in this contribution as in others in this volume, will be potentially powerful factors in the reshaping of families and changing relations of power and mutual support among their members and larger kin group.

MARRIAGE AND THE TRANSITION TO ADULTHOOD

The renovated social contract between the state and families in the new institutional and economic setting as well as rising socioeconomic differentiation within the population leads to a diversification of life-course trajectories, some of which are liable to increase individual emancipation. Indeed, rapid socioeconomic development and the demands of the market system resulted in a complete reconfiguration of production processes, which translated into the rapid growth of a private sector, the fast decline in the proportion of the labor force in agriculture, and the rapid expansion of urban areas and industrialized zones, in addition to the aforementioned intensified migration flows (Dang, Tacoli, and Hoang 2003). On the one hand, economic restructuring now enables individuals to acquire production means through institutions other than the family. Among the urban educated, family and political networks, as factors of integration and success in both the economic and social realms, have, to some extent, lessened in favor of other avenues for social capital accumulation. As a result, individual freedom has increased for those with a high degree of flexibility who possess the qualifications required to succeed in the growing private sector. High-growth economic sectors mostly rely on single young adults, trained under the new system and not yet encumbered by family responsibilities (Dang 1999). On the other hand, the legalization of private property as well as the rebirth of family farms and other family businesses tend to increase parental control over some of the resources that their children depend upon to become adults. Considering the low level of development still characterizing the Vietnam banking and credit systems, relatives in general, and parents in particular, are the most likely providers of the financial capital needed by young people to settle independently.

Despite this well-described context, variations in the sequence of major life-cycle events within the population have not yet been well documented. Peter Xenos and colleagues' chapter in this volume partly fills this gap. Their study is based on an analysis of the nationally representative 2003 Survey and Assessment of Vietnamese Youth. They find that less than one-third of the youths in a representative sample actually follow the classic sequence of leaving school, then leaving home, and then working for pay. A large proportion leaves home before finishing school, with significant differences by sex and social background. The combination of residential and economic independence is identified as a powerful factor in the weakening control over adult children by their elders and larger kin group (Goode 1982). Young men and women who are seeking new educational or economic opportunities are exposed to a wide range of ideas and values through the development of urbanization and communication systems at the expense of social interactions with their kin. The analysis of marriage patterns provides a particularly enlightening example of the reconfiguration of intrafamily relations in this context.

Marriage epitomizes the fundamental nature of the relations between young adults and their parents. Traditionally, in Vietnam, marriage has been perceived as a family obligation, a relationship designed to promote economic security and, through childbearing, the continuity of the family line, which is particularly important in a society dominated by ancestor worship. By regulating access to capital through inheritance rights and by endorsing the material responsibilities of parents toward their young or adolescent children, spouses toward each other, and adult children toward their ageing parents, the state has a direct interest in overseeing marriage as the core component of the family formation process. Though family control over the matching of couples and over marriage ceremonies weakened under socialism, marriage remained tightly controlled by the authorities through a series of laws passed by the Vietnamese government beginning in 1959. After renovation, the state was reluctant to release its grip on an institution that determined the structure of new families. For instance, the Decree on Marriage and the Family, enacted in 1994 to specifically normalize family formation processes and to consolidate the family as a core social institution, devoted half of all sections to the regulation of marriage (Wisensale 1999).

Because they are good indicators of young adults' independence and self-reliance, "differences in age at marriage, residential patterns of married couples, and residential and employment patterns of unmarried adults" coincide with differences in the nature of intergenerational relations (Thornton and Fricke 1987). Increasing delays in the formation of families and change in the characteristics of courtship and in the marriage partner's selection process represent additional meaningful indicators of the degree of personal choice. For example, the fact that people marry later has a marked impact on the family life cycle. It is also highly related to other markers of the transition to adulthood, as showed in Peter Xenos and colleagues' study in this volume. Their analysis indicates that school leaving and, especially, entry into the paid labor force compete with marriage and childbearing to mark this major life cycle transition. Gender differences are significant in this respect, with less than 10 percent of males but more than 30 percent of females having experienced a reproductive-related event by age 20. Reinforcing Peter Xenos and colleagues' findings, Rukmalie Jayakody and Vu Tuan Huy demonstrate in their chapter how such behavior change is accompanied by profound transformations in the value system from one generation to the next. Their study relies on a comparison of three separate cohorts of individuals who married during the Vietnam War, in the early years after reunification, and after the onset of *Doi Moi*. This research design is particularly well suited to an investigation of historical change in relation to political transformations. It demonstrates that while *Doi Moi* did appear to have an impact on some of the investigated mating and marriage behavior (courtship patterns in particular) several of the changes found in this area (such as parental versus individual control over the mate selection process) in fact either preceded or started before the reforms and continued afterward.

In the new context, marriage increasingly involves two individuals rather than two families though as illustrated by Hung Cam Thai's chapter, it remains a major instrument of social promotion. Hung Cam Thai's ethnographic study focuses on overseas Vietnamese men who have taken advantage of globalization to return to Vietnam for marital partners. Though relatives still play an important role, for instance to orient the search and arrange meetings between prospective mates, family pressures are conspicuously absent from these young *Viet Kieu* men's and Vietnamese women's marriage strategies. Hung Cam Thai finds that consumption in late capitalism allows some low-wage immigrant men to recuperate from a loss of status through the convertibility of wage differentials between the first and the third world resulting from international migration, and this convertibility makes it possible for them to use cultural origin to identify a specific marriage market in their home country. As for their Vietnamese brides, the temptation of a transnational marriage is certainly not devoid of similar, though reversed, expectations in terms of status enhancement. In this respect, Hung Cam Thai's research contributes to the growing recognition of the significance of the flows of capital and persons between Vietnam and the outside world for family formation processes (Morgan 2003, 5).

Women and the Family

Historically, Vietnamese women have performed a major productive role (Luong 2003). They were particularly active in the economy during the thirty-year war following independence, and, as in other communist countries, they continued working in the cooperatives afterward. During the previous period, the expectation was that all members of the community, including women, would contribute to the economy, given the requirements of production in all sectors. Since retribution was usually provided in kind, there was little opportunity for the increased independence of household members. This situation has changed with *Doi Moi*. Though, as indicated by Xavier Oudin's research, women's economic activity shows some sign of decline, women who do work increasingly do so in the wage sector, and their earning potentials are much larger than they ever were. They are becoming significant, and sometimes major, contributors to their parents' household budgets, when still unmarried, or to their husbands', after marriage. They also represent a sizeable proportion of household heads, and not only when unmarried.

Studies in other countries have demonstrated the profound impact of women's economic independence on progressively shifting the balance of power in their favor within society, in general, and within the family, in particular. In China, for instance, women's ability to earn a wage "endow[s] them with new resources and the will to attempt to renegotiate their role in the family" (Otis 2003, 209). Studies in this volume tend, however, to qualify this claim, and they collectively conclude—in this area as in many others—that the role of renovation should not be overrated. Their findings support those of other scholars, that is, that the transition to a market economy, as a gendered process, far from resulting in the simple reduction of gender inequalities in Vietnam, emcompasses both constraints and new options for women (Bélanger and Oudin 2007; Drummond and Rydstrom 2004; Luong 2003; Pettus 2003;

Werner 2002). The contributions in this section question the well-known theoretical postulate that a woman's ability to earn money, independent of her husband, larger kin group, or local community, strengthens her decision-making power.

Research carried out in transitional economies of Eastern Europe also indicates that economic restructuring and the transition to a capitalist system are not necessarily associated with increased female autonomy. In a number of such countries, women's forced retreat from the labor force and their return to life as housewives has eroded their status (Werner and Bélanger 2002). Nevertheless, even where women are encouraged to contribute their labor to the new urban economy, as in China, they are channeled into the unregulated sector, compelled to join a growing pool of illegal, temporary workers available for low-wage labor in urban centers, which eventually reinforces their ties to their rural families (Otis 2003, 215). At the same time, however, studies show that "their experience of independence in the urban center leads them to question and revise notions of gender-appropriate behavior, especially those relating to marriage and filiality" (Otis 2003, 208).

Danièle Bélanger and Katherine Pendakis's chapter in this volume provides a number of indications about the complex outcomes of changing economic and social status for women's position and empowerment. Their study of the narratives of single young women who migrated from rural areas to work in garment factories in, or near, urban areas revisits an important topic of sociological and anthropological research in Asia. The "factory daughters," who have been studied since the 1970s and 1980s in Hong Kong and Taiwan, now form an important group of single young women in Vietnam as well. Through their paid work away from their families, these young women challenge parent-daughter relations and the construction of daughters as "the children of others." While their earnings are meager, their premarital working life away from home transforms these young women's visions of their life, their future, and their relations with their peers and with the older generation. Ambiguity is evident in their desire to become independent and their feeling of indebtedness toward their parents, who they are trying to pay back through remittances and frequent visits home. Manifestations of noneconomic empowerment run through these narratives of hope and suffering.

While unmarried women who leave home to work can better fulfill their duty toward their parents, married women in the same situation face more contradictory constructions of womanhood. These women are sometimes larger contributors to the family income than their husbands, but this phenomenon, far from generating feelings of gratification for the women and their close relatives, is a growing source of strain between husbands and wives, as well as between women and their parents-in-law, as found by Truong Huyen Chi's ethnographic study. Her results are also confirmed by a recent survey conducted by Vietnamese researchers at the Institute of Sociology (Vu 2003). Truong Huyen Chi's interviews show that, not only the women themselves, but also their immediate family members, particularly husbands and parents, are compelled to justify why a woman who works, and sometimes lives, away from her community should not be viewed as deserting her traditional family duties. Faced with powerful, and sometimes conflicting, social pressures, women are meeting increasing difficulties in juggling the demands of work and family. Much of the discourse aimed at women conveys the idea that they are responsible for the well-being of immediate family relatives, in particular their children, husbands, and parents-in-law, while they are also under pressure to increase their family well-being through their participation in wage labor. Consequently, women and men alike face much ambivalence in the new Vietnamese society.

Women's contribution to the labor market has been specifically emphasized by the Vietnamese government as a beneficial result of the family planning program. Indeed, the decline in fertility has facilitated the intrahousehold reallocation of labor. Because families are now raising one or two children, instead of five or six as three decades earlier, the demands of childrearing on young parents have lessened, creating new opportunities, particularly for women, by reducing the load of domestic chores, providing relief from childcare and the need to remain close to the household. The self-sacrificing woman who subordinates her own desires and personal development for the sake of her family and larger kinship group, the prototype of the ideal daughter, wife, and mother in classical texts of Vietnamese literature, is both challenged and commonly reproduced. Pettus's analysis of "the governing of feminity in Vietnam" (2003), though demonstrating the collusion between the popular media and the underlying official discourse to promote "the retraditionalization of women as an antidote to the moral costs of market economy" (2003, 209) nevertheless underlines the increasing tensions between an emerging female search for self-fulfillment and the continuous demands of expected filial, marital, and maternal devotion, as vividly illustrated by Truong Huyen Chi's study.

Conversely, women sometimes find themselves left behind, separated from their husbands who were forced to leave home for work. In these situations, women may become official household heads. The strikingly high rate of female heads in Vietnam is the object of Puk Bussarawan Teerawichitchainan's chapter. She questions the social significance of this phenomenon and concludes that it should not be attributed to the new economic position of Vietnamese women, a result also supported by other exploratory research (Vien Xa Hoi Hoc 1996) and contrasting with studies in other countries. Puk Bussarawan Teerawichitchainan's analysis of the 1995 Vietnam Longitudinal Survey and her own fieldwork in two provinces of the Red River Delta in 2002 indicate that the majority of female household heads in these areas report being currently married and living with a spouse and that, for these women, the status of household head does not necessarily translate into increased decision-making power. Her study is particularly useful in calling attention to the risk of wrongly presuming that administrative categories, household headship in this case, carry with them an array of social meanings and practices, such as those related to women's empowerment. In this sense, her contribution speaks to the construction of knowledge in the social sciences.

FAMILY LIVELIHOOD STRATEGIES

Shifts in the labor structure initiated by *Doi Moi* have modified families' livelihood strategies in fundamental ways. Prior to the mid-1980s, the state organized employment in cooperatives and in public services. No one needed to look for work; jobs and workplaces were assigned upon school completion. Individuals received housing, food rations, and basic social services in exchange for their labor. The transition to a market economy has led to the expansion of a cash economy, the massive entry of foreign investment, the development of the private sector, and the nonintervention of the state in the regulation of the new job market, which have all profoundly transformed the employment landscape (Oudin 1999). The state no longer assigns jobs; individuals and their families must find them for themselves. Pressure to enter and stay in the job market has become acute in an environment where the costs of basic services, such as health care and education, are soaring. Recent research conducted in Vietnam suggests, however, that major decisions relative to work are still the result of corporate family interests rather than individual preferences (Korinek et al. 2006). In this respect, the concept of a family adaptive strategy is particularly appropriate. Who is going to work outside the home, in which sector, and in which geographic area are all decided on the basis of the family's collective needs, and on the resources, skills (including nonmarket ones), and power available among its members.

Xavier Oudin's chapter examines how the transformation of work structure and household responsibilities creates new forms of family dependencies and ties. Specifically, he observes these changes through an analysis of household composition and the type of employment held by working household members. Based on the analyses of data from two national surveys, he presents results on the relationship between types of employment and household structure to assess the existence of family ties and solidarities through co-residence. The analysis reveals a weak relationship between employment type and household structure, pointing to a high degree of diversification in family ties and activities, household strategies, and work statuses during the initial phase of renovation.

Hy Van Luong's contribution illustrates the role of networks in migration strategies and points to the relevance of kin and other ties in seizing the benefits offered by the market system. His chapter focuses on regional variations in political economy, family organization, and interhousehold networks in the context of a rapidly evolving economic environment. Hy Van Luong draws upon data from five Vietnamese rural communities, two in the Mekong Delta, two in the southern central coast, and one in the Red River Delta. The comparative analysis of migration into and out of these five communities highlights how local political economies and sociocultural frameworks (including family organization) have shaped the divergent characteristics of migration patterns in different regions of Vietnam. It suggests that stronger migration in Mekong Delta villages, compared to North and Central Vietnam, reflects the long-standing and more open nature of southern villages in general. It also shows that the lesser mutual assistance among Mekong Delta villagers within the same community and the wider extension of social and kinship networks outside of it underlay the migration of many villagers from debt-ridden households to urban areas and their occupational and spatial scattering in the cities. The different pattern of migration in Northern and Central villages compared to the Southern ones reflects a stronger inward orientation and smaller social networks to the outside world. As a result, Central and Northern villagers tend to follow the lead established by a few pioneer migrants and to cluster much more occupationally and spatially in the cities than their Southern counterparts.

This collection concludes with an afterword designed to sum up the most important findings of the twelve analytical chapters in relation to the issues raised in this introduction. The study results are further discussed in a comparative perspective with China and other countries in the region to question the future directions of family change in Vietnam.

Notes

1. Late socialism, in this chapter, refers to the combination of socialist bureaucracy and state apparatus and of market mechanisms regulating the economy. We do not use the term *postsocialism* because we feel that to include in the same category former socialist countries that no longer are led by a Communist Party and countries that have accepted market mechanisms while still led by a Communist Party (Vietnam and China) is somewhat problematic.

2. Such presumption is more common in English-language scholarship on Vietnam. In Europe, and France in particular, where the colonial history has kept France much closer to Vietnam's recent history, the concept of the transition is criticized. See, for instance, An and de Tréglodé (2003) for a critique of the science of "transitologie."

3. Some collections on Vietnam use, as a point of departure, the end of the American War. In the case of the collection edited by Marr and White (1988), *Postwar Vietnam: Dilemmas in Socialist Development*, and the one by Luong (2003), *Postwar Vietnam: Dynamics of a Transforming Society*, most chapters deal in fact with the renovation period (after 1986).

4. Retired members of the army and retired civil servants do receive a pension in Vietnam, but the amount is modest and is not sufficient to cover health care costs.

5. See, for instance, Phan Ke Binh (1975/1980) and Cadière (1930) for works published during the colonial period on the centrality of the family. Recent works, such as those of the Institute of Sociology (1991), Jamieson (1995), Pham Van Bich (1999), and Malarney (2002), also discuss the family as the cornerstone of Vietnamese society.

6. Our translation from French.

7. In an attempt to shed light on what was really happening among Vietnamese family members and in their homes, the French struck up a committee that had the objective of documenting current practices. The report that followed the work of this committee offers interesting evidence about some native practices departing from the Confucian ideal (Protectorat du Tonkin 1930).

8. For a detailed account of some of these campaigns, see Phan Van Bich (1999).

9. In contrast to Malarney, Goodkind has argued that marriage practices were successfully transformed in the North of Vietnam and that there was no return of presocialist elements in the early renovation period (1996).

10. Decisions No.27-ND. and 29-ND of March 1988. A distinction is made in Vietnam between the private sector of production, based on explicit private work contracts between unrelated people, and the household sector of production, based on a consensual agreement among family members. During socialism, the household sector of production was severely restricted but did not completely disappear, as 5 percent of agricultural land was legally attributed to households for their own production.

11. Resolution No. 10 of the Politbureau, April 1988.

References

An, Y. B., and B. de Tréglodé. 2003. Doi Moi et mutations du politique. In *Việt Nam contemporain*, edited by S. Dovert and B. de Tréglodé, 117–148. Paris: Les Indes Savantes.

Anagnost, A. 1995. A surfeit of bodies: Population and the rationality of the state in post-Mao China. In *Conceiving the new world order: The global politics of reproduction*, edited by F. D. Ginsburg and R. Rapp, 22–41. Berkeley: University of California Press.

Bélanger, D. 1997a. Changements familiaux au Vietnam depuis 1960: trente années de formation des couples à Hanoi. *Autrepart* 2: 33–52.

Bélanger, D. 1997b. *Rapport intergénérationnel et raport hommes-femmes dans la transition démographique au Vietnam, de 1930 à 1990*. Ph.D. dissertation, Department of Demography, University of Montreal.

Bélanger, D. 2000. Regional differences in household composition and family formation patterns in Vietnam. *Journal of Comparative Family Studies* 31 (2): 171–189.

Bélanger, D. 2001. Son preference and demographic change in Vietnam. Paper presented at the International Union for the Scientific Study of Population International Conference, Brazil, August 2001.

Bélanger, D. 2002. Childhood, gender and power in Vietnam. In *Communities in Southeast Asia: Challenges and responses*, edited by H. Lansdowne, P. Dearden, and W. Neilson, 380–402. Victoria: Center for Asia-Pacific Initiatives.

Bélanger, D., and Khuat, T. H. 2001. Parents' involvement in children's marriage. In *Vietnamese society in transition*, edited by J. Kleinen, 250–264. Amsterdam: Het Spinhuis.

Bélanger, D., and J. Liu. 2004. Social policy reforms and daughters' schooling. *Vietnam: International Journal of Educational Development* 24: 23–38.

Bélanger, D., and X. Oudin. 2007. For better or worse? Working mothers in late Vietnamese socialism. In *Working and mothering in Asia, images, ideologies and identities*, edited by T. Devasahayam and B. S. A. Yeoh, 106–135. Singapore: National University of Singapore.

Berdahl, D. 2000. Introduction: An anthropology of postsocialism. In *Altering states: ethnographies of transition in Eastern Europe and the former Soviet Union*, edited by D. Berdahl, M. Bunzl, and M. Lampland, 1–13. Ann Arbor: The University of Michigan Press.

Beresford, M. 2003. Economic transition, uneven development, and the impact of reform on regional inequality. In *Postwar Vietnam, dynamics of a transforming society*, edited by H. V. Luong, 55–80. Singapore: Institute of Southeast Asian Studies.

Bersegian, I. 2000. When text becomes field: Fieldwork in "transitional" societies. In *Fieldwork dilemmas*, edited by H. G. D. Soto and N. Dudwick, 119–129. Madison: The University of Wisconsin Press.

Bonker, F., K. Muller, and A. Pickel. 2002. *Postcommunist transformation and the social sciences: Cross disciplinary approaches.* Lanham: Rowman and Littlefield.

Bray, M. 1996. *Counting the full cost: Parental and community financing of education in East Asia.* Washington, DC: The World Bank.

Bui Tran Phuong. 2003. La famille Vietnamienne: Point de repère dans les tourmentes? In *Viêt Nam contemporain*, edited by S. Dovert and B. de Tréglodé, 467–493. Paris: Les Indes Savantes.

Cadière, L. 1930. La famille et la religion en pays annamite. *Bulletin des Amis du Vieux Hue* 17: 353–413. Hue : École Française d'Extrême Orient.

Cho, L.-J., and M. Yada, eds. 1994. *Tradition and change in the Asia family.* Honolulu and Tokyo: East-West Center and University Research Center, Nihon University.

Dang Nguyen Anh. 1999. Market reforms and internal labor migration in Vietnam. *Asian and Pacific Migration Journal* 8 (3): 381–409.

Dang Nguyen Anh, C. Tacoli, and Hoang X. T. 2003. Migration in Vietnam: A review of information on current trends and patterns, and their policy implications. *Regional Conference on Migration, Development Pro-Poor Policy Choices in Asia*, 22–24 June, Dhaka, Bangladesh.

Dang Nguyen Anh, C. Tacoli, and Hoang X. T. 2004. *Stay on the farm, weave in the village, leave the home.* Hanoi: The Gioi Publishers.

Dang Phong. 2004. Stages on the road to renovation of the Vietnamese economy: A historical perspective. In *Reaching for the dream: challenges of sustainable development in Vietnam*, edited by M. Beresford and Tran N. A., 19–50. Copenhagen: Nordic Institute of Asian Studies.

Desai, J. 2000. *Vietnam through the lens of gender: Five years later.* Hanoi: Food and Agriculture Organization of the United Nations.

Desbarats, J. 1987. Population redistribution in the socialist republic of Vietnam. *Population and Development Review* 13 (1): 43–76.

Drummond, L., and H. Rydstrom eds. 2004. *Gender practices in contemporary Vietnam.* Singapore: National University Press.

Edgar, D. 2004. Globalization and the Western bias in family sociology. In *The Blackwell companion to the sociologies of families,* edited by J. Scott, J. Treas, and M. Richards, 3–16. Oxford: Blackwell.

Eng, L. A., and M. Blake. 1998. Introduction. In *Families in Southeast Asia: Facing fundamental changes.* Special issue of *SOJOURN, Journal of Social Issues in Southeast Asia.* 13 (2): 183–192.

Eisen, A. 1984. The family in transition. In *Women and revolution in Vietnam,* edited by A. Eisen, 180–200. London: Zed Books.

Fforde, A., and S. de Vylder. 1996. *From plan to market.* Boulder: Westview Press.

Fraser, S. E. 1993. Vietnam: Schooling, literacy and fertility census 1979, 1989, 1999. *International Journal of Educational Development* 13 (1): 63–80.

Gammeltoft, T. 1999. *Women's bodies, women's worries.* Richmond: Curzon Press.

Ginsburg, F., and R. Rapp. 1991. The politics of reproduction. *Annual Review of Anthropology* 20: 311–343.

Ginsburg, F., and R. Rapp, eds. 1995. *Conceiving the new world order: Local/global intersections in the politics of reproduction.* Berkeley: University of California Press.

Goode, W. 1982. *The family.* Englewood Cliffs: Prentice Hall.

Goodkind, D. 1995a. Rising gender inequality in Vietnam since reunification. *Pacific Affairs* 68 (3): 342–359.

Goodkind, D. 1995b. Vietnam's one- or two-child policy in action. *Population and Development Review* 21 (1): 85–111.

Goodkind, D. 1996. State agendas, local sentiments: Vietnamese wedding practices amidst socialist transformations. *Social Forces* 75 (2): 717–742.

Greenhalgh, S. 1988. Fertility as mobility: Sinic transitions. *Population and Development Review* 14 (4): 629–674.

Greenhalgh, S. 1994. Controlling births and bodies in village China. *American Ethnologist* 21 (1): 3–30.

Greenhalgh, S., ed. 1995. *Situating fertility.* Cambridge, England: Cambridge University Press.

Greenhalgh, S., and J. Li. 1995. *Engendering reproductive policy and practice in peasant China: For a feminist demography of reproduction.* Signs: 601–640.

Haney, L., and L. Pollard. 2003. In a family way: Theorizing state and familial relations. In *Families of a new world: gender, politics and state development in a global context,* edited by L. Haney and L. Pollard, 1–14. New York and London: Routledge.

Hardy, A. 2003. *Red hills: Migrants and the state in the highlands of Vietnam.* Copenhague and Honolulu: NIA Press/Hawaii University Press.

Haughton, J. 1999. Introduction. In *Health and wealth in Vietnam: An analysis of household living standards,* edited by D. Haughton, J. Haughton, S. Bales, Truong T. K. C., and Nguyen N. N., 1–22. Singapore: Institute of Southeast Asian Studies.

Hareven, T. K. 2000. *Families, history, and social change: Life-course & cross-cultural perspectives.* Boulder, CO: Westview Press.

Hirschman, C., and Vu M. L. 1996. Family and household structure in Vietnam: Some glimpses from a recent survey. *Pacific Affairs* 69 (2): 229–249.

Institute of Sociology. 1991. *Sociological studies on the Vietnamese family.* Hanoi: Social Sciences Publishing House.

Jamieson, N. L. 1995. *Understanding Vietnam.* Berkeley, Los Angeles, and London: University of California Press.

Jones, G. W. 1982. Population trends and policies in Vietnam. *Population and Development Review* 8(4): 783–810.

Kerkvliet, B. J. T., A. Chan, and J. Unger. 1999. Comparing Vietnam and China: An introduction. In *Transforming Asian socialism. China and Vietnam compared,* edited by A. Chan, B. J. T. Kerkvliet, and J. Unger, 1–14. Latham: Rowan & Littlefield.

Kerkvliet, B. J. T. 2003. Authorities and the people: An analysis of state-society relations in Vietnam. In *Postwar Vietnam: Dynamics of a transforming society,* edited by H. V. Luong, 27–54. Lanham: Rowman & Littlefield.

Kerkvliet, B. J. T. 2005. *The power of everyday politics: How Vietnamese peasants transformed national policy.* Ithaca, NY: Cornell University Press.

Khuat Thu Hong. 1998. *Study on sexuality in Vietnam: The known and unknown issues.* Hanoi: The Population Council.

Kleinen, J. 1999. *Facing the future, reviving the past: A study of social change in a northern Vietnamese village.* Singapore: Institute of Southeast Asian Studies.

Knodel, John J., and G. W. Jones. 1996. Post-Cairo population policy: Does promoting girls' schooling miss the mark? *Population and Development Review* 22 (4): 683–702.

Kokko, A. 2004. Growth and reform since the Eighth Party Congress. In *Rethinking Vietnam,* edited by D. McCargo, 69–90. London and New York: Routledge Curzon.

Korinek, K., F. Chen, S. Alva, and B. Entwisle. 2006. Household economic transformation and recent fertility in emerging market economies: China and Vietnam compared. *Journal of Comparative Family Studies* 37 (2): 191–234.

Krowolski, N., and Nguyen T. 2005. Femmes et "forêt de rire": La femme à travers les contes à rire au Viêt Nam. In *Le Viêt Nam au Féminin,* edited by N. A. Taylor and G. Bousquet, 153–186. Paris: Les Indes Savantes.

Kruks, S., R. Rapp, and M. Blatt, eds. 1989. *Promissory notes: Women in the transition to socialism.* New York: Monthly Review Press.

Le Van Sinh. 2001. On becoming a more diversified countryside. In *Vietnamese society in transition: The daily politics of reform and change,* edited by J. Kleinen, 133–156. Amsterdam: Her Spinhuis.

Leshkowich, A. M. 2005. Feminine disorder: State campaigns against street traders in socialist and late socialist Viêt Nam. In *Le Viêt Nam au Féminin,* edited by N. A. Taylor and G. Bousquet, 187–207. Paris: Les Indes Savantes.

London, J. 2004. Rethinking Vietnam's mass education and health systems. In *Rethinking Vietnam,* edited by D. McCargo, 127–142. London and New York: Routledge Curzon.

Luong, Hy Van. 1989. Vietnamese kinship: Structural principles and the socialist transformation in Northern Vietnam. *Journal of Asian Studies* 48 (4): 741–756.

Luong, Hy Van. 1993. Economic reforms and the intensification of gender rituals in two north Vietnamese villages, 1980–90. In *The challenge of reforms in Indochina,* edited by B. Ljunggren, 259–252. Cambridge, MA: Harvard University Press.

Luong, Hy Van. 2003. *Postwar Vietnam: Dynamics of a transforming society.* Boulder: Rowman and Littlefield.

Lustéguy, P. 1935. *La femme annamite du Tonkin dans l'institution des biens culturels. Étude sur une enquête récente.* Paris: Librairie Nizet et Bastard.

Malarney, S. K. 2002. *Culture, ritual and revolution in Vietnam.* Honolulu: University of Hawaii Press.

Malarney, S. K. 2003. Return to the past? The dynamics of contemporary religious and ritual transformation. In *Postwar Vietnam: Dynamics of a transforming society,* edited by H. V. Luong, 225–256. Lanham: Rowman & Littlefield.

Marr, D. G. 1981. *Vietnamese tradition on trial 1920–1945.* Berkeley: University of California Press.

Marr, D. G., and C. Pelzer White. 1988. Introduction. In *Postwar Vietnam: Dilemmas in socialist development,* edited by D. G. Marr and C. P. White, 1–15. Ithaca, NY: Cornell University South East Asia Program.

Mason, K. O., N. O. Tsuya, and M. K. Choe. 1998. *The changing family in comparative perspective: Asia and the United States.* Honolulu: The East-West Center.

McCargo, D., ed. 2004. *Rethinking Vietnam.* London: Curzon Press.

McDonald, P. 1994. Families in developing countries: Idealized morality and theories of family change. In *Tradition and change in the Asian family,* edited by L.-J. Cho and M. Yada, 19–27. Honolulu: East West Center.

Meslé, F., and J. Vallin. 2002. Mortalité en Europe: La divergence Est-Ouest. *Population* 1: 1079–1101.

Morgan, D. H. J. 2003. Introduction. In: *Family: Critical concepts in sociology,* edited by D. Cheal, 1–16. London and New York: Routledge.

Nguyen-vo, Thu-huong. 2002. Governing sex: Medicine and governmental intervention in prostitution. In *Gender, household, state: Doi Moi in Viet Nam,* edited by J. Werner and D. Bélanger, 129–151. Ithaca, NY: Southeast Asia Program Publication, Cornell University.

Otis, E. M. 2003. Reinstating the family: Gender and the state-formed foundations of China's flexible labor force. In *Families of a new world: gender, politics, and state development in a global context*, edited by L. Haney and L. Pollard, 196–216. New York and London: Routledge.

Oudin, X. 1999. Le *Doi Moi* et l'évolution du travail au Viêtnam. *Revue Tiers Monde* XL 158: 377–396.

Papin, P. 2003. *Viêt-Nam: Parcours d'une nation*. Paris: Éditions Belin, La documentation française.

Parish, W. L., and M. K. Whyte. 1978. *Village and family in contemporary China*. Chicago: University of Chicago Press.

Perry, E. J., and M. Selden, eds. 2000. *Chinese society: Change, conflict and resistance*. London: Routledge.

Pettus, A. 2003. *Between sacrifice and desire: National identity and the governing of feminity in Vietnam*. New York and London: Routledge.

Pham Van Bich. 1999. *The Vietnamese family in change: The case of the Red River delta*. Richmond: Curzon.

Phan Ke Binh. 1975/1980. Viet-Nam phong-tuc (Moeurs et coutumes du Vietnam). Translated by N. Louis-Hénard. Collection de textes et documents sur l'Indochine. Two volumes. Paris: Ecole Française d'Extrême Orient.

Pickles, J., and A. Smith, eds. 1998. *Theorising transition: The political economy of post-communist transformations*. London: Routledge.

Population and Development Review. 1989. Vietnam's new fertility policy. *Population and Development Review* 15 (1): 169–172.

Protectorat du Tonkin. 1930. *Recueil des avis du comité consultatif de jurisprudence annamite sur les coutumes des Annamites du Tonkin en matière de droit de la famille, de succession et de bien cultuels*. Hanoi: Imprimerie Trung-Bac Tan-Van.

Quinn-Judge, S. 1983. *Indochina Issues* 42: 1–7.

Rousselet, K. 2005. La famille russe: Configurations des relations et évolutions des solidarités. *Informations Sociales* 124: 76–83.

Salecl, R. 1994. *The spoils of freedom: Psychoanalysis and feminism after the fall of socialism*. London: Routledge.

Shkolnikov, V. M. 1995. La crise sanitaire en Russie: Tendances récentes de l'espérance de vie et des causes de décès de 1970 à 1993. *Population* 4–5: 907–943.

Stacey, J. 1983. *Patriarchy and socialist revolution in China*. Berkeley: University of California Press.

Ta Van Tai. 1981. The status of women in traditional Vietnam: A comparison of the code of the Le dynasty (1428–1788) with the Chinese codes. *Journal of Asian History* 15 (2): 97–145.

Taylor, P. 2004. Introduction: Social inequality in a socialist state. In *Social inequality in Vietnam and the challenges to reform*, edited by P. Taylor, 1–40. Singapore: Institute of Southeast Asian Studies.

Thornton, A., and T. E. Fricke. 1987. Social change and the family: Comparative perspectives from the West, China, and South Asia. *Sociological Forum* 4: 746–779.

Tran Thi Thu Trang. 2004. Vietnam's rural transformation. Information, knowledge and diversification. In *Rethinking Vietnam*, edited by D. McCargo, 110–124. London and New York: Routledge Curzon.

Tran Tuyet Nhung. 2006. Beyond the myth of equality: Daughters' inheritance rights in the Le Code. In *Viet Nam: Borderless histories*, edited by N. T. Tran and A. Reid, 121–144. Madison: University of Wisconsin Press.

Turley, W. S. 1993. Introduction. In *Reinventing Vietnamese socialism:* Doi Moi *in comparative perspective*, edited by W. S. Turley and M. Selden, 1–15. Boulder, CO; San Francisco; and Oxford, England: Westview Press.

Turley, W. S., and M. Selden, eds. 1993. *Reinventing Vietnamese socialism:* Doi Moi *in comparative perspective*. Boulder, CO; San Francisco; and Oxford, England: Westview Press.

United Nations. 2005. *Living arrangements of older persons around the world.* New York: United Nations.

Vervoorn, A. E. 1998. *Re orient: Change in Asian societies.* Melbourne and New York: Oxford University Press.

Vien Xa Hoi Hoc. 1996. *Tac dong cua bien doi kinh te-xa hoi den mot so khia canh cua gia dinh Viet Nam.* Nghien cuu truong hop tinh Thai Binh. Hanoi: Nha Xuat Ban Khoa Hoc Xa Hoi

Vu Tuan Huy. 2003. *Mau thuan vo chong trong gia dinh va nhung yeu to anh huong.* Hanoi: Nha Xuat Ban Khoa Hoc Xa Hoi.

Werner, J. 1981. Women, socialism, and the economy of wartime North Vietnam, 1960–1975. *Studies in Comparative Communism* 14 (2 & 3): 165–190.

Werner, J. 1993. Cooperatization, the family economy, and the new family in wartime Vietnam, 1960–1975. In *The American war in Vietnam*, edited by J. Werner and D. Hunt, 77–92. Ithaca, NY: Southeast Asia Program Publication, Cornell University.

Werner, J. 2002. Gender, Household, and State: Renovation (*Doi Moi*) as Social Process in Vietnam. In *Gender, household, State:* Doi Moi *in Viet Nam*, edited by J. Werner and D. Bélanger, 29–47. Ithaca: Southeast Asia Program Publication, Cornell University.

Werner, J., and D. Bélanger, eds. 2002. *Gender, household, State:* Doi Moi *in Viet Nam.* Ithaca: Southeast Asia Program Publication, Cornell University.

White Pelzer, C. 1989. Vietnam: War, Socialism, and the Politics of Gender Relations. In *Promissory notes: women in transition to socialism* edited by S. Kruks, R. Rapp, and M. B. Young, 172–192. New York: New York Monthly Press.

Wiegersma, N. 1988. *Vietnam: Peasant Land, Peasant Revolution: Patriarchy and Collectivity in the Rural Economy.* New York: St. Martin's Press.

Wisensale, S. 1999. Marriage and family law in a changing Vietnam. *Journal of Family Issues* 20 (5): 602–616.

World Bank. 2006. *2006 World Development Indicators*. Washington, DC: The World Bank.

Yan, Y. 2003. *Private Life under Socialism: Love, Intimacy, and Family Change in a Chinese Village 1949–1999*. Stanford: Stanford University Press.

Yu, I. 1978. *Law and Family in Seventeenth and Eighteenth Century Vietnam*. Ph.D. dissertation in History, University of Michigan.

PART ONE

A New Social Contract

Chapter Two

State and the Family

Reproductive Policies and Practices

CATHERINE SCORNET

Paradoxically, just as the Vietnamese state was withdrawing from the economic sphere after the implementation of the *Doi Moi* or "renovation" policy in 1986, it adopted and then strengthened a restrictive, prescriptive family policy. Two years after *Doi Moi* the government introduced a policy limiting families to one or two children, which was energetically applied in many parts of the country in the late 1980s and early 1990s.

This chapter outlines the history of Vietnam's family and birth control policies since the formation of an independent socialist state in the North in 1954, to show how the state is encouraging changes in reproductive behavior. It describes and analyzes how the Vietnamese state has promoted a new norm for family size and composition, highlighting the advantages of a one-or-two-child family. It describes the legislative measures and their local applications. It also analyzes the communication and information campaigns conducted in Ninh Hiep, a rural commune in the Red River Delta region in the North, aimed at persuading people to accept the new norm by presenting its advantages for the individual, the family, and the nation.

Controlling population size began in the North in the 1960s, and for the rest of the twentieth century the focus remained quantitative, concerned with the size and composition of the population. Recently, however, a reproductive health policy based on population quality and individual rights, which was strongly influenced by international and nongovernmental organizations pursuing the recommendations of the 1994 Cairo conference on population and development, has replaced this policy. The Vietnamese state's new position, with its greater emphasis on the population's qualitative characteristics, is set out in the 2003 Population Ordinance. The survival and renewal of the group, the culture, and the population, as a collective entity, have always been major demographic concerns, but there is now, in addition, a new emphasis on a more qualitative dimension, with the integration of the notion of happiness into the population policy. This chapter examines the ideological assumptions behind the population policies adopted in Vietnam since the 1960s.

A New Family for a New Society: Population Policy Measures

The Democratic Republic of Vietnam, established in North Vietnam by the communists after the country was divided under the Geneva Agreement of 1954, was among the first countries in the developing world to introduce a birth control policy and advocate small families as the norm. This chapter describes Vietnam's national policy and then analyzes the role of political players, who have considerable leeway in defining and applying policy at the provincial, district, and communal levels. Vietnamese communism was built on a tradition of decentralized power; even under the old imperial dynasties, local authorities had considerable autonomy and the expression "local State power" was used (Kerkvliet and Marr 2004). As demonstrated by Benedict Kerkvliet (2005), the deep penetration of the state in the villages coincided with a relative degree of autonomy at the local level, in terms of the framework in which to carry out economic and social policy measures. Until the late nineteenth century, local autonomy was based on a literate rural elite that provided the state with its Mandarin scholar-officials through competitive literary examinations. Thanks to their literati, the villages had the means to assert their political autonomy, which was very strong because all Vietnamese identify with their village through a total attachment to the land and their ancestors. "It was the cohesion of society, mainly consisting of peasants and literati, that made Vietnam. Whenever the royal State weakened, social initiative filled the gap"[1] (Hémery 1990, 14). Though the popular adage stating that "village customs carry more weight than the laws of the kingdom" (*Lenh vua thua le lang*) has become somewhat outdated with the strong centralization promoted by the socialist state, it remains true that local authorities continue to play a major role in the implementation of government policy decisions.

Emergence and Establishment of the Socialist Family Norm (1959–80)

From the mid-twentieth century, "the family became a key concern in the endeavor to construct a new society,"[2] under the influence of socialism (Bélanger 1997, 67). From its beginning, the socialist family model sought to break away from the traditional family. Taking advantage of a power vacuum created by the Japanese defeat at the end of World War II and their departure from Vietnam while the French had not yet returned, Ho Chi Minh proclaimed the country's independence on September 2, 1945. The first constitution, promulgated in 1946, abolished legal inequalities between the sexes by stating that: "Women have equal rights to men in all fields" (Article 9). However, the French disputed this bold political move, and an independence war broke out that was to last until the Geneva accords of July 20, 1954. The accords resulted in the division of the national territory along the seventeenth parallel into two separate states, the Democratic Republic of Vietnam in the North and the Republic of Vietnam in the South, with socialist rule in the North only. A first series of legal measures was voted by the socialist government during the war. The first changes to the civil codes introduced by imperial legislators and the French colonial authorities in Tonkin, Annam, and Cochin China came in 1950, with the decrees 97-SL and 159-SL. Patriarchal law was abolished, the age of majority was reduced from twenty-one years to eighteen years (Article 2, 97-SL), and boys and girls were proclaimed equal in the family. Once young people reached the age of majority, their marriages were no longer subject to parental consent (Article 2, 97-SL; Association of Jurists 1987).

However, it was the Family and Marriage Law of December 29, 1959, that took the first major step in establishing a new model of marriage and the family (Pham in Charbit and Scornet 2002). It laid down regulations on marriage, the rights and obligations of spouses, relations between parents and children, and divorce. The new law had two goals. One was to eradicate the remnants of the old family and matrimonial system, key features of which were arranged marriage, early marriage, polygamy, gender inequality, and protection of patriarchal rights. The other was to establish a new system based on four principles: marriage by free consent, monogamy, equality between husband and wife, and protection of children's equality and rights. Conjugal equality and equality between children, regardless of gender and status, formed the basis of the new family norm. According to the 1959 law, "boys and girls have equal rights and duties in the family; adopted children and illegitimate children have the same rights and obligations as legitimate children" (Articles 19 and 23). The new law was the first example of official intervention in family matters, which, until then, had been essentially private.

Once the new legal framework was established, the government turned to the reproductive aspects of the family. The results of the 1960 census in the Democratic Republic of Vietnam alarmed the government; the population had grown at an estimated 3.8 percent per year between 1955 and 1960 (Table 2.1), three times as fast as the 1 to 1.5 percent growth recorded in the colonial era. The country's leaders feared strong population pressure on the land, especially in the Red River Delta, and resulting food shortages.

The first measures to raise the population's awareness of birth control were taken in 1961 (Decision No. 216-CP of the Council of Ministers, December 12, 1961). Smaller household size seemed to be one indispensable way of controlling population growth. The demographic factor affected economic growth, and population growth was liable to slow down economic development; consequently, in 1963, the government launched the birth control policy. For the first time, standards were set for small family size and longer birth interval, and Vietnamese families were advised to have no more than three children, at intervals of five or six years (Decree 99/TTg of October 16, 1963). This directive encouraged people to "combat retrograde ideas about procreation and, through constant, continuing information and education, make family planning a new way of life for the Vietnamese people" (Decree 99/TTg of October 16, 1963). Raising awareness about the small-family norm and the reputedly harmful effects of population growth was, from the start, a major goal of the family planning program. However, the authorities wanted to avoid opposition and resistance, particularly from ethnic minorities and Catholics, and therefore wanted information about the small family norm to be discreetly limited to a few clearly defined groups (officials, Communist Party cadres, etc.).[3] This contrasts with the mass campaigns launched in the early 1990s.

In the 1970s, the government defined the means for regulating fertility; the production and import of intrauterine devices (IUDs) and the practice

TABLE 2.1

Population growth in Vietnam, 1901–2008

Year	Numbers (millions)	Growth rate (%)	Year	Numbers (millions)	Growth rate (%)
1901	13.0	1.2	1980	53.8	2.0
1911	14.7	0.6	1981	54.9	2.4
1921	15.6	0.9	1982	56.2	2.1
1926	16.3	1.7	1983	57.4	2.4
1931	17.7	1.4	1984	58.8	1.9
1936	19.0	1.0	1985	59.9	2.0
1939	19.6	3.2	1986	61.1	2.3
1943	22.2	0.5	1987	62.5	1.9
1951	23.1	2.1	1988	63.7	1.7
1955	25.1	3.8	1989	64.8	2.2
1960	30.2	2.9	1990	66.2	2.4
1965	34.9	3.3	1991	67.8	2.4
1970	41.1	3.0	1992	69.4	2.3
1974	46.2	3.0	1993	71.0	2.1
1975	47.6	3.4	1994	72.5	2.1
1976	49.2	2.4	1995	74.0	0.8
1977	50.4	2.0	1999	76.3	1.5
1978	51.4	2.1	2002	79.7	1.4
1979	52.5	2.5	2008	86.4	

SOURCE: Gendreau, F., V. Favreau, and Dang. 1997; United Nations Economic and Social Commission for Asia and the Pacific 2005; General Statistics Office 2001; Population Reference Bureau 2005; United Nations Economic and Social Commission for Asia and the Pacific, *2008 Population Data Sheet.*

of abortion were vigorously encouraged. This formed the basis of the family planning policy until Vietnam's reunification in 1976. The policy limited family size to three children and to classified areas (towns and densely populated deltas and lowlands) as targets for small-family promotion campaigns. These goals progressively grew more restrictive and the measures extended to the South.[4] In Directive 265/CP of October 19, 1978, the first to cover the whole country, the Council of Ministers stressed the advantages of having only two or three children, four or five years apart, the first being born "when the woman's body has completed its growth and is perfectly developed, at the age of 20 or over." This twenty-year limit coincides with the traditional medical theory that neither the male nor the female principles fully form before the age of twenty. In cases of sterility, masters of the traditional Vietnamese pharmacopeia blame early marriage among other factors (Do 1998). Vietnamese communism did not make an entirely clean sweep of tradition.

Consolidating Policy with Mass Propaganda to Disseminate the New Family Norm (1980s and 1990s)

THE VIETNAMESE STATE ADVOCATES A NEW FAMILY NORM ("WE MUST BUILD A NEW VIETNAMESE FAMILY")

Not until the decisions of the 5th Congress of the Vietnamese Communist Party (VCP) in March 1982 and the creation of the National Committee for Population and Family Planning in 1984 (Decision 58-HDBT of 11 April 1984) was a more energetic family planning policy adopted. The national government publicly proclaimed its normative goal of two children per family in 1988, and the Council of Ministers made it official in their Decision 162 on October 18 of that year. The one-or-two-child policy (*mot hoac hai con*)[5] strengthened the earlier measures to slow down population growth, something considered necessary if living standards of all Vietnamese citizens were to improve. The VCP Congress of 1986 determined that an annual population growth rate of 1.7 percent had to be achieved by 1990. The 1988 decision also sought to mobilize the population on a large scale. "Practicing family planning is the responsibility of all society, of male as well as female citizens, beginning with the ministries and the people's committees on the various levels, whose responsibility it is to provide day to day guidance" (Article 1). It was particularly important for some groups of people to have a maximum of two children. These included political cadres; manual workers; civil servants working for the Communist Party, the state, and mass organizations; soldiers in the armed forces; families who lived in municipalities, cities, or industrial zones (based on the woman's place of residence); and families living in the Red River and Mekong deltas and the lowlands of the coastal provinces.

The family norms were applied in a way that shows how the policy took into account the particular features of ethnic groups and regions and their attendant constraints. The family norm was more flexible for ethnic minorities in the highland provinces of the North and the high plateau; they could have a maximum of three children. Because the population was less dense in the northern highlands (120 per km² in 1989) than in the deltas (1,124 per km² in the Red River Delta), the government's birth control legislation was more flexible. However, fertility rates among ethnic minorities in the highlands were high: the total fertility rate for H'Mong women was 9.3 children per woman in the 1989 census (see Table 2.6 in the section New Goals for Family Policy, later in this chapter).[6]

In January 1993, the Central Committee of the Communist Party adopted a resolution on population and family planning that blamed many of Vietnam's ecological, economic, and social problems on population growth (Communist Party of Vietnam 1993). The two most recent laws on marriage and the family (May 29, 1986 and June 9, 2000) also ratified family planning; "The spouses have a duty to practice birth control" (Article 2, June 9, 2000).[7] Under this law, the minimum age for marriage remained the same as the 1959 law: "A man may not contract a marriage before completion of his 20th year, a woman not before completion of her 18th year" (Article 9).

INSTITUTIONAL ORGANIZATION

These policy statements were not empty verbiage; they were put into practice directly. Until 1984, population control and family planning were the sole responsibility of the Ministry of Health, which is one reason why local political officials did not always pay much attention to demographic issues. Since the formation of the National Committee for Population and Family Planning (NCPFP) in 1984, population problems have been treated as a matter of general policy, not just as a health issue. The chair of the NCPFP,[8] appointed by the prime minister, has ministerial rank. For the first eight years, the NCPFP acted as an independent organization; since 1992, it has reported to the Ministry of Population and Family Planning, which was created that year.

The involvement of representatives from diverse fields, such as economics, education, defense, health, and culture in the NCPFP,[9] shows that the Vietnamese authorities want the new family norm to be very widely disseminated. Each ministry and government agency has a clearly defined task to fill. The Ministry of Defense is responsible for educating members of the armed forces in birth control. The Ministry of Culture is responsible for conducting "Information-Education-Communication" (IEC) campaigns through the mass media. The Ministry of Education is responsible for population-related education at all levels of school and higher education. The task, involving all political and civil players and using propaganda, is to "build a new Vietnamese family."[10]

At the central, provincial, and district levels, the NCPFP network includes over 2,500 people (Figure 2.1). It is particularly dense at the communal level; each of the country's 10,104 communes employs one official, who is aided by

Central:
Party and government

NCPFP - - - - - - - - - - -> Agencies, social organizations
Mass organizations (Fatherland Front)

Province:
Party and authorities

Provincial CPFP - - - - - - - -> Agencies, social organizations
Mass organizations (Fatherland Front)

District:
Party and authorities

District CPFP - - - - - - - -> Agencies, social organizations
Mass organizations

Commune:
Party and authorities

Family planning Team - - - - - -> Agencies, social organizations
Mass organizations (Fatherland Front)

Village:
Party chief and village chief

Assistants - - - - - - - -> Propagandists

Note:

⟶ Leadership   - - - - -> Coordination and supervision

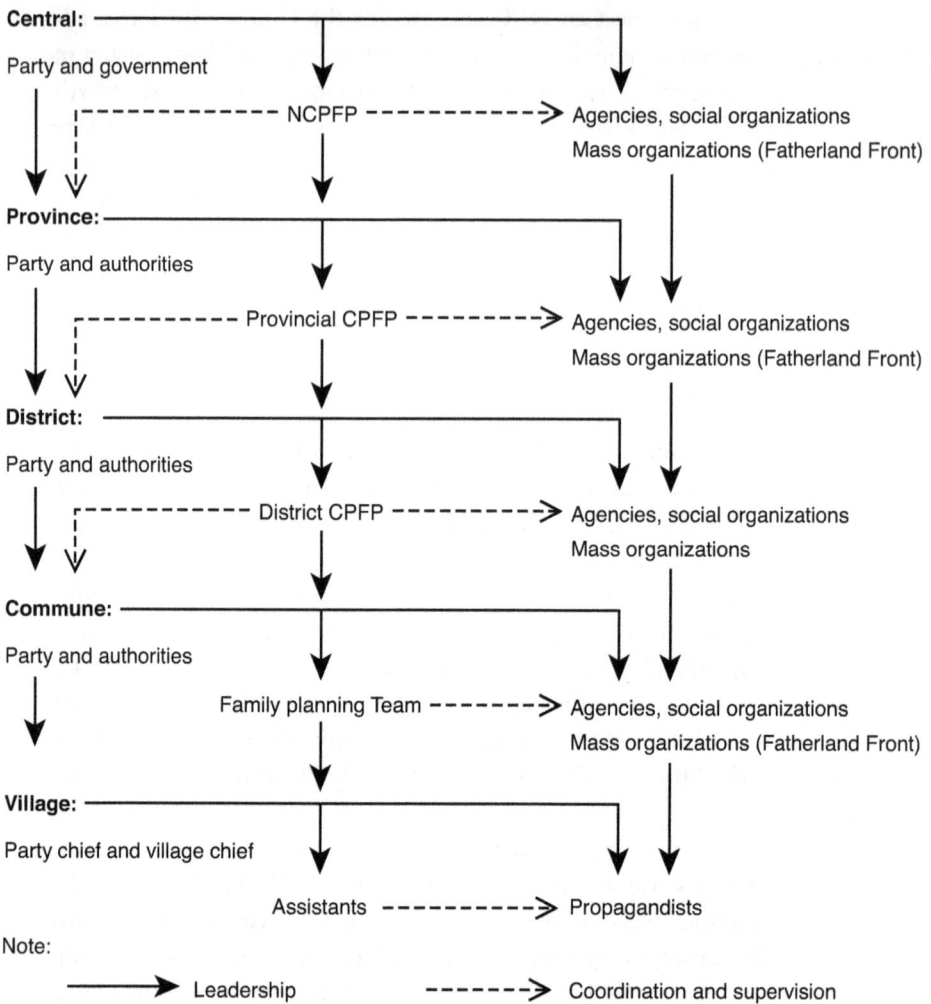

NCPFP: National Committee for Population and Family Planning
CPFP: Committee for Population and Family Planning

Figure 2.1 Organization and management of family planning activities.
Source: Courtesy of author (data collected during field work).

* **The Party**
The Party is responsible for management and supervision of family planning activities in the commune.

* **The Committee for Population and Family Planning**
  - The CPFP is headed by the Chair of the commune People's Committee, who is directly responsible for establishing and assessing population and family planning activities.
  - The Committee includes representatives of mass organizations and social organizations (Fatherland Front).
  - The head of the Committee is assisted by full-time staff to coordinate activities. Local staff is directly responsible for propaganda, for distributing condoms and the pill and for registering family members. They receive monthly payment for their work.

* **The information and education network** *"for the new family norm"*
This is based on:
  - Local staff
  - Propagandists of mass organizations and social organizations (Fatherland Front)
  - Cadres of the commune's cultural and information services (it is they who disseminate messages by loudspeaker), teachers and pupils.
  - Community leaders
Members of village associations.

Figure 2.2 Organization and management of commune level family planning activities.
Source: Author's data.

twelve assistants—130,000 people in all. The organization of the commune-level network reflects the regime's very decentralized supervision of the population. The chair of the commune People's Committee heads the network, which includes representatives of various mass organizations of the Fatherland Front. It has a full-time staff and occasional staff, all chosen from the village community. In *Ninh Hiep*, where we studied the practical implementation of the national policy, each staff member is responsible for encouraging thirty households to adhere to the new family model and for monitoring their reproductive lives, for example, age at marriage, number of children of each gender, and contraceptive method used. They are also responsible for distributing contraceptive pills and condoms. Thus, the organization of family planning activities is highly hierarchical and decentralized, with communal, district, and provincial authorities playing an essential role in the application of the population and family policy.

Large-scale IEC drives aimed at generating popular support for the new model of family and society were fully launched in the early 1990s, when the demographic management and population control system was strengthened at commune level (Figure 2.2). In compliance with the wishes of the government, the mass organizations and social organizations (Women's Union, Farmers' Union, Communist Youth Union, etc.) were required to include IEC messages on family planning in their programs, as stated in the *Population and Family Planning Strategy to 2000:* "The messages on population and family planning issues are included in the projects and programs of economic, cultural and social development so that a varied public belonging to different strata of society clearly perceive the material and spiritual benefits of family planning and small families" (National Committee for Population and Family Planning 1993).

On August 24, 1992, the National Committee defined a program on population and family planning information, education, and communication for the years 1992–2000. It orchestrates and lays the groundwork for mass propaganda campaigns, "to promote the acceptance of a small, healthy, happy and prosperous family as a social norm by adequate provision of information on population, development and family planning methods and by mobilization of every member of community to voluntarily participate in the population and family planning program with a view to achieving the general population objectives of the country" (National Committee for Population and Family Planning 1992, Chapter 1). The strategy focuses on two essential aspects of the new family—size and composition. The family should be small and composed of a couple and their two children, preferably a girl and boy. The benefits for the family are emphasized. "With a small family, parents will have better conditions for carrying and fostering their children, more times reserved for their work to raise income and lessen economic pressure. Children will have more favorable conditions for their advancement in studies and for choosing jobs" (Article 3, para. 5). Equality between girls and boys is also promoted: "To make audiences realize and accept the view that either of the two is also one's born child and deserves one's love. The most important thing is not to have a son or a daughter or many children, but how the child/children are brought up and grow up" (National Committee for Population and Family Planning 1992, Article 3, para. 7).

Propaganda is used at several levels:

- Directly, by local staff, especially for audiences in rural areas.
- Through the mass media (television, radio, the press, loud speakers), usually with easy-to-understand messages, few words, and numerous illustrations (posters, strip cartoons, and animated films) to make the messages accessible to the majority of the population.
- Through live performances (drama, popular songs rewritten for the purpose, shows by folk entertainment groups).

Poster Campaigns

During the *Doi Moi* period, poster campaigns are the most visible way of encouraging couples to adopt the modern family model. These messages are usually drawings or illustrations from strip cartoons, with few words or a short slogan and suggestive images. The most frequent formula is "Each couple can have only one or two children" (*Mot cap vo chong chi co mot hoac hai con*). Posters usually show a couple with one girl or, sometimes, a boy and a girl. One aim of the drive is to persuade families to accept the birth of a girl more readily, even as their only child.

Slogans celebrate the benefits of family planning with illustrations. "To have few children is to eat your fill, enjoy good health, be free in one's mind, be happy" (*It con: an no, khoe manh, tri tue, hanh phuc*). Family planning is also supposed to bring national well-being and women's liberation (*Ke khoach hoa gia dinh: Giai phong phu nu*). Along with messages that encourage small families, the propaganda attacks traditional ideas about fertility conveyed by popular sayings, for example, "These ideas are outmoded: If heaven gives birth to elephants, It must also give them grass. Respect men, despise women. With one boy one has everything. With two girls one has nothing." (*Nhung quan niem loi thoi: Troi sinh voi Troi sinh co; Trong nam khinh nu; Nhat nam viet huu Thap nu viet vo.*)

Drama

To promote the image of girls in a society where most people prefer boys, theater groups put on shows in villages praising the merits and advantages of having a girl child. A girl's main asset is the valuable help she gives her parents, mainly with housework. However, Vietnam is a patrilocal society in which girls only live with their parents until they marry, at which time they leave to look after their parents-in-law. If a family only has girls, no grown-up children will remain with the parents unless they reach a compromise and the husband of one of the girls agrees to live in her parents' home. If there are boys in the family, at least one of them will stay in the parents' home with his wife and children. Then the daughter-in-law will look after the parents. Findings from two other chapters in this volume (see Barbieri, and Jayakody and Huy) support the idea that intergenerational co-residence remains the norm. Jayakody and Huy further show that co-residence with the groom's parents immediately after marriage has increased in recent years by comparison with the most intense war period, as individuals married between 1992 and 2000 are three times more likely to live with parents after marriage than those married between 1963 and 1971. They also indicate that co-residence is more common with the man's parents than with the woman's, though a nonnegligible proportion of daughters remain in their parents' households with their husbands.

Radio

At 11:30 A.M. and 10:15 P.M. every day,[11] the radio broadcasts programs promoting birth control. The daily broadcasts of the radio campaigns have made family planning a community norm and commonplace for many people. Several times a week, stations play jingles like the following:

My sweet, when they call you the woman with only one child,
My eyes burn with desire for you,
But when you're thin and faded for having borne so many children,
Sunny days and rainy days alike are burdensome,
Youth passes so quickly, my sweet.

In these ways, *Doi Moi* is strengthening the norm of an ideal modern family through a restrictive reproductive policy. The political authorities stress that, for sound scientific, medical, and material reasons, Vietnamese families will attain happiness (*hanh phuc*) if they follow these recommendations (Gammelt-oft 1999; Scornet 2001). Contrary to the traditional concepts that associated wealth with large families, family planning campaigns suggest that numerous offspring are associated with poverty. Campaigns promoting the new family constantly revert to images of a thin, exhausted woman, either pregnant or suckling a new baby, surrounded by a gaggle of children in rags. The purpose of the family planning programs is "a small and healthy family to bring about a happy and prosperous life" (Communist Party of Viet-Nam 1993). Conse-quently, only having one or two children ensures a family life of material ease and good health.

All the information campaigns are designed to persuade the Vietnam-ese to accept the one-or-two-child family as a new family and social norm. Family planning campaigns are run like political campaigns, using simple, if not simplistic, slogans to win over the population by mobilizing patriotic sentiments (family planning brings well-being to the nation) and infiltrat-ing the deep structures of Vietnamese society (family, village community, and the heroic tradition, which views mothers of only one or two children as the nation's new heroines). The Vietnamese political system is implemented through the mobilization of the masses in a varied network of grassroot in-stitutions initially designed to promote and monitor the socialist state poli-cies and combined under the overall name of Fatherland Front.[12]

The various member organizations, in charge of closely supervising the population, play a major role in implementing the family planning policy at the local level. The rural population is constantly called upon through large-scale campaigns of demographic, rather than patriotic, emulation in which everyone is involved. The parallel between patriotic emulation and demo-graphic emulation is worth noting. Since both function in the same way, we could call it patriotic demography.

The campaigns have had an undeniable, and still growing, impact on the Vietnamese population. In the 1994 Intercensal Demographic Survey, 72 percent of women said they had heard, read, or seen a message about family planning in the month preceding the survey. According to the Demographic and Health Survey (DHS) in 1997, 87 percent of women had received such messages, while in 2002, the proportion was 88 percent. In fact, the small family is becoming the norm. In the first DHS in 1988, Vietnamese women wanted 3.3 children on average; in 1997 and 2002, they wanted 2.4.

Alongside close supervision of the population, the government has introduced various incentives and repressive measures (moral, political, administrative, and economic) to persuade Vietnamese couples to adhere to the birth control policy. Penalties for noncompliance include dismissal of civil servants, removal from emulation competitions, like the "vanguard worker" awards, exclusion from the Communist Party, and fines of money or in kind, with large variations in the degree of control and of penalties from one area to the next. Indeed, the People's Committees of the provinces, districts, and communes have full leeway in deciding the scale of rewards and sanctions, depending on the demographic, economic, and political environment. In Thai Binh province, for instance, the province which applies the family planning programs most rigorously, penalties can reach the price of a full year's rice harvest (Scornet 2000).

The Major Achievements of the Family Planning Program at the Turn of the Twenty-First Century

THE REPRODUCTIVE TRANSITION

At the turn of the twenty-first century, the government had practically achieved its goal of reducing family size to slow down the country's population growth. Between 1999 and 2002, the population growth rate was 1.5 percent per year (Table 2.1), even below the target, which was 1.7 percent in 2000 (Table 2.2). The crude birth rate is an estimated 20.5 per thousand for 1995–1999 (Table 2.3). In thirty years, the total fertility rate has been reduced from 5.9 children per woman in the early 1970s to 1.9 in 2002 (Committee for Population, Family and Children and Orc Macro, 2003) (Table 2.4 and Figure 2.3) while the goal was 2.4 children for 2005 (Table 2.2). There was a continuing decline in the birth rate, which is clearly visible in the narrowing of the base of the population pyramid (Figure 2.4). Vietnam's fertility is now below replacement. Comparing Vietnam with the nine other countries of Southeast Asia, only Singapore and Thailand have lower fertility, with 1.3 and 1.7 children per woman, respectively.[13] Vietnam's figure is close to that of its giant neighbor, China, where, as of 2005, women have an average of 1.7 children. This low fertility, presented for years as a state norm, is a sign of change in the structure and composition of the Vietnamese family. The United Nations (UN) and the

TABLE 2.2
Demographic targets of the government of Vietnam for 1992–2015

Year	Population size (millions)	Mean annual growth (%)	Crude birth rate (per thousand)	Total fertility rate
1992	70.4	2.18	29.4	3.7
1993	71.9	2.14	28.9	3.7
1994	73.5	2.10	28.4	3.6
1995	75.0	2.06	27.8	3.6
2000	82.6	1.72	23.9	2.9
2005	89.1	1.40	20.3	2.4
2010	95.0	1.24	18.6	2.2
2015	100.8	1.16	17.9	2.1

SOURCE: Appendix 1 of Application Decree of the *Population and Family Planning Strategy to 2000*, approved by Prime Minister Vo Van Kiet on June 3, 1993; National Committee for Population and Family Planning. 1993.

TABLE 2.3
Vital rates and natural increase in Vietnam, 1930–1999

Period	Crude birth rate (per thousand)	Crude death rate (per thousand)	Rate of natural increase (%)
1930–1940	45.0	26.0	1.9
1955–1959	45.0	12.0	3.3
1960–1964	43.9	12.0	3.2
1965–1969	42.3	15.0	2.7
1970–1974	35.5	15.0	2.1
1975–1979	33.2	11.0	2.2
1980–1984	33.5	8.0	2.6
1985–1989	31.0	7.0	2.4
1990–1994	27.4	7.0	2.0
1995–1999	20.5	6.0	1.5

SOURCE: Nguyen 1984; Barbieri et al. 1995; General Statistics Office 2001.[1]

[1]Estimates of mortality after the American War vary widely between sources. The official census figures, used by J. Banister (1992) and Nguyen (1984), give a mortality rate of 7.5 per thousand in 1976, falling to 7 per thousand at the end of the 1970s. Other authors have readjusted these estimates to 10–11 per thousand in 1976 with a more gradual decline over the years that followed, to 8 per thousand in 1990–1994 (Gendreau, Fauveau, and Dang 1997).

TABLE 2.4
Total fertility rate in Vietnam, 1959–2002

Period	Total fertility rate
1959–1964	6.4
1965–1969	6.8
1970–1974	5.9
1975–1979	5.3
1980–1984	4.7
1985–1989	4.0
1990–1994	3.3
1995–1999	2.5
2000–2002	1.9

SOURCE: General Statistics Office 2001; Committee for Population, Family and Children and Orc Macro 2003.

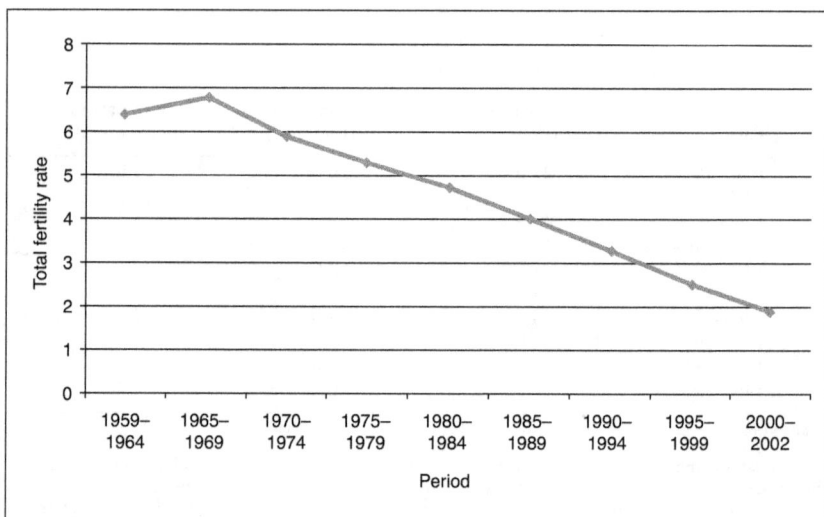

Figure 2.3 Total fertility rate in Vietnam, 1959–2002.

Source: General Statistics Office 2001. 1999 *Population and Housing Census, Completed Census Results.* Hanoi: Statistics Publishing House; Committee for Population, Family and Children and Orc Macro. 2003.

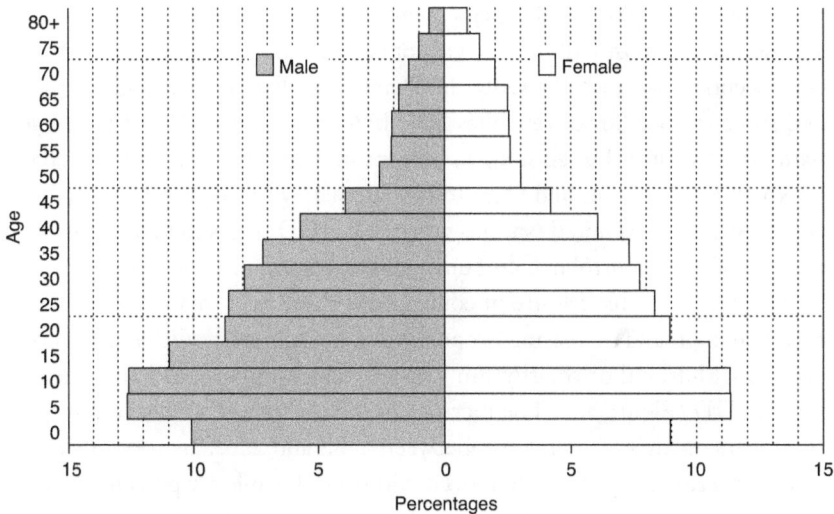

Figure 2.4 Vietnam population pyramid (1999 census).
Source: General Statistics Office 2001.

UN Fund for Population Activities rewarded the Vietnamese state for its efforts in the demographic policy field, by awarding Vietnam, along with Iran, the United Nations Populations Award on June 9, 1999.

HIGH RATE OF CONTRACEPTIVE USE,
WITH LITTLE DIVERSITY

The rapid 25 percent point increase in contraceptive use in less than fifteen years has been the key instrument of the fertility transition. At the time of the first national fertility survey, carried out in 1988, 53.2 percent of women were using contraception. This figure rose to 65 percent in 1994, 75.3 percent in 1997, and 78.5 percent in 2002 (Table 2.5). Today, over three-quarters of Vietnamese women use contraception to control their fertility. The family planning program has achieved its goal of increasing contraceptive use. Contraceptive practice in Vietnam has two notable features.

First, according to all surveys, the IUD is the most widely used method of birth control, far exceeding all other forms (Table 2.5 and Figure 2.5). Between 1988 and 1994, one-third of Vietnamese women were using IUDs. In 1997, the figure rose slightly to 38.5 percent, and, by 2002, it had dropped slightly to 37.7 percent. Almost half (48 percent) of all Vietnamese women who practice contraception use an IUD. Only the Democratic People's Republic of Korea and some former Soviet republics have higher rates of IUD use than Vietnam: 45 percent in Uzbekistan, 39 percent in Turkmenistan, and 48 percent in North Korea. China and Cuba follow Vietnam with 36 percent and 33 percent, respectively (United Nations 2002). The IUD seems to be the preferred method of birth control in communist and ex-communist countries.

The other notable feature of contraceptive practices in Vietnam is that a relatively high and increasing proportion of women use traditional methods, such as withdrawal or the rhythm method, which rank second and third after the IUD (Figure 2.5). The increase in the practice of withdrawal is quite significant, with a 7.3 point rise between 1988 and 2002. In 2002, 14.3 percent of Vietnamese women practiced withdrawal, while 7.5 percent used the rhythm method. Together, these two methods account for 28 percent of current contraceptive use (Committee for Population, Family and Children and Orc Macro 2003).

ABORTION AS BIRTH CONTROL METHOD

For the most part, contraceptive methods are used to control the number of births, though abortion is also practiced extensively. To help achieve its policy goal of smaller households, the Democratic Republic of Vietnam legalized abortion in the North in the early 1960s and in the South in 1976 at the time of reunification (Werner and Bélanger 2002). The law on public health protection of June 30, 1989, stipulated that abortion would be available to women on demand (Article 44) from medical institutions accredited by the Ministry of Health (Article 44). However, in response to certain abusive practices, revisions to the Penal Code in 1999 made the illicit termination of pregnancy[14] punishable. Thus "any person illicitly terminating the pregnancy of another person shall be sentenced to three years' non-custodial re-education" (Article 243) and "the offender may also be sentenced to a fine of 5,000,000 to 50,000,000[15] dongs or banned from exercising a professional activity for five years" (Law No. 15/1999/QU10).

TABLE 2.5
Contraceptive use in Vietnam: Trends and methods, 1988 to 2002

Contraceptive method	Current use, as percentage of women (women in marital union)				Trend 1988–2002 (points)
	1988	1994	1997	2002	
IUD	33.2	33.3	38.5	37.7	+4.5
Pill	0.4	2.1	4.3	6.3	+5.9
Injection	nd	0.2	0.2	0.4	nd
Diaphragm, cream	nd	0.1	0.0	nd	nd
Condom	1.1	4.0	5.9	5.8	+4.7
Female sterilization	2.7	3.9	6.3	5.9	+3.2
Male sterilization	0.3	0.2	0.5	0.5	+0.2
Rhythm method	8.1	9.8	7.3	7.5	−0.6
Withdrawal	7.0	11.2	11.9	14.3	+7.3
Other	0.4	0.2	0.3	0.1	−0.3
At least one method	53.2	65.0	75.3	78.5	+25.3
At least one modern method	37.7	43.8	55.8	56.7	+19.0

SOURCE: *Demographic and Health Surveys* 1988, 1997, and 2002; Intercensal Demographic Survey 1994.

NOTE: Methods classified as modern are the IUD, the pill, condom, diaphragm with cream and male and female sterilization. Traditional methods are withdrawal and the rhythm method.

nd: no data

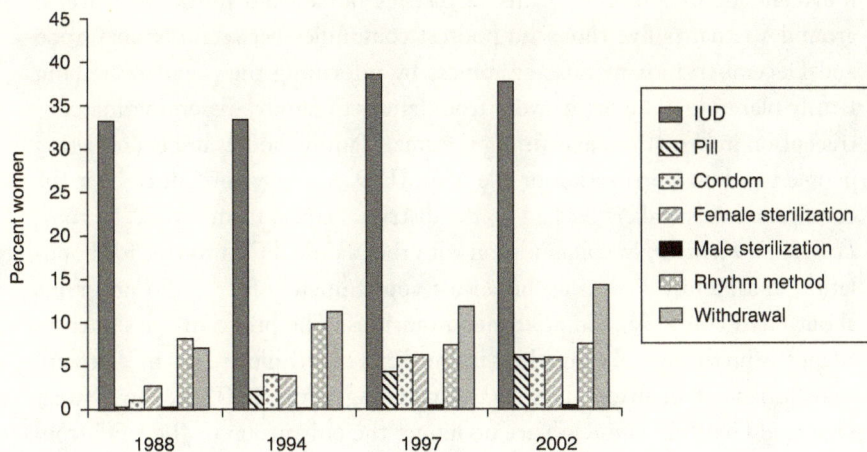

Figure 2.5 Contraceptive use by method in Vietnam, 1988 to 2002.
Source: *Demographic and Health Surveys* 1988, 1997, and 2002; *Intercensal Demographic Survey* 1994.

According to the 2002 Demographic and Health Survey, Vietnamese women have, on average, 0.6 abortions during their reproductive lives.[16] An estimated 22 percent of pregnancies in the three years prior to the survey had been voluntarily terminated (Committee for Population, Family and Children 2003).

New Goals for Family Policy

Although demographic issues still take priority in the country's new socio-economic development strategy decided at the last National Congress of the Communist Party of Vietnam in 2001, the general direction of population policy has shifted significantly. More closely targeted goals have replaced that of reducing population growth nationwide. Efforts are now concentrated on the population groups and regions that are considered problematic. Poor and isolated areas and those where fertility remains high,[17] for example, ethnic minorities in the highlands and island populations, are targeted. Fertility levels differ significantly between ethnic groups (Table 2.6), with Kinh, Tay, Han and Muong women having 2.0 children on average in 1999, H'Mong women having 7.1 children, and Gia Rai women having 5.3 children.

To make up for the shortage of health care facilities in some areas, about fourteen hundred mobile teams of district nurses and midwives traveled around Vietnam's five thousand poorest communes between October 2000 and December 2001 to raise awareness by informing the population about family planning. The teams went from family to family, disseminating contraception information, explaining the small-family model, and encouraging people to adopt sterilization or use of an IUD. Messages broadcast over the commune loudspeakers backed up the district medical team's work. In 2001, *La Voix du Vietnam*, in collaboration with the National Committee for Population and Family Planning, broadcast approximately fifty radio programs about birth control aimed at ethnic minorities. The programs, designed to adapt the birth control campaigns to the different ethnic groups in Vietnam, were broadcast in fifteen languages, including H'mong, Thai, Tay, Nung, Dao, and Gia Rai. The Kinh are no longer the only group to "benefit" from a mass information drive.

The addition of a qualitative goal to the quantitative goal of reducing the country's population has been the most important change. As one government decision expresses it:

TABLE 2.6

Total fertility rate for the ten largest ethnic groups[1] in Vietnam
at the 1989 census and the 1999 census and population in 1999.

Ethnic group	Total fertility rate		Population in 1999 ('000s)
	1989	1999	
Kinh	3.6	1.9	65,796
Tay	4.3	2.1	1,478
Thai	5.7	2.6	1,329
Han	2.9	1.5	862
Khmer	5.3	2.3	1,055
Muong	4.4	2.0	1,138
Nung	5.1	2.9	856
H'Mong	9.3	7.1	787
Dao	6.9	3.6	621
Gia Rai	5.5	5.3	318
Overall	3.8	2.3	76,323

SOURCE: General Statistics Office 2001.

[1]Of Vietnam's fifty-four ethnic groups, the *Kinh* or *Viet* accounted for 86 percent of the population at the 1999 census.

Population activities constitute an important part of the national development strategy, one of the basic goals of which is to raise the quality of life of each person, each family and the entire society, making decisive contributions to the industrialization and modernization of the country. . . . [The overall objective is] to build families with fewer and healthier children, with the aim of eventually stabilizing the size of the population at a reasonable level in order to achieve a prosperous and happy life. To raise the quality of the population, to develop high quality human resources . . . and contribute to the rapid and sustainable development of the country.[18]

The idea is to improve the quality of family planning services and integrate them better into the primary health care networks, in order "to raise the quality of the population physically, intellectually and spiritually. To strive to attain a more advanced Human Development Index (HDI) score by the year 2010."[19] Vietnamese authorities use "quality of the population" to describe the satisfaction of basic human needs and rights (2003 Population Ordinance, Article 21; Uy Ban Thuong Vu Quoc Hoi 2003). Aspects specifically mentioned are the right to physical, intellectual, and spiritual development, better health (measured mainly by anthropometric indicators), longer life expectancy, a higher level of education, and higher average income. Also mentioned are the eradication of famine, access to health for all, quality of education, access to employment for all, and gender equality. Gender discrimination and differential treatment of boys and girls are particularly frowned upon (Article 24). In the eyes of the Vietnamese authorities, diversifying the supply of public goods and services, especially in the areas of education and health, is the only way of achieving these goals.

In accordance with the goals defined at the 1994 Cairo conference, Vietnamese family planning became part of a more general reproductive health policy at the beginning of the twenty-first century and is no longer the sole purpose of focused demographic programs. The idea of a comprehensive, integrated approach to issues of population, health and development has come of age and won approval among Vietnamese policy makers. In November, 2002, as a sign of this new direction, the National Committee for Population and Family Planning, set up under Decision No. 58-HDBT of April, 1984, was renamed the Commission for Population, Family and Children (CPFC) (Decree 94/2002/ND). In 2007, the government abolished this commission entirely and delegated population and family matters to various ministries. Family planning, as such, is no longer a central policy issue.

Vietnamese legislators now stress the individual's right, not only her or his obligation, to control births, as stipulated in the decision of October 18, 1988, which aimed to limit families to one or two children. The population ordinance that came into effect on May 1, 2003, recognizes that people have rights with regard to population: the right to information about population issues and the right to confidential, safe, convenient, high-quality reproductive health services. Every couple and every individual has the right to decide the timing, number, and spacing of births (Article 10). The ordinance also establishes equality between individuals with respect to birth control and reproductive health care (Article 2).

However, in keeping with the earlier, restrictive demographic policies and sometimes in contradiction to individual rights, the legislators maintain that the Vietnamese have duties with regard to fertility. They are responsible for the "use of contraceptive methods and building a small family," one that is therefore "prosperous, equal, advanced, happy and sustainable" (Article 4). Each couple or individual has a duty to practice contraception (2003 Population Ordinance, Article 10). The state is also involved in this duty to readjust population size "to a reasonable level" (Article 8). Thus, everyone must "contribute to the interests of the State, society and the community regarding the size, structure and distribution of the population" (Article 4).

Contradictions between rights and obligations, between the right to choose how many children to have and the obligation to practice contraception, can be explained by pressure from the international community and nongovernmental organizations that promote individual rights on the one hand, and the government's desire to pursue its policy of controlled population growth on the other. The notion of reproductive rights emerged at the same time as that of reproductive health (Gauthier 2000) and is historically associated with feminist demands for sexual freedom, the right to contraception and abortion in the countries of the North, where the intimate links between personal, political, economic, and social rights are now acknowledged. As stated in Cairo, reproductive rights are based on the recognition that "all couples and individuals have the basic right to decide freely and responsibly the number and spacing of their children" and enjoy the right to better sexual and reproductive health (United Nations 1994).

By maintaining the quantitative norm of small family size, while opening up to more qualitative concerns, the Vietnamese authorities have found a compromise. Combining birth control with reproductive health has given family planning and reproductive health programs a new status, independent of demographic goals, such as stabilizing the population. They have become an end in themselves,[20] their legitimacy based on personal, family, and national well-being. At the same time, Vietnamese planners highlight the interests of society and family, along with the individual's interest in reproductive health: "it improves women's status, their health and that of their children, and is in the interests of the whole country, because it improves collective well-being and is a precondition for the country's economic development" (National Committee for Population and Family Planning 2001).

Following this reasoning, there are close links between national, family, and personal dimensions. Family planning programs seek to convince by connecting the family's happiness with that of the nation. This key feature of Vietnamese policy distinguishes it from the program adopted in Cairo, which focused on the individual's reproductive rights, regardless of collective or national considerations.

Linking national, family, and individual interests is in keeping with the traditional "family" view of the world to which Vietnamese communism adapted very well. The Vietnamese state was built on the Chinese Confucian model of the state (both in order to resist it and to take control of the South). The Confucian model extended the notion of family to the kingdom with its "father-king"; in adopting this model, Vietnam made Ho Chi Minh an "uncle-chairman," "Uncle Ho" (*Bac Ho*). *Bac*, the father's elder brother, is almost equal to the father, as *Bac Ho* is to the nation. Confucius (551–471 B.C. in ancient China), who had a major influence on Vietnamese society, particularly among the elites, defined the three basic links (*tam cuong*) to which the individual must conform: sovereign/subject, parents/children, and husband/wife. Thus, the authority of the state (sovereign/subject bond) is the corollary of the unfailing authority of the father (parents/children bond) in the Confucian model. Acceptance of family authority implies acceptance of the political authorities. Educated to respect authority in the family, the Vietnamese have not found it very difficult to accept a strong political authority in the family planning field. This partially explains the success of the birth control campaigns among the Kinh.

Conclusion

As stipulated by Bélanger and Barbieri, "recent sociological work has called for a consideration of global, national and local politics in the shaping of reproductive behavior in families." This chapter shows the role of the state in shaping family behavior and norms with respect to reproduction.

Incorporating qualitative goals, alongside the quantitative, has changed the nature of Vietnam's population policy. Until the start of the twenty-first century, the family institution took precedence over the individual in Vietnam. State policy aimed to achieve a family norm of three or four children in the 1960s, then one or two children, ideally one girl and one boy or even two girls, from 1998 on. Under pressure, mainly from international organizations, the trend now is toward recognizing the rights of individuals and the equality of individual rights.

The history of forty years of family planning in Vietnam shows that the communist leaders are strongly inclined to guide family behavior, particularly reproductive behavior. In the twentieth century, their aim was to reduce population growth by setting quantified targets, but, since the turn of the century, there has been a new focus on improving the population's socioeconomic characteristics. However, with the state's withdrawal from social services provision at the end of the twentieth century and growing private sector involvement in areas such as education, health, and family planning, previously the exclusive responsibility of the state, it is questionable whether the necessary resources are being deployed to implement a more qualitatively oriented population and family policy.

Notes

1. Translated from "La cohérence de sa société, lettrée et paysanne pour l'essentiel, a fait le Viêt-Nam. Que l'Etat royal faiblisse et l'initiative sociale prenait le relais."

2. Translated from "La famille fait figure de cheval de bataille dans les efforts de construction d'une société nouvelle."

3. "In the highlands, information concerning family size limitation will be disseminated only to civil servants and political cadres. It is possible to disseminate this information among the population in Catholic regions, but this must be done prudently. If our fellow countrymen and women are not ready to accept the family norms, there should be no rush." (Decree 99/TTg of October 16, 1963). This cautious approach is symptomatic of the political climate of the time, when ethnic minorities and Catholics represented a potential risk of opposition to the government. Many ethnic minorities had collaborated with the French during the Indochina war, and in 1954 thousands of Catholic families had fled to the South to escape the communist regime.

4. The government of the Republic of South Vietnam disapproved of this family planning policy. A French law of July 13, 1920, extended to Indochina in the 1930s, outlawed incitement to abortion and anticonception propaganda; this law was still in force under South Vietnam's Catholic President Ngo Dinh Diem. From 1971, however, the United States Agency for International Development (USAID) encouraged the nationalist government to promote small family size in the South.

5. Two provinces acted ahead of this government decree: the family directives of Thai Binh province in 1984 and of Hanoi province in 1985 urged families to have only one or two children. The traditional autonomy of local authorities in Vietnam thus asserted itself in defining and applying family policy (Scornet 2000).

6. However, scientists such as Prof. Dang Thu (1996) have calculated that given their high mortality rates and short life expectancy (40 years for the H'Mong, for example), the fertility of certain ethnic minorities should be no less than five children per woman to ensure generation replacement.

7. Official Journal No. 28, July 31, 2000.

8. When the NCPFP was formed in 1984, the prime minister appointed General Vo Nguyen Giap (then vice-chairman of the Council of Ministers but better known for his military exploits at Dien Bien Phu), as chairman of the committee.

9. Each ministry appoints a delegate to the NCPFP: the Ministry of Labor, War Invalids and Social Affairs, the Ministry of Culture and Information, the Ministry of Education, the Ministry of the Interior, the Ministry of Justice. It also includes representatives of Fatherland Front organizations: Women's Union, Farmers' Union, Veterans' Union, and Communist Youth Union.

10. Decision 29-HDBT, approved by the government on August 12, 1981.

11. Observed by the author in 1997 when listening to the *Voix du Vietnam* radio station.

12. According to the Law on the Vietnam Fatherland Front, passed on June 12, 1999: "Vietnam Fatherland Front is a political coalition organization, a voluntary union of political, socio-political and social institutions as well as individuals representing all classes, social strata, ethnic groups, religions and the overseas Vietnamese." (Article 1). Some of its member organizations are the Communist Party, the General Confederation of Labor (VGCL), Farmers Unions, the Youth Union, Women's Union (VWU), and the Association for the Elderly.

13. United Nations Economic and Social Commission for Asia and the Pacific, 2005.

14. For example, without Ministry of Health accreditation.

15. Equivalent to a range of 380 to 3,800 euros.

16. The 2002 Demographic and Health Survey, like the earlier DHSs, does not cover single women but only ever-married women. Excluding single women from the survey sample makes little difference for calculating fertility rates, since births outside marriage are extremely rare in Vietnam and limited to very particular circumstances (Scornet 2000), but it does result in an underestimation of abortion rates. Pregnancy terminations are generally underdeclared in surveys and their number better calculated by the Ministry of Health, which estimates that 30 percent of abortions concern single women.

17. National Committee for Population and Family Planning. 2001. *Vietnam population strategy 2001–2010* adopted by the prime minister on December 22, 2000 (Decision No. 147/2000 QD-TTg).

18. Extracts from Decision No. 147/2000/QD-TTg of December 22, 2000, ratifying Vietnam's population strategy for the period 2001–10.

19. Ibid.

20. Lassonde L., 1996, *Les défis de la démographie. Quelle qualité de vie pour le XXIe siècle?*, La Découverte, Paris.

References

Association of Jurists [Association des Juristes et Union des Femmes de la République Socialiste du Vietnam]. 1987. *Bulletin de Droit* 1.

Banister, J. 1992. *Viet-Nam population dynamics and prospects.* Washington, DC: Center for International Research, U.S. Bureau of the Census.

Barbieri, M., J. Allman, B. S. Pham, and M. T. Nguyen. 1995. La situation démographique du Viêt Nam. *Population* 3: 621–652.

Bélanger, D. 1997. *Rapport intergénérationnel et rapport hommes-femmes dans la transition démographique du Vietnam, de 1930 à 1990.* Thèses et Mémoires No. 46. Montréal, Québec, Canada: Université de Montréal.

Charbit, Y., and C. Scornet, eds. 2002. *Démographie, société et politique de population au Vietnam.* Populations Series. Paris: L'Harmattan.

Committee for Population, Family and Children and Orc Macro. 2003. *Vietnam demographic and health survey 2002.* Hanoi: Macrointernatonial.

Communist Party of Viet-Nam, Central Committee. 1993. *Resolution on population and family planning.* Fourth meeting of the Party Central Committee, 7th session. January 14. Hanoi.

Dang Thu. 1996. *Mot so van de ve dan so Viet Nam* [Reflections on the population of Vietnam]. Hanoi: *Nha xuat ban khoa hoc xa hoi.*

Do Lam Chi Lan. 1998. *La mère et l'enfant dans le Viêt Nam d'autrefois.* Paris: L'Harmattan.

Gammeltoft, T. 1999. *Women's bodies, women's worries: Health and family planning in a Vietnamese rural commune.* Richmond: Curzon Press.

Gauthier, A. 2000. Les droits reproductifs, une quatrième génération de droits ? *Autrepart* 15: 167–180.

Gendreau, F., V. Favreau, and T. Dang. 1997. *Démographie de la péninsule Indochinoise.* Paris: Estem and Aupefl-Uref, collection Savoir Plus Universités.

General Statistical Office. 2001. *1999 population and housing census: Completed census results.* Hanoi: Thê Gioi Publishers.

Hémery, D. 1990. *Ho Chi Minh: De l'Indochine au Viet-Nam.* Paris: Découvertes Gallimard.

Kerkvliet, B. J. 2005. *The power of everyday politics: How Vietnamese peasants transformed national policy.* Ithaca, NY: Cornell University Press.

Kerkvliet, B. J., and D. G. Marr, eds. 2004. *Beyond Hanoi: Local government in Vietnam.* Singapore: Institute of Southeast Asian Studies Publications.

Lassonde, L. 1996. *Les défis de la démographie, quelle qualité de vie pour le XXIe siècle?* Paris: La Découverte.

National Committee for Population and Family Planning. 1992. *Strategy for information education: Communication of population and family planning 1992–2000.* Hanoi: Hanoi Publishing House.

National Committee for Population and Family Planning. 1993. *Population and family planning strategy to the year 2000.* Hanoi: Hanoi Publishing House.

National Committee for Population and Family Planning. 2001. *Vietnam population strategy 2001–2010.* Hanoi: Hanoi Publishing House.

Nguyen Duc Nhan. 1984. Contraintes démographiques et politiques de développement au Viêt Nam, 1975–1980. *Population* 2: 313–338.

Scornet, C. 2000. *Fécondité et politique dans le delta du fleuve Rouge (Vietnam)*, Doctoral thesis in demography, University of Paris V–Sorbonne, Paris, 524.

Scornet, C. 2001. An example of coercive fertility reduction, as seen in the region of the Red River Delta in Viet Nam. *Population* (English Selection) 13 (02): 101–133.

United Nations. 1994. *Report of the International Conference on Population and Development, Cairo, 5–13 September.* New York: United Nations.

United Nations Economic and Social Commission for Asia and the Pacific. 2005. *2005 population data sheet.* New York: United Nations.

Uy Ban Thuong Vu Quoc Hoi [Permanent Committee of the National Assembly]. 2003. *Phap Lenh dan so* [Ordinance on Population]. Hanoi: Nha Xuat Ban Chinh Tri Quoc Gia.

Werner, J., and D. Bélanger, eds. 2002. *Gender, household, state: Doi Moi in Vietnam.* Ithaca, NY: Cornell University Press.

Chapter Three

Health Care and the Family in Vietnam

ANIL DEOLALIKAR

One of the most significant transformations that has occurred in Vietnam during the past two decades has been the significant shift of responsibility for health care from the government to the family. After *Doi Moi*, Vietnam moved quickly from a model of socialist medicine, where the state—brigades, communes, provincial governments, and the central government—was responsible for *both* the financing and provision of health care services, to one where the state was much less involved. Naturally, this had implications for average health outcomes in the population as well as for socioeconomic disparities in health outcomes.

An important consequence of *Doi Moi* was the liberalization of the economy and the ensuing growth of the Vietnamese economy. The growth of the economy dramatically improved family incomes, and these improvements, to some extent, offset the initial declines in access to health services. However, the rising inequality of income during the post–*Doi Moi* period has led to widening health disparities.

Evolution of Vietnam's Health Sector

While Vietnam generally has good health indicators compared to most countries at its level of per capita income, the fact is that many of these health

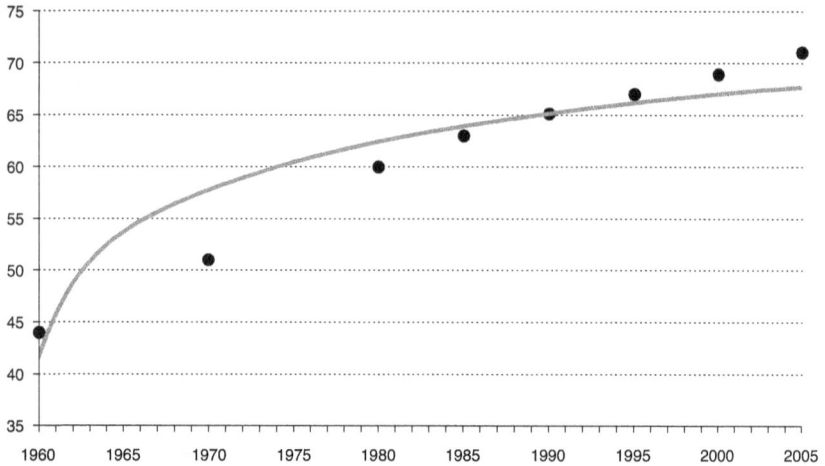

Figure 3.1   Life expectancy at birth, Vietnam, 1960–2005.
Source: World Bank, *World Development Indicators*, various issues.

gains were achieved early during its development. For instance, data on the average life expectancy at birth show that the most rapid improvements in life expectancy occurred between 1960 and the late 1980s—around the time that *Doi Moi* was launched (Figure 3.1). Data on trends in infant mortality tell a broadly similar story (Figure 3.2).

Banister (1993) has likewise argued that the major transformations in health in Vietnam occurred between the 1950s and the 1980s in spite of the country being at war—first with France and then with the United States. Barbieri et al. (1995) have also noted the rapid, albeit uneven, declines in mortality between the colonial era and the late 1970s. Gendreau, Faveau, and Dang (1997) have estimated that life expectancy in Vietnam increased by ten years between 1900 and 1930, which suggests that Vietnam's health transition began early in the twentieth century—significantly earlier than most other developing countries in Asia.

How did Vietnam achieve such impressive health gains so early on? Because of the paucity of historical information on the functioning of the health system, one can only speculate as to what happened to the health sector in the past. It is likely that a number of factors conspired to bring about the dramatic health improvements in the country. The most important factor was probably political resolve and imperative. From the beginning, the

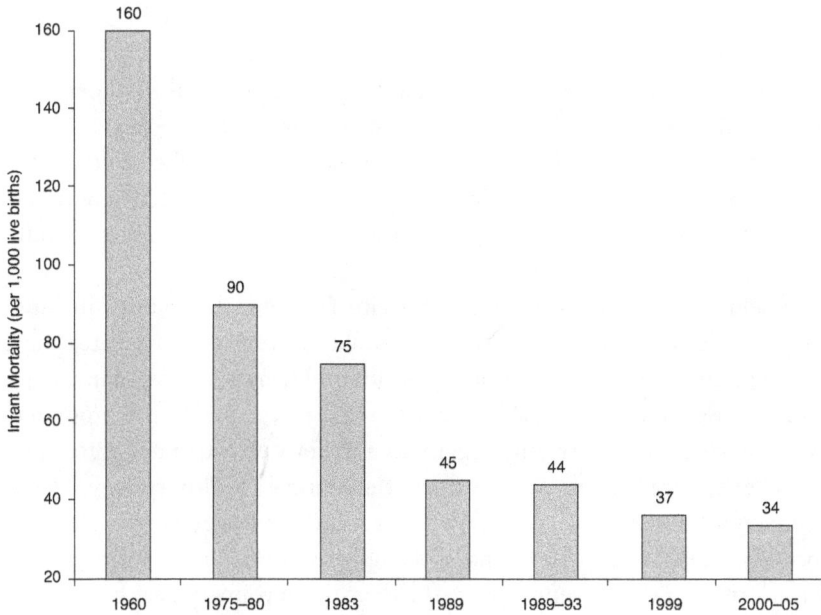

Figure 3.2   Infant mortality rate, 1960–2005.
Source: Ministry of Health, *Health Statistics Yearbook*, various issues.

country's leaders had placed progress in the social sectors—in particular, literacy, education, health, and female emancipation—as one of their highest priorities (Allman 1993; Ladinsky and Levine 1985; Vogel 1987). In this sense, Vietnam was not all that different from other centrally planned, socialist economies, most of which regarded good health as a basic human right and as a political imperative. This resulted in the allocation of considerable commitment and resources to the health sector in Vietnam.

The generous allocation of resources manifested itself in the establishment of a vast network of primary health facilities throughout the country after 1954, but particularly after 1968. The expansion increased people's access to primary health care, except in a few mountainous (and hard-to-reach) provinces. Within provinces, commune health centers and stations were generally well located, since people had a say in the location of health centers via their Commune Councils (Ladinsky and Levine 1985). Unfortunately, since there are no empirical surveys or studies on the functioning of typical commune health centers under the old Democratic Republic of

Vietnam (DRV) system, it is impossible to determine how well the health centers were staffed, what type of useable equipment they had, whether they had adequate supplies of medicines and drugs, and how well they were utilized by the community. However, casual empiricism and anecdotal evidence suggests that even though many of the problems afflicting the health sector today may have been present since early times, they were relatively minor during the 1960s and early 1970s, and they became much more acute only immediately before and after *Doi Moi*.

In addition to the vast network of health facilities, the country invested considerable resources in developing a number of very effective categorical health programs to deal with priority health problems, such as malaria, diarrheal diseases, and immunizable diseases. These categorical health programs, many of which were vertically organized and not well integrated into a primary health care system, were central to the country's health strategy. Again, Vietnam was not unusual in following this strategy. Other centrally planned, socialist countries, such as China, had emphasized categorical interventions for priority health problems despite the rhetoric on primary health care.

The network of primary health facilities and the categorical health programs cannot by themselves account for all of Vietnam's success. In addition to these factors, Vietnam had the advantage of a highly literate population. Of course, near-universal literacy and promotion of education, especially among women, are themselves an achievement of the DRV system. Because of the high literacy rates, the receptivity of the population to health messages and health campaigns was likely to be much greater than in other low-income countries.

Finally, the importance of contextual factors cannot be overlooked. During the period when the health sector achieved its most impressive gains, Vietnam was continuously at war. It was probably easy for the government to mobilize the health cadres, and indeed the entire population, in that political setting.

By the late 1970s, Vietnam had already attained most of the improvements in health that it was to accomplish. After that time, a number of events occurred that adversely affected the health sector. The first of these was reunification. After reunification, the government of the Socialist Republic of Vietnam (SRV) attempted to bring the level of health-services coverage that existed in the North to the South. Since the South had a significantly poorer network of primary health facilities, the extension of health facilities was an enormous task that placed a big burden on the health budget. Health resources had to be spread more thinly, and it is likely that nonsalary, recurrent items in the health budget, such as medical supplies and maintenance, were cut back during this period. The expenditure cutback may have set in motion the process of deteriorating quality of health services and decay of physical infrastructure.

Reunification also brought about with it an enormous loss of skilled health manpower in the South. Because the SRV disallowed private practice, a large number of physicians and highly trained health workers emigrated from the country in 1975. The combination of poor health infrastructure and greatly reduced numbers of health care workers worsened health conditions in the South immediately after 1975.

At the same time, the flow of external resources into Vietnam, which benefited the health sector, began dwindling. After 1979, much of the multilateral aid that Vietnam received was cut off. While the external assistance from the Eastern bloc continued, much of it was directed to sectors other than health. The decline of Western aid and Vietnam's political isolation coincided with a period of hyperinflation and acute macroeconomic instability in Vietnam during the 1980s. The combination of sharply reduced multilateral assistance to the health sector and a deepening macroeconomic crisis adversely affected the flow of resources to the health sector.

The 1980s also marked the end of external hostilities after nearly three decades. In the absence of war, it was difficult for the government to maintain, to the same extent as before, the motivation, enthusiasm, and morale of health workers. With *Doi Moi*, the high priority attached to the health sector by the government probably began diminishing—at exactly the same time as the external hostilities were ending, the macroeconomic environment was worsening, and external assistance to the health sector was falling. With the political imperative lessened, inputs to the health sector—drugs, equipment, medical supplies, maintenance—declined, thereby adversely affecting the quality of care offered by the primary health facilities. This in turn changed the perception of the population about the usefulness of the health services, and lowered utilization rates. Thus, a once well-functioning health service system was breaking down as a result of a number of factors, including the difficult transition from a centrally planned to a market economy.

The experience of the Vietnamese health sector is not unique. The same situation has unfolded in several other centrally planned, socialist economies during the process of transition to a market system. Large health structures and other priority social programs that were built up with considerable resources from the state were left languishing as a result of fiscal crises and changes in political values. As state subsidies to the health sector declined, private households were asked to pick up an increasingly larger share of the burden of health expenditure.

There were, of course, other events that occurred in Vietnam in the aftermath of *Doi Moi* that mitigated, and in some cases even offset, the impact of reduced state support to the health sector. For one, the Vietnamese economy grew rapidly during the 1990s and 2000s. This resulted in a sharp increase in family incomes, which in turn allowed families—at least those whose incomes had risen rapidly—to finance out-of-pocket health expenditures more readily (World Bank 2001).

In Vietnam, as in China, an increasingly market-based economy also meant that income disparities increased significantly in the aftermath of *Doi Moi*. When the burden of health expenditure shifts from the government to families, disparities in income tend to engender disparities in health status. This is what happened in Vietnam. More affluent families, whose incomes grew more rapidly, were able to seek more health care, pay for higher-quality care, and afford more pharmaceuticals and drugs. Poorer families, who had earlier relied on the state for their health care needs, were left to fend for themselves.

Ironically, the reduced presence of the state in the health sector occurred at the same time as it was becoming *more* assertive in formulating and implementing restrictive reproductive policies and family planning. As noted by Scornet in Chapter 2 of this volume, it was in 1988 that the national government publicly proclaimed its normative goal of two children per family and began aggressively mobilizing the population to adopt the two-child norm. Data on the functional composition of government health expenditure show an increase in the share of public health spending on family planning and reproductive health following *Doi Moi*. Thus, the withdrawal of the Vietnamese state from the health sector following *Doi Moi* was not universal; activities related to population control—a renewed priority of the national government—were exempted from this withdrawal.

Of course, as the Vietnamese economy has grown and prospered, especially in the period after 2002, the state has been slowly reversing its neglect of the health sector and increasing state resources to that sector. However, some activities have received greater emphasis than others. As de Loenzien notes in Chapter 4 of this volume, one of these priority activities is HIV/ AIDS prevention. The government has recognized the HIV pandemic as a serious public health issue and devoted significant resources (albeit largely from international donors, such as the World Bank and the World Health Organization [WHO]) to both HIV/AIDS prevention and antiretroviral treatment for HIV/AIDS patients.

Utilization of Health Services

As noted earlier, the pre–*Doi Moi* information base in Vietnam is weak to non-existent. Few, if any, nationally representative household surveys were conducted prior to 1992; those that were, were not available to the public. Beginning in 1992–93, Vietnam established a framework for conducting routine nationally representative household surveys with support from the World Bank. The first Vietnam Living Standards Survey (VLSS) was conducted in 1992– 93 with a sample size of 23,839 individuals drawn from 4,800 households.

A second round of this survey was undertaken from December 1997 to December 1998 with some changes in questionnaire design and a slightly larger sample size of 28,518 individuals from 6,000 households. About 4,300 of the 1997–98 sample households and 17,780 of the 1997–98 sample individuals are the same households and individuals interviewed in 1992–93, thus constituting a substantial longitudinal data set. The survey was conducted by the State Planning Committee (now Ministry of Planning and Investment) and the General Statistics Office (GSO) in 1992–93 and by the General Statistics Office in 1997–98 (General Statistics Office 1993 and 1998). The sample was selected using three-staged random stratified cluster sampling. With sampling weights, the data yield unbiased population estimates at the national level as well as at the regional and urban/rural levels.

More recently, the VLSS sample has been vastly expanded and the questionnaire made much more comprehensive. The new VLSS was administered in 2002 and again in 2004 and 2006. However, this chapter does not use the new VLSS data, instead relying on the original two rounds of the VLSS.

A summary measure of the utilization of health services often used in the literature is the annual per capita number of medical contacts with the health services. Based on administrative data from health facilities, Vietnam's Ministry of Health estimated an average annual health contact rate of 1.7 per

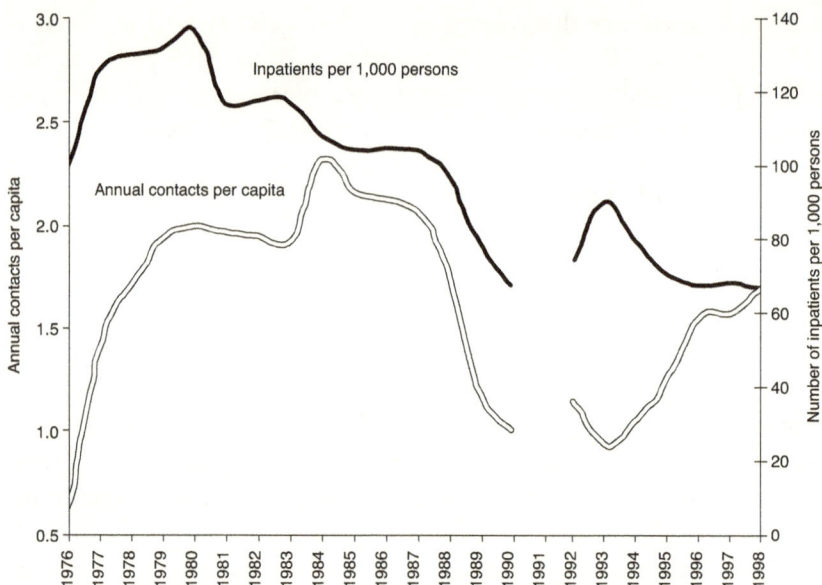

Figure 3.3   Utilization rates at public facilities, 1976–98.
Source: Ministry of Health, *Health Statistics Yearbook*, various issues.

capita and an inpatient admission rate of 68 per 1,000 persons for Vietnam in 1998. Historical data on utilization, shown in Figure 3.3, indicate that annual health contacts per capita increased sharply from 1976 to 1984 (rising from a level of 0.7 to 2.3), then reversed direction to decline all the way back to a level of 1.0 in 1990. After bottoming out in 1990, annual contacts per capita increased steadily during the 1990s to reach a level of 1.7 by 1998.

This is probably the strongest evidence suggesting that in the immediate aftermath of *Doi Moi*, when the health infrastructure collapsed and responsibility for health care was shifted from the state to the family, utilization of health services fell sharply. However, as incomes rose and state spending on health increased again in the late 1990s, health-services utilization resumed its upward trend.

The above data are facility-level data from secondary sources. They obviously do not allow disaggregation by socioeconomic level of persons seeking health care. It is possible to calculate income-specific health utilization rates using data from the first and second VLS surveys. A comparison of the average annual health service contact rate per capita across 1992–93 and 1997–98

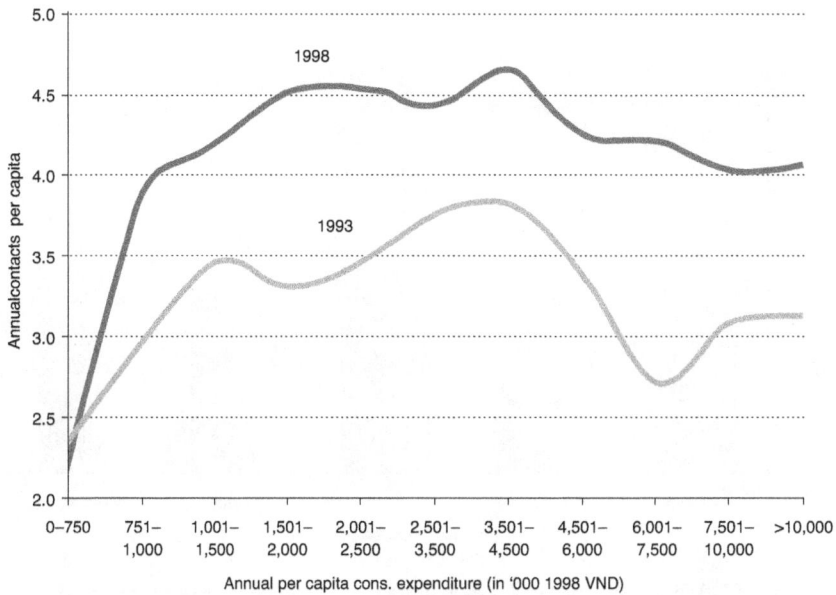

Figure 3.4   Average annual health service contacts per capita, by per capita consumption expenditure, 1993 and 1998.
Source: Author's calculations from the Vietnam Living Standards Survey 1992–93 and 1998–99.

for eleven different per capita expenditure (in constant 1998 dong) groups shows a widening disparity in utilization among different income groups between 1992–93 and 1997–98 (Figure 3.4).[1] The lowest income group (i.e., those whose per capita consumption expenditure was under VND 750,000 in each period) experienced no change in the utilization of health services, while middle- and upper-income groups experienced large increases in utilization. The data thus support our earlier conjecture that health disparities have widened over time in Vietnam.

Self-Medication and Reliance on Drug Vendors

An unintended outcome of the liberalization of the health sector has been to encourage individuals and families to self-medicate. With deregulation in the 1990s, the drug supply situation improved dramatically, and shortages of drugs, which were endemic throughout the Vietnamese health care system

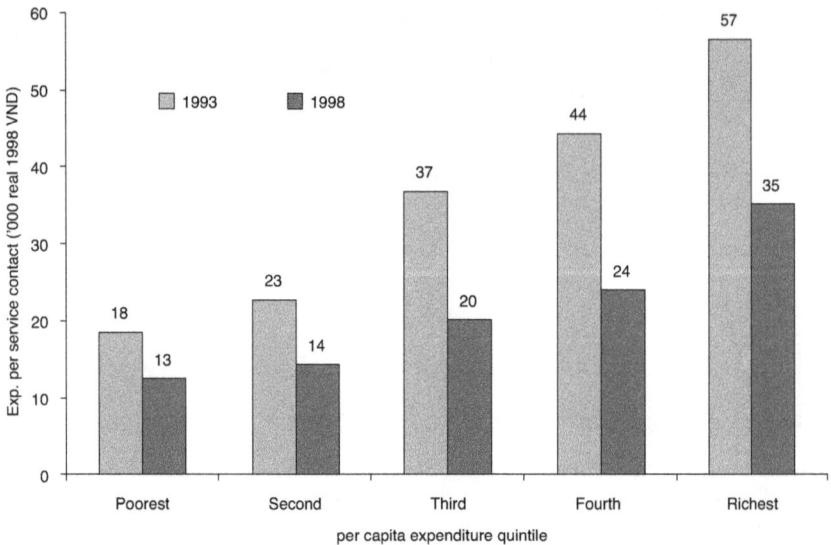

Figure 3.5   Average out-of-pocket expenditure on drugs per health service contact (across all health providers), by per capita expenditure quintile, 1993 and 1997.
Source: Author's calculations from the Vietnam Living Standards Survey 1992–93 and 1997–98.

until the early 1990s, disappeared. The number of drug vendors and pharmacy shops throughout the country mushroomed, with an estimated twenty thousand to thirty thousand or more drug retail outlets being present in the country. Even the smallest village has its own drug shop.

At the same time, deregulation resulted in lower prices of drugs for the consumer. Higher levels of domestic production, greater imports, and a more competitive distribution system all contributed to a decline in real drug prices. This is observed in the VLS survey data in the form of a real decline in out-of-pocket expenditure on drugs per health service contact between 1993 and 1998 for all income groups (Figure 3.5). It is also observed in the behavior of the medicine price index relative to the overall consumer price index over the 1993–98 period. While the price index for medicines was virtually flat between 1993 and 1998, the overall consumer price index and the food price index grew at annual rates of 8 percent and 10.8 percent, respectively, implying a decline of more than 30 percent in the real price of medicines (World Bank 2001).

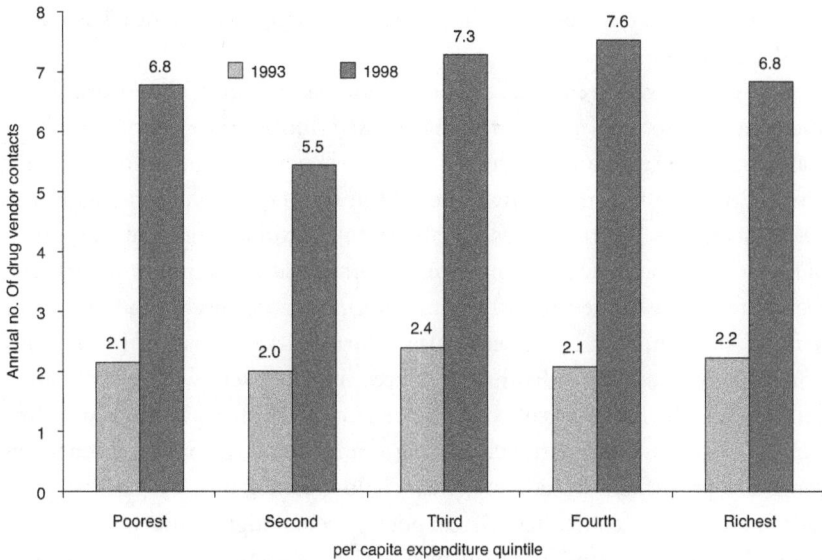

Figure 3.6   Average annual number of health service contacts per capital with drug vendors and pharmacy shops, by per capital expenditure quintile, 1993 and 1998.

Source: Author's calculations from the Vietnam Living Standards Survey 1992–93 amd 1997–98.

The result of these two developments, combined with the collapse of the commune health system, was an alarming increase in self-medication among individuals experiencing illness episodes. The VLSS data show a large increase in the utilization of drug vendors from whom individuals typically obtain drugs without prescription. While individuals made an average of 2.1 annual service contacts per capita with drug vendors and pharmacy shops in 1993, the number had increased to 6.8 annual contacts per capita by 1998. Interestingly, there were no major variations in the annual number of drug vendor contacts per capita across income groups (Figure 3.6). Indeed, drug vendors are the most ubiquitous health providers in Vietnam, accounting for two-thirds of all health service contacts.

What is disturbing is that most of the drug vendor contacts represent purchases of drugs without a prescription. The VLSS 1998 data indicate that 93 percent of all drug vendor contacts were for obtaining medicines without a prescription, with not much variation across economic groups. This effectively means that consumers self-treat their illnesses, perhaps with some advice from the drug vendor.

The unbridled increase in self-medication has resulted in an overuse and abuse of antibiotics. In turn, this has caused antibiotic resistance levels in Vietnam to increase and reach epidemic levels of late. This is an extremely serious problem that threatens to derail the significant achievements in the health sector, as Vietnam loses the ability to control and prevent the spread of many infectious diseases. The spread of antibiotic resistance is directly the result of overuse (unnecessary consumption), irrational use (broad instead of narrow spectrum), and ineffective use (short course instead of full course) of antibiotic drugs by individuals self-treating themselves. The problem is compounded by low levels of competence in clinical pharmacology and clinical pharmacy among pharmacists, drug vendors, and the public. Even when drugs are prescribed by doctors, there is low compliance by patients with rational treatment guidelines. Often, poor patients might limit themselves to a two-day course of antibiotics (instead of the recommended ten-day course) as they do not have enough money to buy the full course (Tornquist 1999).

Child Malnutrition

Another major health problem in Vietnam, especially relating to children, is high levels of child undernutrition. While Vietnam has a significantly lower level of infant mortality than most other Asian countries at its level of per capita GDP, its performance in the area of child malnutrition leaves much to be desired. Indeed, child malnutrition rates in Vietnam are among the highest in the region. The VLSS indicated 36 percent of children under the age of 5 years were malnourished in terms of weight-for-age and 35 percent are undernourished in terms of height for age.[2]

Data from the VLSS 1997–98 show large differences in the rates of child malnutrition across economic groups. For instance, while only 13 percent and 16 percent of children aged 0–59 months belonging to the richest quintile (ranked by consumption expenditure per capita) were stunted and underweight in 1998, the corresponding proportions for children in the poorest quintile were 42 percent. Further, the rate of decline in child malnutrition between 1992–93 and 1997–98 was also significantly greater among the richest quintile than among the poorer quintiles.

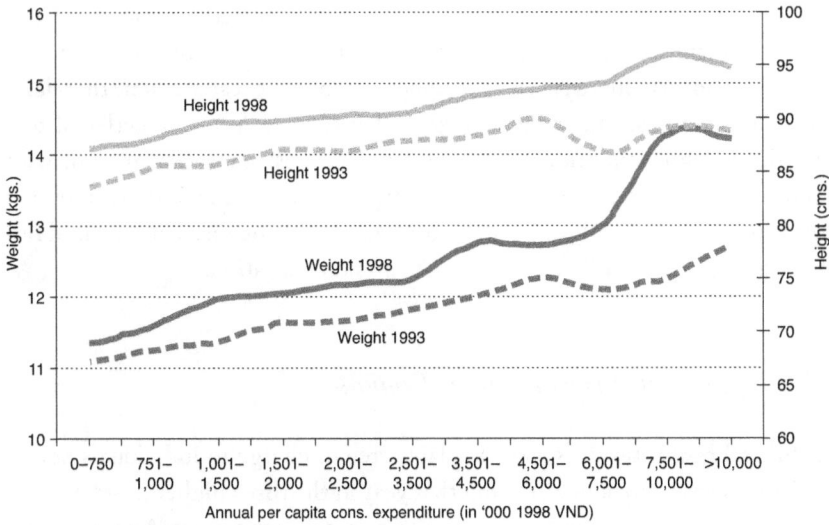

Figure 3.7 Heights and weights of children 0–5 years, by real per capita consumption expenditure, 1993 and 1998.
Source: Author's calculations from the Vietnam Living Standards Survey 1992–93 and 1997–98.

The uneven improvement in child nutrition across economic groups is evident in Figure 3.7, which plots the age- and sex-adjusted weights and heights of children aged 0–5 years in 1992–93 and 1997–98 for eleven real per capita expenditure groups.[3] Since expenditure is defined in constant 1998 dong, the expenditure groups are comparable across the two periods. While the graph shows a definite increase in both heights and weights between 1992–93 and 1997–98 for all expenditure groups, it shows a significantly larger improvement in height and weight for children from better-off families than from poor families. For instance, children living in families with annual per capita expenditure greater than VND 10,000,000 experienced a 12 percent increase in weights and a 7 percent increase in heights, but those in families with less than VND 75,000 annual per capita expenditure experienced a weight gain of only 2 percent and a height gain of 4 percent. Thus, the economic disparity in child nutrition widened during the period.

This finding bears an interesting resemblance to the observation, made by Jayakody and Huy in Chapter 7 of this volume, that education levels aggravated the increase in income inequality experienced by Vietnam during the post–*Doi Moi* period. They find that better-educated families were able to take greater advantage of the economic changes resulting from *Doi Moi*, and consequently increase their incomes to a much greater extent than less-educated families. Our results suggest that income levels exacerbated disparities in child nutritional status during the postrenovation period, with high-income families experiencing a sharper reduction in child malnutrition than low-income families. In this sense, the increasing disparity in child nutrition is ultimately related to levels of parental education.

The Private Cost of Health Care to Families

While all health services were available free of charge to individuals before 1989, fees were introduced during that year in the three higher (district, provincial, and national) levels of the health care delivery system. An explicit fee exemption mechanism was put in place, whereby certain classes of patients, such as the disabled, orphans, individuals able to produce certification of indigency from their neighborhood or village People's Committee, and patients suffering from mental problems, leprosy, and bacille of Koch-positive tuberculosis, were exempted from all or part of the user fees. Health consultations at commune health centers continued (and still continue) to be officially free. However, drugs are rarely provided free of charge at any facility. For the most part, individuals are responsible for obtaining their own supplies of drugs, typically from private pharmacies and drug vendors or from a for-profit pharmacy run by the public health facility.

Table 3.1 shows user fees paid by different population (consumption) quintiles for different types of health care providers.[4] It is observed that per-contact user fees for all providers increased in real terms between 1992–93 and 1997–98. For some providers, the increases were very substantial (e.g., more than 1,000 percent for public hospitals). User fees at commune health centers, which were negligible in 1993, increased significantly as well—to an average of VND 5,260. The latter finding demonstrates that commune health centers rarely provide "free" consultations even though they are supposed to.

Average user fees at health facilities—even public facilities such as public hospitals and commune centers—are prohibitively expensive for the poor. For instance, a *single* service contact with a commune health center costs a typical family in the poorest quintile the equivalent of 4 percent of all its

TABLE 3.1

Average out-of-pocket expenditure on fees
per health service contact (in constant 1998 VND),
by provider and per capita expenditure quintile, 1993 and 1998

Provider	Per capita expenditure quintile					All
	Bottom	Second	Third	Fourth	Top	
			1993			
Public hospitals	3,520	2,460	9,730	11,570	7,360	7,690
Commune health centers	190	170	20	90	770	200
Private clinics, doctors	710	1,020	1,260	2,000	3,540	1,900
Drug vendors	0	0	0	0	0	0
Traditional healers	0	420	340	0	7,280	2,260
			1998			
Public hospitals	32,320	72,660	73,330	99,630	115,320	88,890
Commune health centers	2,820	4,960	6,030	5,390	11,600	5,260
Private clinics	17,400	20,480	3,360	13,000	17,590	12,820
Drug vendors	0	0	0	0	0	0
Traditional healers	5,720	7,030	14,390	31,050	41,040	21,380

SOURCE: Vietnam Living Standards Survey 1993 and 1998.

annual nonfood expenditure. A visit to a public hospital costs significantly more—22 percent of all *annual* nonfood expenditure.

Further, even though the user fees shown in Table 3.1 are observed to increase with the economic status of patients, they are significantly greater for the poor than for the better-off in relative terms. For instance, a *single* service contact with a public hospital takes up 5 percent of all nonfood expenditure for a *year* for a family in the richest quintile—compared to the 22 percent found for a family in the poorest quintile. Thus, health care costs at public facilities—facilities that are intended primarily for the poor—are significantly less affordable for the poor than for the better-off, and the relative burden of user charges falls disproportionately on the poor in Vietnam (Wagstaff and Doorslaer 2003).

While the high costs of health care can in large part be mitigated by the presence of a universal health care system, such a scheme is still in its infancy in Vietnam. The country did introduce two health insurance schemes in 1993: a compulsory scheme covering primarily current and retired civil servants and employees of state and large (i.e., with more than ten employees) private enterprises, and a voluntary scheme aimed at the remainder of the population: farmers, school students, and family members of compulsory scheme enrollees (Ensor 1995; Ensor and San 1996; Jowett and Thompson 1999). The mandatory scheme covers a relatively small proportion of the total population—only those working in the formal sector of the economy. The coverage of the voluntary scheme has been limited, with most of the enrollees in that scheme being students (schools are often under pressure from local authorities to enroll all of their students in the scheme). So far, the scheme has had limited success in enrolling farmers and other rural residents.

Due to the limited success of the voluntary health insurance scheme, the Vietnamese government introduced another scheme—Health Care Fund for the Poor (HCFP)—in 2002–03. The package focuses largely on services delivered by public hospitals and commune health centers, and it does not cover nonprescription drugs purchased from drug vendors and pharmacies, which continue to be extensively used in the country. It is still too early to evaluate the success of the HCFP. However, early reports suggest that the scheme has wider coverage and is better targeted to the poor than its predecessors. Yet, a majority of the rural Vietnamese population (some 80–85 percent) continues to lack any type of health coverage (Axelson et al. 2005; Knowles et al. 2005; Wagstaff 2007).

The Epidemic of Tobacco Use

Another emerging threat to public health in Vietnam is the widespread and rising use of tobacco, an issue also broached upon in the Xenos et al. chapter in this volume. It is widely known that tobacco use is an important contributing risk factor in several diseases, such as respiratory infections, lung cancer, heart disease, and tuberculosis. Vietnam has one of the highest rates of smoking in the world (Wise 1997). Further, smoking rates have been rising over time: the percentage of males aged fifteen years and over increased from 50 percent in 1997–98 to 56 percent in 2002.[5] According to WHO estimates, close to 7.5 million Vietnamese people alive today, or 10 percent of the population, will die of smoking-related causes. Lung cancer is already the most prevalent form of cancer among men.

Lately, the Vietnamese state has recognized the seriousness of the tobacco epidemic and taken active steps to stem the increase in tobacco use. It has tightened restrictions on the imports of U.S. and foreign cigarettes, raised cigarette taxes, prohibited tobacco advertising and promotion, and banned smoking in many public places. However, it is ironic that as the state has tried to discourage tobacco use, it has simultaneously been engaged in manufacturing cigarettes; indeed, the largest domestic cigarette manufacturer in the country is a state-owned firm (Vietnam National Tobacco Corporation or Vinataba). The company has entered into production agreements with Philip Morris, Rothmans of Pall Mall, and BAT to produce and sell their premium brands in Vietnam, using Vinataba facilities. There is thus an inherent conflict of interest in the state being simultaneously engaged in tobacco control as well as in the lucrative business of manufacturing and distributing cigarettes.

In addition, the widespread use of rustic tobacco by rural and poor individuals poses a formidable challenge to health policy makers. While higher taxes on cigarettes raise the price of cigarettes and discourage cigarette use, they do little to curb the use of rustic tobacco; indeed, a study for Vietnam finds that higher cigarette taxes have encouraged low-income cigarette smokers in Vietnam to switch to rustic tobacco, which is as harmful to health as cigarettes (Laxminarayan and Deolalikar 2004). Thus, public efforts to combat cigarette smoking must also address the problem of rustic tobacco use, and measures must be taken to discourage this secondary mechanism of initiation into cigarette smoking.

Conclusion

With the liberalization of the Vietnamese economy (*Doi Moi*) in the late 1980s, there was a major shift in the responsibility for health care from the state to the family. In fact, by some measures, Vietnamese health care is one of the most private-sector-dominated health schemes in developing Asia; it is estimated that nearly three-quarters of health spending is financed by out-of-pocket expenditures by individuals and families (Knowles et al. 2005). Thus, a large proportion of families—especially those in the rural areas—is vulnerable to impoverishment by a catastrophic illness.

Interestingly, government health facilities—especially public hospitals—which used to provide free services in the pre–*Doi Moi* era, are some of the most expensive health facilities in the country. It is ironical that the major proportion of *private* health spending in Vietnam is spent on obtaining services from the *public* sector. One consequence of this trend is that drug vendors have become a health provider of choice for many of Vietnam's poor, and this has resulted in the overuse and abuse of drugs. In turn, this has caused antibiotic resistance levels to increase and reach epidemic rates. Antibiotic resistance is a serious problem that threatens to derail the significant achievements in the health sector, as Vietnam loses the ability to control and prevent the spread of many infectious diseases.

Another consequence of a highly privatized health system is a rapid increase in health disparities. As incomes of a segment of the population have grown sharply owing to rapid economic growth, those who can afford to purchase high-quality health services have managed to improve their access to health care and their health outcomes, while those who cannot have been left behind.

In recent years, the government has tried to mitigate health disparities by launching programs to provide the poor with free or subsidized health care. However, such interventions have had limited success. A national health insurance scheme launched in 1993 has probably exacerbated health disparities, as most of the individuals covered under this scheme are urban dwellers employed by the government and in the organized sector of the economy. Rural residents, especially those in the informal sector and in agriculture, continue to lack coverage, thus being vulnerable to impoverishment by catastrophic health events. A more recent program—Health Care Fund for the Poor—tries to target health care subsidies to the poor, but the coverage of this program is still relatively low. In the years to come, Vietnam's challenge will be to achieve a better balance between public and private financing of health care and to ensure that the poor and indigent are protected from the debilitating financial effects of poor health.

Notes

This chapter draws extensively from two reports written by the author—World Bank (1992) and World Bank (2001).

1. The VLSS data indicate a modest increase of about 29 percent in the annualized per capita health services contact rate between the two periods.

2. As in most of the nutrition literature, a child is considered underweight when his or her weight for age is more than two standard deviations below the National

Center for Health Statistics (NCHS) reference weight. A child is stunted when his or her height-for-age is more than two standard deviations below the NCHS reference. Severe underweight and stunting occur when the relevant nutrition indicator is more than three standard deviations below the NCHS reference.

3. Age and sex adjustments were done on the basis of an estimated regression of height and weight on age and age squared. In addition, a dichotomous variable, representing the method of height measurement (i.e., whether height was measured standing up or lying down), was included in the height equation. All heights and weights shown in the figure are calculated for a "reference" child of age thirty-three months and represent a simple average of male and female values.

4. These user fees do not include expenditure on drugs.

5. Based on data from the 1997–98 Vietnam Living Standards Survey (VLSS) and the 2001–02 VLSS.

References

Allman, J. 1993. Primary health care in Vietnam. In *Reaching health for all*, edited by J. Rohde, M. Chatterjee, and D. Morley, 324–341. Delhi: Oxford University Press.

Axelson, H., Dam V. C., Nguyen K. P., Tran T. M. O., Duong H. L., and Khuong A. T. 2005. The impact of the Health Care Fund for the Poor on poor households in two provinces in Viet Nam. Paper presented at the Global Forum for Health Research Forum, Mumbai, India, 12–16 September.

Banister, J. 1993. *Vietnam population dynamics and prospects*. Berkeley: Institute of East Asian Studies, University of California.

Barbieri, M., J. Allman, Pham B. S., and Nguyen M. T. 1995. La situation démographique du Viêt Nam. *Population* 50: 621–651.

Ensor, T. 1995. Introducing health insurance in Vietnam. *Health Policy and Planning* 10(2): 154–163.

Ensor, T., and Pham B. S. 1996. Access and payment for health care: the poor of northern Vietnam. *International Journal of Health Planning and Management* 11: 69–83.

Fritzen, S. 1999. Decentralization, disparities, and innovation in Vietnam's health sector. In *Market reform in Vietnam: Building institutions for development*, edited by J. I. Litvack and D. A. Rondinelli. Westport, CT: Quorum Books.

Gendreau, F., V. Fauveau, and Dang T. 1997. *Démographie de la péninsule indochinoise*. Paris: Aupelf-Uref.

General Statistics Office. 1993 and 1998. *Vietnam living standards survey (VLSS) 1993 and 1998*. Hanoi: General Statistics Office.

Jowett, M., and R. Thompson. 1999. Paying for health care in Vietnam: Extending voluntary health insurance coverage. Centre for Health Economics, Discussion Paper No. 167, University of York, UK, March.

Knowles, J. C., Nguyen T., Dang B., Nguyen K., Tran T., Nguyen K., and Vu N. 2005. *Making health care more affordable for the poor: Health financing in Vietnam.* Hanoi: Medical Publishing House.

Ladinsky, J. L., and R. E. Levine. 1985. The organization of health services in Vietnam. *Journal of Public Health Policy* 6(2): 255–268.

Laxminarayan, R., and A. B. Deolalikar. 2004. Tobacco initiation, cessation and change: evidence from Vietnam. *Health Economics* 13(12): 1191–1201.

Tornquist, S. 1999. Vietnam–Sweden health cooperation in the area of drug policy and control project document. Ministry of Health, Hanoi, April 24. Mimeo.

Vogel, U. 1987. The whole of Vietnam can be considered as one well-designed project: Some reflections on primary health care experiences in Vietnam, 1945–85. Dissertation submitted in partial fulfillment of the requirements of the M.Sc. (Economics) in Tropical Epidemiology and Health Planning, University of Wales.

Wagstaff, A. 2007. Health insurance for the poor: Initial impacts of Vietnam's health care fund for the poor. World Bank Policy Research Working Paper 4134. Washington, DC: World Bank.

Wagstaff, A., and E. van Doorslaer. 2003. Catastrophe and impoverishment in paying for health care: with applications to Vietnam 1993–1998. *Health Economics* 12(11): 921–34.

Wise, J. 1997. Vietnam tops world smoking league for men. *British Medical Journal* 314(7095): 1641, 7 June.

World Bank. 1992. *Viet Nam: Population, health and nutrition sector review.* Report No. 10289-VN, East Asia and Pacific Regional Office, Washington, DC, September.

World Bank. 2001. *Growing healthy: A review of Vietnam's health sector.* Report No. 22210-VN, Human Development Sector Unit, East Asia and Pacific Region, the World Bank. Washington, DC.

PART TWO

The Redeployment of Family Solidarities

Chapter Four

The Family
A Cornerstone in the Current Fight Against HIV/AIDS

MYRIAM DE LOENZIEN

The fight against HIV/AIDS epitomizes the post–*Doi Moi* strategy developed by the Vietnamese government to compensate for the decline of the welfare state. The strategy explicitly emphasizes the major role of the family in caring for the old and the sick. The main purpose of this chapter is to delineate the functions attributed to the family in the support of HIV-infected individuals by current policy and to explain the context leading to policy shifts over time. The study also evaluates the impact of policies on intrafamily relations and seeks to measure the extent of the ambivalence generated in both care receivers and care providers within the family. The analysis of data from a quantitative and qualitative survey I undertook in 2004, together with an examination of the legal documentation as well as the scientific or organizational literature underlined the following points: (1) HIV/AIDS has been spreading since the 1980s and has gradually become viewed as a serious problem. However, it was only recently addressed mainly as a health problem rather than a social issue. Consequently, solutions for slowing its spread and providing care have been difficult to implement because of widespread stigmatization. (2) The state appealed for a large mobilization against the epidemic. Three main social entities gradually appeared in the discourse of the state and are present in the perceptions of caregivers and HIV-infected persons: society, the community, and the family, the latter being central. (3) Heavy reliance on the family is partly due to the fact that the medical system was initially unable to meet the new demands for prevention and treatment. (4) The family is therefore an essential recourse, but it has complex social and psychological implications for HIV-infected persons. (5) In the context of an increasing openness and the restructuring of the health system—both targeted by *Doi Moi* reforms—the fight against the HIV/AIDS epidemic provides insight on the evolution of the relationship between the state and the family.

This chapter first briefly provides some background on the HIV/AIDS epidemic in Vietnam, the legal context, and the policies implemented to fight the epidemic, as well as changes to these over the past twenty years. It next describes the respective roles assigned to the health care system on the one hand and the family on the other, as well as the interactions between the two. Using information collected by the author through field work, the chapter ends with an analysis of the daily experiences of HIV-infected persons and their families in relation to the broader government strategy in the fight against the epidemic.

HIV/AIDS in Vietnam

In December 2006, 7.8 million people were living with HIV/AIDS in South and Southeast Asia, representing 20 percent of the world's total HIV/AIDS population (UNAIDS 2006a). In this region, the highest national HIV infection levels are in Southeast Asia, mostly Thailand (1.4 percent), Cambodia (1.6 percent), and Myanmar (1.3 percent) (UNAIDS 2006a). With an HIV prevalence of 0.6 percent in 2006 (UNAIDS 2006a), Vietnam is one of the countries, with China, Indonesia and Nepal, in which the epidemic is in transition: a rapid increase in the prevalence of HIV infection has followed a long period of stability at a low level (Ruxrungtham et al. 2004). After the first case of HIV reported in Ho Chi Minh City in December 1990 (Nguyen, Thanh, and Quan 2004), the epidemic remained concentrated in a few provinces, with fewer than 1,500 new cases reported per year at the national level prior to 1993. It then gradually increased to around 5,000 new cases per year. It was not until 1999–2002 that the epidemic spread to the whole country, with more than 10,000 new cases per year (*Cong hoa Xa hoi Chu nghia Viet Nam* 2004, 14) and a prevalence rate over 0.1 percent (UNAIDS 2005). After that, the epidemic entered a phase of rapid propagation. The total number of people living with HIV has doubled since 2000 to reach an estimated 260,000

TABLE 4.1.

HIV prevalence among 15- to 49-year-old adults (%) and number of people living
with HIV/AIDS by provincial cluster (ordered by prevalence rate), 2005 Vietnam

Region	Prevalence of HIV (%)	Number of persons with HIV/AIDS
Ho Chi Minh City	1.25	50,000
North Coast	1.15	21,000
Hanoi	0.86	17,000
Southeast	0.60	28,000
Northeast	0.57	20,000
Mekong River Delta	0.54	61,000
Northwest	0.38	21,000
Red River Delta	0.35	26,000
High Plateau	0.20	5,500
North Plateau	0.20	6,000
Central Coast	0.13	7,100
Total	0.51	263,000

SOURCE: Vietnam Commission for Population, Family and Children, Ministry of Health,
Population Reference Bureau, 2006: 13, 15.

[150,000–430,000] in 2005 (UNAIDS, WHO 2006). HIV is present all over
the country, with great provincial variations (Table 4.1). Prevalence is highest in the northeastern provinces of Quang Ninh and Haiphong, whereas
Ho Chi Minh City has the largest number of HIV-infected persons (Ministry of Health 2007).

As elsewhere in Asia, the progressive spread of the epidemic to the country
as a whole results from the overlap of two major risk-taking behaviors—unprotected sex and injection drug use—with the latter responsible for about
half of all HIV cases (Morrison and Nieburg 2006). However, here more than
elsewhere, the phenomenon is exacerbated by increasing social and economic
transformations and growing internal migration from rural to urban areas as
well as from region to region (Ghys et al. 2003; Gorbach et al. 2002; Grayman
et al. 2005; Nguyen, Thanh, and Quan 2004; UNAIDS 2006a) so other transmission channels are developing, as demonstrated by the prevalence of the
infection among military conscripts and women consulting for prenatal care,
which reached 0.44 percent and 0.35 percent, respectively, in 2005 (Ministry
of Health 2007). This epidemiological change is cause for concern, as it could
result in a generalization of the epidemic in the coming years (Ruxrungtham
et al. 2004). As a direct consequence, the sex ratio—which was six males for one
female among the reported cases in 2006 (Ministry of Health 2007)—could

change as HIV spreads to the whole population. Aware of the potential devastating impact of the epidemic, the government of Vietnam acted early, though its initial approach, developed in the late 1980s and throughout the 1990s, proved ineffectual and resulted in a complete shift in the early 2000s.

Government Policies and Approaches in the Fight Against HIV/AIDS

Initially viewed as an essentially social problem that had to be repressed by punitive measures, the emergence of HIV/AIDS as a public health issue was the result of a change in the political discourse in response to the spread of the epidemic. The year 2003 marked a watershed in the two distinct policy approaches successively adopted by the government in the fight against HIV/AIDS.

HIV/AIDS AS A SYMPTOM OF SOCIAL EVIL

The concept of "social evil" was developed by hygienists in the nineteenth century and used by the French colonial government in Africa and Asia, notably in Indo-China (Monnais-Rousselot 1999, 187). It was subsequently adopted by former French colonies after independence. "Social evils" include all phenomena considered harmful to society from both a moral and a health standpoint. The concept delimits the sphere of activities of a policy targeting social groups "going against the trend of the behavioral model promoted by the authorities" (Diop 1997), a sphere of activities that varies over time and space. In Vietnam, "social evils" mainly consist of prostitution, illegal drug use, gambling, and criminal offences, all prohibited by law (Nguyen, Dinh, and Nguyen 2003). The concept was officially introduced in the context of the struggle against HIV/AIDS in 1991, notably during the 8th Session of the Vietnamese Communist Party and in a number of legal texts.

One of these was the Governmental Resolution of December, 18, 1992, which provides the first general orientation on the control and prevention of the epidemic (*Cong hoa Xa hoi Chu nghia Viet Nam* 1992). Additional regulations were adopted in 1993 and 1994 to organize the prevention of HIV/AIDS in health settings and to provide a legal framework within which to tackle the problems of social evils, namely commercial sex and drug use. The Ordinance of the National Assembly on the Prevention and Control of HIV/AIDS (*Cong hoa Xa hoi Chu nghia Viet Nam* 1995) dated May 31, 1995, was far more extensive than previous texts and represents a second legal benchmark. The social evils approach was further emphasized through the creation of the National Committee for Preventing AIDS, Drug Addiction, and Prostitution in 2000 (*Cong hoa Xa hoi Chu nghia Viet Nam* 2004, 17), an initiative aimed at promoting interministerial collaboration.

As a result, HIV/AIDS was associated with dangerous activities, mainly prostitution and drug addiction (Nguyen, Dinh, and Nguyen 2003) and from 1991 a policy grounded on fear and moral condemnation was implemented in HIV/AIDS prevention and control in Hanoi and Ho Chi Minh City, and then extended to other provinces during the 1990s (National AIDS Committee of Vietnam 1994). It led to the arrest of drug users and prostitutes who were sent to specialized rehabilitation camps, to the execution of drug traffickers, and to public campaigns condemning and stigmatizing drug addiction, prostitution, breaking the law in general, and being HIV-positive in particular (Gorbach et al. 2002; Wolfe and Malinowska-Sempruch 2004). The policy resulted in the marginalization of HIV-infected persons who were excluded from some occupations (Instruction dated October 17, 1999) and forbidden to marry, while their spouses were permitted to divorce (Resolution dated December, 18, 1992, Article 14).

At the end of the 1990s, partly because of pressure from the international community, the government recognized that such an approach was counter-productive since the struggle against the epidemic actually suffered from the assimilation of HIV/AIDS to "social evils." The approach had delayed the establishment of medical intervention appropriate for effectively fighting the disease and contributed to the widespread discrimination of persons with HIV/AIDS, thereby forcing the epidemic underground and complicating the implementation of programs for its prevention and control, or of support of those infected (Le 2005; Morrison and Nieburg 2006; Nguyen, Thanh, and Quan 2004). The ineffectiveness of this policy appeared all the more blatant since neighboring countries such as Thailand and Cambodia, and even more distant countries such as Brazil and a number of others in Sub-Saharan Africa, were recording progress in combating the epidemic by involving HIV-infected persons. Faced with the propagation of the epidemic, the increase in transmissions unrelated to drug addiction or prostitution, and the growing diversity in the type of people infected, the policy was abandoned in 2003.

HIV/AIDS AS A PUBLIC HEALTH ISSUE

From the end of 2003, the Ministry of Health regarded the HIV epidemic as a public health issue to be fought through prevention and treatment (Le 2005). In an August 2004 visit to the country's biggest medical center, Bach Mai Hospital in Hanoi, the president of Vietnam delivered a speech—that received wide media attention—in which he urged the population to stop considering HIV a social evil and to combat discrimination against HIV-positive people. In the same year, the government's "National Strategy on HIV/AIDS Prevention and Control until 2010 with a vision to 2020" (*Cong hoa Xa hoi Chu nghia Viet Nam* 2004) (part V, Article 3) declared the social evils policy to be inadequate and harmful. In 2006, the fourth and most recent legal text, namely the first Law on HIV/AIDS Prevention and Control (*Cong Hoa Xa Hoi Chu Nghia Viet Nam* 2006) was promulgated by the National Assembly to replace the 1995 Ordinance. The National Strategy focuses on the "dangerous" nature of the epidemic and its multidimensional aspect as it "threatens" the health and "lives of individuals and the future of the population" and "directly affects the economic and cultural development, the social order, and the security of the country." The National Strategy includes a quantitative target, which is to hold the HIV prevalence rate in the general population to a level below 0.3, with an overall goal of limiting the impact of the epidemic on the socioeconomic development of the country. Indeed, the economic consequences of HIV/AIDS have served as a powerful argument brandished by international and nongovernmental organizations (NGOs)[1] to convince the Vietnamese government to act against the epidemic. Additional legal texts include governmental decrees, (inter) ministerial instructions, governmental resolutions and decisions, ministerial and governmental directives, directives from the Communist Party, rulings from the Permanent Committee of the National Assembly, and presidential decrees that further built on the new strategy.

A mass-information campaign accompanied the new approach with a series of messages in the media to raise population awareness about the potential risk of contracting HIV and the need to enroll all society's players in the fight against the epidemic. International organizations and NGOs, which had earlier encouraged the Vietnamese government to shift its emphasis, contributed to drawing up the legal texts (Morrison and Nieburg 2006). In recognition of the country's considerable efforts to change its policy, Vietnam was included on the list of eligible countries for funding to tackle the HIV/AIDS epidemic. Thereafter, it participated in the "3 by 5" program (three million people treated in the world by 2005) organized by the World Health Organization (WHO), received large grants from the World Bank's World Funds, and was invited to benefit from the U.S. President's Emergency Plan for AIDS Relief (PEPFAR). In 2006, international donors provided more than $50 million to help the government fight the HIV/AIDS epidemic (Morrison and Nieburg 2006).

The significant policy shift described above was mirrored by parallel changes in the roles respectively assigned to the health system and to the family.

The Institutional Setting

Vietnam has a well-equipped and effective health care system considering its low level of socioeconomic development (National Centre for Social Sciences and Humanities 2001; World Bank et al. 2001). However, the fight against HIV/AIDS arose at a time when the social services were in the throes of reorganization following *Doi Moi*, as explained in the introduction to this book. The increasing difficulties in accessing health care encountered by the poorest strata of the population tended to render ineffective the government efforts to promote treatment of persons with HIV/AIDS. The changing epidemiology of HIV/AIDS in Vietnam also called for changes in the services offered due to the increase in the number of people infected, the new emphasis on treatment in addition to prevention, and the emergence of a new generation of pharmaceutical drugs to cure opportunistic infections, thereby increasing the life expectancy of persons with HIV/AIDS and transforming the infection from an acute to a chronic condition.

THE CHANGING ORGANIZATION AT THE CENTRAL LEVEL

The organization of health institutions in the fight against HIV/AIDS has suffered from continuing changes at the central level.

When *Doi Moi* was launched, the Sub-Committee for the Prevention and Control of AIDS was placed under the auspices of the National Institute of Hygiene and Epidemiology, which had replaced the *Institut Pasteur de Hanoi* in 1987. The institutional mobilization around HIV developed progressively. In 1990, this Sub-Committee became the National AIDS Committee with greater involvement by the Ministry of Health and was promoted to a ministerial level in 1994 with the deputy prime minister as its chairman, thus demonstrating the importance attached to combating the epidemic. This, however, changed when the Committee merged with the National Committee for AIDS, Drug and Prostitution Prevention and Control to become the National AIDS Standing Bureau placed under the supervision of the Ministry of Health. This led to a dual management of activities relating to HIV/AIDS prevention and control, since the social aspects were managed by the Bureau, while the Division of Health was in charge of biomedical aspects. In 2003, the National AIDS Standing Bureau was merged with the Department of Preventive Medicine of the Ministry of Health. Finally, the Vietnam Administration of HIV/AIDS Control (VAAC) affiliated with the Ministry of Health was established in 2005 (Socialist Republic of Vietnam 2006). The provincial level committees are in a process of reorganization that mirrors the redistribution of activities at the national level.

THE PROGRESSIVE DEVELOPMENT OF TREATMENT AND CARE

Health infrastructures have been progressively equipped and their personnel trained, first at the central and then at the provincial level with a gradual decentralization.

The central and regional Hygiene and Epidemiological Institutes first carried out testing for HIV in 1987. Anonymous and free HIV counseling and testing centers were created in 2000. They were spread over forty provinces to test approximately 40,000 people per year (Pham et al. 2002) and reached sixty provinces in early 2006 (Morrison and Nieburg 2006). However, in each province, the number of medical centers offering core services such as voluntary counseling and testing remains limited (CORE, USAID, and CARE 2006). At the beginning of 2000, the Ministry of Health requested systematic testing of women consulting for prenatal care, but by 2002 the obstetrics-gynecological departments of major hospitals were the only structures with the means to offer this (Pham et al. 2002). A study undertaken in Haiphong to evaluate service users' points of view shows that reluctance to HIV testing in pregnant women arose from the perception of poor health care support and worries about a husband's disapproval of the test, leading to a low test acceptance rate and a low level of return for test results (Dinh, Detels, and Nguyen 2005). In addition to infectious departments in the main hospitals, specific centers were set up to provide care for HIV-infected people and AIDS patients, first in Ho Chi Minh City in 2002 (Pham et al. 2002) and then in Hanoi in 2005. HIV care, treatment, and support services have theoretically been extended to more than twenty provinces (CORE, USAID, and CARE 2006) but at the beginning of 2005 medical services qualified to care for HIV-positive patients were only available in the major cities and in a few provinces. Communes[2] were given guidance to implement community and home-based care for HIV-infected persons, but the major tasks of equipping, training, and purchasing medicines remain mostly unfulfilled outside of the largest centers. Most of the staff did not receive the training and resources necessary to care for HIV-positive patients and is unable to cope with the psychological stress resulting from this burdensome type of care. Nonexistent preventive methods for the nursing and medical staff and the lack of systematic protection against accidental exposure to blood partially explain the ostracism and discrimination by local health personnel toward HIV-positive patients. Due to lack of funding and the absence of adequate legislation until 2006, the vast majority of health facilities did not have harm-reduction programs during this period, such as needle and syringe exchanges for injection-drug users.

LIMITED PARTICIPATION FROM THE PRIVATE SECTOR

In 2002, the overall care financed by the private sector represented 71 percent of total health care expenditure in Vietnam (World Health Organization 2005). Most of the private health care system was for profit. In contrast, as in most countries around the world, the participation of private (nonprofit) organizations in combating HIV/AIDS was very low, though the situation tends to improve over time.

The high investment required in both equipment and staff is difficult to secure, especially since international organizations involved in the fight against HIV/AIDS typically aim their funds at the public sector. Only certain specific industrial sectors, such as mining, have their own hospital polyclinics, partly designed to care periodically for HIV-positive patients, although most of their activities target the prevention of HIV transmission. Private sector participation in HIV/AIDS prevention and control mostly occurs through mutual aid associations and support groups that do not have any official legal status and therefore have limited financial and material resources. The growing number of NGOs set up in many countries at the end of the 1980s (O'Malley, Nguyen, and Lee 1996), and which have become significant in Vietnam since the early 2000s, favor a rechanneling of funds to develop private sector participation in the care of HIV/AIDS patients. In Vietnam, NGOs which have a specific institutional context, as mentioned below, play an important role in public programs that offer home-based care and support such as palliative care and community-based services that are not yet fully in place (CORE, USAID, and CARE 2006). An increase in expenditure related to HIV/AIDS prevention and in private-sector involvement, similar to that at world level, is likely to be observed in the future (UNAIDS, WHO 2004, 135). Meanwhile, the family has to cope with the sociomedical emergency and compensate for the deficiencies of the health system.

A COMPREHENSIVE PILOT CARE PROGRAM WITH
ANTIRETROVIRAL (ARV) TREATMENT

Improved access to antiretroviral (ARV) medicines, which has considerably increased HIV/AIDS patients' survival, has led to a change in the role of the family, which used to be mostly limited to providing palliative care and now increasingly revolves around the follow-up and observance of treatments.

Vietnam, along with the Ivory Coast, Chile, and Uganda, was one of the first countries to benefit from the "Access to Medicines" Initiative launched in November 1997 by UNAIDS. This provided free treatment for pregnant women and health workers living with HIV. In 2002, in Vietnam, with the exception of HIV-positive pregnant women, some of whom benefited from preventative prophylaxis, and some health workers who received care following accidental exposure to blood, only 1.1 percent of people who declared themselves to be HIV-positive had received ARV therapy within the framework of a national program (Nguyen, Thanh, and Quan 2004). In 2002–03, in addition to the treatment of specific population groups, some hospitals provided consultations, counseling, and ARV treatment to HIV/AIDS patients. However these services were very expensive.[3] They had to be paid for by the patients themselves and were not accompanied by a comprehensive scheme securing continuum of care.

A turning point was reached in terms of patients' access to the new generation of drugs in 2003, when the Vietnamese Ministry of Health lent its support to a Franco-Vietnamese pilot program for comprehensive ARV treatment within the framework of the French ESTHER initiative. At the time, patients received follow-up care in the Dong Da municipal polyclinic, the reference hospital in the city of Hanoi and the main provider of HIV/AIDS care and treatment. The hospital is relatively small, equipped with only 250 beds. Some patients were already receiving antiretroviral treatment between 1998 and 2000 in this hospital but at their expense. The pharmaceutical drugs used to combat the disease included only one molecule until bi- and tri-therapies were gradually introduced. In October 2003, 94 of the 251 HIV/AIDS patients with a medical file in the hospital were receiving ARV treatment (Tran 2003). The enrollment of patients in the new program, which provided bi- and tri-therapies free of charge, started in April 2004 and continued at a rate of 20 new patients every two to three months. Selected patients had to meet the biological and clinical criteria established by WHO, along with two conditions likely to favor adherence to treatment: they had to live in Hanoi and, if drug addicts, they had to commit to quit. By the end of 2004, among all patients in the ARV program, 82 were receiving a tri-therapy treatment in the Infectious Diseases Department of Dong Da Hospital, the only one in Vietnam to provide such therapy free of charge to HIV/AIDS patients.

Access to ARV medicine gave the family a new responsibility that had to be specified (Decision of March 7, 2005, Article 4.3). A number of regulations attributed specific tasks to patients' kin. The family was expected to ensure correct pharmaceutical drug compliance by the patients (Decision of March 7, 2005, Article 6.1). Indeed, following ARV treatment implies a lifelong commitment. It supposes administering pharmaceutical drugs to the patient at fixed times throughout the day as well as providing meals at regular hours. Regularity is the main factor for a successful treatment to avoid the development of drug resistance.

In December 2005, among the estimated 25,000 patients in need of ARV drugs, only 3,000 (14 percent) were actually treated (WHO, UNAIDS 2006). This treatment rate is close to the average for the Southeast Asian region (16 percent). Although it has been increasing rapidly,[4] the proportion remains quite far from the government's objective[5] to meet 70 percent of treatment needs by 2005. Plans are under way to increase ARV availability in medium-sized towns and to decentralize access at the local level. A system of home-based and community care has been implemented in some provinces. In Da Nang, educators take on the role of instructors for the families of HIV-infected

persons (Pham et al. 2002). Many experiments have demonstrated the usefulness and the cost-effectiveness of this approach in comparison to hospital care
(Le 1999). The change in the government approach to the HIV/AIDS issue
has been accompanied by a growing reliance on the family, whose major role
in the fight against the epidemic has been reemphasized with the development
of the new generation of treatments.

The Role of the Family

From the start, in the political and legal discourse, HIV/AIDS has been the
locus of a mobilization of three social actors: the family, the community, and
society. These three actors are also present in the perceptions of the medical
staff and most people with HIV/AIDS.

THE DISTINCTIVE ROLES OF SOCIETY, THE COMMUNITY, AND THE FAMILY IN LEGAL TEXTS

Society covers a much broader dimension than the other two concepts. Its
position and roles are distinct from those of the community (*cong dong*) and
the family, which gradually have been differentiated. The community is a
common concept in Vietnamese culture and politics and includes the immediate social environment (extended family, friends, neighbors, and colleagues) as well as a network of local associations.

According to the National Strategy, the struggle against HIV/AIDS should
be considered "an important, urgent, and long-term mission that requires a
multi-sector dialogue and the intensive mobilization of the entire society."
The need for society to mobilize against HIV/AIDS is also expressed in the
2006 Law. The family is the first socialization unit within which each individual's position is precisely defined and expressed. Until 2004, the concepts
of family and community as "units of persons sharing common characteristics and forming a coherent social group" (Nguyen 1999) are frequently
confused, as the distinction between the two terms remains fuzzy. In the
legal texts, notably from the mid 1990s, their roles and positions are similar
if not identical. Thus the Decree of June 1, 1996, calls on "the collective responsibility of individuals, families, and communities in the prevention and
control of HIV/AIDS" (Article 1.1). The Directive of September 1997 stipu-

lates that, "for patients affected with AIDS to a low degree[6] (*benh nhan AIDS nhe*), treatment takes place mainly in the community (family)" (Article 2.b). The terms *family* and *community* become interchangeable through the use of parentheses. Where there is no family or when the family is unwilling or unable to cope with the disease, charitable organizations are expected to take its place (Directive of September 24, 1997), a situation that arose when associations and support groups for people infected with and affected by HIV/AIDS began to develop in Vietnam. The first such association was *"Ban giup Ban"* (Friends Help Friends). It was created in Ho Chi Minh City in 1995. In Hanoi, it was not until the end of the 1990s that HIV-infected persons began speaking openly about their condition. Following the development of support groups, a distinction between the family and the community gradually appeared in the legal texts. In the National Strategy on HIV/AIDS Prevention and Control, the family participates with society at large in preventing discrimination and contributes with the rest of the community in controlling transmission of the infection. However, these clarifications were considered insufficient by local and international NGOs. The subsequent 2006 Law on prevention and control of HIV/AIDS distinguishes more clearly between the infected person and his or her family on the one hand, and the community and broader society on the other. It specifically states that people living with HIV/AIDS and their families deserved to be protected against stigmatization and discrimination and that they are entitled to receive information. The family is expected to help its infected member to remain socially integrated within the local community and society at large.

THE CALL FOR FAMILY RESPONSIBILITY

The state has placed the family at the forefront of the fight against HIV/AIDS and called upon its sense of "responsibility." The two terms *family* and *responsibility* are systematically associated in legal texts and in the political discourse around the fight against HIV/AIDS. Three stages may be distinguished in the government vision of the family role in the battle against HIV/AIDS. The emphasis on the involvement of the family in fighting HIV/AIDS was first perceived in the mid-1990s.

Previously, in the early 1990s, the slogans and the iconography used in the awareness campaigns positioned the family as a shield protecting its members from and opposing "social evils," including HIV/AIDS. To summon people's civic-mindedness, references to "Vietnamese citizens" abounded (Decree of December 18, 1992, Article 3). The campaign against the epidemic was considered "the responsibility of all, the State and all of society" (Resolution of December 18, 1992).

Three years later, the word *family* was substituted for the word *state*: "preventing and fighting HIV/AIDS is the responsibility of everyone, every family and the whole of society" (Ordinance of May 31, 1995, Article 1) and "each member of the family must persuade and mobilize as well as educate the other members to carry out the regulations on the prevention and control of HIV/AIDS" (Ordinance of May 31, 1995, Article 11.1). The strategy appealed directly to the family.

Since 2000, however, a number of extensive texts have discussed the issue of HIV/AIDS without systematically mentioning the family,[7] though it is still asked to "participate in the multi-sector mobilization required in the fight against HIV/AIDS" (National Strategy on HIV/AIDS 2004).

Throughout the 1992–2006 period the family was also considered instrumental and an entity to be protected: its "important role" and "great capacity" were to be promoted and enhanced, "linking the prevention and control of HIV/AIDS to the establishment of a civilized Vietnamese family" (*gia dinh van hoa*) (Directive of March 11, 1995, Article 1). This idea was also used in the National Strategy on HIV/AIDS, which elaborated an "approach based on family and community values, support of national traditions of morality, a healthy way of life, and faithful relationships" (Nguyen, Thanh, and Quan 2004).

THE MANY TASKS ATTRIBUTED TO THE FAMILY

The responsibility of the family is moral, social, and health-related (Ordinance of May 31, 1995, Article 11.2).

The association of the family to the public health infrastructures has been progressively emphasized. Whereas, initially, care and treatment of infected people rested only on physicians and the staff of medical facilities (Resolution of December 8, 1992, Article 11), the family became involved in both when ARV drugs were introduced (Instruction of June 21, 1993, Article 2.2.d, and Ordinance of May 31, 1995, Article 11). According to the 1996 decree, the family had to "encourage people living with HIV to attend HIV/AIDS counseling centers" (Decree of June 1, 1996, Article 6.1). Every individual had to be aware of this role, and the information, education, and communication campaigns on HIV/AIDS prevention and control were to emphasize this (Decree of June 1, 1996, Article 1.1). The family was where the administrative management of patients, their care, and their monitoring took place, in relation to the work undertaken (*dam nhan*) by local health centers (Directive of September 24, 1997, Article 2.b). The family was encouraged to participate in the "continued care and support of HIV-positive persons," as organized by the government (Decision of March 17, 2004). In addition, combating stigmatization and discrimination against HIV-infected persons, a task initially attributed to the state (Resolution of December 18, 1992, Article 4.1), became the responsibility of the family in the National Strategy on HIV/AIDS Prevention and Control and the 2006 Law on HIV/AIDS prevention and control.

The family thus lies at the core of the government strategy against HIV/ AIDS. To better understand the tensions and constraints generated by the family's heavy responsibility, I undertook a field study specifically designed for this purpose.

A Study on HIV/AIDS Treatment and Care

Fieldwork was carried out in 2004 and 2005, starting with the first wave of patients treated in the pilot ARV treatment program for HIV-infected persons in Vietnam. This pilot program was undertaken in one center only: Dong Da Hospital in Hanoi. Our sociodemographic study[8] carried out on patients, their families, and caregivers provides a glimpse of the role played by kin in the care of HIV-positive patients, albeit in a specific context. Indeed, in contrast with other, if not most, HIV-infected persons under treatment, those enrolled in the study were not rejected by their families.

METHOD

The research is both qualitative and quantitative. It consists of a series of in-depth semistructured interviews with patients, members of their family, and members of the nursing and medical staff as well as observation of forty-eight consultations held between July 2004 and February 2005, representing three-quarters of all the consultations during that period.

The topics covered included the circumstances of entry into treatment, the way in which the treatment was carried out, its health and psychosocial effects, the patients' family situations, their socioeconomic activities, and their participation in associations and support groups. I asked the majority of the patients if they would introduce me to one or several family members so that they could take part in the study. This was only possible for patients whose families were aware of their ARV treatment. Each interview was held face-to-face, recorded, and lasted from one to two hours. To minimize travel and the time taken up by the interviews, the patients and their family members were invited to participate in the survey during their consultations at the hospital. The interviews were carried out in an office near the consultation room. This solution was particularly suitable for patients whose health or activities limited their mobility. I also offered to interview them in their homes if they preferred, which was indeed the case for many of the patients' kin. The sample of people interviewed is not representative of all HIV-infected persons, as the study only involved patients under ARV treatment. However, it provides in-depth information on the patients and their families in this particular situation, at varying stages of the treatment.

THE STUDY PARTICIPANTS

First, a series of interviews was carried out with members of the staff in Dong Da Hospital, and specifically with the four physicians in charge of the HIV-infected patients, including the head of the Infectious Disease Department, one nurse, one auxiliary nurse, and two pharmacists. These were followed with interviews of patients and their families.

A total of sixty-four patients initiated ARV treatment between April and September 2004. Three-quarters were men. The patients were aged between 21 and 44 with an average of 30 years and a median of 28, which corresponds to the age distribution of HIV/AIDS patients at the national level. As a reflection of the epidemiological situation of the country, more than half of the patients treated and more than two-thirds of the men had a history of drug addiction. The majority of the patients did not report an economic activity. The others were employees, and some reported an independent job, such as trading. Half of them had been married, but only a third still lived with a spouse. Two out of five patients had at least one child, with a maximum of three. Only one unmarried woman had given birth, which is consistent with the strong social norms of nonprocreation outside of marriage (see, for instance, Xenos et al. and Jayakody and Huy, this volume). The majority of patients lived with their families. This is not to be regarded as a consequence of the disease since the rule of virilocality is still predominant in Vietnam, with most married couples co-residing with the husband's parents (Ibid.). Single people in the study also co-resided with their parents and siblings except for two who lived alone. However, they received help on a regular basis from their families nearby. The divorced or separated patients generally also lived with their parents. Interviews were carried out with forty-one of the sixty-four aforementioned patients. Of the remainder, four refused, eight died, and five could not be contacted. The remaining six patients were not contacted because of overlap with information already collected.

Family members interviewed were generally those accompanying the patients or helping them. In nearly half the cases this was the mother, in a quarter the father, and for the remainder a sibling or, more rarely, a member of the extended family. The twenty-two caregivers interviewed belonged to nineteen families. In two instances, family members were interviewed after the patients' deaths.

PERCEPTIONS OF HEALTH CAREGIVERS
AND HIV-INFECTED PERSONS

Mirroring the official discourse, a clear distinction was made between health caregivers, HIV-infected persons, and their kin with regard to the respective roles of society, the community, and the family in the fight against HIV/AIDS.

The staff at Dong Da Hospital considered the family and the community as the main contributors to HIV/AIDS treatment and the prevention of transmission, and they expressed the need for training in how to interact more efficiently with them. The nursing and medical staff, as well as the families, considered that the treatment of HIV-infected persons should not be exclusively limited to the hospital. They regarded the problem of integrating HIV-infected persons into the community as an overriding issue and emphasized the need for good communications about treatment and care of HIV/AIDS patients between families and health services. Patients' perceptions echoed this representation of an environment that could be described as a series of "concentric circles" of responsibility and socialization (Dovert et al. 2004). The first, smallest, circle is the patient him- or herself (*ban than minh*); the second is the family, the very source of an individual's existence, a place of solidarity, control, and care; the third circle is the local community, a frequent source of support but also of stigma; and the fourth is society at large, placed outside of the patient's sphere of action. In fact, some patients view society as responsible for both the infection and its remedy, as an entity which is changing and could provide them with a cure in the years to come (interviews).

The Family: An Essential and Ambivalent Source of Support

The role of the family is ambivalent in several ways, as it is regarded both as a main source of support but also as a source of obligations. This is true in general but is exacerbated in a situation of dependency, such as that of HIV-infected persons, because it aggravates the constraints and tensions to which the dependent and his or her family are subjected. The family is usually the first to identify those infected as HIV-positive persons, often at the time when those are not forced into this status by their own perception since the disease is initially, and sometimes for a very long time, asymptomatic. By often initiating contacts with health care infrastructures, support groups, and other outside interlocutors, the family interferes between the patient and the community in general and the health system in particular, sometimes to the point of depriving the patient of his or her own decision-making power. The family is a shield, protecting the patient from outside stigmatization and discrimination at the same time as it exposes him or her to these attitudes and behavior among its own members. The family provides material, moral, and financial support while exerting control on the patient's whereabouts. These various aspects of the relationship between HIV patients and their families are reviewed below in more detail.

FAMILY AND SELF-IDENTIFICATION AS AN HIV-POSITIVE PERSON

Because of the threat HIV/AIDS represents to life, the awareness of being HIV positive is central to the social identity of an infected person. In the process of accepting a person's HIV-positive status, the family may act as an incentive for action or as a substitute.

The family plays a major role in the decision to undergo an HIV test, whether because of specific events or through explicit encouragement to be tested. Many patients discovered their HIV-positive status when they suffered from independent or opportunistic health problems. The family often occupies a central position in the care and treatment of illnesses in general, and is therefore present during the whole health-seeking process, including before and during the initial HIV test as illustrated by the interviews: "When I did the test, I really didn't think that I could be HIV-positive. I told myself that I was just going to put their [people from my family] minds at rest, but I really didn't think that I could have this damned illness" (he laughs; single male patient, aged 31).

The process of acknowledging one's HIV-positive status may imply the involvement of the whole family and the repetition of the test in case of denial: "Everybody was talking and saying that I should have the test done again to see what would happen. So I went back and had the test done again" (single male patient, aged 27).

The decision to be tested can occur following specific family events, most often a pregnancy or a partner's death: "At the time of my husband's death he had only been ill for 20 days. When he died I didn't know that I was HIV-positive as well. His blood was taken in the day and he died at 6 P.M. that evening. They left the blood at the hospital and it was only the next day that they carried out the test" (widowed female patient, aged 29).

Only a few patients discovered their HIV-positive status during events other than illness, pregnancy, or the death of a spouse. Some of them found out after taking a compulsory health check for recruitment or a checkup before leaving the country, a decision typically supported by the family. Others were forced to take a test when they were arrested, and the result was sent to their home while they were still in a re-education center. Thus, for some patients the family was at the origin of the announcement of their HIV-positive status. Some families took several months before informing the patient.

When the family encourages the patient to take the HIV test, it forces him or her, deliberately or not, to play an active role in the constitution of his or her social identity as an HIV-infected person. Conversely, when the family accompanies the patient at the time of the test or when a family member drops off the blood sample or picks up the results instead of the patient, family intervention can become an obstacle to the process, delaying it and leading to the disclosure of aspects of the patient's private life, as a result of the information sometimes provided about the transmission route. As has been observed for men who have sex with men in another setting (Leask et al. 1997), the central place of the family in the announcement of the HIV test may lead to a "double disclosure" of both HIV status and sexual preference. In Vietnam, this is more often the case for injection drug users: "My parents didn't know that I was living a slightly debauched life, so when the centre [re-education centre for drug addicts] told them [that I was HIV-positive] it was very difficult for them" (single male patient, aged 27).

The family is actively encouraged to interfere by the widely shared perception of a lack of support from the health infrastructure, particularly in terms of poor pre- and postcounseling, as well as the fear of stigmatization. The family may replace the patient without encountering any obstacles from medical services. "At the beginning, [the staff from the testing center] gave me an appointment for the result in the afternoon and my brother-in-law went [instead of me]. They gave him another appointment for the following week. And [when he told me this] I immediately thought then that there was a problem" (single male patient, aged 31).

In extreme cases, a member of the family may decide to double-check the test results after a patient has been diagnosed. For example, the father of a young single male who did not believe his son's positive result, collected the blood sample from the hospital that had carried out the test and took it to the Center for Preventive Medicine to have it tested again. Therefore, the family has a twofold role in the elaboration of an HIV-infected person's self-identification. It both contributes to the process and limits the patient's empowerment. In the asymptomatic phase of the infection, the family's role in the identification process is even more decisive because broader social interactions are not yet influenced by the perception of a biomedical problem.

THE FAMILY: CONDUIT AND BARRIER
TO CONTACT WITH THE OUTSIDE WORLD

In addition to its contacts with health staff, the family intervenes in the many social interactions of the HIV-positive person with the outside world, mainly to help and protect their family member from stigmatization and discrimination. In this way the family may act as either a conduit or a barrier to an independent social life.

The family's intervention to protect the patient is often beneficial, as it provides him or her with information and contacts. In this respect, the family facilitates access to care, treatment, and support. The relationship between health professionals and the patients' families occurs mainly when the patient's health or psychological condition is perceived as too critical for him or her to receive the information directly. In some cases, notably when the patient is physically weak, the family decides by itself to initiate ARV treatment. The following example is typical of such a situation:

> At that time, everyone thought that I was surely going to die. My father asked the doctor to see if there was medicine that I could take that could save me. At the beginning, the physician, Doctor X, said [to my father] "Now your family must consider whether it is necessary for him [the patient] to take the medicine or not because the CD4 count is too low. There are hardly any left. And the therapy is very expensive. I'm just worried that if he [the patient] takes it [the medicine] there won't be any change. You would lose money and it won't solve anything. So the family must seriously consider, because as far as medicine is concerned, it is available." Then my father said, "Good, now there's still an ounce of hope so we must give him the [antiretroviral] medicine." (single male patient, aged 31)

Conversely, the family can set itself up as a barrier between the HIV-positive person and the outside world. For example, parents of injection drug users invoked the fear that their son, through meetings with other patients or support groups for HIV-infected persons, may start using illegal drugs again. These meetings occur in the community or in the health infrastructure, because despite the fact that illegal drug use is one of the main criteria for exclusion from ARV care and treatment in the Dong Da program, many patients continue to use illegal drugs, either because they have not been able to quit or because of a relapse. Within the treatment group, HIV-positive people meet each other in the hospital as consultations are fixed at the same time and the same place for groups of about twenty. Therefore, some parents accompany their child to hospital consultations as well as on other outings to limit the chances of him or her interacting with injection drug users: "My parents are often afraid. They give me advice and say: 'Now that you're taking this medicine, don't go playing around, taking illegal drugs or anything like that.' Often they're scared that I'll meet a friend and go with him. When they are reassured, they leave me alone. They've been reassured for several weeks now and they don't come with me. They're not afraid any more" (single male patient, aged 28).

The extended family is sometimes recruited by parents to help stop their child from taking illegal drugs. The son or daughter is sent to some more- or less-distant relatives in the countryside, far from their usual place of residence. The family receives the antiretroviral treatment from the hospital in the patient's place and reports to the physicians on his or her health. Alternatively, some parents request that their child be sent to a re-education center for injection drug users.

The fear of ostracism is another reason why some parents forbade their HIV-positive son from taking part in support groups for HIV-infected persons: "I often used to participate in all the programs, but my father didn't like it. Because my father said 'now all this stuff has calmed down.' What he meant was that it has been 6 or 7 years since I became HIV-positive, that I have HIV, and everything has calmed down so my father doesn't want people to know what I do, or about my illness" (single male patient, aged 31).

Thus, this interference between the HIV-infected person and health personnel gives the family great influence on the patient's mode of integration in the community and society at large.

THE FAMILY: A SHIELD FROM THE COMMUNITY VERSUS A LOCUS OF EXPOSURE TO DISCRIMINATION

The family is a place where the HIV-positive person can isolate him- or herself and be protected from stigmatization and discrimination by people from the community, but it is also a place where such attitudes and behaviors are expressed by members of the family toward the patient.

The interviews confirmed that HIV-infected persons are generally suspected of partaking in reprehensible behavior, such as having multiple sexual partners or using illegal drugs. However, the stigma varies according to the infected person. As observed in other settings with a similar epidemiological context, such as China (Deng et al. 2007), stigmatization is more common against men suspected of being illegal drug users, than women, who often claim to have been contaminated by their husband, and this stigmatization also exists between HIV-positive people themselves. In the treatment group that was studied, active injection drug users were considered to be cheating, taking a treatment while depriving other patients in need. This perception was reinforced by the behavior of some of them, known to be selling their medicine to buy illegal drugs.

Half the patients who were interviewed declared having suffered from ostracism at some time or another, either from the community or from within the family. This proportion is higher than in Thailand (VanLandingham, Im-Em, and Saengtienchai 2005), probably because of the former "social evils" campaigns described previously (Khuat, Nguyen, and Ogden 2004), though stigmatization and discrimination tend to decrease as the epidemic spreads to the whole population and as new information campaigns are launched.

Apart from factors such as the family's reputation and the personality of the HIV-positive person, two other aspects of the HIV/AIDS epidemic are important in understanding how stigmatization arises: the circulation of information about HIV status and access to care and treatment. The public medical facilities in charge of nonanonymous HIV testing have to report all positive cases to the local health establishment to which the infected person belongs, based on place of residence. This requirement is officially justified by the need to treat infected people. However, senior medical personnel do not always manage this practice in the respect of the patients' privacy. Thus, if a patient has given his or her true name and address as required during the HIV test, and if the medical facility is poorly managed, disclosure of the patient's HIV status can spread around a neighborhood even before the patient has been informed. Consequently, infected persons may face stigma and discrimination in their local community. However, this is becoming less frequent as increasing importance is attached to the anonymity of the tests and voluntary counseling and testing centers are established. Access to care and treatment also tends to reduce stigmatization by eliminating obvious physical signs of opportunistic infections (dermatological problems, fatigue, incapacity) and by allowing HIV people to continue to take part normally in their economic and social activities.

Ostracism of the people who were studied mostly took the form of gossip, but there were cases of HIV-positive patients loosing their jobs and HIV-positive children of HIV-positive patients being excluded from school because of their status. Although stigmatization may be overestimated due to the discrepancy between the perception of oversensitive patients and the reality or because of a misunderstanding by the patients of the interest shown by the community—as has been shown in a study in Thailand (VanLandingham, Im-Em, and Saengtienchai 2005)—this situation led to much suffering in some respondents who tended to remain shut away with their families. Stigmatization was also a reason why some patients were uncomfortable about attending a follow-up consultation at the Department of Infectious Diseases at Dong Da Hospital, since this health infrastructure is clearly associated by the community to HIV/AIDS treatment. Consequently, in the first years of the program, some patients would ask a family member to meet with the medical practitioner and obtain the medicine for them. The practice was later forbidden.

Sometimes the family can be the very place where the HIV-positive person is exposed to stigmatization. Some daughters-in-law who were contaminated by their husbands had to leave their in-laws' homes when they became widowed, sometimes leaving their children behind because the grandparents feared HIV transmission to the grandchildren or poor care as a result of the mother's illness.

To avoid stigmatization within the family, some people kept the information about their HIV status a secret, even from their closest relatives. This was impossible for the first patients in the program due to their lack of access to treatment and care, leading them—sometimes rapidly—to reach a critical physical state. However, patients recently included in the treatment cohort tended to fare much better than earlier patients. In the absence of any visible sign of the disease they did not have to disclose their status to their family. In a few cases, only a part of the patients' nuclear family was aware of their HIV status. This "selective disclosure" has been observed in other contexts, for example in Europe (Leask et al. 1997). In this case, parents and siblings keep the secret from other family members to protect the patient from stigma and its social and psychological consequences. A specific instance is the disclosure by HIV-positive parents to their children. Among the people we interviewed, some infected mothers preferred not to inform their young children about their status even when suffering from related health problems. A young HIV-positive mother under antiretroviral treatment told her child that she was taking food supplements. The reason for this is often the fear of social exclusion of their children, which can occur even when the child is HIV negative. Studies conducted in Europe have shown that the disclosure of a parents' HIV status depends mostly on the age of the children (Thorne, Newell, and Peckham 2000). This result, which remains to be systematically tested in Vietnam, is consistent with our survey findings.

THE FAMILY'S ECONOMIC SUPPORT:
CONTROL OR EMPOWERMENT?

The burden of an adult HIV-positive child is multidimensional as it encompasses physical, psychoemotional, social, and financial costs (Knodel and

VanLandingham 2002; Vithayachockitikhun 2006). Financial support provided by the family is found in many countries and is all the more important when the public health infrastructure is inadequate or access to care is difficult (UNAIDS, WHO 2004, 137). By providing economic support as well as care and treatment, the family is a source of empowerment for the persons infected, although, in turn, it exerts greater control over him or her—a situation that many patients find difficult to accept.

Financing treatment requires a significant amount of money. Overall, total health care expenditure for a household with an HIV/AIDS patient is estimated to reach thirteen times the average household's expenditure in Vietnam (UNDP, Aus-AID 2005). The cost of ARV has dropped but, in the early 2000s, treatment remained expensive. The cost of transportation, of regular and follow-up visits, and of laboratory tests for entering and guaranteeing compliance with the treatment, can be major barriers to care (CORE, USAID, and CARE 2006). The generosity of relatives from the overseas diaspora is sometimes called upon to help gather the necessary funds. After the disappearance of free health care in Vietnam in 1989 (World Bank et al. 2001), a health insurance scheme was created in 1993 and reformed in 1998. However, health insurance only covers 9 percent of all public expenditure and 12 percent of the population (Nguyen, Nguyen, and Palmer 2004, 319), and HIV-positive persons are specifically excluded (Instruction of September 18, 1992). Consequently, the family's material and financial contributions to the care of HIV-infected persons is critical and will remain so until the current program to provide free treatment to all HIV/AIDS patients is fully realized. The reforms have also increased the inequality between rich and poor (Adams 2005; Fritzen 2007; Nguyen and Popkin 2003; also see Deolalikar, in this volume). This problem is particularly relevant as most people affected with HIV/AIDS belong to the poorest 20 percent of the population (UNDP, Aus-AID, 2005). For many participants in our study, economic constraints were a major reason for revealing HIV-positive status to family and close friends: "At that time, I was going to buy medicine but I didn't have any money, and then I hid. So at the start I just told myself 'too bad.' Until the time that I couldn't hide anymore and then that was it. Now the people at home are prepared and have taken care of everything so that I can be treated" (single male patient, aged 32).

In most cases, information about HIV status is shared with the patient's co-residents. The infection is difficult to hide from them given the treatment constraints: medicines have to be administered twice a day, meals have to be taken at fixed hours, and there are frequent follow-up visits to the health care center. Co-residence may also provide a favorable context for help and support. As observed in Thailand (Kespichayawattana and VanLandingham 2003; Knodel et al. 2001), adult HIV-positive people tend to return to their parents or live with a sibling when their health situation becomes difficult. This occurs in a context where most of the parents co-reside with an adult child in any case (Knodel et al. 2000). Dependency on the family increases when HIV-infected persons have an HIV-positive child, since there was no treatment for HIV-positive children at the time of the study.

Conversely, the perception that no potential psychological or economic support was to be expected could prevent the HIV-positive person from disclosing his or her status. Among the people interviewed, only one patient did not inform his parents of his status even though he lived with them and received some form of economic support from them as well as from his siblings: "If I say [that I am HIV-positive], what problem will it solve? Let me ask a question. For example, people in my family are laborers. So if I tell them, it won't solve any problems. It may even be difficult to bear" (single male patient, aged 28). In this respect, access to treatment facilitates the disclosure of HIV-positive status: the HIV-positive person is less reluctant to disclose his or her status because there is hope for a cure.

Support from the family is not only economic but also logistic and psychological. The family provides treatment, care, and social and emotional support. Among the patients observed during consultations, one out of seven came accompanied by a relative. In this area, the HIV/AIDS epidemic highlights the dominating presence of women, notably mothers, in the care of mainly male patients (UNDP, Aus-AID 2005). Fieldwork confirmed this result, which was also found in Thailand (Kespichayawattana and VanLandingham 2003; Knodel and VanLandingham 2002). As elsewhere, such as in the United States (Wight et al. 2006), the care receivers among people who were interviewed were mostly young males, and the caregivers were mostly their mothers. However, they cannot be considered a dyad as in the American context, since in Vietnam caregivers are frequently a group rather than an individual. This is partly due to the many tasks involved in care and treatment, such as paying for medical examinations, overseeing treatment, and providing food and hygiene to the patient. As there is no substitute product for illegal drugs, some families of drug-addicted patients were even compelled to provide drugs to their hospitalized kin.

The family is perceived by some patients as being "too present, burdensome" (*rao can, nang ne*) due to the control that their kin exercise over them. Some patients resist family pressure and wait to be psychologically ready to start treatment, after the shock of the HIV-positive announcement. If the patient does not correctly adhere to treatment, the family sometimes informs the nursing and medical staff. For example, one family in the study provoked the interruption of treatment when the patient resumed his drug habit. The family contacted the medical team to suggest that another patient who would commit to the treatment and not inject drugs should benefit from the ARV treatment instead of their family member. The addicted patient died shortly afterwards.

With the development of free outpatient treatment for the main opportunistic diseases, morbid episodes and their related hospitalization should lessen. Consequently, this may reduce the role of the family in paramedical support. It may also curtail co-residence due to illness because HIV-positive people under antiretroviral treatment will be less likely to suffer from opportunistic infections.

THE FAMILY: A BENCHMARK IN THE LIFE CYCLE VERSUS A CHANGING ENVIRONMENT

Being a member of a family implies assuming roles and a status that are threatened by HIV/AIDS infection. Families try to adapt to these changes.

Being HIV positive places patients, who are typically young, in a situation of dependence at a time when they are supposed to assist their families, notably their parents (see Barbieri's chapter, this volume; Knodel et al. 2000). They express much suffering as a result of their inability to care for themselves and their families, in situations that are difficult to cope with in the absence of any external psychosocial support. Patients without children question their ability to have children while being HIV positive in a context where methods to avoid transmission from males to their offspring and sexual partner are limited, and prevention of transmission from mother to child is weak and typically unknown by the people interviewed. When the infected patient is the only male child and the eldest of the paternal line, the epidemic threatens the continuity of lineage through ancestor worship and the transmission of the family name. In some families this is felt strongly and is very badly perceived by both the family and the infected person: "My mother is very sad, she is desperate. Because at home, first I am the only boy, second I am the chief of the lineage. This means that I deserve to be accused of lack of filial piety because I don't maintain the lineage of my family" (single patient, aged 30).

In this respect, the Confucian model remains a strong norm in many families. This symbolic reference coexists with a family organization that involves greater participation and support from the patient's siblings. This situation creates tensions as the infected person is still present but is presumed unable to assume his role in the future. It influences intrafamily relationships but does not generally involve a complete disruption.

The family also tries to protect itself from social judgment. Indeed, infection by HIV/AIDS throws discredit on the HIV-infected persons as well as on members of their families, notably the parents, who appear to have failed in meeting their responsibility of educating their children. This "courtesy stigma" is evocative of a theme recurrent in the history of state legislation: the collective attribution of compensation or punishment to the entire family in order to sanction the action of one of its individual members.

Discussion: Doi Moi, *the State, and the Family in the Context of the HIV/AIDS Epidemic*

In the study, which took place within a health service catering specifically to HIV/AIDS patients, I did not encounter people living with HIV/AIDS who were deserted by their whole family. Although some patients were rejected by their parents, siblings or spouses, they all received support from at least some members of their kinship group. Thus, overall the findings indicate that the family occupies a central place in the fight against the epidemic even though it often plays an ambivalent role. This ambivalence is a result of the social identity of the person with HIV/AIDS as (1) an HIV-positive individual, (2) a person interacting with support groups for HIV-infected persons, (3) a person evoking socially marginalized groups in society, (4) a patient seeking care and treatment in the health infrastructure and (5) a link in a family lineage. As demonstrated by the experiences related here, the boundaries between these are tenuous and the roles to which they correspond overlap at each stage of the treatment of a person with HIV/AIDS. The social and political pressures exerted on the family to fulfill these numerous functions exacerbate the tensions generated by the disease on the patients and their kin.

The study has also shown that, in order to better understand the role assigned to the family in the fight against HIV/AIDS by the state, it is necessary to examine the historical context of relations between the family and the state and take into account the tendency to a greater integration and globalization, as exchanges with foreign countries are also specific features of the fight against HIV/AIDS.

Compared to the period of collectivization (1958–88) that was marked by the state's appropriation of areas previously controlled by the family, notably domestic production (Yvon-Tran 2002), fertility control and the choice of spouse (Bélanger and Khuat 1996), the current situation constitutes a reversal insofar as the family is being assigned prerogatives that are matters of public policy, especially in the North where many previous functions of the family had been dealt with by community-based organizations, cooperatives, unions, and various associations (Papin 1999).

With the launch of *Doi Moi* in 1986 came "an intensification of family and village relations" (Bélanger 1997), along with strengthened lineage solidarity (Vu 2004), and the family recovered most of its former productive functions. It played a major role in the state scenario to move to a market system as indicated in Bélanger and Barbieri's chapter in this volume. My research shows that a parallel can be made between the recruitment of the family in the economic domain and the role it was assigned in the social domain.

The measures adopted from the year 2000 onward tend to rationalize the role of the family, for example in the search for a more efficient organization for combating HIV/AIDS, based on experiences in Vietnam and among communities abroad.

The ideological dimension of the National Strategy on HIV/AIDS is considerable, but concrete actions have not yet been specified. This is where the role of the family is likely to be restricted. The Ordinance issued by the Permanent Committee of the National Assembly in 2004, and the decree of April 6, 2005, have been hotly debated. One of the issues was the management of confidentiality regarding the announcement of the HIV-positive status. Initially, in 1995, medical chiefs placed the family at the center of the announcement of HIV-positive status (Ordinance of May 31, 1995, Article 18-2) as well as the care for AIDS patients and for the prevention of transmission

(Ordinance of May 31, 1995, Article 20-1). Communication occurred directly between the medical staff and the family for HIV-positive people as well as for persons in detention or re-education centers, drug users, or commercial sex workers, so that families could organize themselves and play an advisory role (Instruction of February 24, 2003, Articles 6 and 7). The concept of confidentiality was initially very vague, as those authorized to receive the information were numerous and varied (Decree of June 1, 1996, Article 5.1). The new law is more restrictive, as the family is informed only when the infected person is a minor, someone under guardianship, or in civil incapacity (Law 2006, Chapter 3, Paragraph 2, Article 30). This is important for the future of HIV care and treatment, and the respective roles and positions of the patient, his or her family, and the medical staff will probably have to be progressively redefined.

The role of the family might shift with its gradual withdrawal from some areas, such as the announcement of HIV-positive status, and its redeployment in others, such as the therapeutic care of patients. In contrast with the previous period, during which the family was mainly responsible for the care of the HIV/AIDS patient, the period after 2006 sees the emergence of a re-appropriation by the patients of their own care, accompanied by attempts at protecting confidentiality. Legislation in Vietnam, thus, draws closer to the United Nation's proposals regarding HIV prevention and control based on a concept of ethics and human rights (UNAIDS 2006b). There is an aspect here of "the return of the individual onto the Vietnamese scene," a phenomenon that is partly linked to developments caused by *Doi Moi* (Dovert and Lambert 2004). This trend also corresponds to the "normalization" of the role of the family in relation to international standards for HIV/AIDS care.

Conclusion

The HIV/AIDS epidemic is one of numerous examples that show that the *Doi Moi* reforms, which initially had primarily economic objectives, largely exceeded this sphere and are significantly transforming social, family, and societal dynamics. Because of the lack of public resources, the family inherited the management of a health problem and took on an adjustment role where less flexible and less reactive medical facilities needed a longer period of adaptation. In this period of profound restructuring of the health system, which led to greater dependence on the family, the state's recognition of its central position in the prevention of HIV and the treatment and care of HIV-infected persons highlighted the trend of the family returning to the center of the sociopolitical arena after a historic period of greater state presence in health care.

Regulation of the family's role through health legislation specifically related to the epidemic, as well as the creation of health facilities and appropriate programs could, paradoxically, reassert the family's position in society by offering alternative solutions. Indeed, this option could reduce the current burden on the family—one that is too heavy and difficult to bear. The family could thus invest more in other spheres, such as the psychosocial care and support of patients, that would alleviate the problems linked to the excessive fear of HIV transmission, which frequently results in the exclusion or confinement of HIV-infected persons within specific groups in the family or society. In the context of the epidemic becoming chronic, this could lead to a reformulation of the family's social role. Future monitoring of the social dimension of the epidemic could prove quite valuable in evaluating the transformation of family welfare functions.

Notes

I would like to thank Mr. Philippe Biberson (French Embassy) for his support and Ms. Catherine Dauphin (ESTHER group) for her careful proofreading of this chapter.

1. Nongovernmental organizations in Vietnam are placed under the supervision of the Vietnam Fatherland Front (Law on the Vietnam Fatherland Front, June 12, 1999).

2. The commune is the smallest administrative division in Vietnam.

3. Approximately US$2.00 to US$2.50 per day, which is the equivalent of a public service salary. This is more than double the cost of tri-therapy in many countries in the same period, notably Africa, due to the low production of antiretroviral drugs in Vietnam, the lack of negotiation on the price of imported medicines, the narrowness of the market, and the lack of compulsory licensing (Kuanpoth and Hoai 2004).

4. The average monthly increase of people receiving ARV was 222 in 2005 (WHO, UNAIDS 2006).

5. The objective of treating 15,000 patients by 2005 (World Health Organization 2004a) was reduced to 5,000 by the end of 2004.

6. The "low degree" can be interpreted as corresponding to clinical stages I and II of HIV infection as defined by the WHO, during which the patient is able to continue with normal activities since the infection is asymptomatic in the first stage, and symptomatic, but at a low level, during the second stage (World Health Organization 2004b, 61).

7. The text of the National Strategy on HIV/AIDS Prevention and Control of 2004 and that of the Ministry of Health's decision of March 7, 2005, are ten times more voluminous than the Ordinance of 1995 and decree of 1996 (25,000 to 27,000 words compared with 2,000 to 2,500). While the word *family* appeared only four and three times, respectively, in the former, it was used ten times in the 1995 Ordinance (2,156 words) and six times in the 1996 decree (2,492 words).

8. This study was carried out with support from the IRD UMR 151 LPED to which the author belongs, in collaboration with the Institute for Population and Social Studies at the National Economic University (NEU) in Hanoi. It was made possible by the French *Groupe d'Intérêt Public ESTHER* in charge of the antiretroviral treatment program at Dong Da Hospital. I would like to take this opportunity to thank Ms. Nguyen Thi Van (Institute of Sociology, Vietnam Academy of Social Sciences) and Ms. Tran Ngoc Yen (NEU) for their participation in this study.

References

Adams, S. J. 2005. Vietnam's health care system: A macroeconomic perspective. Paper prepared for the International Symposium on Health Care Systems in Asia, Hitotsubashi University, Tokyo. Hanoi: International Monetary Fund.

Bélanger, D. 1997. Modes de cohabitation et liens intergénérationnels au Viêtnam. *Cahiers Québécois de Démographie* 26(2): 215–245.

Bélanger, D., and Khuat T. H. 1996. Marriage and the family in urban North Vietnam, 1965 to 1993. *Journal of Population* 2(1): 83–112.

Cong hoa Xa hoi Chu nghia Viet Nam. 1992. *Nghi dinh cua Chinh phu quy dinh mot so van de ve phong va chong nhiem HIV va SIDA* [Socialist Republic of Vietnam 1992. Resolution of the government about decisions relating to issues dealing with prevention and control of HIV infection and AIDS] 16/CP. Hanoi: Bo Y Te Viet Nam.

Cong hoa Xa hoi Chu nghia Viet Nam. 1995. *Phap lenh cua Uy ban Thuong vu Quoc hoi ve Phong, chong nhiem vi rut gay ra hoi chung suy giam mien dich mac phai o nguoi (HIV/AIDS)* [Socialist Republic of Vietnam 1995. Ordinance of the National Assembly Standing Committee about Prevention and Control of the transmission of the virus leading to of the Acquired human immunodeficiency syndrome (HIV/AIDS)] Hanoi: Bo Y Te Viet Nam.

Cong hoa Xa hoi Chu nghia Viet Nam. 2004. *Chien Luoc quoc gia Phong, Chong HIV/AIDS o Viet Nam den nam 2010 va tam nhin 2020* [Government of the Socialist Republic of Vietnam. 2004. National Strategy on HIV/AIDS Prevention and control until 2010 with a vision to 2020] 36/2004/QD-TTg, March. Hanoi: Bo Y Te Viet Nam.

Cong hoa Xa hoi Chu nghia Viet Nam. 2006. *Luat Phong chong nhiem vi rut gay ra hoi chung suy giam mien dich mac phai o nguoi (HIV/AIDS), Quoc Hoi* [Socialist Republic of Vietnam 2006. Law on Prevention and Control of the Human Immunodeficiency Virus and Acquired Immunodeficiency Syndrome (HIV/AIDS), National Assembly], 64/2006/QH11. Hanoi: Bo Y Te Viet Nam.

CORE, USAID, and CARE. 2006. *Mapping HIV/AIDS service provision for most-at-risk and vulnerable populations in the Greater Mekong sub-region.* Hanoi: The CORE Initiative

Dinh Thu Ha, R. Detels, and Nguyen M. A. 2005. Factors associated with declining HIV testing and failure to return for results among pregnant women in Vietnam. *AIDS* 19(11): 1234–1236.

Diop, M. C. 1997. L'administration Sénégalaise et la gestion des "fléaux sociaux. l'héritage colonial." In *AOF: réalités et héritages: Sociétés ouest-africaines et ordre colonial 1895–1960*, Volume 2, edited by C. Becker, S. Mbaye, and I. Thioub, 1128–1150. Dakar: Direction des Archives du Sénégal.

Dovert, S., and P. Lambert. 2004. La relation nord–sud: La clé de la construction nationale Vietnamienne. In *Viêt-Nam contemporain*, edited by S. Dovert and B. de Tréglodé, 31–115. Paris: Les Indes Savantes.

Fritzen, S. A. 2007. Legacies of primary health care in an age of health sector reform: Vietnam's commune clinics in transition. *Social Science and Medicine* 64: 1611–1623.

Ghys, P. D., T. Saidel, Hoang T. V., I. Savtchenko, I. Erasilova, M. S. Yolisa, R. Indongo, N. Sikhosana, and N. Walker. 2003. Growing in silence: Selected regions and countries with expanding HIV/AIDS epidemics. *AIDS* 17 (suppl. 4): S45–S50.

Gorbach, P. M., C. Ryan, V. Saphonn, and R. Detels. 2002. The impact of social, economic and political forces on emerging HIV epidemics. *AIDS* 16 (suppl. 4): S35–S43.

Grayman, J. H., Do T. N., Pham T. H., R. A. Jenkins, J. W. Carey, G. R. West, and Tan M. T. 2005. Factors associated with HIV testing, condom use, and sexually transmitted infections among female sex workers in Nha Trang, Vietnam. *AIDS and Behavior* 9(1) March: 41–51.

Kespichayawattana, J., and M. VanLandingham. 2003. Effects of coresidence and caregiving on health of Thai parents of adult children with AIDS. *Journal of Nursing Scholarship* 35(3): 217–224.

Khuat Thu Hong, Nguyen T. V. A., and J. Ogden. 2004. *Understanding HIV and AIDS-related stigma and discrimination in Vietnam*. Washington, DC: International Center for Research on Women, USAID, 48 p.

Knodel, J., J. Friedman, Truong S. A., and Bui T. C. 2000. Intergenerational exchanges in Vietnam: Family size, sex composition, and the location of Children. *Population Studies* 54(1): 89–104.

Knodel, J., and M. VanLandingham. 2001. *Return migration in the context of parental assistance in the AIDS epidemic: The Thai experience*. PSC Research Report 01-492, December. Ann Arbor: University of Michigan Press.

Knodel, J., and M. VanLandingham. 2002. The impact of the AIDS epidemic on older persons. *AIDS* 16 (suppl. 3): S77–S83.

Kuanpoth, J., and Hoai D. L. 2004. *Thuoc khang virut HIV gia phai chang cho nguoi co HIV/AIDS o Viet Nam: nhung van de phap ly va thuong mai* [Affordable ARV drugs for people living with HIV/AIDS in Vietnam: Legal and trade issues]. Hanoi: Ford Foundation, World Health Organization.

Le Bach Duong. 2005. *Commitment for Action: Assessing leadership for Confronting the HIV/AIDS epidemic across Asia: Focus on Vietnam*. Policy project, January. Washington, DC: USAID,

Le Huu Tho. 1999. *Acceptance behavior of home-based care for PLWHA among family members in Nha Trang City, Khanh Hoa Province, Vietnam*. Master of Public Health Care Management, Asian Institute for Health Development, Bangkok: Mahidol University.

Leask, C., J. Elford, R. Bor, R. Miller, and M. Johnson. 1997. Selective disclosure: A pilot investigation into changes in family relationships since HIV diagnosis. *Journal of Family Therapy* 19: 59–69.

Ministry of Health. 2007. *Program of action on HIV/AIDS surveillance, monitoring and evaluation*. Hanoi.

Monnais-Rousselot, L. 1999. *Médecine et colonisation: L'aventure Indochinoise 1860–1939*. Paris: CNRS editions.

Morrison, J. S., and P. Nieburg. 2006. *HIV/AIDS in Vietnam*. Final report of the CISS HIV/AIDS Task Force Mission to Vietnam, January 8–13, CSIS, June, Washington, DC.

National AIDS Committee of Vietnam. 1994. *Medium term plan for prevention and control of HIV/AIDS in Vietnam 1994–1996 and 1996–2000*. Hanoi: National AIDS Committee.

National Center for Social Sciences and Humanities. 2001. *Doi Moi and human development in Vietnam: National Human Development Report 2001*. Hanoi: The Political Publishing House, UNDP.

Nguyen Minh Thang and B. M. Popkin. 2003. Evolution des revenus et du système de santé au Viêtnam: Réduction de la pauvreté et augmentation des inégalités de prise en charge. *Population*-F 58(2): 279–292.

Nguyen Nhu Y. 1999. *Dai Tu dien tieng Viet* [Dictionary of the Vietnamese Language]. *T. P. Ho Chi Minh: Bo giao duc va dao tao, trung tam ngon ngu va van hoa Viet Nam* [Ministry for Education and Training, Centre for Vietnamese Linguistics and Culture], Nha xuat ban van hoa-thong tin [Publishing House for Culture and Information].

Nguyen Thi Phi Linh, Nguyen N. T., and S. Palmer. 2004. Développement et dynamiques de la santé: Un aperçu du système sanitaire Vietnamien face à ses nouveaux défis. In *Viêt-Nam contemporain*, edited by S. Dovert and B. de Tréglodé, 317–338. Paris: Les Indes savantes.

Nguyen Tran Hien, Thanh L. N., and Quan H. T. 2004. HIV/AIDS epidemic in Vietnam: Evolution and responses. *AIDS Education and Prevention* 16 (June), Academic Research Library: 137–154.

Nguyen Xuan Yem, Dinh K. P., and Nguyen T. K. L. 2003. *Mai dam, ma tuy, co bac, toi pham thoi hien dai* [Prostitution, drug addiction, gambling and crime]. Hanoi: Nha xuat ban Cong an nhan dan, Ha Noi.

O'Malley, J., Nguyen V. K., and S. Lee. 1996. Nongovernmental organizations. In *AIDS in the world*, edited by J. Mann and D. Tarantola, 341–361. New York: Oxford University Press.

Papin, P. 1999. *Viêt-Nam: Parcours d'une nation*. Paris: La Documentation Française.

Pham Bich San, Pham H. D., Khuat T. H., Khuat T. H. O., and Tran T. 2002. *Report evaluation of the national AIDS program January 1996–June 2001 in Vietnam*, conducted by Market and Development Research Center for VIE/98/006 Project—HIV/AIDS Capacity Development, UNDP—United Nations Development Programme; National AIDS Standing Bureau, Ministry of Health; Hanoi: AusAID—Australian Agency for International Development.

Ruxrungtham, K., T. Brown, and P. Phanuphak. 2004. HIV/AIDS in Asia. *The Lancet* 364: 69–82.

Socialist Republic of Vietnam. 2006. *Second country report on following up to the declaration of commitment on HIV/AIDS*, January. Hanoi.

Thorne, C., M-L. Newell, and C. S. Peckham. 2000. Disclosure of diagnosis and planning for the future in HIV-affected families in Europe. In *Child: Care, Health and Development* 26(1): 29–40.

Tran Quoc Tuan. 2003. *Bao cao Hoat dong Cham soc—Dieu tri va tu van nguoi nhiem HIV/AIDS tai benh vien Dong Da—So y te Ha Noi, Benh vien Dong Da* [Report on treatment activities: From treatment to counselling for HIV/AIDS patients in Dong-Da Hospital, Health Service—Dong-Da Hospital]. Hanoi. Unpublished.

UNAIDS. 2005. *A scaled-up response to AIDS in Asia and the Pacific*. June. Geneva: UNAIDS.

UNAIDS. 2006a. *Report on the global AIDS epidemic*. Geneva: UNAIDS.

UNAIDS. 2006b. *International guidelines in HIV/AIDS and human Rights 2006. Consolidated version*. Geneva: OHCHR, UNAIDS.

UNAIDS, WHO. 2004. *UNAIDS/WHO policy statement on HIV testing.* June. Geneva: Joint United Nations Programme on HIV/AIDS.

UNAIDS, WHO. 2006. *2006 AIDS epidemic update.* Geneva: UNAIDS.

UNDP, Aus-AID. 2005. *Impact of HIV/AIDS on household vulnerability and poverty in Viet Nam.* UNDP-Aus-AIDS supported project. Hanoi: UNDP.

VanLandingham, M. J., W. Im-Em, and C. Saengtienchai. 2005. Community reaction to persons with HIV/AIDS and their parents: An analysis of recent evidence from Thailand. *Journal of Health and Social Behaviour* 46 (December): 392–410.

Vietnam Commission for Population, Family and Children, Ministry of Health, Population Reference Bureau. 2006. *HIV/AIDS in Vietnam.* Hanoi: VCPFC, MOH, PRB.

Vithayachockitikhun, N. 2006. Family caregiving of persons living with HIV/AIDS in Thailand: Caregiver burden, an outcome measure. In *International Journal of Nursing Practice* 12:123–128.

Vu Ngoc Bao. 2004. *Sex work in Vietnam: What are the implications for HIV/AIDS prevention?* Translated version (*Mai dam o Viet Nam: cac tac dong toi du phong HIV/AIDS?*), *Cong ty TNHH tu van Dau tu te, Gioi tinh duc va suc khoe tinh duc.* Hanoi: The Rockefeller foundation, *so 4, Nha xuat ban Y hoc.*

Wight, R. G., C. S. Aneshensel, D. A. Murphy, D. Miller-Martinez, and K. P. Beals. 2006. Perceived HIV stigma in AIDS caregiving dyads. *Social Science and Medicine* 62: 444-456.

Wolfe, D., and K. Malinowska-Sempruch. 2004. *Illicit drug policies and the global HIV epidemic: Effects of UN and national government approaches. A working paper commissioned by the HIV/AIDS Task Force of the Millennium Project.* International Harm Reduction Development. New York: Open Society Institute.

World Bank, Sida, AusAID, and the Royal Netherlands Embassy. 2001. *Growing healthy: A review of Vietnam's health sector.* Hanoi: World Bank.

World Health Organization. 2004a. *Vietnam. Summary country profile for HIV/AIDS treatment scale-up.* Geneva. World Health Organization.

World Health Organization. 2004b. *Scaling up antiretroviral therapy in resource-limited settings: treatment guidelines for a public health approach,* revision 2003. Geneva: World Health Organization.

World Health Organization. 2005. *The World Health Report 2005: Make every mother and child count.* Geneva: World Health Organization.

World Health Organization, UNAIDS. 2006. *Progress on global access to HIV antiretroviral therapy. A report on "3 by 5" and beyond.* Geneva: World Health Organization.

Yvon-Tran, F. 2002. The chronicle of a failure: Collectivisation in northern Vietnam, 1958–1988. In *Viet Nam exposé: French scholarship on twentieth-century Vietnamese society,* edited by G. Bousquet and P. Brocheux, 331–355. Ann Arbor: University of Michigan Press.

Chapter Five

Doi Moi and Older Adults
Intergenerational Support Under the Constraints of Reform

MAGALI BARBIERI

The main purpose of this chapter is to investigate the impact of *Doi Moi* on older people and, more particularly, on intergenerational support. In all traditional societies, the family and immediate kin group have the predominant responsibility for taking care of those who are too old or too sick to support themselves. A number of studies around the world have found an increasing tendency for older people to live independently, and a relative weakening of wealth flows from adult children to their ageing parents.[1] This tendency has been attributed to modernization and industrialization processes and is often regarded as being inevitable (International Institute on Ageing 1994). In most of the developing world, where pension and social security schemes remain embryonic, adult children and other immediate kin are still perceived by both the general public and the government as the "natural" caretakers of the elderly. This is especially true in countries influenced by Confucian values of filial piety and family responsibilities. However, in these countries, things are also changing. Research conducted in Japan, Thailand, Taiwan, Korea, and China has confirmed findings previously limited to the West (Cho and Yada 1994; Davis and Harrell 1993; Hermalin, Ofstedal, and Chang 1996; Hong and Byun 1998; Knodel, Chayovan, and Siriboon 1996; Martin and Kinsella 1994; Mason and Miller 1998; Morioka 1996; Traphagan and Knight 2003; Whyte 2003).

Renovation forces in Vietnam tend to resemble globalization processes observed elsewhere around the world, creating a context conducive to a decline in co-residence and financial assistance from children to their parents. In particular, the reforms have led to an intensification of migration flows, a major factor in severing traditional ties between generations (Goody 1996). At the same time, *Doi Moi* has promoted a transfer of social welfare functions from public institutions back to the family, which, at the present, is the unique source of support available to its disabled members for most of the population (Friedman et al. 1999; also see Anil Deolalikar, this volume). The Vietnamese government now stresses that "families should contribute significantly to the care of older persons" (Bui et al. 2000) and previous research does, in fact, underline the central role of children in providing assistance to their ageing parents (Friedman et al. 2002; Knodel et al. 1998; Truong et al. 1997). My study presents evidence of families' strategies to ensure continuous support to their older members in the midst of such conflicting influences. This chapter reviews the demographic context of ageing in Vietnam, contemporary residential patterns of older persons, and the adaptation of family strategies to secure support for ageing relatives since geographic distance between adult children and their parents has increased. It ends with a discussion of the study implications for the future of older people in Vietnam.

The Demographic Context of Ageing in Vietnam

Vietnam is entering a period of rapid ageing due to its recent demographic history. Ageing refers to both a high proportion of older persons in a population and to the process leading to it. It can result from a decline in fertility, from a decline in mortality, or more commonly, from a combination of the two, occurring either in succession or simultaneously. Due to previous demographic trends, all European countries and other industrial regions are faced with the reality of having a large proportion of older people in their population. However, in these countries, the ageing process has been very slow, due to a gradual decline in mortality and fertility associated with steady improvements in the social, economic, medical, and institutional environments, from the nineteenth century to the end of the twentieth century. As underlined by Ham-Chande in a different context, "although there were ample opportunities and time allowances for social and economic adjustments, nevertheless ageing is still imposing great disturbances even upon the wealthiest nations" (Ham-Chande 1994, 46). By contrast, in many Asian countries, including Vietnam, the demographic transition has been extraordinarily rapid. In these settings, imported medical technologies and public health programs had an immediate and dramatic impact on the improvement of life expectancy, while deliberate and strong policies promoting change in reproductive behavior reduced fertility to a level below replacement in hardly more than a generation.

Vietnam initiated its demographic transition from a high level of mortality and fertility to a low level of mortality and fertility well before *Doi Moi*. However, there are reasons to believe that the profound changes associated with the shift from a centrally planned to a market-oriented economic system have been accompanied by an even faster decline in both fertility and mortality. Consequently, the proportion of elders aged sixty and older in Vietnam will double in about thirty years; whereas, it took between seventy-five and one hundred years for this to occur in Western countries.

FERTILITY

Fertility decline is the primary factor responsible for population ageing. Demographic simulations show that it has a much stronger effect on the age distribution of a population than mortality decline during the initial stages of the demographic transition (Keyfitz 2005). Fertility change has a direct influence on ageing at the population level because it determines the level and speed of the process in a population and, at the individual level, because it directly influences the number of potential carers in the immediate family.

As indicated in a number of studies, including a chapter in this volume (Catherine Scornet's), fertility has fallen steadily in Vietnam over the past thirty-five years. Population policy to curb population growth was initiated as early as the 1960s in the North, at a time when the total fertility rate was above six children per woman. Initially ineffectual, it was progressively reinforced and eventually succeeded in deeply transforming reproductive behavior. Far from representing a turning point in the fertility limitation programs of the previous era, *Doi Moi* further consolidated the state commitment and continued the effort as explained in more detail in Catherine Scornet's chapter. The success of the national family planning program is reflected in the dramatically low level that has been reached, as shown by the results of the most recent nationally representative demographic survey.

The survey estimates the total fertility rate to be 1.9 children per woman in the early years of the twenty-first century, a level below that required for the natural replacement of the population (General Statistics Office 2003). This rate is also below that found in a number of developed countries, including the United States.

Because fertility declined relatively slowly until the early 1980s and accelerated only thereafter, most of the impact has not yet been felt. Today's elders, who are in their sixties and above, spent their reproductive years during a period when the total fertility rate was still high (five to six children per woman), even though delayed marriage, widowhood, and spousal separation due to the war were common and tended to reduce fertility. However, even these generations will bear the consequences of rapid fertility decline in the near future as their proportion in the general population progressively increases, a phenomenon further aggravated by the downward mortality trend.

MORTALITY

Mortality increased from about 12 per 1,000 persons at the end of the 1950s and 1960s to a level that is difficult to estimate at the time of reunification, but which probably approximated 15 per 1,000 (Barbieri 2003). Thereafter, it dropped to below 10 per 1,000 at the end of the 1970s, 7.5 at the end of the 1980s, and 5.6 at the end of the 1990s, according to the 1999 Population Census (General Statistics Office 2001). Life expectancy at birth is now above sixty-five years for both sexes combined, with a significant difference between men (63.0 years) and women (67.5 years).

At current mortality levels, 25 percent of each cohort is expected to die before the age of sixty (General Statistics Office 2001). The United Nations forecasts that this proportion will decline by half over the next forty years, with women having a continued advantage over men. By the year 2050, 90 percent of men and 93 percent of women will survive to their sixtieth birthday (United Nations 2005). In addition, those reaching the age of sixty will live longer and longer lives, from an estimated additional 18.5 to 21 years from 2000–05 to 2045–50 for men, and 20 to 24 years, respectively, for women (United Nations 2005). Thus, in terms of survival, women are, and will continue to be, in a more favorable situation than men.

According to the 1999 Census, in addition to living longer, women typically marry men who are their elders by 2.7 years on average (General Statistics

Office 2001). Consequently, women are at a much higher risk of widowhood than men, and this directly translates into higher and increasing proportions of unmarried women at later ages. As shown in Tables 5.1a and 5.1b, while the proportion of unmarried males (i.e., single, widowed, divorced, and separated) increases from 7 percent at ages sixty to sixty-four to almost 70 percent at ages ninety-five and older, it rises from nearly 40 percent at ages sixty to sixty-four to virtually 100 percent at ages ninety-five and older for women, mainly due to widowhood. Ageing is consequently, in Vietnam as elsewhere around the world, typically a female issue. Numerous studies have shown that one's spouse is the most significant helper in later life, as a source of mutual care and psychological support. The high proportion of women alone in the oldest age groups therefore heightens the issue of rapid ageing in the population.

CONSEQUENCES ON THE AGE STRUCTURE

Because of these demographic trends, older people represent a significant minority in Vietnam's population today, with about 8 percent of the total population being sixty and older, and their number is expected to grow faster than any other age group. As a result, the elderly will make up nearly 30 percent of the total population in the mid-twenty-first century, rising in number from about 6 million today to 13.5 million in 2025 and nearly 30 million in 2050.[2] These projections are highly reliable since those who will be aged sixty and older in 2050 have already been born. The only factor liable to influence these numbers is the risk of mortality between now and the projection date, but considering the low level of mortality that already characterizes Vietnam, the margin of error is negligible. The needs of older people are unlike those of any other age group, and time will be needed to develop strategies that are adapted to the particular political, cultural, social, and economic context of Vietnam in order to cope with this fast-growing issue. Consequently, it is by no means premature to collect evidence on the current situation of older people in order to understand the challenges ahead more fully.

OLD-AGE DEPENDENCY

From a socioeconomic standpoint, it is useful to estimate the burden of the dependent elderly on the working-age population. In this respect, the most common indicator is the so-called dependency ratio, which is the ratio of the

TABLE 5.IA

Distribution of the male population by marital status for each age-group (among the sixty years old and above) and for the total (all male ten years old and older), Vietnam 1999 Population and Housing Census (weighted values)

Age group	Single	Married	Widowed	Divorced	Separated	Not reported	Total	Total number of males
60–64	0.4	92.7	5.9	0.3	0.6	0.0	100.0	775,800
65–69	0.4	88.9	9.9	0.3	0.6	0.0	100.0	750,800
70–74	0.5	83.6	15.2	0.1	0.6	0.0	100.0	504,200
75–79	0.4	74.9	23.7	0.1	0.7	0.1	100.0	313,600
80–84	0.6	65.8	32.8	0.1	0.6	0.1	100.0	143,500
85–89	0.8	53.2	45.0	0.1	0.6	0.4	100.0	67,600
90–94	0.5	45.5	53.1	0.3	0.2	0.4	100.0	14,820
95 +	0.0	30.7	67.1	0.0	0.9	0.8	100.0	4,901
Total (10+)	36.4	61.1	1.8	0.4	0.3	0.0	100.0	37,520,000

SOURCE: Author's tabulation from the 3 percent public access microsample, *1999 Population and Housing Census of Vietnam*, General Statistics Office, Vietnam.

TABLE 5.IB

Distribution of the female population by marital status for each age-group (among the sixty years old and above) and for the total (all female ten years old and older), Vietnam 1999 Population and Housing Census (weighted values)

Age group	Single	Married	Widowed	Divorced	Separated	Not reported	Total	Total number of females
60–64	1.6	61.9	34.4	0.8	1.3	0.1	100.0	990,800
65–69	1.4	53.5	43.8	0.4	0.8	0.1	100.0	931,100
70–74	0.9	40.6	57.3	0.3	0.7	0.2	100.0	704,700
75–79	1.0	28.0	69.9	0.3	0.6	0.2	100.0	520,100
80–84	0.9	15.8	82.6	0.0	0.4	0.3	100.0	275,200
85–89	1.0	8.4	90.0	0.0	0.2	0.4	100.0	143,200
90–94	0.8	4.2	94.7	0.0	0.2	0.0	100.0	44,140
95 +	0.3	2.4	93.7	0.0	0.0	0.7	100.0	15,138
Total (10+)	30.1	57.7	10.4	1.0	0.8	0.0	100.0	38,810,000

SOURCE: Author's tabulation from the 3 percent public access microsample, *1999 Population and Housing Census of Vietnam*, General Statistics Office, Vietnam.

population aged sixty and older to the working-age population, typically defined as the population aged from fifteen to fifty-nine. As discussed in detail in Xavier Oudin's contribution to this volume, a more relevant indicator to measure the actual cost of supporting the disabled or retired elderly is to calculate the number of employed people in this group, excluding students and the unemployed, since not all of the adult population is economically active or able to care for others. Due to the increasing level and duration of education, the proportion of students of both sexes older than fifteen is rising continuously (also see Peter Xenos et al., this volume). A further limitation results from the fact that many older persons are forced to continue working to an advanced age due to economic constraints. However, it is much easier to obtain reliable statistics on the demographic characteristics than on the employment status of a population, so it is customary to approximate the latter, economic, indicator by the former, demographic, index.

In Vietnam, as in most Asian countries, the ageing process, as measured by change in the old-age dependency ratio (the ratio of the population aged sixty or older to the working-age population), is anticipated to be very rapid during the next four decades or so, due to the demographic trends described above. The cost of supporting one person aged sixty plus, borne by more than seven people aged fifteen to fifty-nine at the moment, will be borne by only two people in that age group by the mid-twenty-first century. The real economic burden will depend on the proportion of the population actually working in both age groups. In addition to future demographic trends, there may be an increase in the age at entering the job market, due to a longer duration of education, an increase in the age at retirement, as well as lower rates of disability among the elderly due to improved health. In any case, as already shown by current indicators, the increase in the old-age dependency burden will likely be more pronounced in rural than in urban areas because of differences in the age distribution of the population, an issue that is more thoroughly investigated later in this chapter.

With an increasing number of older people living longer, with fewer close relatives, the traditional pattern of intergenerational co-residence is likely to be placed under great strain. Concurrent changes related to rapid socio-economic development fostered by the transition to a market system exert further pressure on co-residence while, at the same time, the present policy of welfare retrenchment is reducing government support to older people (see Bélanger and Barbieri, this volume). The following sections examine current residential patterns of older people in general and, more specifically, in the particular context of accelerating migration flows, before considering alternative forms of support. A brief description of the data used for the analyses is first provided.

Data

Two quantitative sources of information, both representative at the national level, were used in this analysis: the 3 percent public access microdata sample extracted from the 1999 Vietnam Population Census, and the 1997–1998 Vietnam Living Standard Survey.

THE 1999 POPULATION AND HOUSING CENSUS OF VIETNAM

The 1999 Population Census is the most recent census in Vietnam. The General Statistics Office of Vietnam distributes an electronic extract representing 3 percent of the overall dataset with detailed information at the individual and household levels that includes all the variables collected in the Census. The advantage of using this microsample dataset is that it is very large, covering nearly 2.4 million household members. Because the proportion of people over sixty is relatively low in the general population (less than 8 percent), survey samples are typically too small to provide statistically significant information on the elderly, unless they are specifically designed for this purpose.[3] In the 1997–1998 Vietnam Living Standard Survey, for instance, there are fewer than 3,000 people aged sixty or older, compared with nearly 200,000 in the microsample of the 1999 Population Census.

The main drawback of the 1999 Census dataset is the limited amount of information included. The basic demographic characteristics of age, sex, and marital status are precisely documented, but the primary variable necessary to investigate household composition—family relationships among all household members—provides only a small number of categories and all of them in relation to the household head. These categories include "household head," "spouse of household head," "child of household head," and "father or mother of household head." All other types of relationship are classified as "other." Thus, there is no way to identify parents, spouses, or children of household members other than the household head. Socioeconomic characteristics are restricted to the level of education, literacy, and the main occupation. Information on migration is limited to change in residence over an extended period (five years), and does not measure shorter residential movements or return migration flows; however, we know which administrative borders were crossed during the move (commune, district, province, country). In spite of its limitations, the 1999 Census, with its large sample size and nationally representative quality, is a powerful source of information, possibly the only one available to document general household structures and intergenerational coresidence patterns in relation to migration. However, it is obviously not appropriate for studying other forms of support. To do so, we rely on another source of statistical information.

THE 1997–1998 VIETNAM LIVING STANDARD SURVEY

The General Statistics Office of Vietnam conducted the first Vietnam Living Standard Survey (VLSS) in 1992–93 on a nationally representative sample of 4,800 households (World Bank 2001). As part of the more global survey program carried out under the auspices of the World Bank in developing countries since the 1980s, the purpose of the 1992–93 VLSS was mainly to estimate variations in living standards and evaluate government policies. The 1997–98 VLSS updated information on the socioeconomic situation of the population and changes in living standards that occurred during the five intervening years (General Statistics Office 2000). In the second survey, 4,305 households from the original 1992–93 sample were reinterviewed, to which were added 1,255 households drawn from the total sample of the 1995 Multi-Purpose Household Survey (MPHS) conducted by the General Statistics Office of Vietnam, along with 439 replacement households randomly selected in the same village or city block as those households in the original 1992–93 VLSS or 1995 MPHS that were unavailable or unwilling to respond. The total number of households interviewed in the 1997–98 VLSS was 5,999, of which 2,116 (35 percent) included at least one person aged sixty or older.

In addition to its relatively small sample size, the 1997–98 VLSS contains limited information on migration. Indeed, most of the sample is, by design, comprised of nonmigrant households—those households that had remained in the same location since the 1992–93 or 1995 surveys. The proportion of households lost from the 1992–93 sample, due to out-migration, totals, for instance, about 7 percent, which is very close to the individual migration rate at the national level (6.5 percent). We have no information about the whereabouts of these households other than the fact that they moved out of the community.

Compared with the 1999 Census, the VLSS provides a wealth of useful information on the demographic, social, and economic characteristics of the households and of each of their members. As in the census, we know the relationship between each household member and the household head but, in contrast with the census, the information is very detailed. In addition to categories used in the census like "household head," "spouse of the household head," "child of the household head" and "father or mother of the household head," the survey also includes specific categories for "sons- and daughters-in-law," "fathers- and mothers-in-law," "grandchildren," "siblings," "grandparents," "nieces or nephews," "adopted or stepchildren," "other relatives" and "non-relatives."

Furthermore, the 1997–98 VLSS contains information on the survival of each household member's biological father and mother, as well as the age, sex, marital status, and province of residence for all non–co-resident children of the household members. However, an important limitation for our purpose is that, for those non–co-resident children living in the same province as their parents, we lack information on the degree of geographic proximity. Since adult children living close by, though in a separate household, are in nearly as good a position to help their ageing parents as those who co-reside with them, as suggested by ethnographic studies of the type presented elsewhere in this volume (see Truong Huyen Chi, this volume), we underestimate the proportion of those in a position to provide daily care and emotional support. Notwithstanding this caveat, the survey is extremely valuable for comparing the potential versus actual living arrangements of the elderly, given their demographic and socioeconomic characteristics as well as that of their children. Indeed, because the VLSS provides specific identification codes for the biological fathers, mothers, and children of each household member residing in the same household, it is possible to link household members to their closest co-residing relatives, independent of the household head.

In addition to enabling a detailed analysis of older people's living arrangements, the survey also allows for an exploration of other forms of support. It includes, in particular, information on remittances received by each household. It is possible to investigate financial transfers from non–co-resident adult children to their ageing parents because both the senders and beneficiaries are identified.[4]

In summary, the current study utilizes census data, with a large sample of older persons and information on migration status, and the 1997–98 VLSS dataset, with information on kinship patterns, socioeconomic characteristics, and financial transfers.

Methods

Both the census and survey data were analyzed using the STATA© software. In this study, the elderly are defined as all individuals aged sixty and older in both the 1999 Census dataset and the 1997–98 VLSS data. All results are weighted, although the number of unweighted cases used is shown in the tables. While census data are used to investigate the impact of migration on the household structure of older persons, survey data are used to analyze living arrangements in relation to the number of children alive, and to examine alternative forms of support, more specifically financial assistance.

Together, the two datasets answer a number of initial questions, and they are of much value in guiding the discussion on the issue at stake. The four major findings include the following: (1) co-residence does remain widespread in Vietnam, and the large majority of ageing parents live with their children; (2) elders are less likely than younger people to migrate, but the proportion of those moving is not insignificant; (3) migration of the elderly appears to increase the odds of co-residing with adult children, suggesting that when older people do move, they do so to follow or join their children and immediate families; (4) remittances from non–co-resident children to their ageing parents' household is a major, and probably growing, form of support. The remainder of this chapter documents and discusses each of these findings.

RESIDENTIAL PATTERNS OF THE ELDERLY

Confucian ideology, with its strong emphasis on the family as the basic social unit, has dominated traditional Vietnamese society. The family system was rooted in virilocal residential patterns and patriarchy. The idealized multiple-generation household, consisting of a patriarch, his wife, adult children, and numerous grandchildren, illustrates the importance placed on family cohesion and integration, and on the continuity of the family line (Luong 1992). A study of family structure during the French colonial period suggests a different reality, with a relatively small household size (fewer than six people) and an equal proportion of nuclear and extended households (Bélanger 1997). However, the same study also demonstrates that the difference between observed and idealized family forms resulted largely from the very high mortality rate recorded at the time, since an overwhelming proportion of older people actually lived with their adult children and their families (Bélanger 1997).

My analysis of the 1999 Census data shows that, overall in Vietnam, the proportion of elders co-residing with their children is very high: over three out of every four persons (77 percent), aged sixty and older, co-reside with at least one adult child. Furthermore, a recently published study comparing the 1999 Population Census with that of 1989 found that this proportion has been very stable over time, with no indication of decline in the recent period (Knodel and Truong 2002). It is comparable to that found in Thailand or in the Philippines, higher than in some Eastern Asian countries, such as Japan or South Korea, where it is closer to 60 percent, and considerably higher than in Western countries, such as the United States or Germany, where it reaches a low 15 percent (Phillips 2000).

The high proportion of elders living with adult children is fairly uniform, with only small differences by age, sex, and area of residence. Regarding age, the proportion progressively declines from around 80 percent at ages sixty to sixty-nine to close to 70 percent at seventy and older. Variations by sex do not exhibit a systematic pattern. Men are slightly more likely to live with children than women at ages sixty to sixty-nine and less likely to do so at ages eighty and older. Generally, the proportion of ageing parents living with children is significantly higher in urban areas, where it reaches 80 percent, compared with rural areas, where it is 75 percent. The stronger pattern of co-residence found in urban areas could result from the higher cost of housing. It could also result from migration patterns, as will be further discussed below.

Given the very high proportion of the ageing parents co-residing with children, the percentage living alone or living with a spouse only is small (below 20 percent), compared with countries outside the region. In Japan, for instance, a country which is much more developed but belongs to the same geographic and cultural sphere, this proportion is above 40 percent (Raymo and Kaneda 2003). The overall proportion living with a spouse only is larger than the proportion living alone (11 percent and 6 percent, respectively). Due to rising widowhood (from 4 percent among those aged sixty to sixty-nine to 9 percent among those aged eighty and older), the proportion living with a spouse tends to decline at older ages (from over 10 percent below age eighty to 8 percent after age eighty), while the proportion living alone follows the opposite trend. Furthermore, among all individuals living alone in the overall population, about half are aged sixty and older.

Among those not living with children, the difference by sex is striking: men are more likely to live with a spouse while women are more likely to live alone. The proportion of older persons living with a spouse only is 15 percent for men and 9 percent for women, while the proportion living alone is 3 percent for men and 8 percent for women (Table 5.2). This contrast is especially true in rural areas, where the percentage of women living alone is more than three times higher than that of men. It is a little more than twice as high in urban areas (results not shown). These variations likely reflect sex differences in life expectancy, since older women are more often widowed than older men. Thus, women are less likely to live with a spouse and more likely to live alone. The higher rate of solitude for women also reflects their higher rate of childlessness. Indeed, living arrangements of the elderly are probably constrained by demographic patterns. The number of surviving sons, the total number of surviving children, and adult children's residential strategies all determine the likelihood of co-residence.

SURVIVING CHILDREN

An analysis of the 1997–98 VLSS data, using the information on all biological co-resident and non–co-resident children, shows that the proportion of persons aged sixty and older who are childless is small (below 4 percent) (Table 5.3). This is a result of the high fertility regime under which today's older people lived most of their reproductive years. Indeed, the mean number of surviving children in these cohorts is high (4.3, on average). It reaches its highest level at ages sixty to sixty-nine (5.2) and then declines progressively and significantly to 4.6 at ages seventy to seventy-nine and 3.0 at eighty and older.

The data show significant variations by sex, with women being twice as likely to be childless than men (4.8 percent versus 2.3 percent for those aged sixty and older). Women are also much less likely to have a surviving son, especially in the highest age group (eighty and older) in which the proportion without a son reaches 30 percent versus 14 percent for men. During the thirty-year war suffered by the country through the 1950s, 1960s, and 1970s, women experienced a combination of early widowhood, nonmarriage, and high mortality (of children, in particular) at a time when they were going through their reproductive span. By contrast, marriage rates were high for those men who survived the war, and men who are widowers at the time

TABLE 5.2

Percent distribution of the population by household type
in each sex and age group sixty and above (weighted values)

Age group and sex		Percentage of population aged 60+ that is living			
	Alone	with a spouse only	with children	with others	Total
Male					
60–69	1.7	12.2	82.3	3.8	100.0
70–79	3.6	18.2	72.3	5.9	100.0
80+	6.1	16.7	69.1	8.1	100.0
All 60+	2.7	14.5	78.0	4.9	100.0
Female					
60–69	5.8	9.7	78.7	5.9	100.0
70–79	10.2	9.6	72.3	7.9	100.0
80+	10.7	3.4	75.2	10.7	100.0
All 60+	7.9	8.8	76.1	7.2	100.0
Both sexes					
60–69	4.0	10.8	80.3	5.0	100.0
70–79	7.6	13.0	72.3	7.1	100.0
80+	9.2	7.7	73.2	9.9	100.0
All 60+	5.8	11.2	76.8	6.2	100.0

SOURCE: Author's tabulation from the 3 percent public access microsample, *1999 Population and Housing Census of Vietnam*, General Statistics Office, Vietnam.

TABLE 5.3

Percent distribution of the population aged forty and over by proportion childless,
sonless, and number of surviving children by age group and sex, 1997–1998 (%)

Age group	Male			Female			Total		
	% with no surviving child	% with no surviving son	Mean number of surviving children	% with no surviving child	% with no surviving son	Mean number of surviving children	% with no surviving child	% with no surviving son	Mean number of surviving children
40–49	3.63	12.69	3.6	7.44	16.92	3.6	5.68	14.96	3.6
50–59	2.64	7.19	4.8	5.92	12.52	4.7	4.44	10.12	4.7
60–69	2.16	6.89	5.4	3.68	9.70	5.1	2.99	8.43	5.2
70–79	2.39	6.65	5.2	3.48	13.92	4.1	3.04	10.95	4.6
80+	3.19	13.83	4.0	13.00	30.00	2.6	9.86	24.83	3.0
All 40+	2.93	9.52	4.5	6.06	14.62	4.2	4.67	12.34	4.3

SOURCE: Author's tabulation from the *1997–1998 Vietnam Living Standard Survey* data, World Bank, 2001.

of the survey presumably became so after the war. The probability of them having children is thus much greater.

The war also explains why the proportion of people aged sixty and older without a son (11 percent) is so much higher than the proportion of those without any children (4 percent). This is particularly so for people aged eighty and older, of which 25 percent do not have a son. Indeed, sons of people in this age group would have been in their twenties in the late 1960s and early 1970s. According to one study, "war mortality [was] highest in 1965–1975, the period of escalation of the American war, among men, especially young men between ages 15 and 29, and to a lesser extent among middle-aged men" (Merli 2000, 8). Nevertheless, close to 98 percent of men and 95 percent of women over sixty have at least one surviving child, and over 90 percent of men and 85 percent of women in this group have at least one surviving son. The potential for co-residence between ageing parents and their adult children is thus high.

Survey data confirm the findings from the Census data analysis which indicate that a high proportion of older people are living with their children. Restricting the analysis to parents with at least one surviving child shows a systematic pattern with age that was not perceptible using census data (Table 5.4). While 80 percent of people aged sixty and above with at least one surviving child co-reside with adult children, the proportion drops to 60 percent at ages seventy and above. There is no clear difference between men and women in the probability of living with a child, except at higher ages: three out of four women aged eighty and above co-reside with a child, whereas the proportion is below 50 percent for men at that age. This results from the higher rate of female widowhood and the association between widowhood and co-residence with children, which is revisited below.

For both men and women in every age group, the data show that the proportion of older people living with a son (and no daughter) is about 50 percent higher than the proportion living with a daughter (and no son). The result persists even when we restrict the analysis to parents who have a choice between living with a son or daughter. The proportion of both men and women living with a son only is about 60 percent, while the proportion living with a daughter only is 30 percent for those aged sixty to sixty-nine, nearly 40 percent and 20 percent for those aged seventy to seventy-nine, and approximately 30 percent and 15 percent for those aged eighty and over. The proportion of men and women living with both a son and a daughter is higher than the proportion living with a daughter only.

TABLE 5.4
Differences in parents' living arrangements
by age and sex relative to own children (%)

Survival of children and co-residence	Men			Women			Total		
	60–69	70–79	80+	60–69	70–79	80+	60–69	70–79	80+
Percent living with									
at least one child of any sex*	80.1	58.1	44.7	79.6	64.6	74.1	79.9	60.9	58.1
at least one son*	70.0	47.9	32.8	71.9	53.3	51.5	70.9	50.1	39.1
at least one daughter*	49.3	31.0	25.5	50.8	40.7	57.9	50.0	34.7	39.1
at least one son and one daughter**	36.8	19.0	10.7	37.6	19.5	4.2	37.2	19.2	9.0
at least one son and no daughter**	62.5	39.7	27.7	54.0	30.8	28.4	58.7	36.6	27.9
at least one daughter and no son**	36.6	21.1	16.8	28.1	15.4	16.0	32.6	19.0	16.6

*Among all individuals with at least one surviving child/son/daughter; because siblings sometimes co-reside with their parents, especially when unmarried, the percentage of parents living with a male child and the percentage living with a female child do not add up to the percentage living with any child.

**Among all individuals with at least one surviving son and one surviving daughter.

SOURCE: Author's tabulation from the *1997–1998 Vietnam Living Standard Survey* data, World Bank, 2001.

In conclusion, the most interesting finding, in the Vietnamese cultural context, is that the proportion of parents living with a daughter (and not with a son), even when sons are alive, is not insignificant. About 20 percent of those aged sixty and older, with approximately 30 percent of those aged sixty to sixty-nine, and slightly below 20 percent at older ages, live in this situation. It is certainly higher than Confucian values would have led us to expect. Indeed, Confucianism emphasizes the role of male children in caring for their ageing parents, but adaptation strategies to the new socioeconomic context are likely to have played an important role in altering traditional patterns, assuming that those have ever been predominant as suggested by Haines' review of historical evidence (Haines 2006). Considering the continuous decline in fertility, the proportion of couples with one female child only will increase in the future, further reinforcing this trend.

Intergenerational Support and Migration

Demographic factors, like the number of surviving children, and the geographic distance between adults and their ageing parents determine the number of potential caregivers among children. The 1990s witnessed a re-markable increase in migration flows in Vietnam, with about 6.5 percent of the population, nearly 4.5 million people, having experienced a change in residence between 1994 and 1999, a restrictive definition of migration that undoubtedly underestimates the phenomenon (Dang, Tacoli, and Hoang 2003). Furthermore, this is a national average that conceals major variations by region; for example, the proportion of migrants increases to one out of every five persons (20 percent) in Ho Chi Minh City, the main economic center, when using the census definition.

A recent study on migration in Vietnam has clearly identified three main mechanisms through which *Doi Moi* has influenced population movement and distribution in the country (Dang, Tacoli, and Hoang 2003). On the supply side, the decollectivization of agriculture produced an increase in productivity and released a significant proportion of the rural labor force. The growth of foreign investment in industries and services concentrated in certain regions and in large- and medium-size cities especially, has created new economic opportunities in these sectors and areas for workers released by the agricultural sector. Finally, the relaxation of governmental controls on internal migration enabled workers released by the agricultural sector to take advantage of the new employment opportunities. Such opportunities mainly benefited the newly educated young, since approximately half of all migrants are below twenty-five years of age (Dang 1999; Djamba, Goldstein, and Goldstein 2000). About 45 percent of the 4.5 million migrants moved across provincial boundaries and, for the majority of them, the move involved a change of region (Dang, Tacoli, and Hoang 2003).

Migration is a good example of a process associated with rapid economic transformations, which has a strong, potentially detrimental, impact on the traditional role of the immediate relatives caring for and supporting elderly family members. It shows how the well-being of the older population is being threatened in the context of *Doi Moi*. Indeed, long-distance migration of the young is expected to have a considerable and multidimensional impact on the well-being of older people in a country where government assistance to the elderly has virtually disappeared in recent years and where most of the responsibility for old-age caregiving now falls on the immediate family and community (Bui et al. 2000). Young adults' migration reduces the availability of physical and emotional support for older relatives left behind and results in a loss of potential caregivers to ageing parents, as already demonstrated in other countries of Southeast Asia (Chang 1992). Because of intensifying

TABLE 5.5A

Percent distribution of the population aged forty and over by number
of surviving children by age group and sex in rural areas, 1997–1998 (%)

Age group	Male				Female			
	0	1	2+	Total	0	1	2+	Total
40–49	1.4	1.5	97.1	100.0	5.5	4.1	90.3	100.0
50–59	1.6	1.7	96.6	100.0	5.0	5.4	89.6	100.0
60–69	2.0	2.3	95.7	100.0	2.7	4.3	93.0	100.0
70+	1.9	8.4	89.7	100.0	5.9	20.7	73.4	100.0
All 40+	1.7	2.7	95.6	100.0	4.9	7.5	87.7	100.0

SOURCE: Author's tabulation from the *1997–1998 Vietnam Living Standard Survey* data, World Bank, 2001.

TABLE 5.5B

Percent distribution of the population aged forty and over by number
of surviving children by age group and sex in urban areas, 1997–1998 (%)

Age group	Male				Female			
	0	1	2+	Total	0	1	2+	Total
40–49	7.2	5.9	86.9	100.0	11.2	8.2	80.6	100.0
50–59	4.8	2.9	92.3	100.0	7.6	5.7	86.7	100.0
60–69	2.8	2.4	94.8	100.0	6.5	9.2	84.4	100.0
70+	4.4	13.9	81.7	100.0	7.3	25.1	67.6	100.0
All 40+	5.4	5.3	89.3	100.0	8.8	10.7	80.5	100.0

SOURCE: Author's tabulation from the *1997–1998 Vietnam Living Standard Survey* data, World Bank, 2001.

migration flows from rural to urban areas, the burden of older people is heavier in rural areas.

For the moment, however, the greater availability of immediate kin in rural areas compensates for the differential rate of support in the overall population between rural and urban areas. Because fertility declined earlier in urban than in rural areas, the average number of children alive is higher for people aged 40 years and over in rural than in urban areas (Tables 5.5a and 5.5b). Cangping and Peng's analysis of ageing in China is particularly relevant for Vietnam. They show how economic development has increased the demand for young workers, and how differential fertility trends have contributed to the geographic imbalance of labor demand:

It is easy to ascertain that the areas receiving migrants are almost all those recording low fertility rates whereas the areas sending migrants are primarily rural ones, particularly the interior provinces. Outcome of transition is the shift of young persons from primary industry to secondary and tertiary industries, with agriculture work relying on "outsiders." On the one hand, the migration of a large number of peasants to the cities in pursuit of a better life tends to alleviate the ageing process and helps to rejuvenate their population. On the other hand, the problems associated with rapid ageing in a rural environment, such as income security, medical and emotional care of the elderly, pose an increasing challenge. (Cangping and Peng 1994, 62)

LIVING ARRANGEMENTS OF AGEING PARENTS WITH CHILDREN ON THE MOVE

Analyses confirm that older persons are the least likely to migrate. Figure 5.1 represents the age and sex distribution of migrants, as defined in the 1999 Population Census (those individuals who lived in another commune five years before). As expected, the population pyramid is heavily skewed toward younger people and women, a phenomenon well documented throughout Asia. The proportion of migrants is higher among people aged twenty to twenty-four (around 15 percent) and lower among people aged sixty and older (from 3 percent among those aged sixty to sixty-four to 2 percent among those aged eighty and older).

However, the data show that older people who do migrate are more likely to live with their children than those who do not. We carried out a logistic regression using the 1999 Census data to estimate the odds of co-residing with a child for all older people aged sixty and above by migration status. We restricted the analysis to ever-married individuals, as the social and historical context makes it virtually impossible for the never-married to have children. Because, as we have seen above, co-residence varies by sex, age, marital status, and place of residence, we introduced these factors into the multivariate model. We also controlled for literacy, the best proxy for social class available in the 1999 Census considering the strong emphasis traditionally placed on education and its associated social status (Nguyen 2001). Table 5.6 presents the results of this analysis. Odds ratios (OR), rather than coefficients, are shown for easier reading. The level of statistical significance is also indicated for each individual category.

The main finding here is that the probability of living with a child is *higher* for migrants moving out of their immediate geographic neighborhood

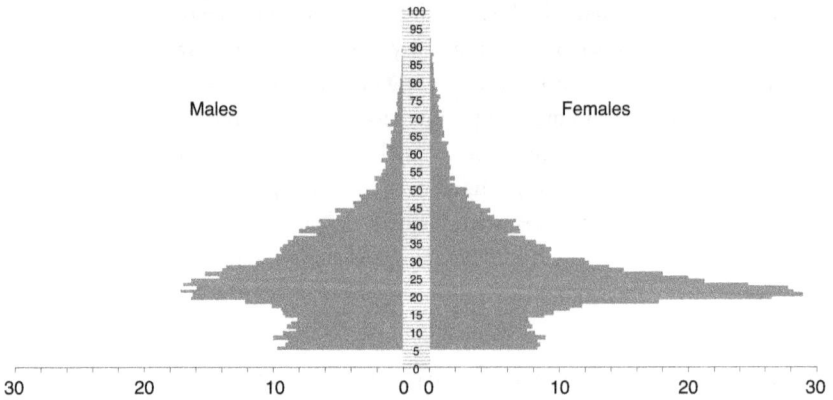

Figure 5.1   Age pyramid of migrants (per 1,000 total) 1999 Vietnam Population Census.

Source: Author's calculations from the 3 percent public access microsample, *1999 Population and Housing Census of Vietnam*, General Statistics Office, Vietnam.

(out of the district) than for nonmigrants, and this is especially true for older people living in urban areas. As previously noted, older persons in urban areas are more likely than their rural counterparts to live with children (OR = 1.34). Because of a multiplication effect, their odds of co-residing with a child are more than twice the odds of those living in a rural area if they have moved into their current urban place of residence within the previous years, by leaving another district (urban or rural) in the same province or in another province.

The other variables in the model, except for sex, operate in the expected direction. Indeed, the one unexplained finding is that, accounting for all factors, including age and marital status, women are less likely than men to co-reside with a child (OR = 0.75). This is true whatever the marital status. However, within each sex, the odds of living with a child are significantly higher for unmarried elders. Therefore, widowed men are more likely to live with a child than married men are, and widowed women are more likely to live with a child than unmarried women, although less than widowed men. Odds ratios for other variables confirm previous findings. The older a person, the less likely he or she is to co-reside with a child: compared with the reference category of those aged sixty to sixty-nine, the odds are about a third below for those aged seventy to seventy-nine, and a half below for those aged eighty and above. Illiteracy, our one measure of poverty, increases the odds of liv-

TABLE 5.6

Predicted odds of living with a child (all ever-married people aged 60+)

Independent variable	Odds ratio $p > z$
Sex	
Male (ref.)	1.000
Female	0.747***
Age group	
60–69 (ref.)	1.000
70–79	0.661***
80+	0.517***
Marital status	
Married (ref.)	1.000
Widow/sep/div	1.863***
Literacy	
Literate (ref.)	1.000
Illiterate	1.135***
Zone of residence	
Rural (ref.)	1.000
Urban	1.339***
Migration status	
Non migrant (ref.)	1.000
Same district	1.092
Same province	1.080
Other province	1.217
Abroad	2.577
Interaction urban residence* migration	
Non migrant (ref.)	1.000
Same district	0.835
Same province	1.709*
Other province	1.536*
Region of residence	
North (ref.)	1.000
Centre	1.113***
South	1.602***
Interaction urban residence* region	
Urban North (ref.)	1.000
Urban Center	0.730***
Urban South	1.085*
Number of observations	79,344
Prob > Chi2	0.0000
Log-likelihood	–36,780
Pseudo R2	0.0333

***p <0.01 ; **p <0.05 ; *p <0.1

SOURCE: Author's analysis of the 1999 Population Census (3 percent microsample)

ing with a child by a small but significant amount (OR = 1.1). The type and region of residence interact in an interesting way so that living in the South systematically increases the odds of living with a child (OR = 1.6), especially in urban areas, where the odds are about twice that of the reference category (rural North). Living in the urban Center hardly modifies the odds of living with a child (OR = 1.1), compared with the reference category, and does not raise them compared with living in the rural Center (OR = 1.1 also in the rural Center).

In conclusion, this analysis demonstrates that, when older people move to an urban area, they are more likely to follow or join their adult children. This is especially true for men, widows, the younger old, the illiterate, and those living in the South. However, since a much higher proportion of young adults migrate, in most families, children who move often leave their parents behind. Financial support, in the form of remittances, is a likely substitute for physical proximity, especially when the move is associated with upward social mobility for the adult children, a situation observed for most permanent migrants (Djamba, Goldstein, and Goldstein 2000). Indeed, findings from two regional surveys conducted among Vietnamese older people in 1996 and 1997 revealed that many report receiving remittances from non–co-resident children (Bui et al. 2000). To further investigate alternative forms of support, we carried out an analysis using the information on remittances from the 1997–98 VLSS dataset.

REMITTANCE AS A MAJOR ALTERNATIVE FORM OF SUPPORT

To examine the receipt of remittances from non–co-residing children, we restricted the analysis to older people with at least one non–co-residing child. Similarly, to examine differentials by sex of the sender, the study limited the analysis of remittances from sons to older persons with at least one non–co-residing son and the analysis of remittances from daughters to those with at least one non–co-residing daughter.

The analysis shows that slightly over 20 percent of all people aged sixty and older have received remittances from a non–co-residing child in the previous twelve months, 16 percent from a son, and 12 percent from a daughter.[5] However, it is unlikely that each member of an elderly couple would receive remittances from their children. Indeed, the VLSS phrases questions referring to remittances in such a way that it obliges the respondent to designate a single beneficiary, while the actual intent in sending money to ageing parents would probably have been to benefit both of them. This would also explain why the proportion of women who received remittances is so much lower than that of men (10 percent and 30 percent, respectively). Accounting for this bias, I estimated the proportion of all households with an older person in which remittances had been received from a child over the past twelve months. The percentage of beneficiary households then increases to 35 percent. In addition, this approach also indicates that women are more likely than men to live in a household that receives remittances from children. The proportions are 37 percent of women and 33 percent of men. Women benefit from remittances both directly, when they are widowed and living alone, and indirectly, through their husband when they are still married. Since remittances from children are sent twice as often to a one-person household (the proportion reaches 60 percent) than to a couple-only household (33 percent), and, since women are more often living alone, they are also more likely to receive remittances than men.

The data further show that sons send support more often (to 25 percent of all households in which at least one older person lives) than daughters do (to less than 20 percent of such households), though the difference between the two sexes is unexpectedly small considering the cultural context. It is quite possible that daughters, especially while single but also possibly after marriage, have always been a source of support to their ageing parents in Vietnam. This might have been particularly so in the southern part of the country where Southeast Asian cultural patterns, more egalitarian than those of Eastern Asia, prevailed. The contribution of adult daughters to their parents' households could also be a new phenomenon, resulting from the rising age at marriage and the increasing participation of unmarried women in the labor force, as discussed in other chapters of this volume (see in particular those written by Danièle Bélanger and Katherine Pendakis; Rukmalie Jayakody and Vu Tuan Huy; Truong Huyen Chi; and Peter Xenos et al.). However, had I been able to take into account the amount sent, the gap might have been significantly larger.

Age of the recipient also appears as a factor, with the oldest old receiving support more often than others. The proportion of households with an older person having received remittances over the previous twelve months increases from 30 percent when at least one member is aged sixty to sixty-nine, to nearly 60 percent when a person aged eighty or older resides there. Wealthier households and households located in urban areas are also more likely to receive remittances from non–co-residing children. The proportion is about three times higher for the richest household compared with the poorest (50 percent and 17 percent, respectively), and those in urban areas are about fifty percent more likely to receive remittances than those in rural areas (46 percent and

31 percent, respectively). However, many of these factors are interrelated. For instance, wealthier households are more frequently found in urban than in rural areas. Women are also more likely to be older and widowed, while men are more likely than women to live in a couple-only household rather than in a one-person household. A multivariate analysis is thus required to disentangle the separate influence of each variable and to estimate their net effects, independently from that of the others.

Three logistic regressions using the 1997–98 VLSS data estimate the odds of having received remittances during the previous twelve months, depending on the sex of the sending child. We obtained results from non–co-residing children (Table 5.7, first model in column 1 under "Remittances received from"), from non–co-residing sons (second model in column 2), and from non–co-residing daughters (third model in column 3) for the people aged sixty or older. The covariates in the models include the following characteristics of the beneficiary: sex (male versus female), age group (sixty to sixty-nine, seventy to seventy-nine, and eighty and older), household structure (one-person, couple only, couple with unmarried children, single head with unmarried children, parents with married children, other structure), household income group (five categories from poorest to richest as defined in the survey), and place of residence (rural or urban).[6] All variables were dichotomized. The reference category for all models is men, aged sixty to sixty-nine, living alone, in the lowest income group, in a rural area. The analysis results in Table 5.7 present odds ratios, rather than coefficients, to facilitate interpretation of the results. A ratio significantly above one indicates a positive relationship between the independent variable (having received remittances from a child over the previous twelve months) and the indicator tested; a ratio significantly lower than one indicates a negative relationship between the two variables.

Multivariate analysis confirms that women are more likely to receive remittances from either sons or daughters than men (OR = 1.27 versus 1). They are also more likely to receive some form of support as they become older (OR = 1.88 at ages seventy to seventy-nine and 2.32 at ages eighty and older versus 1.00 at ages sixty to sixty-nine in the first model). Furthermore, the analysis confirms that isolated older people (those living either alone or with a spouse only) are more likely to receive remittances from their children than those who are co-residing with a married or unmarried child. The possible exception is those in a single-headed household (the odds ratio is below one, but

TABLE 5.7

Odds ratios for three logistic regressions on the reception of remittances over the previous twelve months from non–co-residing children in Vietnam (all individuals aged 60+ with at least one child/son/daughter)

Independent variable	Remittances received from		
	Any child Odds ratio *p*>z	Any son Odds ratio *p*>z	Any daughter Odds ratio *p*>z
Sex			
Male (ref.)	*1.000*	*1.000*	*1.000*
Female	1.267*	1.209	1.256
Age group			
60–69 (ref.)	*1.000*	*1.000*	*1.000*
70–79	1.884***	1.521***	1.857***
80+	2.319***	2.616***	3.099***
Household structure			
One-person (ref.)	*1.000*	*1.000*	*1.000*
Couple only	1.119	1.847	1.109
Couple with unmarried children	0.363**	0.645	0.451
Single head with unmarried children	0.694	0.764	1.463
Parent(s) with married children	0.349**	0.538	0.548
Other structure	0.710	1.036	1.206
Household income group			
Poorest (ref.)	*1.000*	*1.000*	*1.000*
Poor-mid	3.140***	2.550***	3.508***
Middle	3.152***	2.769***	3.460***
Mid-upper	2.627***	2.960***	2.487**
Richest	4.939***	4.346***	4.881***
Place of residence			
Rural area (ref.)	*1.000*	*1.000*	*1.000*
Urban area	1.611***	1.325*	1.939***
Number of observations	1502	1299	1332
Prob > Chi2	0.0000	0.0000	0.0000
Log-likelihood	−867.41	−713.75	−645.28
Pseudo R2	0.1071	0.0878	0.0981

***p <0.01 ; **p <0.05 ; *p <0.1

SOURCE: Author's analysis of the *1997–1998 Vietnam Living Standard Survey* data, World Bank, 2001.

it is not significant). Indeed, the odds of receiving remittances for the first two household categories are three times higher than those for elderly couples living with married or unmarried children. However, there is no significant difference in the odds of receiving remittances between one-person and couple-only households. Socioeconomic characteristics also appear to influence significantly the odds of receiving remittances, as older people living in urban areas and in wealthier households are more likely to receive support from non–co-residing children than the rural and poor elderly. Though both variables show a significant net effect, it is smaller for area of residence (OR = 1.61 for older people in urban areas versus 1.00 for those in rural areas). By contrast, the effect of wealth is very strong. In fact, it is the strongest effect of all variables in the model, with an odds of receiving remittances five times larger for older people in the richest households than for those in the poorest (OR = 4.94 versus 1.00). This finding can be explained either by the fact that remittances represent the main source of the recipient's wealth or by the fact that offspring of wealthy households are themselves more likely to be wealthy, and, thus, in a position to send money or goods to their ageing parents. Other authors have interpreted results of this type as reverse causality: children of wealthier parents would be more likely to send assistance in the hope of receiving a larger share of the inheritance (Knodel, Chayovan, and Siriboon 1996).

The variables operate in the same direction whether we consider remittances from any child (model in first column under "Remittances received from" in Table 5.7) or whether we look separately at remittances sent by sons (second column in Table 5.7) and remittances sent by daughters (third column in Table 5.7). However, the one interesting difference is that for every significant variable, the effect is stronger in the third than in the second model. In other words, though overall, daughters are less likely than sons are to send remittances to their ageing parents, their sending behavior is more strongly influenced by their parents' circumstances than that of sons. For instance, the odds of a daughter sending remittances to her parents are three times higher when the parents are very old (age eighty and older under "Independent variable" in Table 5.7) than when they are younger (age sixty to sixty-nine), while, for sons, they are only about 2.5 times higher. Similarly, the odds of a daughter sending remittances are about twice as high when the parents live in an urban area than when they live in a rural area. For sons, the odds are only 30 percent higher.

In conclusion, the results of multivariate modeling indicate, as initially hypothesized, that geographic distance between adult children and their ageing parents should not be interpreted as a sign of indifference. They also point to the often underestimated role of daughters compared with that of sons. Though the study found that daughters are less likely to live with their ageing parents than sons are and equally less likely to send financial assistance, their contribution is not insignificant. All of these results confirm earlier findings in other, more geographically restricted, studies (Knodel, Chayovan, and Siri-boon 1996). The research findings imply that the intensification of migration does not necessarily jeopardize intergenerational solidarities and that children continue to take responsibility for their ageing parents even when they live apart and especially when the parents are in a particularly vulnerable situation, such as without a spouse or in age groups when disability increases.

Conclusion

Combining information from two different sources of quantitative data, I found that though increasing geographic mobility puts pressure on traditional family patterns because younger people are more likely to move than older persons, co-residence between adult children and their ageing parents remains the norm in Vietnam, with about 75 percent of all people aged sixty and older living with at least one child, most often a son. This finding runs counter to modern theory of the necessary shift in household composition prior to rapid economic development (Cain and McNicoll 1988; Goody 1996). Families in Vietnam have developed alternative strategies of elderly support in response to their changing environment, in keeping with firmly rooted values of elderly care by their immediate family. When still young, and presumably healthy enough, ageing parents follow or join their adult children moving out. For those who are too old or fragile to follow their migrant children and especially for those left without co-residing children, intergenerational support takes the form of remittances. Such a situation is certainly a source of strain on both the parents and their adult children. Sons, in particular, must be torn between the cultural obligations of caring for their ageing parents and the social pressure, possibly originating from within their family, to seize the new economic opportunities and move away from their original household. I acknowledge however that reducing intergenerational support to co-residence and financial transfers is an oversimplification likely to underestimate the true level of exchange between generations. Such a reduction overlooks a whole set of other major forms of support, such as the type of general care that can be provided by children who do not live in the same dwelling but who live in the same village or neighborhood. The oversimplification results from the constraints of the data available as well as those of statistical analysis with its binary decision (co-residence versus

non–co-residence), which ignores the diversity of living arrangements between married children and their ageing parents. Other forms of goods and
service transfers from children to their ageing parents' households, as well as
emotional support in the form of frequent visiting or daily phone calls, are
similarly overlooked. In spite of such limitations, I believe that the analysis
has succeeded in demonstrating the continuity of traditional support of the
older generation by the younger and that, had the data allowed me to take
into account all forms of exchange, the results would have simply reinforced
our main conclusion.

There are, however, a number of troublesome points highlighted by the
study for the future of older people in Vietnam. For one thing, a sizeable
proportion of isolated older people—about 15 percent of those aged sixty-
five to sixty-nine and 20 percent of those aged seventy and older—live by
themselves or with a spouse only. Among them, quite a significant proportion is childless (40 to 45 percent) or has received no material help from their
children over a relatively long period of time (one year).

The proportion of the population aged sixty and older will increase only
moderately during the first two decades of the twenty-first century. However, the proportion of very old adults will be significantly greater over that
period, given the faster growth occurring among the "oldest old" (those aged
seventy-five and older) compared with the "younger old." This is relevant to
this discussion because the "oldest old" are more likely to be disabled. They
stand a much greater risk of long-term illnesses and loss of independence,
and they are in much greater need of extensive care. The sex imbalance that
leads to a higher risk of widowhood for women also increases with age so
that, even though the overall proportion of older people in Vietnam over the
next twenty years does not pose a threat, the proportion of dependent and
isolated older people will likely grow significantly.

Furthermore, future demographic trends do not cast an optimistic light
on the situation of older people. The continuing decline in the average number of offspring, which resulted from the rapid fertility transition experienced in Vietnam, has yet to show most of its effects on the situation of older
people. This trend will only be slightly counterbalanced by the increasing
odds of the children surviving to adulthood. The significant proportion of
daughters supporting their ageing parents, though considerably lower than
that of sons when we combine co-residence and remittances, could be a sign

of adaptation to this context. However, whether sons or daughters, adult children will be under considerable strain when, together with their spouses, they become the only potential caregivers to both their own parents and their parents-in-law. In addition, the major socioeconomic changes, which continue to characterize Vietnam, are likely to foster a further increase in migration flows. This is particularly likely considering the relatively low rate of urbanization in the country, compared with the rest of the region or even to countries in other parts of the world with a comparable level of socio-economic development. Intensifying migration will result in an increasing proportion of isolated older people.

In particular, one might wonder whether geographic distance will eventually make it more difficult for ageing parents to rely on their migrant children. As for those parents who move with or join their children, they may find it difficult to adjust to a new geographic setting, especially when moving from a rural to an urban area. Furthermore, to the extent that housing conditions are better in rural than in urban areas, the move is likely to be detrimental to their quality of life.

On the bright side, however, this very socioeconomic development also means that young adults who are willing to migrate in search of economic opportunities will more likely benefit economically and socially from their change of residence. Thus, they will be in a better position to provide some kind of material support to their ageing parents.

In conclusion, the current period, with its relatively low proportion of older persons in the population, should be one of experimentation and close monitoring in which the government can develop programs designed to help young adults care for their ageing parents before the gains in mortality and the accelerated fall in fertility, observed during the past two decades, show their full effects on the ageing population. While the well-being of the elderly might not be a current priority for the government, since fewer than 10 percent of the population is over sixty, it will most likely become a major one after 2020 when this proportion more than doubles to reach 25 percent. Therefore, the current period is a window of opportunity for the research community and policy makers alike to better understand the phenomenon before pressure becomes too strong to ignore it any longer.

Notes

1. For a recent review of the elderly residential patterns in a variety of geographical settings, see United Nations, *Living Arrangements of Older Persons Around the World*, Economic and Social Affairs, New York, 2005.

2. The United Nations projection used here is the low variant, as the other variants are based on fertility levels significantly higher in 2000–2005 than those recorded in the latest Demographic and Health Survey (2002). The Total Fertility Rate is 1.9 in the low variant versus 2.1 in the medium variant, 2.4 in the high variant, and 2.3 in the constant variant, while the DHS showed a level already as low as 1.87 for the period 1998–2002 (National Committee for Population, Family and Children and ORC Macro 2003).

3. To our knowledge, there have only been two such surveys carried out in Vietnam, namely the 1996 Survey of the Elderly in the Red River Delta, undertaken by the Hanoi Institute of Sociology, and the 1997 Survey of the Elderly in Ho Chi Minh City and Environs, undertaken by the Ho Chi Minh City Institute of Economic Research. Both surveys were conducted on a local sample, and the number of interviewees was quite small (930 and 840, respectively, in each survey) (Truong et al. 1997). Data from these two surveys are not available for public access.

4. The questions on remittances asked in the 1997–98 VLSS were phrased as follows: "During the past 12 months, has any member of your household received money or goods from persons who are not members of your household?" If the answer was "Yes," then the household head was asked, "What is the relationship of [name of the people who sent money or goods] to the person who received money?" "Child" was one of the possible answers. The sex of the sender and the place of residence relative to that of the respondent were documented.

5. Because an elderly person might have received remittances from several of his or her children, both sons and daughters, the percentage having received remittances from any son and the percentage having received remittances from any daughter do not add up to the total percentage of those having received remittances from any child.

6. In fact, because of the previously discussed bias, we did not distinguish between those older adults who directly received remittances, for example those specifically designated by the survey respondent as the beneficiary, from those who received remittances through spouses.

References

Barbieri, M. 2003. Le Viêt-Nam: Guerre, communisme et libéralisme. In *La population du monde. Géants démographiques et défis internationaux*, edited by J.-C. Chasteland and J.-C. Chesnais, 417–434. Les Cahiers de l'INED no. 149, Second updated edition. Paris: PUF-INED.

Bélanger, D. 1997. Modes de cohabitation et liens intergénérationnels au Vietnam. *Cahiers québécois de démographie* 26(2): 215–245.

Bui The Cuong, Truong S. A., D. Goodkind, J. Knodel, and J. Friedman. 2000. Older people in Vietnam amidst transformations in social welfare policy. In *Ageing in the Asia-Pacific region, issues, policies and future trends*, edited by D. R. Philips, 334–359. London and New York: Routledge.

Cain, M., and G. McNicoll. 1988. Population growth and agrarian outcomes. In *Population, food, and rural development*, edited by R. D. Lee et al. Oxford, U.K.: Oxford University Press.

Cangping, W., and D. Peng. 1994. The demographic aspects of population ageing in China: Social and economic implications. In *Short-term training in the demographic aspects of population ageing and its implications for socio-economic development, policies and plans*. Report of the expert group meeting held in Malta, December 6–9, 1993: 54–65. International Institute on Ageing. Malta: United Nations.

Chang, T. P. 1992. Implications of changing family structures on old-age support in the ESCAP region. *Asia-Pacific Population Journal* 2: 49–66.

Cho, L.-J., and M. Yada, eds. 1994. *Tradition and change in the Asian family*. Honolulu: East-West Center.

Dang Nguyen Anh. 1999. Market reforms and internal labor migration in Vietnam. *Asian and Pacific Migration Journal* 8(3): 381–409.

Dang Nguyen Anh, C. Tacoli, and Hoang X. T. 2003. Migration in Vietnam: A review of information on current trends and patterns, and their policy implications. *Regional Conference on Migration, Development Pro-Poor Policy Choices in Asia*, 22–24 June, Dhaka, Bangladesh.

Davis, D., and S. Harrell, eds. 1993. *Chinese families in the post-Mao Era*. Berkeley, Los Angeles, and London: California University Press.

Djamba, Y. K., S. Goldstein, and A. Goldstein. 2000. Migration and occupational changes during periods of economic transition: Women and men in Vietnam. *Asian and Pacific Migration Journal* 9(1): 65–92.

Friedman, J., D. Goodkind, Bui T. C., and Truong S. A. 1999. *Work and retirement among the elderly in Vietnam*. Population Studies Center Research Reports no. 99-442. Ann Arbor: University of Michigan.

Friedman, J., J. Knodel, Bui T. C., and Truong S. A. 2002. *Gender and intergenerational exchange in Vietnam*. Population Studies Center Research Reports no. 02-529. Ann Arbor: University of Michigan.

General Statistics Office. 2000. *Vietnam living standards survey 1997–1998.* Hanoi: Statistical Publishing House.

General Statistics Office. 2001. *1999 Population and housing census. Census monograph on marriage, fertility and mortality in Viet Nam: Level, trends and differentials.* Hanoi: Statistical Publishing House.

General Statistics Office. 2003. *Vietnam demographic and health survey 2002.* National committee for population, family and children, population and family health project. Hanoi: Statistical Publishing House and Calverton: ORC Macro.

Goody, J. 1996. Comparing family systems in Europe and Asia: Are there different sets of rules? *Population and Development Review* 22(1): 1–20.

Haines, D. W. 2006. *The limits of kinship: South Vietnamese households 1954–1975.* DeKalb: Southeast Asia Publications, Northern Illinois University.

Ham-Chande, R. 1994. Mexico: Does a young society have to worry about ageing? In *Short-term training in the demographic aspects of population ageing and its implications for socio-economic development, policies and plans.* Report of the expert group meeting held in Malta, December 6-9, 1993: 41–53. International Institute on Ageing. Malta: United Nations.

Hermalin, A. I., M. B. Ofstedal, and M.-C. Chang. 1996. Types of supports for the aged and their providers in Taiwan. In *Ageing and generational relations: Life-course and cross-cultural perspectives,* edited by T. K. Hareven: 179–216. New York: Aldine de Gruyter.

Hong, M.-S., and Y.-C. Byun. 1998. Intergenerational relations in South Korea. In *The changing family in comparative perspective: Asia and the United States,* edited by K. Oppenheim Mason, N. O. Tsuya, and M. K. Choe: 175–192. Honolulu: East-West Center.

International Institute on Ageing. 1994. *Short-term training in the demographic aspects of population ageing and its implications for socio-economic development, policies and plans.* Report of the expert group meeting held in Malta, December 6–9, 1993. Malta: United Nations.

Keyfitz, N. 2005. *Applied mathematical demography,* 3rd ed. New York and Berlin: Springer.

Knodel, J., J. Friedman, Truong S. A., and Bui T. C. 1998. *Intergenerational exchanges in Vietnam: Family size, sex composition, and the location of children,* Population Studies Center Research Reports no. 98-430. Ann Arbor: University of Michigan Press.

Knodel, J., N. Chayovan, and S. Siriboon. 1996. Familial support and the life course of Thai elderly and their children. In *Ageing and generational relations: Life-course and cross-cultural perspectives,* edited by T. K. Hareven: 217–240. New York: Aldine de Gruyter.

Knodel, J., and Truong S. A. 2002. *Vietnam's older population: The view from the census,* Population Studies Center Research Reports no. 02-523. Ann Arbor: University of Michigan Press.

Luong, Hy Van. 1992. *Revolution in the village: Tradition and transformation in North Vietnam, 1925–1988.* Honolulu: University of Hawaii Press.

Martin, L. G., and K. Kinsella. 1994. Research on the demography of ageing in developing countries. In *Demography of ageing,* edited by L. G. Martin and S. H. Preston: 356–403. Washington DC: National Academy Press.

Mason, A., and T. Miller. 1998. Family and intergenerational income transfers in Taiwan. In *The changing family in comparative perspective: Asia and the United States,* edited by K. Oppenheim Mason, N. O. Tsuya, and M. K. Choe: 215–234. Honolulu: East-West Center.

Merli, G. 2000. Socioeconomic background and war mortality during Vietnam's wars. *Demography* 37(1): 1–15.

Morioka, K. 1996. Generational relations and their changes as they affect the status of older people in Japan. In *Ageing and generational relations. life-course and cross-cultural perspectives,* edited by T. K. Hareven: 263–281. New York: Aldine de Gruyter.

National Committee for Population, Family and Children, Hanoi, Vietnam, and ORC Macro. 2003. *Vietnam demographic and health survey 2002.* Calverton, MD: ORC.

Nguyen Van Chinh. 2001. Work versus education? An empirical study of rural education in a transitional economy of Vietnam. In *Vietnamese society in transition: The daily politics of reform and change,* edited by J. Kleinen: 64–101. Amsterdam: Het Spinhuis.

Philips, D. R., ed. 2000. *Ageing in the Asia-Pacific region, issues, policies and future trends.* London and New York: Routledge.

Raymo, J. M., and T. Kaneda. 2003. Changes in the living arrangements of Japanese elderly: The role of demographic factors. In *demographic change and the family in Japan's ageing society,* edited by J. W. Traphagan and J. Knight: 27–52. Albany: State University of New York Press.

Traphagan, J. W., and J. Knight. 2003. *Demographic change and the family in Japan's ageing society.* Albany: State University of New York Press.

Truong Si Anh, Bui T. C., D. Goodkind, and J. Knodel. 1997. Living arrangements, patrilinearity and sources of support among elderly Vietnamese. *Asia-Pacific Population Journal* 12(4): 69–88.

United Nations. 2005. World population prospects: The 2004 revision, population division. New York: United Nations.

Whyte, M. K. 2003. *China's evolutions and intergenerational relations.* Ann Arbor: University of Michigan Press.

World Bank. 2001. *Vietnam living standards survey (VLSS), 1997–98. Basic information,* April. Washington, DC: World Bank, Poverty and Human Resources Division.

PART THREE

Marriage and the Transition to Adulthood

Chapter Six

From Youth to Adulthood
Benchmarks and Pathways in Modern Vietnam

PETER XENOS, NGUYEN DUY KHE, NGUYEN HUU
MINH, MARGARET SHEEHAN, VU MANH LOI,
LE THI MINH CHAU, AND NGUYEN DINH CHUNG

That significant social change accompanies large scale economic transformation is axiomatic, and it is equally apparent that many of the most dramatic social changes involved affect youth disproportionately. In societies undergoing rapid change, young people find themselves in a whirlpool of society-wide adjustment and change just as they are navigating critical personal transformations and, along the way, making crucial long-term choices for their lives. The proximate context for this tumultuous experience includes families, schools, communities, and labor markets—the institutions in which the majority of young people are most directly imbedded.

The adolescent and young adult years are being reshaped nearly everywhere by changes in these institutions. Today's youth are much more likely to spend a longer period in formal schooling, outside the formal system of labor and, very often until the third decade of life, outside marriage, thus, removed from the concerns of marriage and childbearing. That is to say, in these institutional terms, today's youth are experiencing key transitional events—leaving school, entering the formal workforce, forming a union, getting pregnant, becoming parents—much more slowly, much later in their lives, than in the past. One can think of a "lengthening ladder" or "raised bar" for adulthood (Larson 2002).

In contrast, young people today are more likely to be physiologically mature at a younger age than in the past. In most societies, they are likely involved, from an ever-earlier age and sometimes quite intensely, in an emergent set of distinct "youth institutions" centered, generally, on peer groups and, in particular, heterosexual relationships. At the same time, the social worlds of today's youth are often extraordinarily large and complex, relative to the experiences of earlier generations. The ongoing transportation and communication revolutions and, more recently, the Internet and cell phone have shaped this new and formative feature of modern youth culture. Much contemporary theorizing on youth explores these aspects of modernity under the broad rubric of globalization (Brown and Larson 2002; Bucholtz 2002; Lloyd 2005; Ruddick 2003; Schlegel 2000).

All this is certainly happening, and with even greater intensity, in modern Vietnam, and one is tempted to suggest that the government's policy of *Doi Moi* is the primary cause. Economic renovation or the "opening" began in 1986 and since then has generated a corresponding social opening of Vietnamese society on a very broad front. The new policies have introduced a combination of opportunity and choice, along with uncertainty, into the lives of the nation's youth. The gradual shift toward markets as arbitrators of value has had considerable impact on the key youth institutions (Jeffrey and McDowell 2004; Schlegel 2000; for a focus on Vietnam, see Long et al. 2000; Marr and Rosen 1998; Nilan 1999).

At the same time, certain other aspects of young people's lives seem to offer a measure of stability. Notably, today's youth are more likely to have surviving parents and siblings (though in smaller numbers) than in the past, their families are likely to be intact, and emotional and social connections with families remain strong. In fact, youth are very likely to continue living with their families of origin throughout most of their adolescent and young adult years. Evidence establishes the continuing importance of the family of orientation or upbringing as the material, social, and emotional context for young adult experiences. Facilitating the successful transitions of offspring to adult life is certainly one of the core tasks of families. Therefore, understanding changes in these transitions, and the role of families in them, provides an interesting and potentially important window on the broader question of interest in this volume: how recent economic transformations in Vietnam may be reorganizing the social fabric in general, and the family in particular.

In this chapter, we examine a recent national survey of Vietnamese youth to provide a perspective on the functioning of Vietnamese families in the era of *Doi Moi*. Although it was designed for a rather different purpose, the 2003 Survey and Assessment of Vietnamese Youth (SAVY) provides some interesting glimpses into Vietnamese family life through the responses of the young people living in those families. The interviewees were aged fourteen through twenty-five years in 2003. The oldest, therefore, reached their teenage years just as the *Doi Moi* era was beginning, while the youngest became teenagers after Vietnam had witnessed more than a decade of rapid social change. We examine the questionnaire responses of 7,584 young people. We have provided further details on the survey in an appendix at the end of the chapter. For a full exposition of the survey methodology, see Ministry of Health and General Statistics Office (2005).

Families exist everywhere because some type of family system is required to carry out certain critical functions of society, among these are material survival, the regulation and enabling of reproduction, and the preparation of offspring for adult life (Coser 1974, xv–xxviii; Waite 2001). In this chapter, we focus on one of these critical functions: the preparation of children for adult life. We examine some of the important events in the transitions toward adulthood, as reported by survey respondents, and then look for ways to gauge the significance of young people's families in those events.

A "transition to adulthood" framework is generally relevant to the study of adolescent and young adult segments of life (Furstenberg et al. 2002; Hogan and Astone 1986; Lloyd 2005; Modell, Furstenberg, and Hershberg 1976; Shanahan 2000). This framework highlights key markers of the transition, including *school leaving, work for pay, home leaving, entrance to marriage, first pregnancy* and *first birth*. These events are all described in the SAVY interviews, as understanding the transition to adulthood was one of the core interests underlying SAVY's design and questionnaire content, particularly as it relates to young people's adaptation to modern social and economic life. In addition, a policy and program interest in risk behaviors among Vietnamese youth (Ridge and Murphy 2002) motivated questioning in SAVY about events reflecting the first experience of certain risk behaviors, such as smoking, drinking, premarital sex, and early pregnancy. The survey also measured age at puberty as a fundamental biological marker (Marshall and Tanner 1986). This information supports a detailed analysis of transitional events and their configurations, including their variability, sequencing, extent of co-occurrence and the life segments defined by them (Shanahan 2000). In this chapter, we extract a general overview of the patterns and then relate them to the respondents' family situations, both at the time of the interviews and earlier in their lives.

It is important to note certain limitations inherent in the SAVY data. Though providing a nationally representative sample of teenagers and young adults, SAVY cannot give us a complete picture of the transition to adult-hood among them, because modern Vietnamese cohorts do not generally complete the full transition to adulthood until the mid-to-late twenties.[1] The cross-sectional survey design and the size of the SAVY sample is more suited to an analytic approach that focuses on experiences up to twenty years of age among those survey respondents aged twenty years and older at the time of the survey. For this reason, we are really considering life experiences dur-ing the second decade of life (through age nineteen) and the place of families as the social context for those experiences.

This is an important segment of life everywhere—a time of discovery and new experiences. The pattern and tempo of benchmark events during these years varies across societies, but one generalization seems to be valid: in all settings studied, there is an extraordinary burst of new experiences during the adolescent and young adult years (Rindfuss 1991; see Xenos et al. 2006 for Asian examples and Nahar 2007). Rindfuss emphasizes that these years are "demographically dense" and diverse as to the range of roles and event sequences experienced. The pattern is worth noting even if one does not take a classic "storm and stress" (Arnett 1999) perspective with regard to likely implications. Subsequently, we will offer evidence of the same kind of high demographic density among teenagers in modern Vietnam.

SAVY provides a limited, but useful, set of indicators of family life and function. Without being at all comprehensive, we are able to glean some important elements of the overall picture. First, we describe how very high proportions of the reported events occurred while respondents were still living at home. This certainly is true of early events, such as *school entrance* and *puberty*, but it is also often true of events at somewhat older ages, such as *school leaving* and *entrance to marriage*. Second, we illustrate several of the numerous connections, causal and otherwise, that exist among family life, family influences, and one or more of the transition events. We focus on the events most closely related to personal independence (*school leaving, home leaving*, and starting *work for pay*).

Comparative Transitional Patterns

Personal life course changes lie at the heart of all the modern macroscale demographic transitions, including Vietnam's demographic transformation over the last few decades. With effective control over many causes of death, mortality rates have declined sharply. Vietnamese born recently are looking forward to nearly seven decades of life (see Barbieri, this volume). This carries important implications, not only for population-level and personal-level ageing, but for the young as well. When overall mortality is low, mortality after childhood, especially in the teenage and young adult years, is a rare experience. Moreover, almost all of those who reach age twenty will go on to complete their entire family-building careers and working lives.[2] The personal implication of this for a young person is evident; however, there is an additional important implication for the society as a whole. Resources expended by families, or by the national government, aimed at making better transitions to adulthood possible can translate efficiently into many effective and productive years of adult life.

This is the positive side of the marked policy and program emphasis on youth in recent years (Blum and Nelson-Mmari 2004; Greene, Rasekh, and Amen 2002; Kirby 2001; Mortimer and Larson 2002; for a focus on Vietnam, see Committee on Population, Family and Children 2003; Ministry of Health and General Statistics Office 2005; Ridge and Murphy 2002). However, much more often, we hear the negative side, in the form of grave concerns over incomplete or dysfunctional transitions to adulthood, very often associated with diverse, and even multiple, patterns of risk taking during the transition (Bell and Bell 1993; Jessor, Turbin, and Costa 1999). Many of the programs in Vietnam and around the world that seek to limit the prevalence of risk behaviors utilize some form of a risk and resilience model focused on "reducing factors known to increase the potential for problem behaviors ("risk factors"), while emphasizing those factors known to promote resilience, or young people's capacity to cope in difficult times ("protective factors")" (Ministry of Health and General Statistics Office 2005; see Blum and Rinehart 1997; Kirby 2001).

The overall conclusion for Vietnam, presented in the main report and based on SAVY analysis, reads as follows:

> Considering young people in the context of their own family dynamics is a useful lens through which to consider the values of the risk and protective framework. SAVY establishes that most young people, even those in difficult situations, appear to remain connected to family, are prepared to work hard for their families, respect their families, and look forward to having a family of their own. These are all significant protective factors that can strengthen

young people's self-esteem and boost resilience. At the same time, there are adolescents who are not connected to their families, and this can pose potential problems in terms of the status of their physical and mental health. (Ministry of Health and General Statistics Office 2005, part 1, 16)

Lying behind these modern concerns about risk behaviors is the recognition that contemporary youth in Vietnam, as throughout much of the developing world, find themselves caught at the conjuncture of dramatic and multiple social transformations, which they must negotiate with the support of their communities and especially their peer groups and families. These transformations are essential background to the present analysis.

THE EXTENSION OF SCHOOLING

Mass education is a modern phenomenon, with the necessary institutions appearing in the early nineteenth century for a very few societies and by the second half of the twentieth century for others, including most Asian societies (Benavot and Riddle 1988; Boli, Ramirez, and Meyer 1985). In the initial phase of the revolution, there were more changes in the lives of children, compared to adolescents and young adults. Nevertheless, at a later point, mass education and the advent of large tertiary enrollments extended well into the second half of the teenage years and even beyond. Asia, including Vietnam, has participated fully in this historic transformation in the lives of young people. Figure 6.1 illustrates the magnitude of the change by showing gross enrollment ratios at the secondary level for males and females in Vietnam and neighboring countries of Southeast Asia at available dates. Clearly, Vietnam has been a strong participant in the region's education revolution, surging well ahead of Myanmar, the Lao Peoples Democratic Republic, and Cambodia and somewhat behind Brunei, the Philippines, and Singapore. Among all these countries, regardless of the prevailing enrollment level in 1970, there had been roughly a 50 percent increase in secondary enrollment ratios by 1995. The much higher levels prevailing in East Asia and the much lower levels found in much of South and West Asia are not shown. Vietnam's pattern does have certain features of its own. There was little increase (but relative to an already-high level) between 1970 and 1985, then a decline in enrollment rates in the early years of *Doi Moi* (see Glewwe and Jacoby 1998; Le 1991), followed by a surge in enrollment rates during the 1990s. This surge is evident at the tertiary level as well (c.f. Institute of International Education 2004, 5). There are two

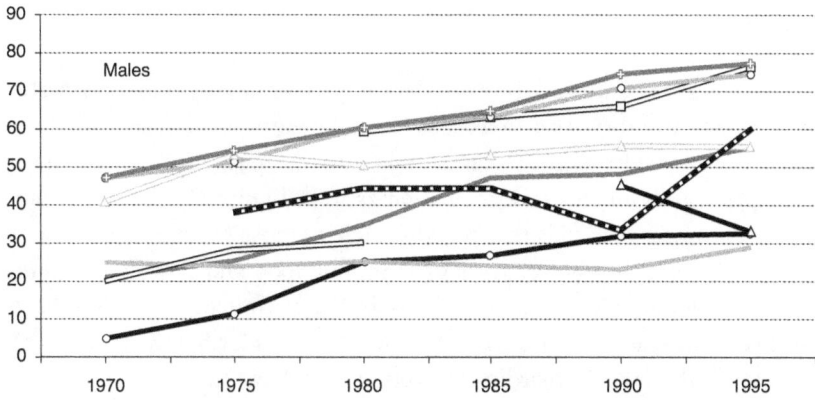

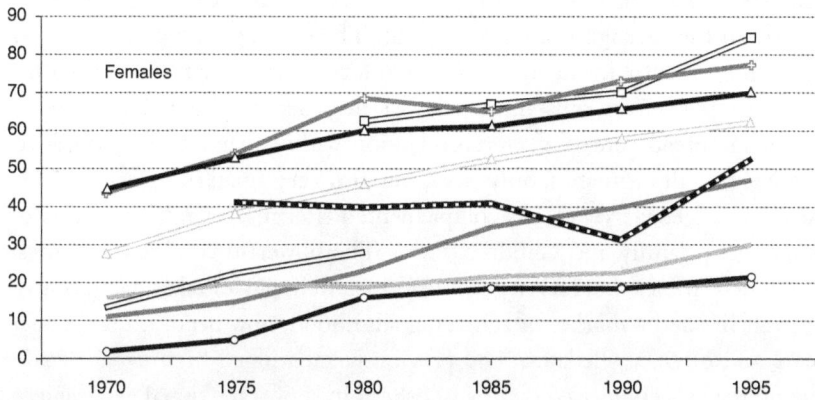

Figure 6.1 Secondary enrollment ratios, Southeast Asia, 1970–1995.
Source: UNESCO 1999, Table II-8, and General Statistics Office 2000, Table 2.3.1.

implications, in particular, to note here. First, in the cross-section or snapshot provided by any recent census or survey of Vietnam, the proportion currently enrolled in the youth age range will be high. By the time SAVY was conducted in 2003, the majority of both males and females aged fifteen to nineteen years in Vietnam were currently enrolled in school (58 percent in the SAVY sample), and even 13 percent of those aged twenty to twenty-four years were currently enrolled. Second, the age at *school leaving*, a key event in the adulthood transition, has risen markedly as we will be seeing shortly.

THE EXTENSION OF SINGLEHOOD

Another well-documented transformation is a dramatic, and remarkably uniform, shift across Asia, toward much later ages at marriage for both men and women (Jones 1997; Xenos and Gultiano 1992, 2002). Vietnam has participated fully in this transformation as well. Figure 6.2 shows the percent of 20- to 24-year-olds that remain single in most Asian countries, with Vietnam indexed by the censuses of 1989 and 1999 and the SAVY results for 2003. Vietnam's levels and trends are in line with many other Southeast Asian countries, and females are well above the levels for South Asia, though much lower than the extraordinary levels in East Asia.[3]

These two trends—more time spent in school and considerably more time spent prior to the formation of lifetime unions—intervene quite obviously in the teenage years and beyond. They are emerging patterns that figure prominently in the event-history information described shortly. Both trends support a very substantial delay in the onset of childbirth and parenting. Widespread control over reproduction within marriage that produces relatively small ultimate family sizes, but also very small numbers of births during the teenage years, has complemented later marriage (Committee on Population, Family and Children 2003). The powerful confluence of these trends determines that marriage and family building, viewed as being central to adult life and a marker of achieving adulthood, now occur after the teen years and often much later. The previously mentioned high event-density among teens is comprised mainly of other kinds of transitional experiences, such as *school leaving*, and *work for pay*.

Economic Liberalization, Teenagers, and Families

It is worth pausing to recognize that this changing life course demography conspires with the ongoing renovation of economic and social policies to form a remarkable conjuncture. One underlying set of changes relates to the configuration of experience during the teenage years, as this has shifted toward long periods of school enrollment and even longer periods of single status, prior to marriage. *Doi Moi* adds another set of changes, creating competitive markets for jobs, schooling opportunities, and in other areas of life as well. This entirely new context for growing up tends to widen social and economic gaps between generations and, in particular, between parents and children by

100 ┬
 90 ┤
 80 ┤
 70 ┤
 60 ┤
 50 ┤   2003
 40 ┤   Vietnam
 30 ┤   1989 1999
 20 ┤
 10 ┤
  0 ┴
  1890 1900 1910 1920 1930 1940 1950 1960 1970 1980 1990 2000 2010
                          Year

Percent Single

100 ┬
 90 ┤
 80 ┤
 70 ┤   2003
 60 ┤   Vietnam
 50 ┤   1999
 40 ┤   1989
 30 ┤
 20 ┤
 10 ┤
  0 ┴
  1890 1900 1910 1920 1930 1940 1950 1960 1970 1980 1990 2000 2010
                          Year

Percent Single

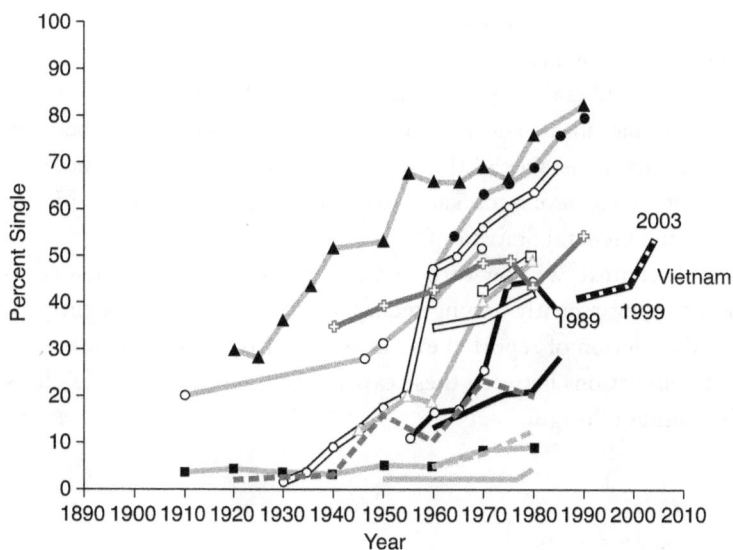

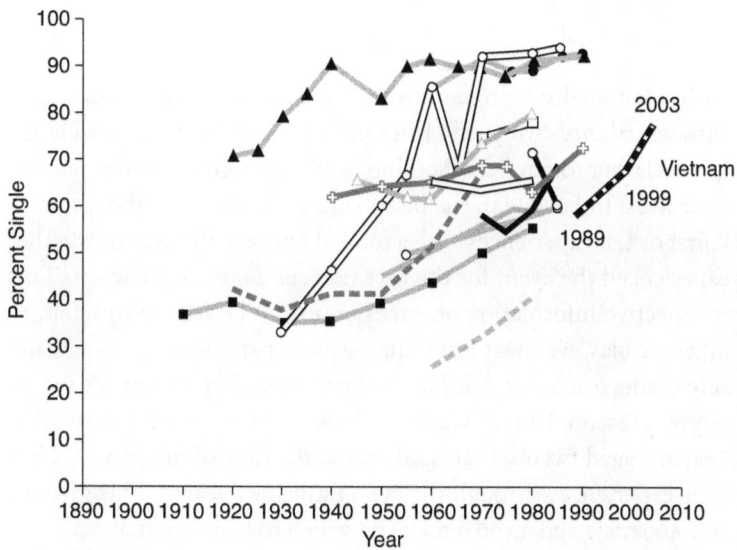

Bangladesh   Indonesia   Philippines
Burma   Japan   Singapore
Brunei   Korea   Sri Lanka
China   Malaysia   Taiwan
Hong Kong   Nepal   Thailand
India   Pakistan   Vietnam

Figure 6.2 Asian historical trend toward late marriage: Percent single at ages twenty to twenty-four.

creating new choices and experiences which were not available to older Viet-namese. The generation gap widens further with the important globalization aspect of economic liberalization, which inevitably takes the form of greater contact with people, ideas, and products from outside Vietnam. The most evident and dramatic instance of this is in the modern global mass media to which teenagers today have remarkably easy access (Berry et al. 1996; Minis-try of Health and General Statistics Office 2005; Nilan 1999).

Within this context, we now turn to SAVY to investigate what has actu-ally been occurring recently among teenagers in Vietnam. We begin with a statistical description of reported events and their patterns. Then we seek to illustrate connections between these experiences and young people's lives with their families of origin.

Events During the Teenage Years

ANALYTIC APPROACH

SAVY 2003 is a nationally representative sample of 7,584 Vietnamese, aged fourteen through twenty-five years. Interviews provided data on a wide va-riety of topics relating to family, schooling, work, peer group, and other do-mains of their lives. Imbedded in the interviews were questions about the re-spondents' first or last experiences with a total of fourteen life events: whether they had experienced the event for the first time, and if so, at what age. This kind of retrospective information on experiences can be very useful, but, to avoid an inherent bias, we must limit analysis to a particular age range and consider only events occurring prior to the lower boundary of that age range. In the analysis presented here, we have drawn retrospective information from respondents aged twenty years and over at the time of the survey. They describe their experiences through the age of nineteen years.[4] This gives us 2,975 cases (1,469 male and 1,506 female) on which to base our analysis.

Table 6.1 presents some general information on the SAVY data available for each set of events. The experiences described range from a physiologi-cal marker (*puberty*) that occurs only once, to some of the most conventional transition-to-adulthood events (*school entrance, school leaving, home leaving, work for pay, entrance to marriage*), to several events indicating the establishment of independent life as an adult (*entrance to marriage, first pregnancy, first birth*), and to events indicating behavioral choices sometimes associated with ado-

TABLE 6.1

General indicators for event information in SAVY 2003

INDICATOR Age Yrs	Physiological			Social					Marriage & Reproduction		
	Puberty	School Entrance	School Leaving	Work for Pay	Home Leaving	First Sex	First Smoking	First Drinking	Entrance to Marriage	First Pregnancy	First Birth
Persons at selected current ages reporting an event by that age (% of all those at specified age)											
16	87.4	97.7	30.2	36.5	13.5	0.9	10.0	38.9	0.1	0.0	0.0
18	96.1	96.5	55.2	52.7	29.8	7.0	21.7	54.6	4.5	3.5	2.4
20	96.5	94.9	76.2	67.2	39.3	26.2	29.3	57.9	19.1	4.3	9.8
22	96.3	94.3	77.9	81.2	50.7	47.6	30.6	58.5	38.9	25.7	21.2
25	97.2	92.9	89.1	87.8	47.6	65.0	39.3	61.6	43.5	33.3	31.1
Persons 20 to 25 years at the survey reporting this event (% of all those at specified age)											
15	48.0	92.6	42.5	17.4	5.3	0.6	5.0	6.1	0.4	0.0	0.0
17	85.4	93.8	55.4	34.7	13.2	4.1	12.9	16.8	2.6	1.4	0.8
19	94.5	100.0	70.3	50.8	32.6	18.8	26.2	38.8	13.6	7.7	5.4

SOURCE: Tabulated by the authors from Survey and Assessment of Vietnamese Youth (SAVY).

NOTE: Each event is defined by its first (and often only) occurrence. Puberty refers to the first wet dream for males or the first period (menarche) for females. School entrance and leaving are defined in terms of the formal school system. Work for pay includes work for family, but only if monetary remuneration is involved. Home leaving is defined by the earliest experience of being away from the family of upbringing for one month or longer. Sex refers to sexual intercourse. Smoking refers to ever trying tobacco products. Drinking refers to ever finishing a glass of beer or cup of liquor. Marriage refers to a socially acknowledged event. Birth refers to live parturition.

lescence (*first sex, first smoking, first drinking*). It is evident from Table 6.1 that these events are characterized by their timing (early or late) and by whether they commonly occur at all by age twenty or twenty-five. *Puberty, school entrance*, and to a degree *school leaving* and *work for pay* occur relatively early. *Puberty* and *school entrance* have occurred to the great majority of respondents by age sixteen. For 30 to 37 percent of respondents *school leaving* and *work for pay* have occurred by age sixteen, and for 67 to 76 percent of respondents they occurred by age twenty. In contrast, *home leaving* and *entrance to marriage* are uncommon experiences by age sixteen, or even age eighteen as well, and only 39 percent have left home and 19 percent have married by age twenty. Later, we examine the apparent gap between the experiences of leaving home and marriage. Similarly, the difference between the occurrence of marriage and first sexual experience warrants attention, but is not considered in this chapter (see Ministry of Health and General Statistics Office 2005, 46). The two additional behaviors, smoking and drinking, illustrate how the timing of events can reflect behavioral norms. The initiation of smoking is rare by age sixteen, but it reaches 39 percent by age twenty-five, whereas the consumption of alcohol begins at a much earlier age with 39 percent drinking by age sixteen and the majority by age twenty.[5]

Within this overall framework, we turn our discussion to the patterns of occurrence for *school leaving* and *work for pay* through age nineteen for both sexes (Figures 6.3a and 6.3b). For each of these events, a standard life-table framework gives us four interdependent pieces of information—four ways of looking at the experience. We have the distribution of events,[6] the distribution of cumulative events, and the number of "survivors." Survivors refers to those who have not experienced the event by each successive age (in traditional life-table usage the event of interest is death). Finally, we have the age pattern of rates. Each of these is the age-specific probability of occurrence in the life-table sense.[7]

The cumulative events curves rise across ages, and the survival curves correspondingly fall; only the tempo of the experience across ages varies with the event and by sex. Among the events shown in Table 6.1, there is a considerable difference between the puberty event and first marriage event. Puberty starts at a relatively young age and overtakes the sample cohort very rapidly (most puberty events are reported to occur within a three-year span for both sexes), while first marriage starts later and occurs over a much broader range of ages.

The pattern of age-specific events versus age-specific rates is particularly interesting. Typically, the peak rates of occurrence are a few years older than the peak number of events, since the rates have progressively smaller denominators (the survivors to the various ages). For example, rates for the *work for pay* event increase among males to high levels in the late teenage years because the young men who did not begin working for pay by age seventeen are highly likely to begin working in the following year or two.

Some other events (details not shown here) follow that general pattern (for example, *school entrance, school leaving, work for pay, first smoking, first drinking*). Other events such as *home leaving* and *entrance to marriage* reflect the fact that a large part of the cohort will experience these events only after age twenty. This applies also to *first sex, first pregnancy,* and *first birth.*

It is important to recognize that reports on the puberty experience are relatively complete, while reports on the marriage experience are somewhat

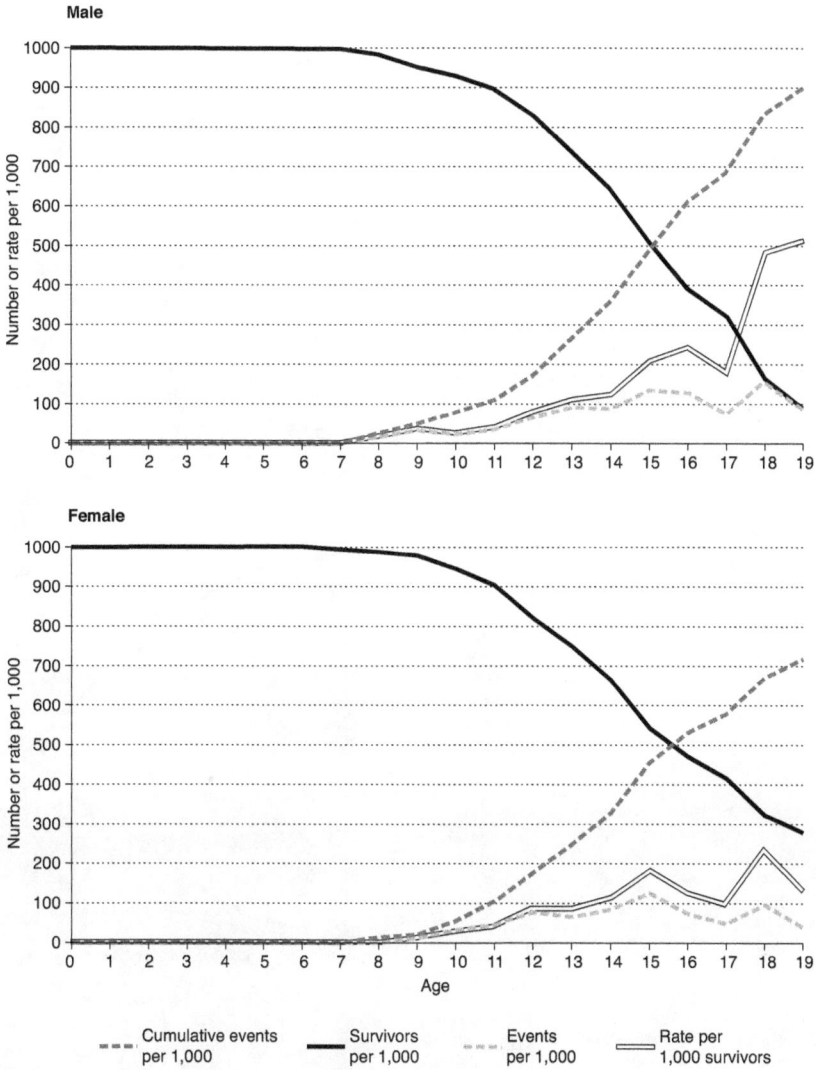

Figure 6.3a Patterns of school leaving.
Source: Tabulated by the authors from Survey and Assessment of Vietnamese Youth (SAVY).

incomplete. Very high percentages of respondents will eventually experience both these events, yet only 27 percent of males and 49 percent of females had done so by age twenty. In fact, among those aged twenty-five at the time of the survey, only 50 percent of males and 68 percent of females had married.[8] Unfortunately, due to a lack of evidence, we cannot address an important

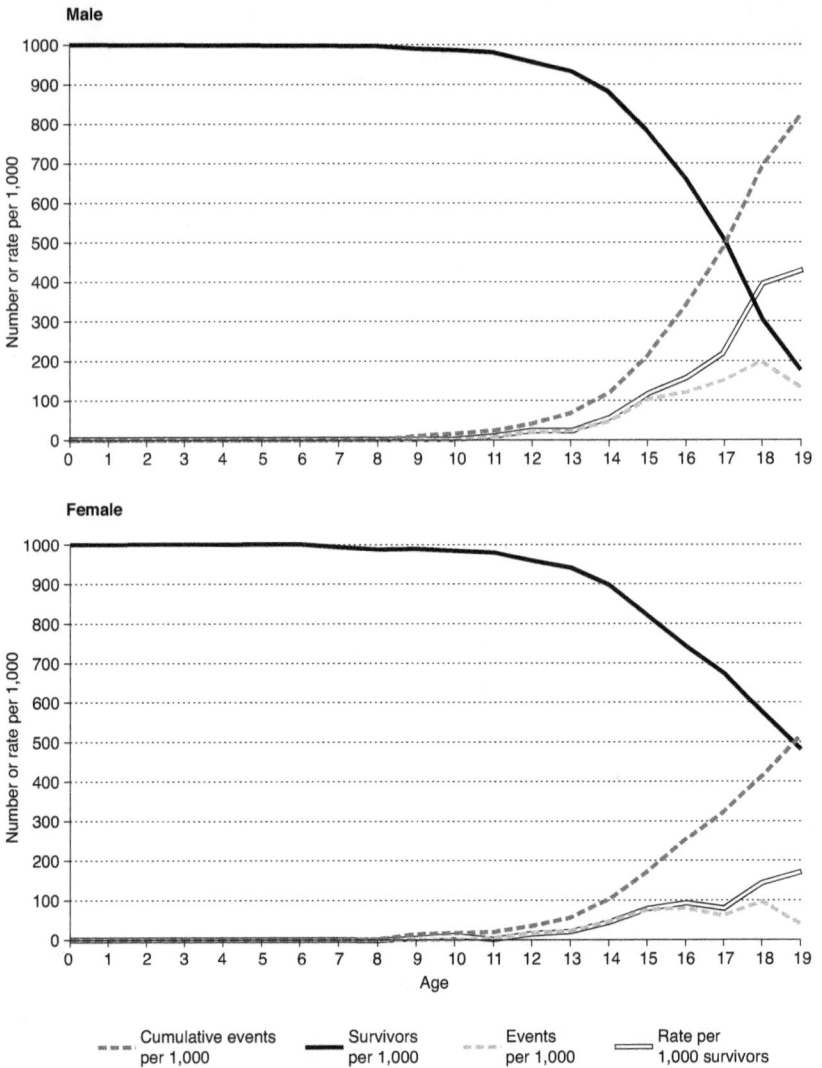

Figure 6.3b Patterns of work for pay.
Source: Tabulated by the authors from Survey and Assessment of Vietnamese Youth (SAVY).

question regarding the proportion of the cohort that will ultimately experience the other events in the list here. This highlights a notable shortcoming of the "youth survey" research strategy, which does not provide comparable information on older age groups in the population.

Before turning to any further specific events and their patterns, we want to establish as graphically as possible the eventful character of the teenage years—that is, the high density of new experiences during these years (Rind-fuss 1991). One way of portraying this (Figures 6.4a and 6.4b) is to graph the rates of occurrence for the full set of events available from the survey, stacking them so their coincidence and cumulative character during the teenage years is fully evident. The concentration of new experiences, starting in the early teenage years, then growing and accelerating in the later teenage years, is apparent in Figure 6.4 for both males and females. However, it is notable that, for many of the events, females peak at eighteen years of age, whereas males' rates generally continue to rise through age nineteen. We will consider this later in relation to individual events in the discussion. In addition, we note that one event among those shown, *school entrance*, is a childhood event—probably the single most important transitional event experienced before the second decade of life.

A TYPOLOGY OF EVENTS

To understand these events and their patterns more fully, we form them into groups. For the present purpose, we have identified "Child and Early Teen" events (*puberty* and *school entrance*) which occur no later than age sixteen or so; achievement of "Independence" from the family events (*school leaving, home leaving, work for pay*); "Lifestyle" events (*first smoking, first drinking,* and *first sex*); and, finally, "Family Formation" events (*entrance to marriage, first pregnancy,* and *first birth*). In Figure 6.5, we display the distribution of the sample (separately for males and females) by the age at which each of these events first occurred. The separation between the occurrences of these various events is readily apparent, although the temporal overlaps are also of interest.

The "Child and Early Teen" events, *school entrance* at around ages five through seven and *puberty* at around ages twelve to sixteen, are close to universal experiences in Vietnam. Among males in our sample, 95 percent had entered school by age twenty, and, of these, 94 percent had done so before age ten. Among females, for the same ages as males, these figures are 95 and 95 percent, respectively. These ages mark off a period when young people are highly enmeshed in both their families and their schools. There is only

Male

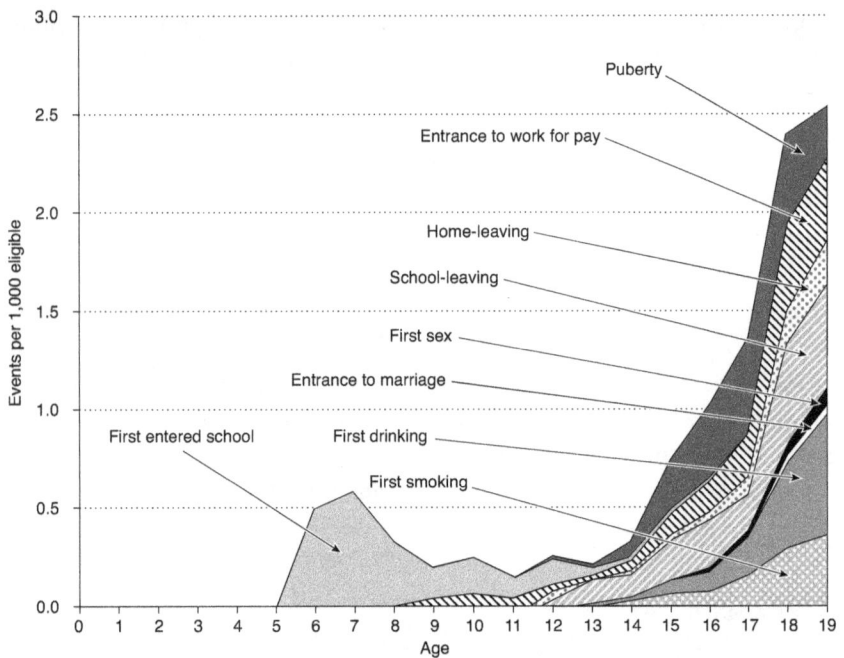

Figure 6.4a The Density of First Experiences (Vietnamese males aged twenty and over in 2003).
Source: Tabulated by the authors from Survey and Assessment of Vietnamese Youth (SAVY).

a limited temporal connection between this segment of life and the various other events examined here. There is a delay until later in the teenage years for the "Lifestyle" events. In our sample, only about 17 percent reported at least one "Lifestyle" event before at least one "Child and Early Teen" event. However, there is a sharp gender contrast. Only 3 percent of females reported a relatively early "Lifestyle" event, compared with 32 percent of males. In these instances, the "Lifestyle" event involved is usually smoking (20 percent) or drinking (23 percent).

The onset of "Independence" events (*school leaving, home leaving, work for pay*) usually begins with *school leaving*. There is considerable dispersion across ages for those who experience at least one "Independence" event. Among males, about 10 percent had experienced one of these events by age fourteen, about

Female

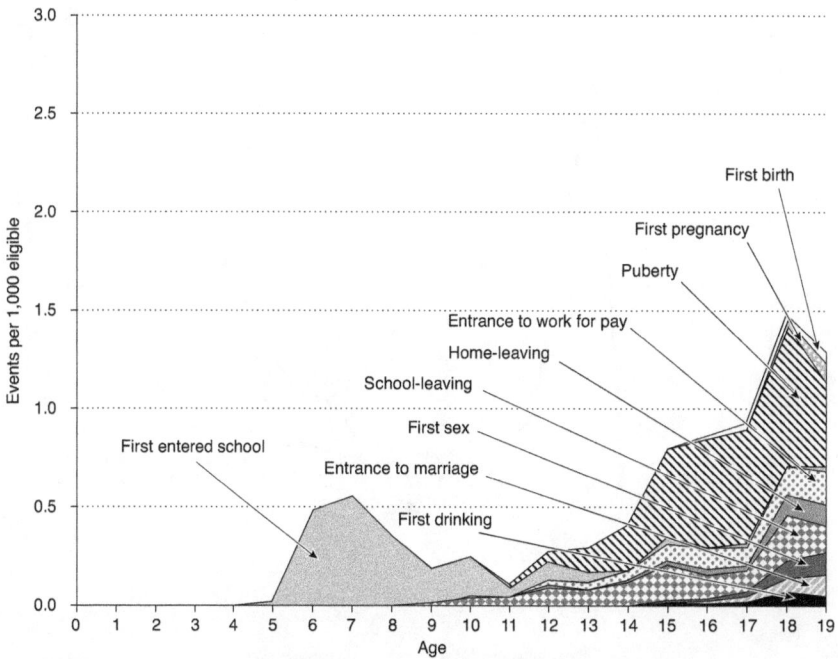

Figure 6.4b   The Density of first experiences (Vietnamese females aged twenty and over in 2003).
Source: Tabulated by the authors from Survey and Assessment of Vietnamese Youth (SAVY).

25 percent by age sixteen, about 60 percent by age eighteen, and 90 percent by age twenty. About half of these occurrences took place between the ages of fifteen through nineteen. This means that many of the "Independence" events occur after age twenty. The patterns for females are similar.

In sharp contrast, the "Family Formation" events do not begin to occur until age fifteen among both males and females, and even then only rarely. Most "Family Formation" events, of course, occur much later, and only 1 percent of either males or females in the sample reported a "Family Formation" event during the "Child and Early Teen" stage of life. There is a considerable gender gap in the timing of "Family Formation" events. Only 10 percent of male youth and 30 percent of female youth had experienced a "Family Formation" event by age twenty. The great majority will experience these events in the third decade of their lives.

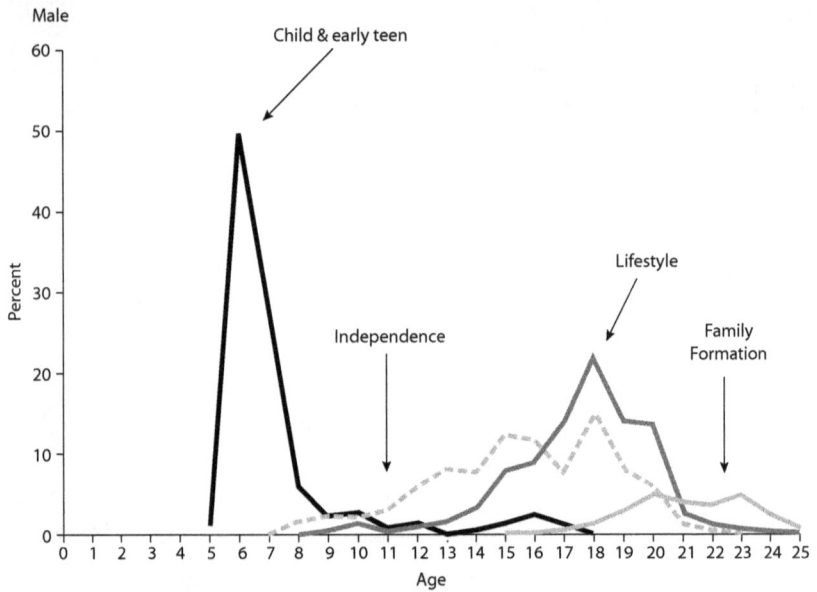

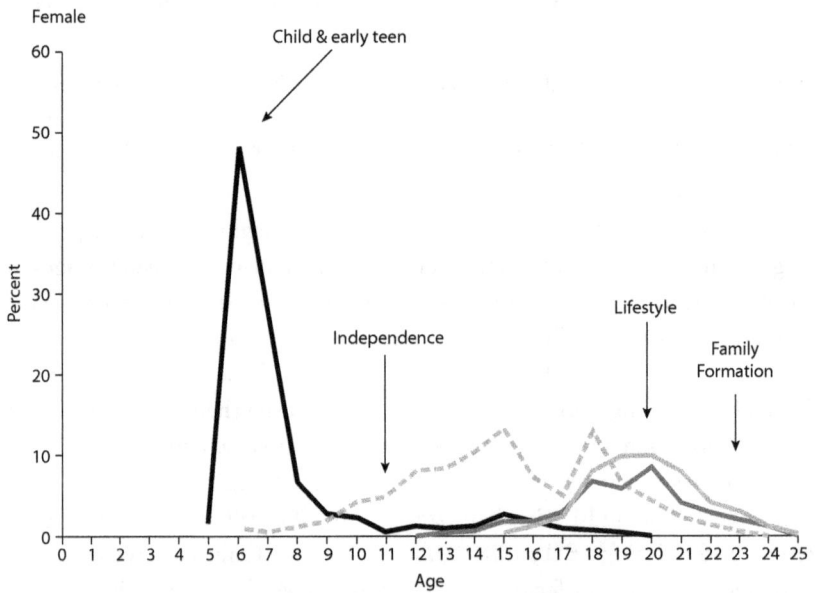

Figure 6.5   Age patterns of first experience for types of event, by sex.
Source: Tabulated by the authors from Survey and Assessment of Vietnamese Youth (SAVY).
Note: Based on responses of persons aged twenty to twenty-five at the time of the survey.

Of considerable policy interest are the "Lifestyle" events that mark these transitional years. We see this label as appropriate because smoking, drinking, and premarital sex are behavioral choices that vary markedly across the youth population. In this analysis, we document differences by gender and by family class/residence background (defined below). Figure 6.5 shows that the onset of "Lifestyle" events begins around ages fifteen to seventeen years and peaks at eighteen to nineteen years, by which time approximately 75 percent of males and less than 30 percent of females report having experienced one. The cumulative percent of those experiencing a "Lifestyle" event by the age of twenty reaches over 90 percent for males and just under 40 percent for females.

We could pursue a further study of these patterns and their interconnections, but such an investigation lies beyond the intent of our analysis. In the remainder of this chapter, we focus our attention on interconnections between *home leaving* and some of the other events.

Transitional Events and Families

We will look at these events from the standpoint of the families in which these young respondents grew up to examine, at least in a preliminary way, whether we can discern any influences and connections. The first step is to tabulate our age at *home leaving* to determine, for each event and each age of occurrence by sex, the percentage of other experiences that took place while respondents were still living at home with their parents.[9] Table 6.2 presents this information, with the limitation that available case bases at single years of age do not allow us to estimate all cells in the table. In Table 6.2, we see that the overall proportion of events occurring while youth are still living at home is high, ranging from 60 to 92 percent for all events except *first sex* and *entrance to marriage* for males, which occurred in 54 to 55 percent of the cases, respectively, before *home leaving*. These patterns reflect the combined effects of ages of *home leaving*, ages of occurrence of events, plus any association that may exist between the behavior itself and residence at home.

Certain events that may have been prevalent among young people in the past have become uncommon in recent years. These include the death of a mother, father, or sibling (not available in SAVY). Only 7 and 3 percent of the respondents report the death of a father or mother, respectively, and, of these, 85 to 92 percent were living with the parents at the time. The loss of parents

TABLE 6.2
Proportion of transition events occurring while still living
with parental family by age of occurrence

| Event | Age | | | | | All ages |
	12	16	20	22	24	
Physiological						
Puberty						
Male	*	88.5	47.7	*	*	87.2
Female	96.8	88.6	*	*	–	91.8
Social						
School entrance						
Male	*	*	*	*	*	99.3
Female	*	*	*	*	*	98.9
School leaving						
Male	98.9	84.5	58.0	16.2	*	83.2
Female	90.0	90.9	55.2	34.3	*	87.2
Death of father						
Male	*	*	*	*	*	88.1
Female	*	*	*	*	*	91.7
Death of mother						
Male	*	*	*	*	*	84.8
Female	*	*	*	*	*	88.2
Work for pay						
Male	88.7	67.7	47.3	40.2	*	69.0
Female	76.5	75.9	54.0	54.9	*	71.4
First sex						
Male	–	*	48.4	51.1	38.8	54.4
Female	–	63.9	58.5	46.8	*	64.5
First smoking						
Male	95.4	80.9	49.8	46.4	*	71.6
Female	*	*	*	*	*	80.6
First drinking						
Male	91.4	84.5	48.3	60.7	*	76.4
Female	*	74.4	57.8	53.4	*	72.4
First drug use						
Both sexes	*	*	*	*	*	50.8
Marriage and Reproduction						
Entrance to marriage						
Male	–	*	64.9	52.5	32.5	55.4
Female	–	63.8	61.1	46.2	*	64.0
First pregnancy						
Female	–	*	61.0	54.4	46.0	61.4
First birth						
Female	–	*	66.4	58.1	53.3	62.5

SOURCE: Tabulated by the authors from Survey and Assessment of Vietnamese Youth (SAVY).

NOTE: – No events for this age; * Insufficient cases to estimate (<30); see text for definition of *home leaving*.

is an experience that usually comes later in life and, in all likelihood, after *home leaving.*

Since *puberty* is an event that occurs in a very narrow age range, typically between twelve and fifteen years, it occurs while the youth are still at home in roughly nine out of ten cases. Rates for males are slightly lower because males enter puberty somewhat later (Eveleth and Tanner 1976). When puberty is relatively late, the respondent is much more likely to have left his or her parents, but this is uncommon and, certainly, no causal connection with *home leaving* is implied. *Puberty* takes much of its importance from the fact that it signifies the appropriateness of certain other events (Brooks-Gunn 1988). Moreover, such influences may not be limited to the most obvious ones—*first sex, first pregnancy,* and *entrance to marriage.*

SAVY provides an interesting piece of information about the social context of puberty, specifically, whether respondents talked to anyone about their puberty experience at the time of puberty and, if so, to whom. Among the half or so of respondents who spoke with someone at the time of puberty, 85 percent of the females say they talked with their parents, while only 17 percent of males reported doing so. Of the males, 72 percent say they talked with their friends. This pattern highlights the importance of family sources of information on a key personal event, but only among females. The considerably lower level of family communication regarding puberty among males illustrates how family influences can be very different for each sex. We have considered whether the gender difference might reflect the later ages of males at puberty, but find that the difference remains even when residence at home is taken into account.

School entrance occurs in a very narrow range of ages and virtually always in the context of the parental home. However, there is a wide variance in the ages for *school leaving* across the teenage years and beyond. Whether this occurs while living at home or after *home leaving* is highly dependent on the age when *school leaving* occurs. Until sixteen years of age, 90 percent or more of the *school leaving* events occur while still living at home, but this drops to 55 to 58 percent for those who left school at age twenty and between 16 and 34 percent among those who left school at age twenty-two. These late school leavers are at the tertiary level of education, which is often not available in the same locality as the parental home.

It is important to note that, overall, between 83 and 87 percent of respondents left school while still living at home. Also notable is the fact that more females who stayed in school into their twenties still lived at home, as compared with the similar group of males. SAVY documents the reasons for leaving school, and both direct and indirect family influences are clear. The indirect effect results largely from family economic circumstances; 44 percent of males and 47 percent of females say they left school either because they could not afford to continue or because they had to work for the family instead. The much smaller direct effect, where the family did not want the respondent to continue, is 1 percent for males and 3 percent for females. Other influences, such as distance of the family residence from the school, are indirect family influences, but these are not statistically important. It is difficult to classify some other influences, such as the respondent's desire to leave, poor grades, or failure to pass to the next grade, which account for 30 to 36 percent of all reasons given.

The timing of *work for pay* and the timing of *school leaving* are somewhat linked, as is suggested by the similar percentages living at home versus elsewhere when these events occurred. When *work for pay* occurs at age twenty, about half were still living at home compared with 55 to 58 percent for those who left school at that age. We find the same gender difference in *work for pay* as for *school leaving*—at older ages of occurrence, females are more likely than males to be still living at home.

Most *entrance to marriage, first sex, first pregnancy,* and *first birth* events— which we might call the reproduction sequence, though the actual sequence might vary—take place in close connection with one another in a usual sequence having both biological and cultural/normative roots. This sequence of events spreads across the young adult years and well into the years of adulthood. These four events take place after leaving the family of orientation in approximately 38 to 40 percent of the cases, and in a slightly lower proportion for *entrance to marriage* and *first sex* among males. This probably reflects the Vietnamese pattern of residence with the husband's relatives immediately after marriage (Hirschman and Nguyen 2002). Those experiences in the sequence that occur relatively late are more likely to occur outside the context of the family of orientation. Half of the *first sex* and *entrance to marriage* events from age twenty-two and onward occur after *home leaving*, and half the *first pregnancy* and *first birth* events at age twenty-four occur after *home leaving*. Nevertheless, the striking element in these series is really how common it is, even when *first sex, entrance to marriage, pregnancy,* and *first birth* occur at relatively late ages, for these events to take place in a familial context.

We can add two items of information regarding family influences to the analysis. One is that for 61 to 65 percent of respondents, the decision whom to marry is shared with their families. For most respondents, this very important decision is clearly something in which their families are substantially involved. We cannot always presume that a powerful family influence is protective; however, SAVY also tells us that among the unmarried who reported sexual experience, their first sexual experience usually took place in their own homes or the homes of their sexual partner (60 percent of males and 93 percent of females).

First smoking and *first drinking* occur while living at home for 70 percent or more for both males and females who report these experiences. This information is valuable for policy consideration regarding the pro- versus anti-smoking and drinking atmosphere families provide. When looking at the association of family smoking and respondent smoking, 65 percent of males report that someone within their family smokes (usually a father, sometimes a brother), and slightly more than 45 percent of respondents in such families also smoke themselves. Nevertheless, these data show that this particular family influence is not a determining factor. Many young men report that their father (or some other person in the family) smokes, yet they do not smoke themselves. Also, male respondents report that a high percentage of their friends smoke (71 percent). Moreover, whether a young man's friends smoke is highly associated with whether he smokes (13 percent among those with friends who do not smoke versus 56 percent among those with friends who do). These results remind us of a very important feature of families— they are determined by kinship and not by voluntary association—as compared with peer groups about which young people have some measure of choice. This point may suggest why family influences on smoking (and perhaps other issues) may be weak, relative to peer influences. The formation of peer groups, unlike families, depends on shared views and activities, as well as simple homogeneity and proximity.

We must be cautious about interpreting the limited number of responses concerning drug use, but it is worth noting that, while the ages of occurrence are similar, these events are much less likely to occur while living at home (only 51 percent versus 71 to 82 percent for smoking and drinking). It is possible that drug use is imbedded in a social syndrome that includes early *home leaving.* In any case, we can suggest that messages to youth about use of these substances should, at least in the case of smoking and drinking, take advantage of family avenues of communication and contain messages that can counteract the negative influences of families where these behaviors are common.

"INDEPENDENCE" EVENTS, GENDER, AND FAMILY BACKGROUND

The final segment of our analysis focuses on the three events most directly involved with the move toward independence: *school leaving, home leaving,* and *work for pay.* In many other societies, these events are of crucial importance to the overall transition to adulthood (Kerchoff 2003; Lloyd 2005, chapters 3 and 5). In Vietnam, these events tend to occur late in the teenage years, well after any of the "Child and Early Teen" events as we have noted, but well before any of the "Family Formation" events. Our analysis also shows that they occur in a variety of sequences. We seek to cast some light on the role of families in these "Independence" events. In order to accomplish this, we disaggregate the descriptive results on event sequences by respondents' sex and by a simple measure of family background based on a combination of information regarding father's schooling and the degree of urbanization for the family of origin. This simple classification scheme distinguishes young people with "urban/high education" families, "rural/low education" families, and those with families located somewhere between these two extremes. Among those aged twenty years or over in our sample, 17 percent are classified as "urban/high education," 55 percent as "intermediate," and 27 percent as "rural/low education."

Table 6.3 illustrates that the timing of various events does indeed vary, sometimes markedly, by gender and family background. Shown in the table is the mean age of each event for each gender and family background. The "Child and Early Teen" events begin to occur slightly earlier for males than for females, and substantially later for those with less-advantaged family backgrounds. There is a well-defined gradient and a consistent male-female differential. These patterns reflect the fact (detailed results not shown here) that both *puberty* and *school entrance* occur later for females and for those with disadvantaged family backgrounds. The *puberty* differential between the sexes averages 0.3 years, whereas the differential across family backgrounds (comparing the highest and lowest) averages 2.2 years. Next, in terms of timing, are the "Independence" events, which are initiated an average of 8.1 years later. This timing difference is smaller for females than males, and

TABLE 6.3
Mean age at first events by type, sex, and family background

Event Type	Male Urban/High Education	Intermediate Backgrounds	Rural/Low Education	Female Urban/High Education	Intermediate Backgrounds	Rural/Low Education
Child and Teen Event	6.4	7.0	8.4	6.6	7.1	9.0
Independence Event	17.0	15.7	14.7	16.9	15.2	13.6
Lifestyle Event	17.6	17.6	17.3	19.6	19.4	18.2
Family Formation	22.2	21.4	20.7	20.4	19.9	19.4

SOURCE: Tabulated by the authors from Survey and Assessment of Vietnamese Youth (SAVY).

NOTE: Based on SAVY respondents aged twenty years and over.

much smaller for the most disadvantaged family background. Expressed differently, we see that the age of the first "Independence" event ranges from 17.0 years among "urban/high education" males to only 13.6 years among "rural/low education" females.

Those from disadvantaged backgrounds experience "Lifestyle" events earlier, although the family background differential is very small here. However, the gender differential ranges from two years among the urban and highly educated to just under 1 year among those with rural backgrounds and relatively low educational levels. With "Family Formation" events, we again see a substantial differential by family background, as those from disadvantaged backgrounds start family formation 1.5 years earlier for males and 1.0 years for females. At the same time, the gender difference is substantial, averaging 1.5 years. There is nearly a three-year difference between males of advantaged family backgrounds and females of disadvantaged backgrounds.

We now turn to the sequences of "Independence" events (presented in Table 6.4). We began with an expectation that the most common sequence would be *school leaving*, then *home leaving*, and then *work for pay*. We find, however, that this sequence describes only about 25 to 38 percent of the sample providing the necessary information. Moreover, we have included those with incomplete experience of the three events, but for whom the expected sequence remains a possibility, in this category.[10] There is a sharp gender difference, with females being more likely to report this anticipated sequence. In Table 6.4, we have condensed a considerable array of sequences into two patterns of interest given our focus on the role of families. Of those not reporting our expected pattern, two-thirds or so have experienced one or both

TABLE 6.4

Distribution by sequence of three independence events, by sex and family background

Event Type	Male			Female		
	Urban/High Education	Intermediate Backgrounds	Rural/Low Education	Urban/High Education	Intermediate Backgrounds	Rural/Low Education
On track for School-Home-Work	0.25	0.27	0.28	0.33	0.35	0.38
Events while still at home	0.51	0.52	0.52	0.46	0.50	0.52
Left home early	0.24	0.21	0.20	0.21	0.15	0.11
All sequences	1.00	1.00	1.00	1.00	1.00	1.00[a]
N	325	1,253	746	347	1,385	661

[a] Discrepancy due to rounding.

SOURCE: Tabulated by the authors from Survey and Assessment of Vietnamese Youth (SAVY).

NOTE: Based on SAVY respondents aged twenty years and over.

remaining "Independence" events while still living at home with their parents. This pattern is largely consistent across gender and family backgrounds, dipping somewhat only among females with an urban/high education background. The remainder of the sample reports that they left home relatively early, defined in relation to our expectations. That is, they report *home leaving* before *school leaving*. The higher prevalence of this pattern among those with advantaged backgrounds, and the very low prevalence among females with disadvantaged backgrounds, suggests that leaving home relatively early is further evidence of the strong role of families, rather than the failure of family to support young people. We can confirm from the SAVY responses that young people from relatively advantaged backgrounds are able to move to other households in order to continue their schooling. This is least likely to occur among females of disadvantaged family backgrounds, and most likely to occur among males from advantaged family backgrounds.

Conclusion

We began by recognizing the powerful forces influencing Vietnamese youth today, some associated with demographic transition and structural change, and some associated broadly with globalization. It is worth emphasizing that the underlying fertility changes associated with the demographic transition were well under way by the time *Doi Moi* was initiated (Haughton 1997: figure 1) —an illustration of the broader reality that the social impacts of *Doi Moi* are playing out in the context of ongoing processes (see Bélanger and Barbieri's introduction, this volume). Patterns of transition to adulthood are seen in our chapter to reflect a confluence of policy (*Doi Moi*), demography, and broader social and economic changes. We have explored the consequences of this by looking at a set of events during the adulthood transition as reported in 2003 in the Survey and Assessment of Vietnamese Youth. We demonstrate the dramatic concentration of first-time experiences during the teenage years. Distinguishing "Child and Teen" events, "Independence" events, "Lifestyle" events, and "Family Formation" events, we find that during the teenage years "Independence" and "Lifestyle" events dominate, while the "Family Formation" events are largely delayed until the third decade of life. We then seek to understand the role of families in these experiences. We are able to show that very high proportions of most events take place while young people are still living in their households of upbringing. Approximately 25 percent of our sample report that they left home before stopping their schooling, and even the "Family Formation" events, though occurring relatively late, take place in the familial context. Another measure of the family's importance is the fact that many youth "Lifestyle" events and even "Independence" events occur while they are still living at home. Our examination of the sequences of "Independence" events, including *home leaving*, elaborates on this.

There is much more to learn about the issues that we have explored here. It will be valuable to examine the transition events much more thoroughly, in terms of temporal configurations of events and common versus uncommon paths, which may be associated with higher or lower levels of social problems, including the common risk behaviors. With regard to families in the lives of young people, the SAVY research agenda includes an investigation of risk-behavior outcomes in relation to family strengths and weaknesses as "protective" versus "risk" factors in young people's lives. In many societies, research is suggesting that "family connectedness" is a crucial element in steering youth safely through their adulthood transitions. SAVY research is thus far suggesting that, for the majority of Vietnamese youth, their families provide a positive foundation for the transitions they face.

Appendix: Notes on Data and Methods

Figure 6.1. The gross enrollment ratios were extracted from UNESCO (1999), table II-8. In a few instances, an adjacent date was used when the precise data were not available. These are ratios of numbers enrolled at each level divided by the estimated numbers at the ages appropriate for each enrollment level. These ratios can exceed 100 and sometimes do, especially at the primary level. The Vietnam estimates were supplemented with estimates for 1995 based on the Vietnam Living Standards Survey 1997–1998 (General Statistics Office 2000: table 2.3.1).

Figure 6.2. Marital status is available in every census conducted across Asia since 1891. For the few adjustments necessary to obtain the age-sex specific indicators see Smith (1980) and Xenos and Gultiano (1992).

The Survey and Assessment of Vietnamese Youth (SAVY). Questionnaire design and pretesting of the questionnaire and field procedures took place during April–June, 2003, and field data collection took place in September 2003 and onward. The multistaged, probability sample includes 449 enumeration areas as defined for the General Statistics Office's national multipurpose sampling frame. The SAVY questionnaire included an interview part covering a broad range of social and economic topics, and a self-completed part, which covered a set of issues deemed sensitive to respondents. Data collection encompassed a range of important risk behaviors including substance risks, sexual risks, and other kinds of risk-taking behavior as deemed relevant. In order to analyze and understand these risk behaviors, data were also collected on a set of background or "social setting" indicators covering the school, peer group, community, and family settings of youth and designed to identify important risk factors and protective factors in the lives of youth. The survey was designed to provide an overall statistical description of youth characteristics and problem indicators, sufficient to inform discussion of a national youth health policy framework and policy statement on youth (Ministry of Health 2006) and detailed analysis to support program planning in certain key sectors.

The SAVY sample is a national representative sample of youth (persons ages fourteen to twenty-five) living in households across the eight economic regions of Vietnam.[11] The sample was drawn from the subsample of 45,000 households in the 2002 Vietnam Living Standards Survey (Phung and Nguyen 2006) with a multistaged and stratified design. The youth in the

SAVY sample design are sufficient to represent the nation as a whole as well as the urban and rural sectors separately. The largest cities (Hanoi, Ho Chi Minh City) were oversampled in order to provide for increased statistical power in that segment of the total population of youth.

Forty-two out of sixty-one provinces were selected for the SAVY sample,[12] using the probability proportional to size (PPS) method to maintain representativeness. At the next stage of sampling, enumeration areas (EAs) in each province were selected. In those EAs sampled, all youth aged fourteen through twenty-five, were identified (i.e., those born between 1978 and 1989, male and female, married and nonmarried from the twenty households that had been selected for VLSS 2002). The youth cohort represents all youth living in households, but not youth living in institutional settings of various kinds (barracks, jails, social protection centers, factory dormitories, etc.).

In the actual SAVY field experience, the mobilization rate was 85 percent and the number of completed interviews is 7,584. The SAVY mobilization rate is reasonably good by the standard of such surveys of youth, though it is slightly lower than the General Statistics Office had expected. As noted in the survey report (Ministry of Health and General Statistics Office 2005), SAVY has certain characteristics that might have lowered the mobilization rate, particularly the manner in which its sampling frame was derived from another survey using household lists created one year earlier, and the way that local people's committees were called upon to mobilize youth. These two features may have combined with the relatively high rate of geographic mobility of the youth population to diminish the mobilization rate somewhat.

Among those who agreed to go to the central location for interviewing, almost none refused to answer the questions or to fill in the self-completed part of the survey. The survey method (face-to-face interview with a self-administered second part), the quality of interviewers and the organization of the fieldwork, including extensive supervision, were important factors that ensured the quality of the SAVY data.

The Method of Analysis. It has been necessary to recognize and avoid an analytic problem due to truncation of the full experience of each respondent. There is no truncation at the younger ages since respondents were free to indicate ages of occurrence back to their first days of life. However, there is certainly a significant amount of "right side" or upper age limit truncation, since in 2003 individuals could only report on the events they had experienced up to their ages at that time. The effect of this truncation varies with the event. Puberty occurs within a fairly narrow range of ages, and virtually every female at age sixteen will have experienced this event (98 percent of the SAVY sample sixteen years of age, though only 78 percent of males at that age). At age twenty all but 0.05 percent of males and 1.6 percent of females say they have experienced puberty. However, union formation begins at a much later age and then is experienced at a wide range of ages. By age sixteen, in the SAVY sample, only 0.2 percent of females (and 0.0 percent of males) report that they had married. By twenty-five years of age, 32 percent of females and 49 percent of males had not formed a union. The puberty event is barely truncated at all above age sixteen or so for females, but union formation is substantially truncated for both sexes, even among those aged twenty-five years when they were interviewed.

Two general approaches have been devised for analyzing data in such circumstances. One is a multivariate life-table approach—survival models, including proportional hazard models (Retherford and Choe 1993, chapters 7–8). The other, and the one taken for the present purpose since we are not engaged in multivariate modeling, is a life-table-based presentation of events during the teenage years in which the truncation bias is avoided by limiting analysis to a particular age range of respondents and limiting the events and ages under consideration to those reported to have taken place before and up to the chosen age cutoff. We have drawn retrospective information from respondents aged twenty and over at the time of the survey describing their experiences through age nineteen. That experience is reported without the truncation bias. The arbitrary cutoff at age twenty gives us 2,975 cases (1,469 male and 1,506 female) on which to base our analysis.

Notes

1. This is the case for any reasonable list of benchmark events. Thus, in the SAVY sample, leaving home and marriage, to cite just two iconic events, are only 39.4 and 19.1 percent complete, respectively, at age twenty.

2. This paragraph is based on Coale and Demeny (1983), reading from the West model for females. In a life table corresponding to a life expectancy at birth of seventy years, about 96 percent of those born will reach age ten, and 95 percent will reach age twenty. Moreover, 78 percent or so of those who complete their teenage years then will go on to reach age sixty-five. It is worth noting that deaths among family members and peers are also rare.

3. Vietnam's trend here is not as dramatic as some other countries in Asia, but by 2003 more than half of all females and about three-fourths of all males, ages twenty to twenty-four, were unmarried, and nearly 100 percent of each sex aged fifteen to nineteen were unmarried. We must note that this combination of census and SAVY survey results for Vietnam may perhaps exaggerate the upward trends slightly, because there is some indication that married persons were underrepresented in SAVY (Ministry of Health and General Statistics Office 2005).

4. For more on this see the Appendix.

5. Dramatic gender differences are concealed here. Among males at age twenty-five years, 78 percent have initiated smoking, compared with only 0.8 percent among the corresponding group of females. For drinking, these levels are 90 percent and 37 percent, respectively.

6. For clarity of presentation, we have adjusted the actual sample numbers to express the numbers by age that would be reported by one thousand persons. This facilitates comparison of males and females, for example, which exist in the sample in unequal numbers and, in another context, makes it easier to compare Vietnam's results with those of other countries and samples (e.g., Xenos et al. 2006).

7. Each "rate" is the ratio of reported events during that age divided by the population "surviving" to the beginning of that age not yet having experienced the event.

8. Based on recent experience, we expect that over 95 percent of males and females among our respondents will ever marry, though this is a preliminary judgment and the percent remaining single throughout their lives may rise from the current level (Jones 1997).

9. The term *parents* here includes parent-substitutes as identified in the survey. *Home leaving* can be gauged in SAVY only with the responses to a question on whether the respondent had ever lived away from the parental home for a month or more, and at what age this occurred.

10. For example, included are those who have left school (before *home leaving* if they have left home) but do not report any work event.

11. The main report on the survey (Ministry of Health and General Statistics Office 2005: chapter 2) includes a statement of sampling design and other aspects of the data collection methodology. The SAVY questionnaire is given in English translation; the Vietnamese language version is available on request.

12. At the time of the sample, there were sixty-one provinces; however, at the time of printing, Vietnam had sixty-four provinces.

References

Arnett, J. J. 1999. Adolescent storm and stress reconsidered. *American Psychologist* 54(5): 317–326.

Bell, N. J., and R. W. Bell. 1993. *Adolescent risk taking.* Newbury Park, CA: Sage Publications.

Benavot, A., and P. Riddle. 1988. The expansion of primary education, 1870–1940: trends and issues. *Sociology of Education,* 61(July): 191–210.

Berry, C., D. Birch, S. Dermody, J. Grant, A. Hamilton, M. Quilty, and K. Sen. 1996. The media. In *Comparing cultures, Australia in Asia series,* edited by A. Milner, 193–223. Melbourne: Oxford University Press.

Blum, R. W., and P. Mann Rinehart. 1997. *Reducing the risk: Connections that make a difference in the lives of youth.* Minneapolis: AddHealth.

Blum, R. W., and K. Nelson-Mmari. 2004. The health of young people in a global context. *Journal of Adolescent Health,* 35:402–418.

Boli, J., F. Ramirez, and J. Meyer. 1985. Explaining the origins and expansion of mass education. *Comparative Education Review,* 29(2): 145–70.

Brooks-Gunn, J. 1988. Antecedents and consequences of variations in girls' maturational timing. *Journal of Adolescent Health Care,* 9(5): 365–373.

Brown, B. B., and R. Larson. 2002. The kaleidoscope of adolescence: Experiences of the world's youth at the beginning of the 21st century. In *The world's youth: Adolescence in eight regions of the world,* edited by B. B. Brown, R. Larson, and T. S. Saraswathi, 1–20. New York: Cambridge University Press.

Bucholtz, M. 2002. Youth and cultural practice. *Annual Review of Anthropology,* 31: 525–52

Coale, A. J., and P. Demeny. 1983. *Regional model life tables and stable populations.* Second Edition. New York: Academic Press.

Committee on Population, Family and Children. 2003. *Adolescents and youth in Viet Nam.* Hanoi: Committee for Population, Family and Children.

Coser, R. L. 1974. *The family: Its structures and functions.* New York: St. Martin's Press.

Eveleth, P. B., and J. M. Tanner. 1976. *Worldwide variation in human growth.* Cambridge, U.K.: Cambridge University Press.

Furstenberg, F. F. Jr., T. D. Cook, R. Sampson, and G. Slap. 2002. Preface. *The Annals of the American Academy of Political and Social Science* 580(March): 6–15.

General Statistics Office. 2000. *Vietnam living standards survey 1997–1998.* Hanoi: Statistical Publishing House.

Glewwe, P., and H. Jacoby. 1998. School enrollment and completion in Viet Nam: An investigation of recent trends. In *Household welfare and Vietnam's transition,* edited by D. Dollar, P. Glewwe, and J. Litvack, 201–234, World Bank Regional and Sectoral Studies, Washington, D.C.: The World Bank.

Greene, M., Z. Rasekh, and K.-A. Amen. 2002. *Sexual & reproductive health policies for a youthful world.* Washington, DC: Population Assistance International.

Haughton, J. 1997. Falling fertility in Vietnam. *Population Studies* 51(2): 203–211.

Hirschman, C., and Nguyen H. M. 2002. Tradition and change in Vietnamese family structure in the Red River delta. *Journal of Marriage and the Family* 64: 1063–1079.

Hogan, D. P., and N. Astone. 1986. The transition to adulthood. *Annual Review of Sociology* 12: 109–130.

Institute of International Education. 2004. *Higher education in Vietnam.* Hanoi: Institute of International Education.

Jeffrey, C., and L. McDowell. 2004. Youth in a comparative perspective. *Youth and Society* 36(2): 131–142.

Jessor, R., M. S. Turbin, and F. M. Costa. 1999. Risk and protection in successful outcomes among disadvantaged adolescents. *Applied Development Science* 2(4): 194–208.

Jones, G. W. 1997. The demise of universal marriage in East and South-East Asia. In *The continuing demographic transition,* edited by G. W. Jones, R. M. Douglas, J. C. Caldwell, and R. M. D'Souza, 51–79. Oxford, U.K.: Oxford University Press.

Kirby, D. 2001. *Emerging answers: Research findings on programs to reduce teen pregnancy.* Washington DC: The National Campaign to Prevent Teen Pregnancy.

Kerchoff, A. C. 2003. From student to worker, chapter 12. In *Handbook of the life course,* edited by J. T. Mortimer and M. J. Shanahan, 251–267. New York: Kluwer Academic/Plenum Publishers.

Larson, R. 2002. The future of adolescence: Lengthening ladders to adulthood. *The Futurist,* 36(7): 16–20.

Le Thac Can. 1991. Higher education reform in Vietnam, Laos, and Cambodia. *Comparative Education Review,* 35(1): 170–176.

Lloyd, C. B., ed. 2005. *Growing up global: The changing transitions to adulthood in developing countries.* Washington DC: The National Academy Press.

Long, L. D., L. N. Henderson, L. T. P. Mai, and C. Haub. 2000. *The Doi Moi generation: Coming of age in Vietnam today.* Hanoi: Population Council.

Marr, D., and S. Rosen. 1998. Chinese and Vietnamese youth in the 1990s. *The China Journal,* 40: 145–172.

Marshall, W. A., and J. M. Tanner. 1986. Puberty. In *Human growth,* edited by W. A. Marshall and J. M. Tanner, 171–209. London: Plenum Press.

Ministry of Health. 2006. *National master plan on protection, care, and promotion of adolescent and youth health (for the period 2006–2010 and strategic orientation until 2020).* Hanoi: Medical Publishing House

Ministry of Health and General Statistics Office. 2005. *Survey assessment of Vietnamese youth.* Hanoi: Vietnam Ministry of Health.

Modell, J., F. F. Furstenberg Jr., and T. Hershberg. 1976. Social change and transitions to adulthood in historical perspective. *Journal of Family History*, 1: 7–32.

Mortimer, J. T., and R. Larson. 2002. Macrostructural trends and the reshaping of adolescence. In *The changing adolescent experience: Societal trends and the transition to adulthood*, edited by J. T. Mortimer and R. Larson, 1–17. New York: Cambridge University Press.

Nahar, Q. 2007. *Risk, vulnerability and protection among Bangladeshi adolescents.* PhD dissertation, Department of Sociology, University of Hawaii, Honolulu.

Nilan, P. 1999. Young people and globalizing trends in Vietnam. *Journal of Youth Studies*, 2(3): 353–70

Phung Duc Tung and Nguyen P. 2006. *Vietnam household living standard survey (VHLSS), 2002 and 2004: Basic information.* mimeo, Hanoi: General Statistics Office.

Retherford, R. D., and M. K. Choe. 1993. *Statistical models for causal analysis.* New York: John Wiley and Sons.

Ridge, D., and B. Murphy. 2002. *Consultancy on youth for the United Nations interagency programme working croup—Final report.* Hanoi: United Nations.

Rindfuss, R. R. 1991. The young adult years: diversity, structural change, and fertility. *Demography*, 28(4): 493–512.

Ruddick, S. 2003. The politics of ageing: Globalization and the restructuring of youth and childhood. *Antipode*, 35(2): 334–362.

Schlegel, A. 2000. The global spread of adolescent culture. In *Negotiating adolescence in times of social change*, edited by L. J. Crockett and R. K. Silbereisen, 71–88. Cambridge, U.K.: Cambridge University Press.

Shanahan, M. J. 2000. Pathways to adulthood in changing societies: variability and mechanisms in life course perspective. *Annual Review of Sociology*, 26: 667–692.

Smith, P. C. 1980. Asian marriage patterns in transition. *Journal of Family History*, 5(1): 58–97.

Waite, L. J. 2001. Family as an institution. In *International encyclopedia of the social and behavioral sciences.* Vol. 8, edited by N. J. Smelser and P. B. Baltes, 5311–5314. Amsterdam: Elsevier.

Xenos, P., S. Achmad, Nguyen D. K., H. S. Lin, P. K. Luis, C. Podhisita, C. Raymundo, and S. Thapa. 2006. Delayed Asian transitions to adulthood: evidence from national surveys of youth. *Asian Population Studies*, 2(2): 145–189.

Xenos, P., and S. A. Gultiano. 1992. *Trends in female and male age at marriage and celibacy in Asia.* Honolulu: East-West Center Program on Population (Sandra E. Ward. Papers of the Program on Population; No. 20).

Xenos, P., and S. A. Gultiano. 2002. *The marriage ratios of Asian countries and cohorts.* Paper prepared for the 2002 IUSSP Regional Population Conference "Southeast Asia's Population in a Changing Asian Context," Bangkok, Thailand, June 10–13.

Chapter Seven

Family Change in Vietnam's Red River Delta
From War, to Reunification, to Renovation

RUKMALIE JAYAKODY AND VU TUAN HUY

Vietnam has enjoyed dramatic economic growth since the implementation of renovation policies (*Doi Moi*) from 1986, resulting in a transition from a centrally planned to a market-based system and an opening up of Vietnam to the rest of the world. Although reform efforts in the former Soviet Union and Eastern European states centered on political change, Vietnam's reforms concentrated on economic liberalization and growth (Norlund, Gates, and Dam 1995). Initiated after China adopted reforms in 1978, Vietnam's restructuring occurred in three interrelated areas: (1) the transformation of the administratively planned economy into a market economy; (2) the establishment of international economic relations, particularly with non-Soviet countries; and (3) the restructuring of the administration to eliminate corruption, to increase efficiency, and to promote law-based governance. The most significant measures are discussed in detail in Bélanger and Barbieri's Chapter in this volume.

The economic consequences of *Doi Moi* are well documented: the gross domestic product grew by nearly 9 percent annually; inflation fell from 400 percent in 1988 to 17 percent in 1994; Vietnam went from being a rice importer to the second largest rice-exporting country in the world; and there were substantial reductions in poverty and increases in living standards (Haughton, Haughton, and Phong 2001; Lamb 2002). *Doi Moi's* economic successes are well illustrated by the dramatic drop in poverty rates: while nearly 60 percent of the population was living in poverty (measured as the caloric intake associated with expenditures) in 1993, the proportion declined to 37 percent in 1998 and 29 percent in 2002 (World Bank 2003, 1). Although the economic consequences of *Doi Moi* are well known, little information is available on how renovation policies and the resulting changes have affected family relationships and dynamics (see Bélanger and Barbieri's chapter in this volume). In this chapter, we examine marriage formation patterns and characteristics as a particularly good illustration of intrafamily transformations.

We focus on aspects of mating and marriage in northern Vietnam's Red River Delta and examine how couples and individuals have responded to a rapidly changing society. The hypothesis is that changes resulting from *Doi Moi*, including the spread of the Western media, increased migration and urbanization, labor force diversification, higher educational attainment, improved living standards and may influence union formation in a variety of ways. Our analyses document the extent of change in various aspects of mating and marriage and the factors associated with these changes.

Although *Doi Moi* is an important event in Vietnam's recent history, it is one of several changes affecting individuals and families. Vietnam's recent history also includes prolonged periods of war, collectivization efforts, the country's reunification after a half century of division, and severe food shortages and economic crises following reunification. Understanding the extent to which *Doi Moi* has affected families must include information on these prior events. Focusing only on postrenovation conditions may overstate the extent of change, as some changes attributed to *Doi Moi* may actually have preceded renovation policies. Therefore, when trying to assess the consequences of *Doi Moi* it is important to determine the correct baseline. Rather than focusing exclusively on conditions after *Doi Moi*, we also include data from earlier periods to better identify continuities and changes in mating and marriage patterns and the extent to which the changes are attributable to *Doi Moi*.

Vietnam's history differs by region, with the North and the South characterized by markedly different economic, political, and social structures. Although these differences were most obvious during Vietnam's fight for independence, first against the French and then against the United States, some evidence indicates that differences in kin structure predate French colonization. In terms of kinship, researchers have argued that in Vietnam the north is closer to East Asian patterns, with the predominance of the Confucian culture, while the South is less patriarchal and more favorable to gender equality, and more closely resembles Southeast Asia (Hirschman and Vu 1996). Additional differences in inheritance and elder care are also evident. In the North, it is the oldest son who receives the largest share of the inheritance and is responsible for the care of his parents in old age, while these rights and obligations fall to the youngest son in the South (Do 1991). Consequently, although we refer to Vietnam throughout the chapter, it is important to keep in mind that the information on which our findings are drawn originates from the Red River Delta Region, the cradle of Vietnamese civilization located in the North, and should not be systematically generalized to the country as a whole.

Data are utilized from the Red River Delta Family Survey (RRDFS), a probability survey designed to document and explain changes in family life that have taken place within the context of major social changes and events occurring over the past four decades.

Theoretical Background

There are several reasons why we would expect the reforms, as well as earlier changes in Vietnam's recent history, to affect mating and marriage patterns. A key tenet of the modernization theory, for example, is that economic development is linked to cultural changes affecting social life. Goode (1963) specified that structural forces accompanying modernization, including education, industrialization, and urbanization, would strengthen conjugal family ties and weaken extended family obligations. In terms of mating and marriage, Goode's model predicts that changes associated with modernization would result in a loss of parental control over children's courtship and mate choice, increased age at marriage, and a rise in nuclear households.

However, there is growing recognition across the globe that structural forces alone are insufficient to fully understand family change, leading many researchers to look at alternative explanations (Jayakody, Thornton, and Axinn 2008). Among these alternative explanations are broad ideational and normative forces related to new ideas about the place and role of individuals relative to the family and larger community, and to changing norms concerning marriage, relationships between men and women, intergenerational ties, and the place of children in families. Especially relevant are ideas about marriage and the ways it connects and affects women and men and influences relationships across generations (Jayakody, Thornton, and Axinn 2008). Therefore, along with the structural changes brought about by the economic reforms in *Doi Moi*, ideational changes resulting from the increased spread of Western mass media after renovation, and the increased openness of Vietnam to the rest of the world, may also result in new patterns of mating and marriage, especially in urban areas, as indicated in recent studies by Nguyen An Phuong (2005, 2007).

One problem in examining family change in Vietnam is the lack of available data describing what families were like in the past. Some information about families in the past is available from studies of the Imperial legal codes and, in particular, inheritance rules and laws on family behavior and responsibilities (Yu 1978). As suggested in Bélanger and Barbieri's chapter in this volume, additional information on families in the more recent past can be usefully drawn from the analysis of Marriage and Family Laws (also see Jayakody and Vu 2008). We elaborate on these historical documents and the accounts of other scholars to provide some ideas of what families were like in the past in order to assess the extent of change.

One of the first areas of interest is the extent to which marriage systems more closely resemble an arranged marriage or a free-choice system. Traditionally, marriages in Vietnam have been parentally arranged (Nguyen 1996), as described by the saying translated literally as "where the parents put, children sit" (Ha 1992, 31), meaning who parents choose, children marry. Historically, marriage was regarded as a social contract between two families, and it was arranged by parents through intermediaries. The Le dynasty law code specifically mentioned parental control over mate selection and marriage procedures, and the later Gia Long dynasty code further detailed and strengthened parents' roles in marriages. For instance, Article 49 of the latter stated that marriage is legal only when it is approved by the senior male in the kinship hierarchy (Vu 1991). Arranged marriages seem to have been the rule among the rich, with more freedom of choice among the poor (Yu 1994). However, unlike in China, young adults were often consulted by their family when making the final choice of a spouse (Belanger & Khuat 1996).

These traditional ideas were challenged by Communist Party doctrine during the Marxist era and by the demands of the Colonial and American wars and reunification efforts. For example, along with calls for independence and freedom, the constitution of the new Democratic Republic of 1946 contained directives encouraging marriages based on love rather than arranged by the family (Vu 1991). Consequently, for several decades, most marriages in Vietnam appear to have been free-choice based. For instance, the proportion of respondents in our survey who indicated that their marriages "were arranged solely by their parents" declined from 3.5 percent for those who married during the American War to 0.5 percent at the time of reunification and 0.9 percent after renovation. The proportion of respondents who indicated that their marriages were "arranged by parents, but with my approval" declined from 8.1 percent to 3.5 percent and 1.9 percent, respectively. Considering that the topic of arranged marriage has been extensively covered by the authors in another publication (Jayakody and Vu 2008), we have chosen to concentrate here on other aspects of mating and marriage.

We focus on the following topics: (1) the characteristics sought in a marriage partner, (2) the circumstances in which respondents met their spouse, (3) the number of people courted and the duration of courting, (4) perceptions regarding the ideal age at marriage, (5) premarital sexual activity, and (6) living arrangements after marriage. Most of these topics have already been covered in a series of ethnographic studies conducted by Nguyen An Phuong on a very selective subgroup of the population, namely university graduates in Hanoi (see Nguyen 2005 and 2007 in particular). Our aim is to assess on a broader basis the extent to which her findings can be generalized to the larger population, as well as to determine the impact of *Doi Moi* by contrast with that of prior historical events. We anticipate that the structural and ideational transformations brought about by the succession of historical events over the past forty years have resulted in the transformation of personal relationships, particularly well illustrated by changes in mating and marriage attitudes and behavior (Goodwin 1998; Jayakody, Thornton, and Axinn 2008). We begin by reviewing some of the literature on these aspects. Next, we focus on how differences in education and rural/urban residence, particularly significant post-*Doi Moi*, may have resulted in increasingly divergent mating patterns for the most recent marriage cohorts. In the rest of this chapter, we successively review the current evidence on each of the topics of interest, then present our hypotheses about the impact of socioeconomic factors before presenting the results of our statistical analyses using the Red River Delta Family Survey (RRDFS) data and ending with a discussion of the findings.

Mating and Marriage

One of the most researched areas in the mating process is that of the characteristics sought in a partner. In particular, Buss has conducted a number of studies on partner selection in cross-cultural settings. Using a sociobiological approach, he argues that men value features in women that are tied to their reproductive capacity, youth, and beauty (Buss 1989, 1990). Women, on the other hand, look for characteristics that emphasize the provision of social and material resources, such as earning potential and industriousness. He tested these hypotheses with data collected in more than thirty-seven countries from over ten thousand respondents and found that, indeed, women value good financial prospects more than men do in thirty-six of the thirty-seven countries; in twenty-nine of the thirty-seven countries, women, more than men, sought out hard-working spouses with ambition. In all thirty-seven countries, men rated physical attractiveness as more important than did women. Buss further concluded from his analyses that variability across countries is associated with social development (Buss 1990).

Stereotyped gender differences in qualities sought in a mate are reflected in Vietnam by the following saying: "Girls look for talented boys while boys seek out beautiful girls" (Nguyen 1957, 126). However, because traditional Vietnamese society relied on an arranged marriage system, parents' preferences outweighed children's desires, particularly among the rich (Yu 1994). Therefore, mate selection characteristics that have historically been important in Vietnam include social endogamy and residential propinquity (marrying someone from the same village). The importance of residential propinquity is illustrated in the following Vietnamese saying: "It is better to marry a poor man in one's own village than a rich man from another village" (Nguyen 1957, 174), though how the proverb translated into reality in traditional Vietnam remains to be demonstrated. A study conducted before the reforms points to gentleness and virtue as highly valued characteristics for women, whereas being good-natured and hardworking were particularly appreciated in men (Tran 1991). Postrenovation evidence from Vietnam indicates that the traits desired in a wife include physical attractiveness, a high level of education, a high-status occupation, and a good family background. For men, desired traits include aggressiveness, a high income, ambition, and, as for women, a prestigious occupation and a good family background (Vu 2004).

Parents' historically strong role in the mate selection process implies that couples generally met each other through family. Parents' declining role in mate selection, particularly after 1945 in the North, meant that fewer couples met through their parents and relatives. Instead, meeting through friends and while working together became increasingly important (Barbieri and Vu 1996; Bélanger and Khuat 1995). However, parental control was, to a certain extent, replaced by state intervention so that the degree to which socialism entailed more freedom of choice in the selection of a mate by young men and women remains to be assessed (Nguyen 1997).

Data from a number of national surveys, including the 1991 Vietnam Life History Survey (VLHS), the 1997 and 2002 Demographic and Health Surveys, and the 1999 Census indicate significant increases in age at marriage over the last few decades (Nguyen 1995). Policy changes specified in a series of marriage and family laws probably influenced this increase. Currently, the minimum legal age of marriage in Vietnam is eighteen for women and twenty for men (Dinh 2000). The National Family Planning campaign calls for even later ages—twenty-six for men and twenty-two for women. Following renovation policies, marriage has tended to occur at an even later age due to increases in the duration of education and returns from education. As education becomes even more discriminating for finding employment and securing a good income, men and women are motivated to postpone marriage until they leave school or establish themselves in a job. Women appear to be further motivated by the desire to fully enjoy their premarital freedom and to delay—as long as social and family pressure so permits—the duties attached to a married status (Nguyen 2005). The relationships among education, employment, residential independence, and marriage are further discussed by Xenos and colleagues in this volume.

The Confucian tradition prohibits premarital sexual activity, particularly for women. The traditional arranged marriage system further helped control young people's sexual activity. As the traditional system gave way to free choice, the lessening of parental control and supervision produced more opportunities for sex before marriage. As vividly illustrated by Nguyen An Phuong's 2005 and 2007 studies, increased urbanization and the migration of young unmarried people may also expose them to more opportunities for premarital sexual activity. Additionally, increased globalization and the spread of new ideas through the modern media may contribute to changing attitudes about the acceptability of sex before marriage (Bélanger and

Khuat 1996; Nguyen 2007). During renovation, there have been growing concerns about the perceived increases in premarital sexual activity, particularly among adolescents (see de Loenzien, this volume). However, recent research argues that this concern is misplaced as there is little evidence of such an increase (Mensch, Clark, and Dang 2002).

An important aspect of Vietnamese family life has been postmarital living arrangements, where traditionally the young couple would spend some time residing with the husband's parents immediately after marriage. According to Vietnamese customs, co-residence of the newly married couple with the groom's parents was an obligation at least until the marriage of another brother who would then be joined by his wife in his parents' household (Pham 1998). Patrilocality remains a key feature of Vietnam kinship organization (Hirschman and Nguyen 2002). Data from the VLHS indicate that approximately 75 percent of couples lived with their parents after marriage. Though intergenerational co-residence is sometimes temporary, statistical evidence suggests that it generally persists over time. Indeed, as discussed in detail in Barbieri's chapter in this volume, nationally representative data show that the majority of today's elderly live with their adult children and their family. However, her chapter also underlines that the substantial social and economic changes that occurred during the 1990s may ultimately alter the traditional pattern.

Education, Urban Residence, Mating, and Marriage

We hypothesize that educational attainment and growing up in an urban area (compared to a rural area) produce important variations in mating and marriage. Theoretical explanations of family change highlight the influence of education and urbanization as forces of change, with education perceived as the primary engine transforming society (Macaulay 1974). Growth in the number and types of schools and an increase in school attendance can profoundly transform relationships within the family and the community (Cleland 2001; Jejeebhoy 1995; Thornton and Lin 1994). Increasing educational attendance may lead to a decline in parental authority as teachers, instead of parents, increasingly supervise and socialize children. Schools may impart values, attitudes, and ideas not necessarily shared by parents. A generational gap in education may result, reducing the prestige of the older, less educated generation (Caldwell 1982). Most important in the context of economic reforms, skills increase with education level, opening up more job opportunities for the better educated.

Barbieri's and Chi's chapters in this volume show that urbanization and migration from rural to urban areas are frequently associated with new living arrangement patterns (also see Thornton and Lin 1994 for similar trends in other Asian countries). In the same way, the place of childhood residence is expected to influence family structure and relationships. Rural/urban differences in nonfamilial employment opportunities, access to new information and ideas, leisure-time activities, patterns of association with others, and transportation and communication networks are all likely to affect mating and marriage (Nguyen 2005). In addition, the population density in urban areas often implies interactions and communication patterns different from those in rural areas due to the specialized and unfamiliar nature of social relations in cities.

When examining the influence of educational attainment and urban residence on mating and marriage, we expect both a *direct effect* and an *interaction effect* on mating and marriage. The direct effect specifies that an individual's education level and rural/urban residence will be significantly associated with mating and marriage, most notably in terms of parental control on mating and the prevalence of premarital sexual activity. In addition, we hypothesize that, for some aspects of mating and marriage, there will be an interaction between education, the place of residence (in urban versus rural areas) and the marriage cohort. This interaction effect hypothesizes that, while education and urban residence will significantly affect mating and marriage for all three cohorts, the nature of the association will be different for the renovation cohort compared to the American War and reunification cohorts. We hypothesize that the level of education and the place of residence will operate differently in the renovation cohort because inequality by education and rural/urban residence has increased during *Doi Moi*. As a result, the experience of growing up in an urban area has been different for the youngest individuals compared to older generations. In a similar way, differences in educational attainment by cohort are in large part explained by changes in the opportunities for education, the cost of education, and returns to education over time.

Indeed, Vietnam's postrenovation economic growth provides evidence of increasing inequality by education and rural/urban residence. While renovation has clearly resulted in a dramatic reduction in poverty (for example, consumption poverty fell from 54 percent in 1992–93 to 37 percent in 1997–98 [World Bank 1999]) and improvements in human development indicators (Justino and Litchfield 2003), this economic growth success story masks rising economic disparities (Binh et al. 2003; Glewwe, Gragnolati, and Zaman 2002; Minot et al. 2003; World Bank 1999).

Education level and rural/urban residence appear to aggravate these inequalities. Although poverty reductions during the mid-1990s were dramatic, the pattern of poverty reduction has been uneven. For example, while all education groups experienced poverty declines, individuals and households with higher educational attainment experienced proportionally larger declines. Among households headed by someone with a university education, the poverty rate declined from 13.4 percent in 1992–93 to 4.5 percent in 1997–98. In contrast, the poverty rate for households headed by individuals with no education has remained high, with a decline from 69.9 percent in 1992–93 to 57.3 percent in 1997–98. Increasing inequalities suggest that households headed by well-educated individuals were better able to take advantage of the economic changes resulting from *Doi Moi* (Glewwe, Gragnolati, and Zaman 2002). There are also substantial differences in poverty by rural/urban area, with urban areas characterized by lower poverty rates and sharper poverty declines than rural areas. While urban households enjoyed a 63.9 percent decline in poverty between 1992–93 and 1997–98, the decline for rural households was only half that (Justino and Litchfield 2003). In fact, Liu's calculations indicate that increases in rural/urban inequality account for 76 percent of the increase in total inequality between 1992–93 and 1997–98 (Liu 2001).

In summary, this chapter examines the extent of change in various aspects of mating and marriage in Vietnam's Red River Delta. To assess change, data from three different marital cohorts are used, including two cohorts marrying prior to *Doi Moi*, enabling us to better assess the extent of change attributable to renovation policies versus other significant changes in Vietnam's recent history. In assessing the extent of change, we highlight the role of education and urban residence, examining whether the influence of these two key variables has been strengthened or weakened since renovation. After describing our data and methods, we present our results, first by commenting on some basic descriptive measures that differentiate the three marriage cohorts, then by discussing a series of multivariate models.

Data

Assessing family change in Vietnam is difficult due to the lack of empirical data. Information was gathered in a population census in 1979; however, this data has not been published and is unavailable for analyses. The first available census data is for 1989, after the implementation of economic renovation policies. Other large surveys, such as the Demographic and Health Surveys and the Living Standards Surveys, also first occurred after renovation. Therefore, little empirical information exists on what families were like prior to renovation. The RRDFS, a collaborative project between the Institute of Sociology in Hanoi, in Vietnam, and the Population Studies Center at the University of Michigan, in the United States, was designed specifically to address this problem. The RRDFS uses a cohort design to assess the impact of recent social changes on Vietnamese families and provide some baseline data on families for future studies. Data were collected in 2003, and one of the authors, Vu Tuan Huy, directed all aspects of the fieldwork. To measure change over time and the influence of historical events on life course trajectories, the sample included individuals in three marriage cohorts, with each cohort corresponding to an important historical period in Vietnam's recent political history:

1. The War Cohort—the first cohort—married between 1963 and 1971, the period during Vietnam's war against the United States for reunification. Aggressive collectivization efforts and mass mobilization characterized this period in the North.
2. The Reunification Cohort—the second cohort—married between 1977 and 1985, the early postunification period, when economic hardship and social upheaval were most severe and when a centrally planned economy was pervasive. Economic growth was stagnant during this period and food shortages were common.
3. The Renovation Cohort—the final cohort—married between 1992 and 2000, the period when economic reforms and the opening of Vietnam to global influences were well under way. As more specifically

214 JAYAKODY AND VU

described in Bélanger and Barbieri's chapter, even though *Doi Moi* was proclaimed in 1986, it was not until the early 1990s that the reform efforts brought noticeable change.

The RRDFS is comprised of a representative sample of 1,296 currently married individuals, equally divided between men and women, rural and urban settings, and the three marital cohorts. Either the husband or the wife, but not both, participated in face-to-face interviews. The survey contains extensive information about marriage patterns, family structure and organization, and their potential determinants. Some of the topics not covered in this chapter have been reviewed elsewhere in detail (see Jayakody and Vu 2008 in particular). It also documents a number of potential covariates, namely the place of origin, the current place of residence (rural or urban), and the level of education of the respondents and their spouses. A stratified multistage cluster sampling approach was used. Figure 7.1 provides information on our sampling region. All eleven provinces of the Red River Delta were included in our sampling frame.

Respondents reported on events and experiences that had occurred in the past. We controlled for age by asking people to report experiences at a similar point in the life course, in our case at the time of marriage and during the first years of childrearing. The war cohort serves as the reference cohort with the assumption that historical change will account for differences in experiences or behaviors with the other two cohorts. Although this approach can separate period effects from age effects, we cannot distinguish between period effects and cohort effects. That is, when we use the war cohort as our historical marker, each successive marriage cohort is also associated with a different period, so that period and cohort are confounded.

An additional concern in analyses using cross-sectional data to examine social change is truncation. Because our sample criteria requires currently married couples, our oldest cohort is likely to be less representative of the population, as both individuals in the couple must still be alive. That is, some couples and individuals who married during the war cohort are absent from our study because one or both spouses have died. We therefore have age truncation for the oldest cohort. Comparisons between the RRDFS sample and the 1999 Vietnam Census 3 percent microdata sample file enabled us to identify potential problems of representativeness. Results suggest that mortality is not likely to have contributed a great deal to the selectivity of respondents.

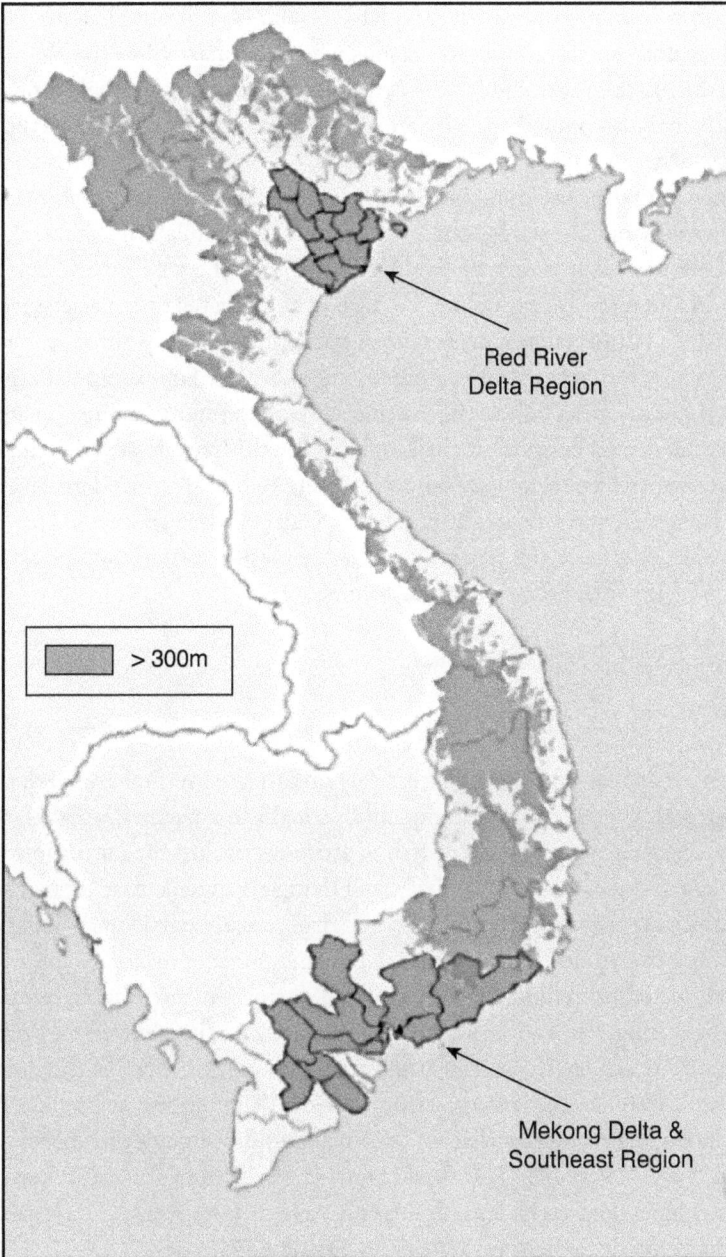

Figure 7.1   Vietnam map and study regions.

Migration into and out of the Red River Delta also means that the sample does not correspond exactly to persons who were married in the Red River Delta during the years under consideration. Therefore, our sample more specifically includes individuals who are currently married and living in the Red River Delta.

Since our study design involves retrospective information, recall bias may differentially operate across our three cohorts. Individuals in the war cohort may be more likely to recall events occurring in the past incorrectly than those in the more recent cohort because of the greater time lapse since the event. In addition, changing norms of social acceptability across the three cohorts may result in inaccurate reporting of events. For example, individuals in the renovation cohort may be more likely to report having engaged in premarital sexual behavior if the sanctions for this have lessened, compared to the prior two cohorts. Extensive pretesting in both rural and urban areas, with both men and women, attempted to address these concerns. However, we cannot eliminate the possibility of these biases, and this should be considered in any interpretation of our results.

Measures and Methods

As previously mentioned, we successively investigated several areas related to mating and marriage, including qualities sought in a partner, ways in which spouses became acquainted, courtship, attitudes toward the ideal age at first marriage, premarital sexual activity, and living arrangements after marriage. In examining aspects of mating and marriage, we are particularly interested in change over time and therefore include measures of marriage cohort, indicating whether individuals were married during the war, during reunification, or during renovation, with the war cohort as the omitted category in our multivariate analyses. Also, the respondent's sex (female is the omitted category) and age at marriage are included. Although the age at marriage is included, we recognize that we are unable to disentangle the direction of effects for this variable. The causal connectedness between age at marriage and the dependent variables is ambiguous, as age at marriage can be a determinant of the dependent variable or an outcome of it.

In addition, we included in our models the respondents' level of education and residence during childhood (in a rural or an urban area). The former is

TABLE 7.1

Independent and dependent variables by marriage cohort[1]

Indicator	War cohort	Reunification cohort	Renovation cohort
Mean age at marriage for men	25.32	25.64	26.41
Mean age at marriage for women	21.56	22.23	21.51
Grew up in urban area	17.13	23.15	30.56
Less than 12th grade education	65.28	65.74	55.79
Met spouse through parents or relatives	27.31	17.36	11.81
Courted two or more people	43.98	43.98	48.38
Courted for a year or more	57.17	54.68	60.65
Ideal age for women to marry 22 or older	28.94	45.83	56.71
Ideal age for men to marry 25 or older	44.44	64.12	79.17
Premarital sexual activity	4.86	8.56	21.53
Living with parents after marriage	61.11	70.37	74.77

[1]Table 7.1 presents the proportion for all categories, except mean age at marriage, which uses age in years as the unit. The total sample size is 1,296 with 432 respondents in each marital cohort.

a dichotomous measure contrasting individuals with fewer than twelve years of schooling, defined as the lower level of education, and those with twelve or more years of schooling (the omitted category). Questions used to determine whether the respondent grew up in a rural or urban area included the following: "At the time you were growing up (between the ages of five and fifteen years) was that area rural or urban?" Due to high postrenovation migration rates and because substantial time has elapsed since marriage for our older individuals, the area of residence while growing up is expected to be a more meaningful determinant of mating patterns than the current area of residence. Table 7.1 provides basic descriptive information on our dependent and independent variables for each of the three cohorts.

Tables 7.2 and 7.3 present further statistical results by cohort for each of our mating and marriage measures. For selected variables, we have conducted additional multivariate analyses that include our key control variables and test for potential interactions between the renovation cohort and education on the one hand, and the renovation cohort and residence during childhood on the other (Table 7.4). Due to the categorical nature of our mating and marriage measures, we implement logistic regression models. Because it is difficult to make meaningful interpretations from logistic regression coefficients, we present the odds-ratios calculated from the unstandardized beta coefficients and provide the level of significance for each coefficient. An odds-ratio greater than one indicates a higher likelihood for the indicated category compared to the omitted category, whereas an odds-ratio below one indicates a lower likelihood. We illustrate the impact of significant interactions by presenting graphs of the predicted probabilities.

Results

QUALITIES SOUGHT IN A PARTNER

We begin by examining the qualities sought in a marriage partner and the extent to which these differ across the three marital cohorts. Respondents were presented with a list of seventeen traits and asked to rate the importance of each one. These traits were chosen based on their predominance in both Vietnamese and international studies on mating (Buss 1990) and on pretest work conducted by the authors in Hai Duong (Red River Delta). Respondents were asked to think back to the time when they were getting married rather than to provide their current opinion. The question was phrased as: "Could you please tell me how important were each of these characteristics for your spouse to have before you got married?" Possible answers were: very important, somewhat important, not that important, and not at all important. Table 7.2 presents the results on the percentage of respondents who considered various traits to be very important, shown separately by traits sought in a husband (the responses given by female respondents), in a wife (the responses given by male respondents), and by marriage cohort. Results indicate significant differences in the mean values between men and women and among the marriage cohorts.

The most desirable characteristics include being hardworking, responsible, considerate, and having a gentle personality. Despite economic and social change, there is substantial similarity across the three cohorts in the characteristics desired in a husband or in a wife. No single trait showed consistent change across all three cohorts. There were no significant differences across cohorts by sex of the respondent in the importance of having a spouse who was hardworking or had a gentle personality. There was a change from the war cohort to the reunification cohort in the importance of having a husband who was responsible and considerate (these characteristics became more important) while there was no change across the three cohorts in the importance of these two traits in a wife.

TABLE 7.2.
Percentage of respondents who declared each trait as "Very Important" for a husband or wife

Trait	War cohort(1)			Reunification cohort(2)			Renovation cohort(3)			Husband[b]		Wife[c]	
	Traits sought in a wife	Traits sought in a husband	Significance[a]	Traits sought in a wife	Traits sought in a husband	Significance[a]	Traits sought in a wife	Traits sought in a husband	Significance[a]	1&2	2&3	1&2	2&3
Attractive looking	18.5	6.9	**	17.1	14.8	ns	14.8	8.8	*	**	*	ns	ns
Gentleness	75.9	51.9	ns	73.6	47.2	—	74.5	44.9	na	ns	ns	ns	ns
Hard working	80.1	74.1	—	74.5	76.9	ns	68.1	75.0	na	ns	ns	ns	ns
High level of education	10.2	25.0	*	15.3	27.8	**	19.9	25.0	na	**	ns	ns	ns
Stable occupation	27.8	37.0	**	38.4	50.0	**	31.5	50.0	—	**	ns	*	ns
High income	7.9	15.2	ns	13.4	25.9	**	15.7	31.0	**	**	ns	*	ns
Zodiac sign compatibility	8.9	7.9	ns	9.3	18.5	**	15.3	21.2	ns	*	ns	ns	*
Being responsible	69.9	72.7	ns	68.9	81.9	**	70.4	77.3	ns	ns	ns	ns	ns
Good family background	44.4	44.9	ns	44.9	44.9	ns	42.1	33.3	*	ns	*	ns	ns
Being obedient	52.8	20.8	*	48.1	15.7	—	49.1	23.1	—	**	*	ns	ns
Sharing interests &hobbies	13.9	12.0	ns	18.9	22.7	ns	21.8	28.2	ns	**	ns	ns	ns
Good sense of humor	4.6	8.8	ns	10.2	17.6	*	9.7	15.7	*	**	ns	*	ns
Being considerate	73.4	67.1	—	73.6	77.8	ns	71.8	75.9	ns	*	ns	ns	ns
Not a heavy drinker	31.0	50.9	**	33.8	59.7	—	33.8	53.2	—	**	ns	ns	ns
Intelligence	18.1	31.0	**	34.7	43.9	*	34.3	42.2	*	**	ns	—	ns
Not having a hot temper	27.3	37.9	ns	31.9	43.9	**	30.9	40.7	*	ns	ns	ns	ns
Ambition	2.8	5.6		4.6	6.9	ns	6.0	10.6	*	ns	ns	ns	ns

[a]This column indicates whether there is a significant difference between husband and wife on the importance of each characteristic.

[b]This column indicates whether there is a significant difference in the characteristics sought in a husband between the War (1) and Reunification (2) cohort and between the Reunification (2) and the Renovation (3) cohort for each characteristic.

[c]This column indicates whether there is a significant difference in the characteristics sought in a wife between the War (1) and Reunification (2) cohort and between the Reunification (2) and the Renovation (3) cohort for each characteristic.

*$p < .05$; **$p < .01$; ***$p < .001$; ns (not significant) $p > .05$

Additionally, when a significant change in the importance of a trait is evident, it appears to have occurred between the war and the reunification cohort, rather than between the reunification and the renovation cohort. For the traits sought in a husband, the following showed a significant change from the reunification to the renovation cohort: having a husband who was attractive, with a good family background, and obedient (more important for individuals in the reunification cohort than in the renovation cohort). Zodiac sign compatibility was the only characteristic that showed significant change in importance between the reunification and the renovation cohorts for a wife. Men in the renovation cohort were significantly more likely than men who married right after reunification to consider zodiac sign compatibility a "very important" characteristic to have in a wife. Due to the lack of further information on this issue in our data, we are unable to provide an explanation for this finding.

Although there is a remarkable similarity across cohorts in the characteristics rated as being "very important" to have in a spouse, there are substantial sex differences within each cohort. Previous research found that men value beauty more than women do, while women look for characteristics related to men's provider role (Buss 1989, 1990). For both the war and the renovation cohorts, there was a significant difference by sex in the importance of a spouse being attractive; having an attractive wife was significantly more important for men than having an attractive husband was for women. About 19 percent of men in the war cohort, 17 percent in the reunification cohort, and 15 percent in the renovation cohort indicated that finding an attractive wife was "very important" for them at the time they were getting married (compared to 7 percent, 15 percent, and 9 percent, respectively, of wives who felt that finding an attractive husband was "very important"). Interestingly, there is some speculation that Vietnamese men actually want a less attractive wife—"[marrying] a beautiful girl often results in a miserable fate" as the saying goes (Nguyen 1957, 140). A spouse with a gentle personality was ranked significantly higher for men than for women in all three cohorts.

In terms of characteristics measuring the provider role, a good job and a good income were significantly associated with better marriage prospects across all three cohorts. Additionally, for the renovation cohort, seeking a husband who was ambitious was significantly more important than seeking an ambitious wife. While having a good education was more important for a husband to possess than for a wife in the war and reunification cohorts, there was no significant difference by sex in the renovation cohort. Given women's high labor force participation in Vietnam, a good education is indeed an important factor for the economic status of the family.

Two of the characteristics considered very important by the highest percentage of respondents—being hardworking and being considerate—show no sex differences in all three cohorts. Because recent research on partner preferences tends to emphasize sex differences (Buss 1989), the extent to which men and women agree on what they are seeking in a mate has been generally overlooked, though cross-country studies have found that for prime partner preferences, such as kindness and honesty, there are few sex differences (Buss 1989; Goodwin 1999).

MEETING A SPOUSE

One hypothesis is that social and economic changes over the past four decades have created new social arrangements and institutions affecting how individuals meet their spouses. Though still fairly limited in scope, the rapid spread of Internet dating among Vietnamese urban youth is one extreme example of such changes (Nguyen 2005). In our survey, respondents were asked: "Thinking back to the time before you were married, how did you first become acquainted with your spouse? Did your spouse live in the same place as you? Did you meet him/her through work, through school, through friends, through parents or relatives, or in some other way (specify)?" We used separate questions to identify the different ways of meeting a spouse so as to allow several possible answers. The results are displayed in Table 7.3. They are presented separately by cohort and rural/urban residence during childhood.

Differences in how respondents met their spouses are evident both across marriage cohorts and by the childhood place of residence. For example, among the war cohort, one of the most common ways of meeting a spouse was by working together. The prevalence of meeting one's spouse through work declined for those in the reunification cohort and declined further in the renovation cohort. Additionally, regardless of the cohort, meeting through work was more prevalent for individuals growing up in urban than in rural areas. We also see substantial declines across the three marital cohorts in the proportion of respondents who met their spouse through parents or relatives. On the other hand, meeting a spouse through friends or in a place of entertainment has increased. Only 1 percent of rural residents in the war

TABLE 7.3
Percentage distribution of respondents on the circumstances
of their meeting their spouses by cohort and current place of residence

Circumstances of meeting one's spouse	War cohort		Reunification cohort		Renovation cohort	
	Rural	Urban	Rural	Urban	Rural	Urban
Working together	24.0	41.9	19.0	27.0	6.7	18.2
Going to school together	10.3	13.5	10.0	12.0	8.0	9.9
Through friends	18.2	24.3	20.5	33.0	27.0	33.3
Through parents or relatives	28.5	21.6	19.6	10.0	10.3	15.2
Through entertainment places	3.9	1.4	5.4	4.0	12.7	15.2
Through a matchmaker	3.4	2.7	0.9	1.0	0.7	0.0
By myself	11.7	1.4	23.2	18.0	33.3	15.2
Lived in the same village	22.1	6.8	22.9	6.0	19.7	6.1
In a common social association	2.0	1.4	1.5	1.0	1.7	1.5
Other	2.0	4.1	2.1	3.0	1.7	3.8

cohort reported meeting their spouse in a place of entertainment, whereas 15 percent of urban residents in the renovation cohort reported doing so.

We were particularly interested in comparing the experience of meeting one's spouse through more "traditional" family-based means, such as meeting through parents or relatives, versus other ways of meeting. As nonfamilial social institutions become increasingly important, parents and relatives are likely to play less of a role in finding a marital partner. To examine whether the influence of family in meeting a spouse has changed across the three cohorts, we constructed a dependent variable contrasting individuals who met through parents or relatives (coded as 1) with all others (coded as 0). We then estimated a logistic regression model, including marital cohort, sex, age at marriage, growing up in urban areas, and having fewer than twelve years of education as the independent variables (results not shown). However, such a model does not adequately describe the effect of the residential context (urban versus rural) on how individuals met their spouse under the assumption of a differential effect of this variable by cohort. We thus tested a more complicated model in which we included two interaction terms, namely an interaction between the childhood place of residence and the renovation cohort and another interaction between the level of education and the renovation cohort. As the fit statistics indicated that the first interaction term had a statistically significant effect but not the second, our final model included only the former.

The results are presented in Table 7.4, Model 1. They indicate that the probability of meeting a spouse through parents or relatives declined significantly across the three cohorts. The odds of meeting one's mate through parents or relatives for those marrying after reunification and those in the renovation cohort were, respectively, 44 percent and 72 percent lower than for those in the war cohort, controlling for all the other variables in the model. This finding shows that the influence of family declined from the war to the reunification and again to the renovation period. Another finding was that the odds of meeting one's mate through parents or relatives are 30 percent lower for men than for women, suggesting that family influence is greater for the latter than for the former. By contrast with education, which appears not to be statistically significant, growing up in an urban area is associated with the probability of meeting one's spouse through parents or relatives. Additionally, the significant interaction term indicates that the nature of this effect is different for the renovation cohort compared to the war and reunification cohorts.

To better illustrate the effect of this interaction, we calculated predicted probabilities using the estimates from Model 1, Table 7.4, and displayed them in Figure 7.2. The probability of meeting one's spouse through parents and relatives has declined across the three cohorts. Individuals who grew up in a rural area and who married during the war are the most likely to have met their spouse through parents or relatives (24 percent), whereas individuals who also grew up in a rural area but married during renovation are the least likely to have met their spouse in this way (8 percent). Figure 7.2 also illustrates how growing up in a rural or urban area differentially affects the probability of having met one's spouse through parents or relatives by cohort. Whereas growing up in a rural area increased the probability of having met a spouse through parents or relatives for the war and reunification cohorts, individuals in the renovation cohort who grew up in an urban area are surprisingly more likely to have met through parents or relatives, a finding that partly contradicts conventional thinking about these issues and the role of urbanization on increased individual freedom.

COURTSHIP

The following two questions provided information on courtship: (1) "How many people did you court before you got married, including your spouse?"

TABLE 7.4
Logistic regression models[1]

	MODEL 1 Meeting spouse through parents or relatives	MODEL 2 Courting two or more people	MODEL 3 Courting a year or more	MODEL 4 Marrying after age 20 is ideal for women	MODEL 5 Marrying after age 22 is ideal for men	MODEL 6 Premarital sexual activity	MODEL 7 Living with parents after marriage
	odds ratio	odds ratio	odds ratio	odds ratio	odds ratio	odds ratio	odds ratio
Constant							
Marital cohort							
Reunification	.56***	.95	.88	2.04***	2.17***	1.88*	1.64**
Renovation	.28***	1.13	1.23	3.09***	4.11***	3.14***	3.08***
Male	.67*	.69**	.96	.38***	.59***	1.16***	1.55**
Marital age	1.03	1.10***	.99	1.17***	1.17***	1.02	.91***
Grew up in an urban area	.59*	1.05	1.63	2.74***	1.80**	1.71*	.90
Low education	1.32	1.01	.45***	.55***	.71*	.47**	2.11***
Interaction							
Renovation* urban	2.68*				4.05*		
Renovation* education			.51*			2.73***	.55*

[1]This table presents the odds-ratios and the significance level for each coefficient. When the inclusion of an interaction term significantly improved model fit, the model with the interaction terms is presented. Otherwise, the base model with no interaction terms is presented. *p < .05; **p < .01; ***p < .001

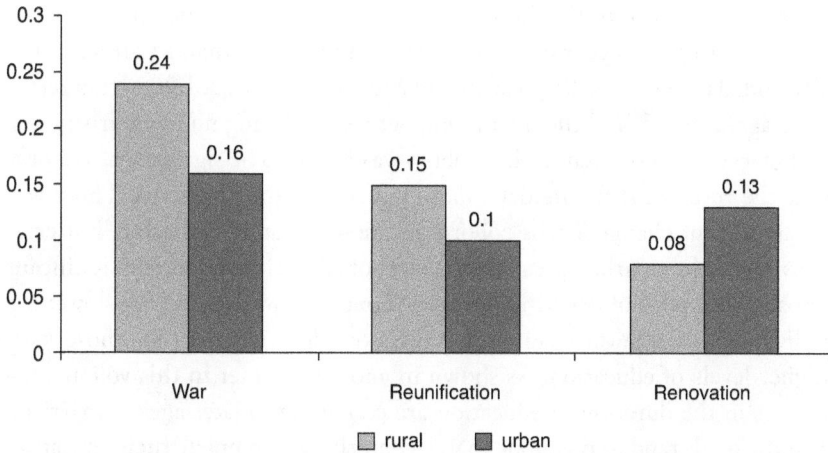

Figure 7.2   The Probability of Meeting One's Spouse Through Parents or Relatives
NOTE: Predicted probability calculated for men with lower education who married at age 20.

and (2) "How long did you and your spouse court before you got married?" The majority of the respondents in our sample courted fewer than two persons—about 10 percent did not court; 45 percent courted only one person; 21 percent courted two; 18 percent courted three; and only about 7 percent courted four or more. To assess change across our three cohorts, we created a dichotomous variable for the number of people courted, coding those who courted two or more people as 1 and those who courted no one or only their spouse as 0. Model 2, Table 7.4, shows these results. Although interaction terms between education and the renovation cohort, and between growing up in an urban area and the renovation cohort, were tested, the coefficients were not statistically significant and the variables did not significantly improve our model fit. Consequently, only direct effects are included in the final model. Findings indicate that the odds of multiple courtship for men were significantly lower (by about 40 percent) than for women. The age at marriage also was significantly associated with courtship patterns with, not surprisingly, a higher probability of multiple courtship for those marrying later. Growing up in a rural area and the level of education did not significantly affect the number of people courted. Additionally, there was no change across cohorts in the number of people courted.

Next, we turned to the duration of courtship and examined the probability of courting for a year or more (coded 1) and for less than a year (or not at all) (coded 0), with results presented in Model 3, Table 7.4. Interaction terms were again tested, and the interaction between growing up in an urban area and marrying in the renovation cohort was found to be significant. We present the results for the model containing this interaction term. There was no significant change across cohorts in the duration of courtship; however, growing up in an urban area and the level of education did have a significant impact. The odds of courting for at least one year were 55 percent lower for individuals with fewer than twelve years of education than for those with higher levels of education. As shown in another chapter in this volume, increases in the duration of education are conducive to later ages at marriage as individuals tend to postpone marriage until they complete their education (see Xenos et al., this volume).

Figure 7.3 shows the predicted probabilities that illustrate the interaction effect. For those marrying during the war or just after reunification, the probability of courting for a year or more does not exhibit any significant difference by the place of childhood residence, in contrast with those who married during renovation, for whom growing up in an urban area significantly increases the duration of courtship compared to those who grew up in a rural area. This finding may indicate that the prerequisites for marriage, such as becoming financially independent and securing housing, have taken longer to achieve in urban areas after renovation, thereby lengthening the courtship period for urban respondents.

AGE AT FIRST MARRIAGE

Table 7.1 shows the mean age at first marriage for men and women in each cohort. Although the actual age at marriage has increased slightly for men in the renovation cohort, there has been little change for women. In addition to actual age at marriage, we examine whether there has been any attitudinal change in the ideal age at which men and women are expected to marry. Respondents were asked: "Thinking back to the time when you got married, what would people think about a man who got married before age 18? Would people think this age was too early to get married or about right?" If respondents indicated that this age was "about right," they were asked no further questions. If respondents answered that this age was "too early," they were

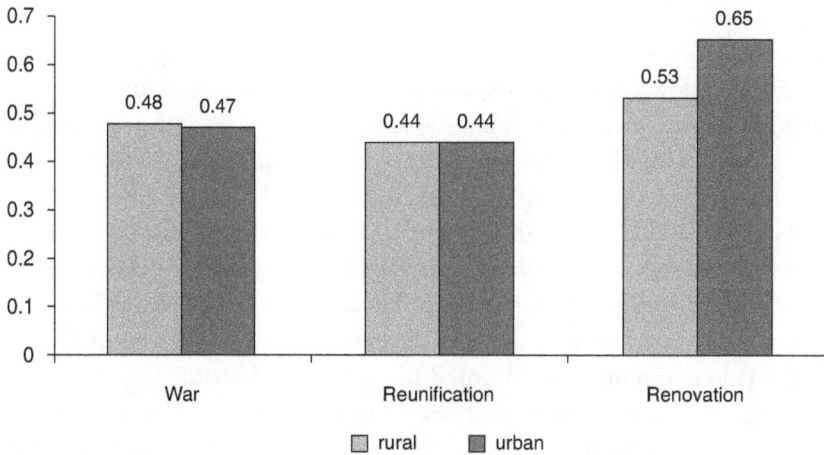

Figure 7.3   The Probability of Courting a Year or More
NOTE: Predicted probability calculated for men with lower education who married
at age 20.

then asked whether getting married by age twenty was "too early" or "about
right." Respondents continued to be asked about subsequent ages (twenty-
two, twenty-five, thirty) until they indicated an age that was "about right."

Model 4, Table 7.4, presents the results from a logistic regression model
where the dependent variable indicates whether respondents felt marrying after age twenty was ideal for women (coded 1), or whether they felt the ideal age
for women to marry was up to twenty (coded 0). Although the actual ages at
which women marry did not change across our three cohorts, there has been
a substantial attitudinal shift in what is regarded as the ideal age at first marriage for women. Compared with those in the war cohort, individuals marrying in the reunification cohort were twice as likely, and individuals marrying
during the renovation cohort were three times as likely, to think that the ideal
age for women to marry was after age twenty. Investments in education and
career training and their economic returns have increased since renovation,
and people may therefore believe that individuals should marry at a later age
in order to first accumulate human capital skills. Further evidence on the relationship between the ages at which young Vietnamese now leave school,
start working, and get married is provided elsewhere in this volume (see Xenos et al.). Although most of the respondents think that women should marry

after twenty, there is a difference depending on the sex of the respondent: the odds of declaring an ideal age at first marriage for women past twenty are significantly lower for male respondents (by 60 percent) than for female. In addition, those who married at older ages were more likely to think marrying past twenty was ideal for women. There were no significant interactions between education, growing up in an urban area, and the renovation cohort.

Model 5, Table 7.4, examines the probability that individuals declare that the ideal age at first marriage for men is twenty-two and above (coded 1), compared to below twenty-two (coded 0). The coefficient on the interaction between growing up in an urban area and marrying during the renovation cohort significantly improved the model fit. As with the ideal age at marriage for women, there has been a significant change across the three cohorts in attitudes toward the ideal age at marriage for men. Compared to the war cohort, the odds of declaring the ideal age at first marriage for men to be twenty-two years or more are twice that of declaring an ideal age below twenty-two for individuals in the reunification cohort and four times that for individuals in the renovation cohort. Again, male respondents were significantly less likely than female respondents to think that marrying after age twenty-two was ideal (with an odds ratio about 40 percent below that for women), while individuals who married at older ages were more likely to think marrying after twenty-two was ideal for men. Individuals whose education level was fewer than twelve years of schooling were also less likely to think marrying after age twenty-two was ideal (with an odds ratio about 30 percent below that for individuals with higher levels of education).

Figure 7.4 displays the predicted probabilities and illustrates the interaction between growing up in an urban area and marrying in the renovation cohort. It shows how, regardless of the childhood place of residence, the probability of considering an ideal age at marriage of twenty-two years or more for men increases with the marriage cohort. For all three cohorts, individuals who grew up in a rural area are less likely than those who grew up in an urban area to think that marrying after age twenty-two is ideal for men. The main finding implied by the interaction term is that the difference in attitude toward the ideal age at marriage for men between respondents who grew up in a rural area and those who grew up in an urban area has increased over time, that is, there is a larger difference between these two groups for the renovation cohort than for earlier cohorts. This supports our hypothesis that the increasing rural/urban inequality following the reforms has trans-

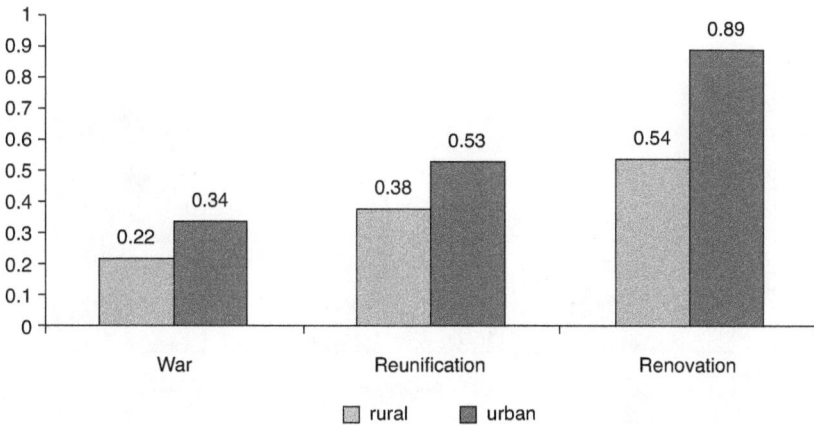

Figure 7.4   The Probability of Age 22 or Later as Ideal Age for Men to Marry
NOTE: Predicted probability calculated for men with lower education who married at age 20.

formed the nature of the effects of a rural versus an urban childhood for this cohort, compared to earlier cohorts.

PREMARITAL SEX

Premarital sexual experience is measured by self reports to the following two questions: "Was the first time you had sexual intercourse with your spouse before or after you got married?" and "Did you ever have sexual intercourse with someone else before you got married?" A dichotomous variable indicates whether the respondent had sex before marriage, either with his or her spouse or with someone else. The logistic regression model presented in Model 6, Table 7.4, shows the impact of our independent variables on this dependent variable. The coefficient attached to the interaction between the level of education and the renovation cohort is significant, and we focus our discussion on this model.

A significant difference across cohorts in the probability of reporting premarital sex is evident. Individuals in the reunification and renovation cohorts have a higher probability of reporting that they have had premarital sex than those in the war cohort. The odds for those in the reunification cohort are almost twice as high, and the odds for those in the renovation cohort are

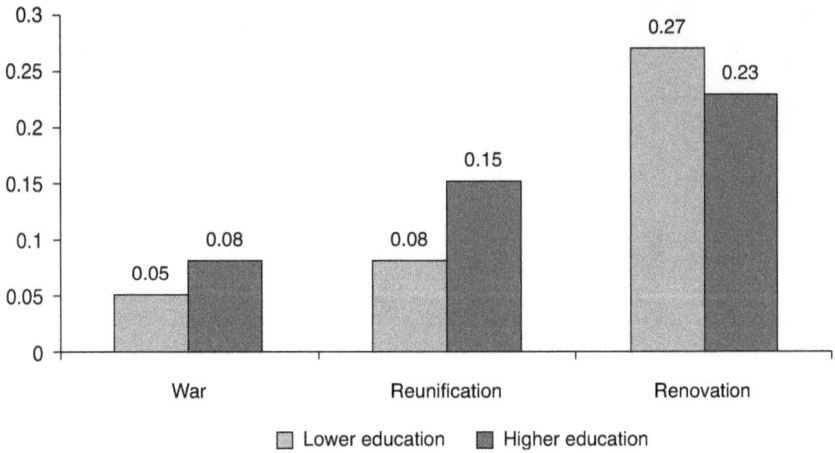

Figure 7.5   The Probability of Premarital Sexual Activity
NOTE: Predicted probability calculated for men growing up in rural areas who married at age 20.

over three times as high as in the war cohort. Men are significantly more likely than women to have had premarital sex. Individuals who grew up in an urban area are also more likely to have sex before marriage than are those who grew up in a rural area, controlling for the other variables in the model (the odds ratio is about 70 percent higher for the former than for the latter). This finding supports the results of other studies which have suggested that there is less supervision, weakening parental control, and more opportunities for privacy in urban areas, especially for young people who have moved from rural areas, and also that attitudes toward premarital sex are more lax in urban areas (Khuat 2003; Nguyen 2005, 2007). It is also possible that a higher rate of premarital sexual activity in urban areas reflects a greater exposure to commercial sex.

Figure 7.5 displays the predicted probabilities for the interaction term between education and marrying in the renovation cohort. As illustrated, regardless of the level of education, the probability of premarital sex has increased from one marriage cohort to the next. Whereas only 5 percent of the less educated and 8 percent of the better educated respondents declare premarital sex in the war cohort, the proportions increase to 27 and 23 percent, respectively, for the renovation cohort. These proportions also indicate that the relationship between education and the probability of declaring pre-

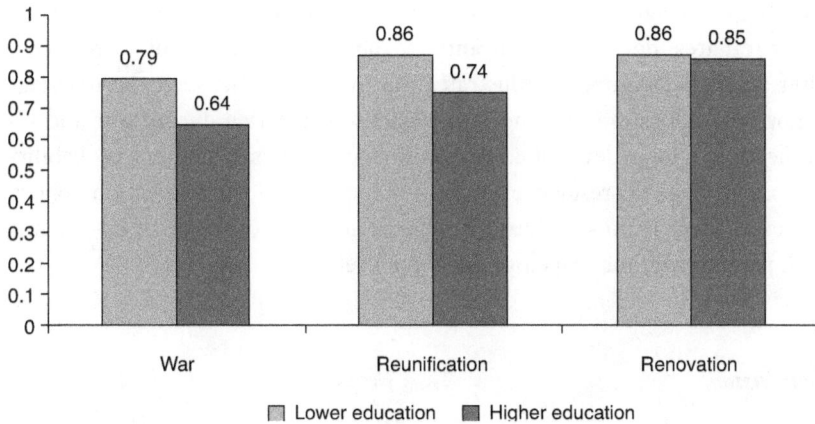

Figure 7.6   The Probability of Living with Parents After Marriage
NOTE: Predicted probability calculated for men growing up in rural areas who married at age 20.

marital sex has become stronger over time. Among the war and reunification cohorts, the higher educated individuals are more likely to declare premarital sex than those with lower levels of education. In the renovation cohort, however, individuals with lower levels of education are more likely to declare premarital sex than those with twelve or more years of education.

LIVING ARRANGEMENTS AFTER MARRIAGE

Next, we examined the probability of co-residing with parents (including in-laws) right after marriage (coded 1) compared to other types of living arrangements (coded 0), such as independently or with nonparental others. Because the introduction of an interaction term between the level of education and the marriage cohort significantly improved the model fit, we focus our discussion on the model containing the interaction effect (Model 7 in Table 7.4). There are significant changes across our three cohorts in the probability of co-residing with parents after marriage. The odds of co-residing with parents are about three times higher for respondents in the renovation cohort than for those in the war cohort, a finding supported by other studies (Hirschman and Nguyen 2002). Men are significantly more likely to live with parents after marriage, and the probability of co-residence after marriage declines slightly with increased age at marriage. Having grown up in an urban area, compared to a rural area, does not significantly change the probability of co-residence after marriage. Figure 7.6 illustrates the interaction between the marriage cohort and education. Among individuals who married during war and re-unification, a lower level of education is associated with a higher probability of postmarriage co-residence. Among individuals in the renovation cohort, however, there is no significant difference in the probability of co-residing with parents after marriage by education level.

Conclusion

Although many have speculated that economic reforms have resulted in dra-matic changes in Vietnamese society, the lack of longitudinal data had so far limited the empirical examination of the extent and nature of these changes. Data from the RRDFS, with its cohort design, can be used to examine such changes in mating and marriage, either as a consequence of *Doi Moi* or be-cause of significant political events in the previous periods. The three co-horts design provides information relevant for periods both before and after renovation, enabling a more accurate assessment of change. While the data indicate substantial changes in many aspects of mating and marriage behav-ior, it is important to note that many of these changes preceded *Doi Moi*. For several of our measures, changes from the war cohort to the reunification cohort are as large, and even larger in some cases, than those from the reuni-fication cohort to the renovation cohort. This long-range view is necessary to avoid overattributing change to the recent reforms.

While mating and marriage behavior during renovation appears to be a continuation and, in many cases, an acceleration of changes already under way, an analysis of interaction effects highlights the unique nature of family change after *Doi Moi*. Interactions were introduced in our models to allow for a differential relationship between the dependent variable and education on the one hand, and the place of residence in childhood on the other, for the renova-tion marriage cohort compared to the other two cohorts. Their effects show that significant structural change has indeed occurred in the relationship between education and the place of childhood residence on the one hand, and attitudes and behavior in mating and marriage on the other, during *Doi Moi*. These results also demonstrate that examining direct effects alone does not adequately capture the influence of education and urban residence on mating and marriage. In many of our base models, the level of education and the type of residence in childhood were not significantly associated with the mating and marriage outcomes (results not shown). It was only after the interaction was included that education and urban area became significant. The changing nature of education and place of childhood residence after renovation, along with an increasing difference between respondents by education and rural/urban residence, helps explain these significant interactions. The importance of the interaction effects demonstrates the growing divergence between individuals in rural and urban areas and with different levels of education. While economic studies on rising inequality after *Doi Moi* illustrate the increasing gap in income and living standards by education and place of residence, our research demonstrates other areas of difference, as illustrated by a growing dissimilarity in mating and marriage behavior and attitudes.

Many of our findings concerning these interaction effects may be due to economic differences. In other words, educational attainment and having grown up in an urban area may in fact interact with mating and marriage through their association with income levels (not measured in our models due to the lack of information). Since we recognize this potential confounding effect of education and place of residence with income, we do not argue for a pure education effect or a pure urban effect and believe that income differences may explain part or all of the difference in postrenovation behavior. The importance of education and urban residence, however, does not mean that changes in mating and marriage cannot be entirely attributed to compositional effects, or to economic versus cultural factors. In fact, Goode (1963) hypothesized that links exist between economic development and cultural change, and the best explanation for change is likely to be an interaction between structure and ideation and between economic development and "culture" (Jayakody, Thornton, and Axinn 2008).

Our examination of mating and marriage focuses on those marrying between 1962 and 2000. Many individuals who married during the renovation period grew up and were socialized before the substantial changes resulting from *Doi Moi* had taken place. Therefore, this research likely underestimates the effects of renovation, and future research is expected to uncover further changes. As indicated by other chapters in this volume, the substantial social and economic changes currently experienced by Vietnam are likely to

234 JAYAKODY AND VU

fundamentally alter family and personal relationships. Although it is doubtful that Vietnam will suddenly abandon its traditional kinship structure, accommodation and adaptations to respond to new social conditions are likely.

References

Barbieri, M., and Vu T. H. 1996. *The impact of social-economic changes on some aspects of the family in Vietnam: A case study in Thai Binh province.* Hanoi: National Political Publishing House.

Bélanger, D., and Khuat T. H. 1995. Some changes in marriage and family in Hanoi during 1965–1992. *Sociological Review* 4: 27–41.

Bélanger, D., and Khuat T. H. 1996. Marriage and the family in urban North Vietnam, 1965–1993. *Journal of Population* 2(1): 83–111.

Binh T. Nguyen, J. A. Albrecht, S. B. Vroman, and M. D. Westbrook. 2003. *A quantile regression decomposition of urban-rural inequality in Vietnam.* Working paper. Washington, DC: Department of Economics, Georgetown University.

Buss, D. M. 1989. Sex differences in human mate preferences: Evolutionary hypotheses tested in 37 cultures. *Behavioral and Brain Sciences* 12: 1–49.

Buss, D. M. 1990. International preferences in selecting mates. *Journal of Cross-Cultural Psychology* 21: 5–47.

Caldwell, J. C. 1982. *Theory of fertility decline.* New York: Academic Press.

Cleland, J. 2001. The effects of improved survival on fertility: A reassessment. *Population Development Review* 27: 60–92.

Dinh Trung Tung. 2000. *Introduction to the basic contents of Vietnam marriage and family law in 2000.* Hanoi: Ho Chi Minh Publishing House. [Available in Vietnamese only]

Do Thai Dong. 1991. Modification of the traditional family in the south of Vietnam. In *Sociological studies on the Vietnamese family,* edited by R. Liljestrom and Tuong Lai, 69–83. Hanoi: Social Science Publishing House.

Glewwe, P., M. Gragnolati, and H. Zaman. 2002. Who gained from Vietnam's boom in the 1990s? *Economic Development and Cultural Change* 50(4): 773–792.

Goode, W. J. 1963. *World revolution and family patterns.* New York: Free Press.

Goodwin, R. 1998. Personal relationships and social change: The "realpolitik" of cross-cultural research in transient cultures. *Journal of Social and Personal Relationships* 15(2): 227–247.

Goodwin, R. 1999. *Personal relationships across cultures.* London: Routledge.

Ha Van Cau. 1992. *Wedding customs in Vietnam.* Hanoi: Government Publishing House. [Available in Vietnamese only]

Haughton, D., J. Haughton, and N. Phong. (Eds.). 2001. *Living standards during an economic boom: Vietnam 1993–1998.* Hanoi: Statistical Publishing House.

Hirschman, C., and Nguyen H. M. 2002. Tradition and change in Vietnamese family structure in the Red River delta. *Journal of Marriage and the Family* 64: 1063–1079.

Hirschman, C., and Vu M. L. 1996. Family and household structure in Vietnam: Some glimpses from a recent survey. *Public Affairs* 69: 229–249.

Jayakody, R., Thornton, A., and Axinn, W. 2008. Perspectives on international family change. In *International family change: Ideational perspectives*, edited by R. Jayakody, A. Thornton, and W. Axinn, 1–18. Mahwah, NJ: Lawrence Erlbaum Associates.

Jayakody, R., and Vu T. H. 2008. Social change and marriage in Vietnam: From socialist State to market reform. In *International family change: Ideational perspectives*, edited by R. Jayakody, A. Thornton, and W. Axinn, 199–222. Mahwah, NJ: Lawrence Earlbaum Associates.

Jejeebhoy, S. J. 1995. *Women's education, autonomy, and reproductive behavior: Experience from developing countries.* Oxford, U.K.: Clarendon Press.

Justino, P., and J. Litchfield. 2003. Welfare in Vietnam during the 1990s: Poverty, inequality and poverty dynamics. *Working paper, Poverty Research Unit at Sussex, Paper No. 8, Sussex, United Kingdom.*

Khuat Thu Hong. 2003. *Adolescent and youth reproductive health in Vietnam: Status, issues, policies, and programs.* Hanoi: Policy.

Lamb, D. 2002. *Vietnam, now.* New York: Public Affairs.

Liu, A. Y. C. 2001. Markets, inequality and poverty in Vietnam. *Asian Economic Journal* 15(2): 217–235.

Macaulay, C. 1974. *Letters of education.* New York: Garland Publishing.

Mensch, B., W. H. Clark, and Dang N. A. 2002. *Premarital sex in Vietnam: Is the current concern with adolescent reproductive health warranted?* (No. 163). New York: The Population Council.

Minot, N., B. Baulch, B. Epprecht, and M. Epprecht. 2003. *Poverty and inequality in Vietnam: Spatial patterns and geographic determinants.* Washington, DC: International Food Policy Research Institute and Institute for Development Studies.

Nguyen An Phuong. 2005. Courtship and marriage of university graduates in Hanoi: Changing values in a time of market liberalisation. *South East Asia Research* 13(3): 385–416.

Nguyen An Phuong. 2007. "Relationships based on love and relationships based on needs": Emerging trends in youth sex culture in contemporary urban Vietnam. *Modern Asian Studies* 41: 287–313.

Nguyen Huu Minh. 1995. *Age at first marriage in Vietnam: Patterns and determinants.* Unpublished Working Paper, University of Washington, Seattle.

Nguyen Huu Minh. 1996. *Tradition and change in Vietnamese marriage patterns in the Red River delta.* Unpublished dissertation, University of Washington, Seattle.

Nguyen Van Ngoc. 1957. *Proverbs and Folk-Songs.* Hanoi: Minh Duc Publishing House. [Available in Vietnamese only]

Norlund, I., C. L. Gates, and Vu C. D. 1995. *Vietnam in a changing world*. Richmond: Curzon. Pham Van Bich. 1998. *The Vietnamese family in change: The case of the Red River delta*. London: Curzon Press.

Thornton, A., and H. S. Lin. 1994. *Social change and the family in Taiwan*. Chicago: University of Chicago Press.

Tran Dinh Huou. 1991. Traditional families in Vietnam and the influence of Confucianism. In *Sociological studies on the Vietnamese family*, edited by R. Liljestrom and Tuong L., 25–47. Hanoi: Social Science Publishing House.

Vu Manh Loi. 1991. The gender division of labour in rural families in the Red River delta. In *Sociological studies on the Vietnamese family*, edited by R. Liljestrom and Tuong L., 149–163. Hanoi: Social Science Publishing House.

Vu Tuan Huy. 2004. *Tendency of the family: Some features from pilot study in Hai Duong*. Hanoi: Social Science Publishing House. [Available in Vietnamese only]

World Bank. 1999. *Vietnam development report 2000: Attacking poverty*. Hanoi: World Bank.

World Bank. 2003. *Vietnam development report 2004: Poverty*. Hanoi: World Bank.

Yu, Insun. 1978. *Law and family in seventeenth and eighteenth century Vietnam*. PhD dissertation in History, University of Michigan.

Yu, Insun. 1994. *Law and Vietnam society in the 17th and 18th century*. Seoul: Asiatic Research Center.

Chapter Eight

The Legacy of *Doi Moi*, the Legacy of Immigration

Overseas Vietnamese Grooms Come Home to Vietnam

HUNG CAM THAI

The mass out-migration of Vietnamese to the West was part of a specific phase in global history. The political turmoil of the mid-1970s in Southeast Asia resulted in more than two million people leaving Vietnam, primarily as political refugees, and relocating in more than eighty countries worldwide (Tran 1997). More than 90 percent of these post-1975 international migrants reside in the core countries of the United States, Canada, Australia, and France (Merli 1997). Vietnamese out-migration can be categorized into six different waves which were closely associated with socioeconomic origins and whether one came from an urban or rural background. In general, the earlier waves came from more affluent urban backgrounds (Chan 1991; Kibria 1993; Whitmore 1995).[1] While they continue to be associated with refugee out-migration or "the scatterings of war," as Zhou and Bankston (1998) call them, the majority of Vietnamese immigrants currently enter such countries as the United States through family sponsorship, as is the case for the general immigrant population.[2] Scholars continue to write about this group's sense of displacement and their experiences as refugees in settlements worldwide (Freeman and Huu 2003; Thomas 1997; Zhou and Bankston 1998) but have paid little attention to the global links Vietnamese emigrants have maintained with their families and networks of kin in Vietnam over the past three decades.

By attending to the emergence of a transpacific marriage market that has been made available to women in Vietnam and Vietnamese men who live overseas, I disembark from the refugee model of Vietnamese migration. This marriage market is invariably gendered because very few Vietnamese women return from overseas to Vietnam to find husbands as I discovered in my investigation of case studies and confirmed by consulting marriage registration lists at the Vietnamese Department of Justice. This gendered pattern resulted from a high male mortality rate during the Vietnam War (known in Vietnam as the American War) and the emigration of more men than women during the last quarter of the twentieth century. This has produced what demographer Daniel Goodkind (1997) calls the "double marriage squeeze," a situation resulting in a "surplus" of women of marriageable age in Vietnam and a "surplus" of men of marriageable age in Vietnamese communities overseas.[3]

In this chapter, I argue that the recent return of immigrant Vietnamese men to their homeland to find wives is not just a matter of an emigration history, nor is it simply a matter of demographic skews. It has emerged in the context of global forces and transnational ties that have changed Vietnamese society on many levels, and as a consequence of changing gender relations in postmigrant overseas Vietnamese communities that are only partly related to demographic skews (Kibria 1993). After having no contact with most of the Western world between 1975 and 1986 for the south, and much longer for the north, in 1986, Vietnam adopted a new socioeconomic policy called *Doi Moi*[4] (renovation) which did not end state ownership or central planning, but moved the country from complete state-sponsored socialism to partial free-market capitalism (Ebashi 1997; Morley and Nishihara 1997). Vietnam was admitted to the Association of Southeast Asian Nations (ASEAN) in 1993, but it was not until August 1995 that former U.S. President Bill Clinton established full diplomatic relations with the country (Morley and Nishihara 1997).

The normalization of economic and social ties by 1995 gradually increased the number of individuals from the Vietnamese diaspora, known as *Viet Kieu*, who returned to Vietnam to visit family members or to vacation. Incentives provided by the state for the overseas population, like the ability to purchase land and make investments, have created an extraordinarily important *Viet Kieu* economy. For instance, remittances grew dramatically from only $35 million in 1991 to more than $2 billion by 2002 (Nguyen 2002). The Vietnamese government estimates that there are currently more than one million *Viet Kieu* who return to visit annually, a dramatic increase

The Legacy of Doi Moi   239

from eight thousand in 1988 and eighty-seven thousand in 1992. The traffic of *Viet Kieu* goods, people, and ideas has manifested itself in profound gendered ways, one of which is the ability for men overseas to improve their social status in their pursuit of marriage when they return to Vietnam.

In Vietnam, family life has undergone dramatic socioeconomic changes since *Doi Moi*. This chapter joins others in this volume to shift the spotlight from macrotransformations to daily activities by focusing on global economic changes on the subjective experiences encountered by family and kinship across the Vietnamese diaspora (see Bélanger and Barbieri, this volume). In this chapter, I point to the significance of Vietnamese international migration and international marriages on a particular segment of Vietnamese families. As noted by Jayakody and Huy as well as by Xenos et al. in this volume, a number of significant changes have taken place in mate selection and union formation since *Doi Moi*, including diminished parental influences and the rise of personal choice. Others in this volume, including Luong, Chi, and Bélanger and Pendakis, have shown how migration has modified families' economic circumstances and social practices. This chapter provides an exploratory look at the nexus between international migration and international marriage against the backdrop of a *Viet Kieu* economy and the 1986 policy shift of *Doi Moi*.

I identify the logics of consumption, defined here as the usage of goods and services at the end of the chain of production,[5] that allow some low-wage-earning Vietnamese immigrant men to create definitions around social worth, status, and national identity when they return to Vietnam for marriage. I establish that consumption among *Viet Kieu* provides a crucial platform from which to understand *Doi Moi* and the dynamics of change among a specific segment of families in Vietnam. In describing the lives of low-wage immigrant men in the context of Vietnam's post-1975 emigration to the West, this chapter engages in two important conversations among scholars doing work on globalization and national identity. First, I address the power of status across transnational social fields by highlighting relations between class and masculinities in globalization (Connell 1995, 2000; Goldring 1998, 2003; Jones-Correa 1998a, 1998b; Smith 1998). Second, by bringing questions of masculinity into the discussions on globalization, I join the dialogue of feminist theorists who have demonstrated that gender plays a key role in the constitution and formation of national subjectivities and collectivities (Abu-Lughod 1998; Alonso 1994; Chatterjee 1993; Espiritu 1997; Lowe 1996). Focusing on men, this chapter draws upon a study consisting of 189 interviews with men, women, and their families who have participated in the recent formation of the Vietnamese transpacific marriage market that links Vietnamese men overseas and women in Vietnam (Thai 2008). In a larger study, about 80 percent of the men in my sample who returned to Vietnam for wives were part of the low-wage, low-status labor market in their diasporic locations.

Interviews used in this analysis come from the narratives of two *Viet Kieu* whom I shall call *Teo* and *Toan*.[6] Teo was a thirty-two-year-old man who worked for his parents at a small sandwich shop in the Silicon Valley, where the second highest concentration of *Viet Kieu* reside. Thirty-year-old Toan was the afternoon janitor at a public elementary school in urban Los Angeles, the metropolitan area with the highest concentration of *Viet Kieu* in the diaspora. Since both Teo and Toan wanted to marry women of Vietnamese origin, they had recently returned to Vietnam to obtain wives through the arrangements of family and kin in the Vietnamese diaspora, despite the demographic advantage of living in two heavily populated Vietnamese metropolitan areas in the United States.

The stories of Teo and Toan illuminate the linkages between certain historical and structural factors, including the demography of marriage markets in postimmigrant communities and to what Constable (2003) calls "marital subjectivities" in global space. Their narratives illustrate how some immigrant men of color, particularly those in low-wage work, utilize globalization as a gender strategy to increase their sense of self-worth by converting their social status across national boundaries (Hochschild with Machung 1989).[7] This international convertibility allows men, in turn, to feel as if they have more options available to them in the global hierarchy of marriage markets. These narratives also reveal how "subaltern men" construct their own masculinity and sense of respectability given that their lives are placed "at the intersection and interstices of vast systems of power: patriarchy, racism, colonialism, and capitalism, to name a few" (Chen 1999, 589).

Similar to Mexicans in the United States, as described in Goldring's study of transmigrants, Vietnamese immigrant men orient their lives to their place of origin because the "locality of origin provides a unique social and spatial context within transnational communities for making claims to and valorizing social status" (1998, 165). Thus, the place of origin provides an important social space to which immigrants can return and improve their social position based on material consumptions, which are often translated into symbolic power, since enormous differentiation in purchasing abilities exists between unequal nation states in the global economy. I assert that, at this junction in the twenty-first-century global economy, it is necessary to situate Vietnamese society in relation to transnational links from abroad, and, when speaking of the family, it is crucial to identify the links and manifestations of Vietnamese post-1975 emigration history.

Following research questions concerning immigrant men, social status, and transnational practices that have been raised by scholars like Goldring (1998, 2003), Jones-Correa (1998a, 1998b), and Smith (1998), I address the questions of how social status is converted across transnational social fields, and, more importantly, how this convertibility is gendered across transnational space. In Bourdieu's (1984) view, as a point of reference, social status and distinctions are not only based on economic capital (for example, income) but they are also linked to other forms of capital, namely cultural, social, and symbolic. Status distinctions and class boundaries are sites of conflict for Bourdieu because differentiations are made by social groups in order to legitimize symbolic and material power. For scholars of globalization, one of the most insightful and relevant critiques of Bourdieu is the question of convertibility across national boundaries, for while Bourdieu's approach "does not preclude the notion of transnational social fields, he does not directly discuss the implications of social fields that are not coterminous with state boundaries" (Schiller 2005, 442).

One of the most striking observations regarding the question of convertibility across national boundaries was Espiritu's compelling argument that it is not often possible to use standard measures, such as education or occupation, to talk about class status among transnational and immigrant populations. As Espiritu (2001) suggested in her study of the Filipino community in San Diego, California, the class status of most of her informants was both ambiguous and transnational. Espiritu explained: "I met Filipinos/as who toiled as assembly workers but who, through the pooling of income and finances, owned homes in middle-class communities . . . I encountered individuals who struggled economically in the United States but owned sizable properties in the Philippines. And I interviewed immigrants who continued to view themselves as 'upper class' even while living in dire conditions in the United States" (2001, 425).

As I will demonstrate, the case of convertibility among the Vietnamese reflects, in some ways, Espiritu's observations, but the Vietnamese situation is also significantly different given the specific histories of migration from the Philippines and Vietnam that are linked to specific colonial moments. Filipinos/as were much more likely to have migrated as professionals, whereas the Vietnamese were initially part of a refugee dispersion that flung them to different parts of the world, tremendously affecting their job prospects when they arrived on Western soil. The Vietnamese continue to be one of the lowest income-earning groups in Asia America (Yamane 2001). In my years of fieldwork in Vietnam, I have witnessed and read about numerous *Viet Kieu* who, indeed, do return to invest and buy property. Yet, I have found that, as with diverse patterns of migration and return in the global economy, there are enormous variations in patterns of who returns to Vietnam and why.

In my study of international marriages in the Vietnamese diaspora I found that, while most *Viet Kieu* who return could partake in consumption patterns that they otherwise could not afford in the West, most *Viet Kieu* transpacific husbands, in fact, lived in minimal housing situations, could not afford properties in Vietnam, and had very modest self-worth in their overseas contexts. It is the power of convertibility in globalization at the everyday level of food consumption, small gift-giving activities, and recognition of differences from very poor kin members in third world Vietnam that allow some *Viet Kieu* to recuperate from the loss of self-worth caused by migration.

Methods

The empirical evidence for this study originates from a larger ethnographic, mainly interview-based, research project that I conducted between June 1997 and March 2001 among women in Vietnam and Vietnamese men overseas who had recently married across the Pacific. During fourteen months of fieldwork done in phases in Vietnam and the United States, I studied sixtynine transpacific marriages. In this distinct and emergent global marriage market, the immigrant Vietnamese men typically return to Vietnam to marry through arranged marriage and, subsequently, return to their place of residence in the Vietnamese diaspora (usually, the United States, Canada, France, and Australia) to initiate paperwork to sponsor their wives as immigrants. The couples in these marriages were, therefore, in a "migration waiting period." That is, they were transnationally separated as the women waited to be united with their husbands. During this waiting period, I met the brides in Vietnam and later the grooms in the United States.[8]

I present two life histories and purposely move away from the conventional technique of weaving in multiple stories from several respondents. Of course, the technique of using in-depth life histories is limited, namely in achieving any sort of generalizeability. Nevertheless, I have taken this approach in order to provide analytical clarity. In addition, in this chapter, I have avoided relating stories of specific women or particular marriages, as I have done elsewhere (Thai 2002, 2003). Rather than focusing on decisions around marriage selections, this chapter concentrates on the ways in which low-wage men convert their social status across transnational social fields in the wake of the *Doi Moi* policy in Vietnam. To develop my analysis, I begin by briefly tracing the chronological paradox to the literature on gender and (trans) migration. I then chronicle the migration and marriage narratives of Teo and Toan to illustrate how globalization is used as a gender strategy. I echo Constable's observations on global marriage options—they should not be understood as a "simple unilinear movement from East to West, from underdeveloped 'South' to developed 'North,' from so-called traditional societies to so-called modern ones, or from oppression to liberation" (Constable 2003, 165). In this contribution, I imply that international marriages among coethnics living in different parts of the world are not only anchored in a history of migration that dispersed this group of people involuntarily from their homelands, but are also motivated by the need for material, as well as emotional, recuperations of self-worth that make such marriages necessary.

Gender and Transmigration

There is a chronological paradox to research on gender and transmigration. From the 1950s to the 1970s, scholarship on migration focused almost exclusively on men as the "birds of passage," while women, children, and the elderly were seen as following in their paths (Bodnar, Simon, and Weber 1982; Handlin 1951; Howe 1976; Piore 1979; Simon and Brettell 1986). This earlier research assumed that males were more inclined and better able to take risks and to journey abroad in search of better job opportunities, whereas women, if they migrated at all, were depicted as emotional caretakers who accompanied men to ensure family and community stability. This ear-lier research suppressed women's (and children's) agency in family migra-tion processes and assumed that "children are carried along by their parents, willy-nilly, and wives accompany their husbands though it tears them away from the environment they love" (Lee 1966, 578).

In the 1970s and 1980s, scholars and policy makers began to focus on women as central actors in the migration process, in part because of the dra-matic growth in feminist scholarship and women's studies programs. As well, demographic reports showed that more women than men were migrating to the United States (Hondagneu-Sotelo 2003; Houstoun, Kramer, and Barrett 1984; Pessar 1999). By the late 1990s and early twenty-first century, numerous migration scholars included women in their research. This effort resulted in a collection of important anthologies, articles, and books focusing on women and the migration process (for example, Brettell and deBerjeois 1992; Brettell and Simon 1986; Buijs 1993; Chant 1992; Donato 1992; Gamburd 2000; Hondagneu-Sotelo 1994, 2001; Hondagneu-Sotelo and Avila 1997; Parre-nas 2001a, 2001b; Pedraza 1991; Phizacklea 1983; Romero 1992; Simon and Brettell 1986).

The most recent collection of essays assembled by pioneering gender and immigration scholar Hondagneu-Sotelo (2003) suggests that, currently, there is relatively little attention paid to the situation of men in the contemporary literature on "gender" and migration. Furthermore, very few studies have highlighted gender in transnational social fields. Notable exceptions include the works of a few scholars doing research on domestic workers in the new global economy (Ehrenreich 2002; Ehrenreich and Hochschild 2002; Gam-burd 2000; Hondagneu-Sotelo 2001; Parrenas 2001b). Mahler (1999) was one of the first to critique the bipolar approach to understanding gender and transmigration. She argued that the emergence of transnationalism as a "criti-cal optic" mirrors the emergence of gender in migration scholarship (693). "Migration was (and continues to be) gendered long before scholars perceived it as a fundamental axis," Mahler writes, "transnationalism itself is not com-pletely new, yet the predominant doctrine of bipolar migration deterred its de-tection and investigation"(694). The research by Jones-Correa (1998a, 1998b) and Smith (1998) strongly suggests two important gendered patterns among Mexican, Dominican, Colombian, and Puerto Rican transmigrants. First, compared to immigrant women, immigrant men are more likely to shift their orientation to their home countries and to the prospect of return migration as

The Legacy of Doi Moi 245

they lose status in the United States. Second, correlated with the first finding, immigrant women are more likely to interface with American institutions.

More recently, Goldring (2003) has documented how Mexico's outreach programs reinforce gendered projects of transmigrants because they "offer a context for exercising substantive citizenship that enhances immigrant men's status and citizenship vis-à-vis the Mexican State while marginalizing women by excluding them from positions of power and status" (347). In all these studies, mainly men on the lower rung of the U.S. labor market are compelled to maintain strong ties with their homeland. I have not systematically interviewed Vietnamese women overseas in order to compare their situations to those of Vietnamese men overseas; however, my data suggest, at least through the prism of marriage during fieldwork in Vietnam, that immigrant Vietnamese men are more likely to orient themselves to "home" in order to valorize social status. I have found, for example, that in Vietnam it is *Viet Kieu* men, as opposed to *Viet Kieu* women, who are more visible in the growing leisure economy catering to the overseas Vietnamese population, like Western style cafes, bars, and dance clubs. Also, in my interviews I have found that it is overwhelmingly men who initiate remittance relationships and consumption chains, such as buying small gifts and inviting large groups of people out to eat. Thus, this chapter adds, in an exploratory way, to the small body of literature on gender and transmigration by drawing on studies of masculinity and consumption and by focusing specifically on the meanings of masculinity and consumption in globalization among immigrant men of color.

Gender Strategies and the Convertibility of Social Status in Transnational Social Fields

A Vietnamese immigrant man utilizes globalization as a gender strategy when he "performs" transnationalism in order to "achieve" masculinity. He deliberately converts his relatively low status in the West to a higher status when he goes to Vietnam. To do this, a Vietnamese immigrant man engages in small-scale conspicuous consumption, such as everyday drinking and eating activities and simple gift-giving practices (that are often beyond his Western means). This convertibility becomes most, sometimes only, meaningful when he establishes and maintains translocal relations which "are constituted within historically and geographically specific points of origin and migration established by transmigrants" (Guarnizo and Smith 1998b, 13). He thereby forms a "triadic connection that links transmigrants, the localities to which they migrate, and their locality of origin" (Ibid.). Convertibility across national borders benefits a Vietnamese immigrant man by offering him the ability to cross international borders geographically and go from the status of low marriageability to relatively higher marriageability.

Hochschild (with Machung 1989) argues that gender strategies are utilized by women as well as men. I also found that both men and women pursue gender strategies based on their gender ideologies. In Hochschild's study, men from various social class backgrounds pursued gender strategies, meaning that gender strategies were important for both working-class and middle-class men. In this study, I found that both men and women of the diaspora pursue convertibility of economic capital. Likewise, men from across social class backgrounds also take part in convertibility, which is to say that convertibility across social fields was important for both working-class as well as middle-class men. But I make the point here that the interrelated issues of global convertibility, social status, and masculinity are particularly central, salient, and relevant to the lives of low-wage immigrant men because of their very marginal economic status in their overseas locations. This is especially true when one considers that about 80 percent of the men in my sample of sixty-nine marriages were low-wage workers who, because of their low-wage status, found it difficult to find marriage partners in their overseas locations. These men viewed their jobs as not being highly respected, which they felt also made them unmarriageable overseas.

In the following pages, the narratives of Teo and Toan illustrate the following argument. First, low-wage Vietnamese American men are able to convert their "low-income" status in the first world to a relatively "higher-income" status when they visit third-world Vietnam. Second, material convertibility through small-scale, conspicuous consumption translates into symbolic status that is used to "trade off" in the Vietnamese transpacific marriage market. Third, convertibility of material and symbolic differences is usually, if not always, anchored in a tangible transnational relation that people recognize as having differential purchasing power in the first and third worlds. If the convertibility goes unnoticed, it is often meaningless to the person doing the converting. Finally, convertibility is practical, if not necessary, to increase self-worth among low-wage Vietnamese immigrant men, but it is tremendously costly.

Bottom Among Men, Top Among Nations

In many ways men like Teo and Toan belong to the lowest social status group in their local overseas contexts. Although Asian Americans are reputed for having the highest median income of all racial groups in the United States, Vietnamese American men earn on average 30 percent less than their white counterparts and are one of the lowest income-earning ethnic groups in the United States (Yamane 2001). Except for a few men who worked in ethnic enterprises, such as nail salons where average hourly wages ranged from $8 to $12 per hour, I refer to low-wage Vietnamese American men in this study as men who generally earned from $6 to $8 per hour, on average. These low-wage workers usually worked in jobs that offered them very little stability. Their yearly salaries ranged between $8,000 and $20,000, and many fall below the U.S. poverty level. Yet, compared to Vietnamese men globally, they are at the top since the United States holds enormous social and economic power in the global economy and makes wage differentials dramatically obvious. For example, at the time of my research for this project, 2 million Vietnamese Dongs (US$133) was usually considered the typical monthly wage earned in Vietnam among professionals, such as foreign translators, pharmacists, and even some medical doctors (General Statistics Office [GSO] 2003). Thus, while some of the low-wage men in this study experienced tremendous downward social and economic mobility after migration, their overseas low wage takes on different economic and social meanings when they return to Vietnam. Most of the men felt that they had experienced nonmobility, as most entered very low-paying jobs after migration that, as Teo said, only allowed them "to survive" (*de song*).

I met Teo in the Vietnamese enclave of the Silicon Valley, approximately one hour south of San Francisco, where Teo grew up as the middle child in a relatively comfortable home. His parents were able to move to the Silicon Valley because their kin networks helped them settle there after migrating as boat refugees in 1984. His parents' lifestyle, as exhibited by the house they lived in and the cars they drove, indicated that they were at least economically middle class. But, because his parents, both in their late fifties, owned a simple sandwich shop catering to the mixed-income ethnic community in which they lived, Teo thought of his parents, and by extension himself since he also worked at the shop, as being part of the working class (*tang lop lao dong*). Each day, his parents woke up at four in the morning to prepare for the shop's early opening hour and worked until past eight in the evening. The "style" (*kieu*) of their lives, as Teo emphasized, is one of "laborers who work with [their] hands so [they] can have enough to survive."

Teo had internalized his style of living in his early adulthood, particularly when his older brother and younger sister both earned educational credentials to secure "office jobs." Because Teo did not have an "office job," as he explained, he had unofficially assumed responsibility for his parents' elderly years in place of his brother who was two years older. He assumed this responsibility, in part, because he was also working for his parents at the sandwich shop and still living in their home (which saved him a tremendous amount of money in the expensive Silicon Valley). This was partly an economic exchange for Teo since he did not have better alternatives. Working in his parents' sandwich shop seemed to be a better option than obtaining a low-wage job that tended to offer little autonomy. As Teo told me, "I work whenever I want and can take vacations whenever I want."

When Teo spoke about his brother, he spoke with a sense of discomfort about the fact that his brother and his brother's wife were both professionals. "They are very critical people (*phe binh*)," he remarked. Teo said that they were critical of the fact that he had never earned a college degree, which would likely make him unmarriageable. Yet, when I was able to persuade him to talk about his romantic history, Teo was moderately confident about his ability to court women in the United States. Like many men in this study, he made sure to convey that he did not go to Vietnam to marry because he was simply *e vo* or *unmarketable*, a term frequently referring to commodities at markets that remain unsold and metaphorically used to stigmatize those at the marriageable age and not yet married. Teo went a little further than most men, however, by taking out photo albums to show me pictures taken with about half a dozen ex-girlfriends throughout his early adulthood, as if to offer evidence of masculinity. When we spoke at length about his last serious relationship, Teo explained that it was a very difficult breakup "for her." As I continued in this line of inquiry, I learned that it took Teo two years to realize that he was "over" [*xong*] the relationship. He met this ex-girlfriend at the community college in the Vietnamese Student Association in 1988 when he was nineteen. According to Teo, she courted him more aggressively than he courted her. They had a very romantic beginning and he even bragged that they once took a trip together to Hawaii—something he felt only married people do.

Two years after they started dating, when Teo was midway through his community college education, his ex-girlfriend was accepted into one of the best University of California campuses. Although they remained committed to each other while she went to university, he felt that she lost interest when she was accepted into another University of California school to earn her pharmacy degree. He said he always felt comfortable going out with her school friends; however, she did not like to meet or go out with his community college friends—a sign of disrespect to him. According to Teo, he eventually broke up the relationship due to her disinterest. "She was fine with the break up," Teo explained, "but I know *she* was in pain." Several more visits with Teo revealed that he had broken up that serious relationship because he could not envision himself marrying a woman who he felt had so much more education than he did. As he explained to me:

> I know I should be happy if my wife is successful, but when *the wife* feels she is better than the husband, it is not a good situation [*hoan canh khong tot*]. My ex-girlfriend and I almost got married, but I think she did not feel very easy with me not having an advanced college education. And you know how Vietnamese people are: they are very snobby if they have advanced degrees like they only care about doctorates (*si*).

Teo's ability to court women in his early adulthood did not follow him through his early thirties when people he knew obtained "careers," rather than the sort of job that Teo took. Moreover, the fact that he felt his last ex-girlfriend did not "respect" him because of his lack of high education prompted Teo to look elsewhere for a marriage partner. "As a man," Teo said to me with a strong sense of depth, "you have to have a certain kind of status." However, as Teo looked elsewhere in the highly populated Vietnamese enclave of the Silicon Valley, he found that social status was relatively difficult to achieve, regardless of what social circles he entered, because he was still a sandwich shop worker. "Vietnamese people here [in the United States] only pay attention to how much money you make or what kind of degrees you have," Teo said. "The women don't want to marry men who don't have comfortable jobs."

When Teo began seriously looking for marriage prospects, he moved out of his Silicon Valley cultural corner and, in effect, turned to a transnational space in which he could convert his relatively low social status. Teo had a good friend, Manh, who had a single younger sister still living in Vietnam. According to Teo, Manh was also a low-wage worker who had been to Vietnam several times and had each time tried to persuade Teo to take the trip with him, in part because Manh had wanted to arrange a marriage for Teo with his younger sister. The two men took their first trip together in 1998, and by early 1999 Teo had married Manh's younger sister. When I asked Teo to chronicle that first trip back to Vietnam, he immediately raised the issue of convertibility:

> I felt like a different person when I went to Vietnam for the first time, like I had another life in another world. Everything was so cheap, and I could just spend money on luxuries. I didn't have to worry about the cost of anything, like you can take twenty people out to eat a huge feast and it could cost you less than what you would spend on two people in San Jose. It's very luxurious (*sung suong lam*)!

Partly as a reflection of his low level of education, Teo barely earned $1,500 per month, which did not go far in the United States, especially living in the expensive Silicon Valley. Both the low-income and absence of a college degree in the United States meant that Teo had little opportunity for social mobility in the formal U.S. labor market, or, in Teo's eyes, to acquire social status, particularly in the Vietnamese American marriage market. Like many *Viet Kieu* who journey home, Teo converted his low income into the ability to enjoy luxuries that he could not otherwise usually afford in the United States, like taking "twenty people out to eat a huge feast." The convertibility of money is linked immediately to the convertibility of status and esteem. This process of convertibility allows men like Teo to participate in a marriage market because they feel they have something to offer, and, in turn, something to obtain. As Teo explained:

> In America, I don't have any class/rank (*hang*), because I only work as a laborer (*nguoi lao dong*), but when I go to Vietnam, I only need to spend a few hundred dollars and people see the value in me (*gia tri*). In the U.S., single women see me as nothing because I have nothing. In Vietnam, I have a lot. I can drink and eat much more with the money I make in the U.S. than if I try to spend it there . . . I think it is better (*tot hon*) that I married someone in Vietnam, because we can try to spend more of our time there. We both have family there, and they

don't judge me because of my education. In Vietnam, it's all about money, you know (*cai gi cung la tien*).

When men like Teo talk about consumption and being in Vietnam, it is most often in the context of being under the watchful eyes of family and kin. The anchoring of transnational ties to specific communities of origin means that Teo had a particular network to validate his social worth. There seems to be a need for an audience of convertibility, as Teo explained:

> When you are a *Viet Kieu*, people in Vietnam watch you. They want to see that you have the ability (*kha nang*) to buy what they cannot. And, if you cannot, they will think of you as one of them. And then you are a useless (*vo dung*) *Viet Kieu*. If you love your family, you also want to show them that you can afford what they cannot, that you can take care of them . . . But for yourself, you also don't want to have a reputation (*tieng tam*) as someone who cannot buy the things they cannot. Like me, I have been gone for over fifteen years so I have to show that I did something important. I don't want to be a useless *Viet Kieu*.

The Lowest-Wage Among Low-Wage Men

Among the low-wage earners, there were different types of "lowness." If income level and the type of work each man did were associated with his sense of self-worth, then the lowest of the low had internalized his low-status in compelling ways. The lowest-wage men tended to powerfully avoid anchoring themselves in the overseas community, as one way of avoiding being contextualized and compared with other overseas Vietnamese, or as Katrak (1996) succinctly describes some transmigrants—they "live here in body and elsewhere in mind and imagination" (125). This was especially true among the most recent arrivals, like thirty-year-old Toan who, because of the timing of his migration, had more concrete and tangible connections with people in Vietnam than those men who had been gone for longer periods.

I met Toan one weekday afternoon in January 2001 at an inner city elementary school in urban Los Angeles where he worked as an after-school janitor. Toan, like other lowest-wage men, perceived his job, which usually barely paid the legal minimum wage and sometimes less, as being a site of degradation. "It is maybe better not to work at all," as Toan told me, "than to work at a job where you feel humiliated (*nhuc*) to tell people you know." Such feelings of humiliation led Toan eventually to globalize his marriage options. Prior to leaving Vietnam in 1996, Toan had a serious relationship with a woman he met in the eighth grade from his home village in the province of *Se Long* (name changed). When Toan left Vietnam through the sponsorship of his father, he said he did not intend to keep the long-distance relationship with this long-term girlfriend. Nevertheless, after being in the United States for only a few months, Toan soon realized that his prospect for marriage in the United States was low, in large part because of his low-wage job. As Toan explained:

> I know I came to America late and that is why I have to work like a buffalo in this school, clean the toilet. There is no status with society in this job. No woman will want to marry a man like me. I can barely make enough money to feed myself, how can I provide for a woman in America? No woman here will respect me for what I do. If I married a woman here, she will get tired of seeing me with this job and she will leave me. If a woman does not respect what you do, she won't respect you. And what kind of marriage will you have if there is no respect?

Thus, after having been in the United States for only two years, Toan returned to Vietnam to propose marriage, having kept in touch with his serious girlfriend in *Se Long*. Like my interviews with most men in this study, I asked Toan to recount his feelings and experiences with the first visit home. He said:

> We live overseas, we have nothing. We just work. When we go to Vietnam, we have happiness (*co su sung suong*). [Why?] Because we have money when we go to Vietnam. There are people who will look at us, people who will pay attention to us because we have the behavior of a person (*tu cach con nguoi*) that is enough for others to have a relation with (*quan he*), we are not an ordinary person (*nguoi tam tuong*) [in Vietnam].

Indeed, as a janitor in Los Angeles, Toan viewed himself as an "ordinary person," someone who was embarrassed to tell people what he did for a wage. For in the landscape of urban Los Angeles, Toan's hourly income of $6.75 meant that he literally could not afford the sort of lifestyle that he enjoyed whenever he visited Vietnam. I have heard and witnessed hundreds of stories of *Viet Kieu* who barely made minimum wages in their overseas contexts, but who consumed haphazardly when they visited Vietnam. Regarding his consumption patterns, Toan succinctly confessed: "In the U.S., I often spend a whole day thinking about whether I should go and eat a five dollar bowl of beef noodle soup (*pho*) when I get off work, but in Vietnam, I don't even think twice when I go to a bar or café and pay 2 million Vietnamese dongs (US$133) for a bottle of Hennessy (cognac)."

How is the convertibility of money, status, and consumption related to marriage choices? If Teo felt that an absence of a college degree meant that he could not earn respect by marrying his ex-girlfriend who was studying for a pharmacy degree, then Toan's very low-wage job led him to believe that he was completely unmarriageable in the United States. "If I want to find a wife in the U.S," Toan said, "I will have to wait for the next life (*kiep sau*)." Both Teo and Toan felt marginal in their overseas marriage markets, although in different ways. Whereas Teo sensed that he deliberately rejected the marriage market in the United States, Toan felt he was rejected. Both experiences of rejection were anchored in the same way as both men sought to participate in small-scale conspicuous consumption in Vietnam. They returned to Vietnam in order to convert their low income to a relatively higher income as a gender strategy to make themselves marriageable in the Vietnamese global hierarchy of marriage markets. Although some men like Teo and Toan are successful at achieving their goals of upgrading their sense of self-worth, their use of globalization as a gender strategy comes at a cost that often results in sacrifices at the everyday level in their overseas contexts.

As Packard (1999) observes, "over time, stereotypical images of rich, ostentatious and arrogant *Viet Kieu* on the one side, and of ignorant, backward and beggarly 'country bumpkins' on the other, have been replaced by more nuanced views" (82). Indeed, the initial view of Vietnamese nationals was that *Viet Kieu* had an impressive purchasing power because of income differences between Vietnam and the West. Initial views have changed, although not entirely, as locals learned that, while the *Viet Kieu* salaries could purchase a luxury life in Vietnam, they, in fact, could not go far in the West. Thus, men like Teo and Toan gradually realized that, in order to keep up their images of *Viet Kieu* who were "ready to play" (*trieu choi*), they must spend all their savings during the few weeks or months that they visit Vietnam. Meanwhile, they live minimal lives in their overseas locations for the rest of the year; they, in effect, reverse their "worlds of consumption."

Materially, they live a first-world life in Vietnam and a third-world life in the United States. Many *Viet Kieu*, including Toan succinctly explained this reversion to me: "I abstain from eating and drinking (*nhin an nhin uong*) as much as possible in the United States so that I can live like a king when I go to Vietnam." This means that, for example, Toan survives on the most basic needs when he is in Los Angeles, in part, he says, "because there is no one to look at you and judge what you eat and drink." Toan told me that in Los Angeles, he ate instant ramen noodles for dinner at least three or four times a week, packed all of his lunches for work, and rarely ate at a restaurant. In contrast, he says, in Vietnam, "instant noodles are for the poor," and, as a *Viet Kieu*, he needs to demonstrate his ability to pay for expensive food items, like jumbo shrimp or abalone shellfish (two items he said he never consumed in the United States). Toan's explanation of the social meanings of consumption in the West and in Vietnam was as follows: "When I am in Vietnam, people know that I have money, and they expect me to pay for everything. It is embarrassing when a *Viet Kieu* goes back to Vietnam and he is cheap (*keo*). And you can never let anyone in Vietnam pay for you when you go back there. People expect you to be able to afford anything (*nghi rang co du kha nang*)."

Thus, in order to recuperate from their loss of status in their overseas locations, low-wage Vietnamese immigrant men attempt to live up to the expectation that they can afford anything in Vietnam. This means that they often deprive themselves of necessities in their overseas contexts in order to accumulate resources, which then allows them to consume "like a *Viet Kieu*" when they visit Vietnam. Some family members in Vietnam have realized that, while income disparities exist between the West and Vietnam, some *Viet Kieu* do struggle financially to make ends meet in their daily overseas lives. This knowledge sometimes leads kin members in Vietnam to prevent *Viet Kieu* from overspending by, for example, cooking at home rather than eating huge feasts at restaurants with the entire family and kin.

For the most part, however, I found that most kin members in Vietnam attempt to "save face" for all involved, particularly for the visiting *Viet Kieu*, by embracing and participating in small-scale conspicuous consumption when the *Viet Kieu* visits. They do so in order to prevent any embarrassment for the visiting *Viet Kieu*, especially men, since men most often pay in the leisure economy of Vietnam. Family members save face even as they know that it comes at a tremendous cost for their overseas loved ones; they, in effect, help the visiting *Viet Kieu* garner a sense of self-worth in the public's eyes, especially when there is a large network of people observing the visitor.

Kin members in Vietnam who benefit materially from *Viet Kieu* small-scale conspicuous consumption patterns often do not want to undermine it. In fact, they go to great lengths to commend *Viet Kieu* for having a "luxurious life in the West," even to the extent of recognizing that *Viet Kieu* can "burn money." On many occasions, transpacific husbands confided in me the burden of consumption when they go to Vietnam. Toan recounted numerous stories of how kin members in Vietnam did not fully understand his income in the United States was very low. In one story, Toan told me of a twenty-something female cousin of his wife who, in the presence of over twenty kin members, publicly asked Toan to buy her a bottle of perfume at a department store that had just opened in central Saigon. In her public request, Toan told me, she jokingly said, "A $50 bottle of perfume means nothing to you, Toan. You can burn money when you visit here, right?" Toan described that, as the noisy and attentive audience watched for a reply, Toan simply said, "Fifty dollars is nothing (*khong co gi*)." When I asked what happened afterwards, Toan said some family members laughed, some clapped their hands at Toan's reply, and that eventually, but reluctantly, Toan bought the cousin the bottle of perfume. "Fifty dollars could buy me several hundred packages of instant noodles in Los Angeles," Toan explained with laughter.

The Meaning and Masculine Politics of Consumption Across Transnational Social Fields

This contribution focuses on the meaning of consumption across national boundaries, that is, to recognize social action, according to Max Weber (1978), we must examine the meanings that people attach to their own behaviors and experience. I have found that, in an effort to recuperate from a loss of status after migration to overseas communities, Vietnamese immigrant men engage in small-scale consumption and, subsequently, attach a particular social meaning to their consumption pattern in the home country in order to upgrade their social status and improve their sense of self. As shown, Vietnamese low-wage immigrant men convert "low-income" status to a comparatively "higher-income" one when they return "home," draw upon this convertibility to raise their marriageability, and anchor the practice of convertibility in translocal relations. As the stories of Teo and Toan illustrate, convertibility is tremendously costly because low-wage Vietnamese immigrant men often deprive themselves of basic needs in their diasporic locations so that they can save money to convert when they go home.

This chapter provides an exploratory look at low-wage immigrant men, thereby contributing to other research that examines the constitution of gender in migration streams (see Goldring 2003; Grasmuck and Pessar 1991; Hondagneu-Sotelo 1994, 2003; Hondagneu-Sotelo and Avila 1997; Jones-Correa 1998a, 1998b; Smith 1998). Various scholars have explored what Hondagneu-Sotelo calls the "third," or current, stage of immigration research that examines the "extent to which gender permeates a variety of practices, identities, and institutions implicated in immigration . . . in ways that reveal how gender is incorporated into a myriad of daily operations and institutional, political, and economic structures" (Hondagneu-Sotelo 2003, 9).

Although I do not have insight into whether overseas Vietnamese immigrant women also practice convertibility across national borders, in many ways I echo what other scholars have found regarding gender and migration among Mexican and Latino men (Goldring 2003; Hardy-Fanta 1993; Jones-Correa 1998a, 1998b; Smith 1998). In Vietnam, I found that men are overwhelmingly more visible and more discursively exposed than women when it comes to drawing upon meanings of home while in diaspora, as well as once they are at home in the natal country. For the most part, men, compared to women, are more likely to be compelled to claim social positions at "home"— social positions that are often denied to them in the country of migration.

The "ageing" Vietnamese diaspora has only recently witnessed a dramatic return of *Viet Kieu* to the natal country. My work moves away from the "refugee model" that characterizes many studies on Vietnamese in exile and builds on the important research on transnationalism from "below" (Guarnizo and Smith 1998a) by foregrounding everyday life and the emotional side of migration (Hochschild 2002; Hondagneu-Sotelo and Avila 1997; Parrenas 2001a). Studying low-wage Vietnamese immigrant men who are beginning to anchor themselves in the natal country in response to labor market marginality in the host country provides a different vantage point in the research on gender and migration. It examines gender as a "constitutive" element of immigration by linking gender with other categories, like social class, migration history, colonial past, and a particular racialized experience (Hondagneu-Sotelo 2003, 9), which helps explain, if only partially, why certain low-wage immigrant men are seduced by home in Vietnam.

Notes

This chapter is based on a presentation given at the 2004 Annual Meeting of the Association for Asian Studies in San Diego, California. It is also a revised version of a shorter essay previously published in *Critical Globalization* (2004) edited by William Robinson and Richard Appelbaum. I would like to express gratitude to Jane Zavisca for supplying me with ideas on consumption studies, and to the anonymous reviewer for comments on a previous draft of this chapter. Special thanks to Magali Barbieri and Danièle Bélanger for organizing the conference in Paris on Vietnamese families, and for their helpful comments on this chapter.

1. The first exodus of Vietnamese immigrants who arrived as political refugees began days before the fall of Saigon on April 30, 1975, after American troops withdrew from Vietnam. The second wave, which included mostly ethnic Chinese, left in 1978 and 1979; the third wave included those who escaped by boat or overland between 1978 and 1982. The fourth and fifth waves occurred between 1983–89 and after 1989, respectively, and mostly included asylum seekers and those who sought resettlement from refugee camps in countries such as Thailand and the Phillipines. Currently, those arriving in the United States and elsewhere enter primarily through family reunification programs.

2. *Legal* immigrants are defined by U.S. immigration law as persons admitted to the United States for legal permanent residence. They comprise two categories: those with immigrant visas obtained from abroad and those adjusting their status in the United States from temporary to permanent residence (see United States Immigration and Naturalization Service 2002, 13–18, for a detailed discussion of this point). Vietnamese migrants arrived on the American scene mostly as refugees from the 1970s to the early 1990s, with the largest flows coming between 1978 and 1988. By the mid-1990s, Vietnamese refugee flows dramatically declined so that by 1999, refugees accounted for only a little over 20 percent of all Vietnamese immigrants. As the proportion of Vietnamese refugees declined and as earlier arrivals settled and became naturalized U.S. citizens, the proportion of family-sponsored immigrants increased. The proportion of Vietnamese immigrants arriving through family-sponsorship between 1992 and 1999 increased notably from about 30 percent in 1992 to nearly 75 percent in 1999 (United States Immigration and Naturalization Service 2002).

3. A shortage of one sex or the other in the age group in which marriage generally occurs is often termed a marriage squeeze (Guttentag and Secord 1983). The Vietnamese double marriage squeeze specifically refers to the low ratio of males to females in Vietnam and the unusually high ratio of males to females in the Vietnamese diaspora, especially in Australia and in the United States. Among the fifteen most populated nations in 1989, Vietnam had the lowest ratio of men to women among those at the peak marrying ages. By 1999, among people between

the ages of thirty to thirty-four years in Vietnam, statistically speaking, there were approximately 92 men for every 100 women. In 1990, for Vietnamese Americans in all age groups, there were about 113 males for every 100 females (Zhou and Bankston 1998).

4. Literally, "changing for the new."

5. For an excellent up-to-date and critical literature review on consumption studies, see Zavisca (2004).

6. To protect the privacy of informants, all names have been changed. As well, I have changed the names of villages in Vietnam and small towns in the United States. I have kept the real names of all metropolitan areas. And while full Vietnamese names are usually indicated in the order of last, middle, and first names, I will use "American" standards of referencing names since I used this format when I got to know informants.

7. According to sociologist Hochschild (with Machung 1989), there are differences between what people say they believe about their marital roles and how they seem to feel about those roles. Furthermore, what they believe and how they feel may differ from what they actually do. Hochschild distinguishes between gender ideologies and gender strategies to point out that ideology has to do with how men and women draw on "beliefs about manhood and womanhood, beliefs that are forged in early childhood and thus anchored to deep emotions" (Hochschild with Machung 1989, 15). "Gender strategies" refers to people's plans of action and to their emotional preparations for pursuing them.

8. I began to set up this research project with an initial visit in June 1997, with the most intensive research periods beginning with the "bride phase" in Vietnam from December 1999 to August 2000 and the "groom phase" in the United States from January to March 2001. In 1999, the Vietnamese Department of Justice provided randomly generated lists of 200 names of couples who had marriages registered in Saigon and 120 names of couples who had marriages registered in a Mekong Delta province I call *Se Long* (220 kilometers southwest of Saigon). These lists contained names of both grooms and brides who registered their marriages between September and December 1999. These couples were in a migration-waiting period as the grooms returned to their places of residence and work to initiate paperwork for sponsoring their wives as immigrants. I systematically selected every fourth name from top to bottom of each list and literally went to the brides' houses, knocked on their doors, and invited them to participate in the study. The response rate for the brides was 86 percent (sixty-nine of eighty brides). Once I captured the experiences of brides in Vietnam, I went to the metropolitan areas of San Francisco, Los Angeles, Seattle, and Boston to interview grooms who married the brides I met in Vietnam. Of the twenty-eight grooms I contacted, all participated in the study. In total, I learned about sixty-nine marriages, some from brides only, and some from both grooms and brides. In addition to formal tape-recorded interviews with brides, grooms, and their families, I was a participant observer of eight

families in Saigon, maximizing variation (for example, by age, level of education, income, contexts of transnational networks). I transcribed and translated about half of the interviews, and two research assistants in the United States did the rest.

References

Abu-Lughod, L. 1998. *Remaking women: Feminism and modernity in the Middle East.* Princeton, NJ: Princeton University Press.

Alonso, A. M. 1994. The politics of space, time and substance: State formation, nationalism, and ethnicity. *Annual Review of Anthropology* 23: 379–405.

Bodnar, J., R. Simon, and M. P. Weber. 1982. *Lives of their own: Blacks, Italians, and Poles in Pittsburg, 1900–1960.* Urbana: University of Illinois Press.

Bourdieu, P. 1984. *Distinction: A social critique of the judgment of taste.* Cambridge, MA: Harvard University Press.

Brettell, C. B., and P. A. deBerjeois. 1992. Anthropology and the study of immigrant women. In *Seeking common ground: Multidisciplinary studies of immigrant women in the United States,* edited by D. Gabaccia, 41–64. Westport, CT: Greenwood Press.

Brettell, C. B., and R. J. Simon. 1986. Immigrant women: An introduction. In *International migration: The female experience,* edited by R. J. Simon and C. B. Brettell, 3–21. Totowa, New Jersey: Rowman and Allenheld Press.

Buijs, G. (Ed.). 1993. *Migrant women: Crossing boundaries and changing identities.* Providence, RI: Berg Publishers.

Chan, K. B., and L.-J. Dorais. 1998. Family, identity, and the Vietnamese Diaspora: The Quebec experience. *Journal of Social Issues in Southeast Asia* 13(2): 285–305.

Chant, S. 1992. *Gender and migration in developing countries.* London: Behaven Press.

Chatterjee, P. 1993. *The nation and its fragments: Colonial and postcolonial histories.* Princeton, NJ: Princeton University Press.

Chen, A. S. 1999. Lives at the center of the periphery, lives at the periphery of the center. *Gender & Society* 13: 584–607.

Connell, R. W. 1995. *Masculinities.* Berkeley: University of California Press.

Connell, R. W. 2000. *The men and the boys.* Berkeley: University of California Press.

Constable, N. 2003. A transnational perspective on divorce and marriage: Filipina wives and workers. *Identities* 10: 163–180.

Donato, K. M. 1992. Understanding U.S. immigration: Why some countries send women and others send men. In *Seeking common ground: Multidisciplinary studies of immigrant women in the United States,* edited by D. Gabaccia, 159–184. Westport, CT: Praeger Press.

Ebashi, M. 1997. The economic take-off. In *Vietnam joins the world,* edited by J. Morley and M. Nishihara, 37–65. Armonk, NY: M. E. Press.

Ehrenreich, B. 2002. Maid to order. In *Global woman: Nannies, maids, and sex workers in the new economy*, edited by B. Ehrenreich and A. R. Hochschild, 85–103. New York: Metropolitan Books.

Ehrenreich, B., and A. R. Hochschild. 2002. *Global woman: Nannies, maids, and sex workers in the new economy*. New York: Metropolitan Books.

Espiritu, Y. L. 1997. *Asian American women and men: Labor, laws and love*. Thousand Oaks, CA: Sage Publications.

Espiritu, Y. L. 2001. We don't sleep around like white girls do: Family, culture and gender in Filipina American lives. *Signs* 26: 415–440.

Freeman, J. M., and Nguyen Dinh Huu. 2003. *Voices from the camps: Vietnamese children seeking asylum*. Seattle: University of Washington Press.

Gamburd, M. R. 2000. *The kitchen spoon's handle: Transnationalism and Sri Lanka's migrant housemaids*. Ithaca, NY: Cornell University Press.

General Statistics Office (GSO). 2003. *Statistical yearbook 2002*. Hanoi: General Statistics Office.

Goldring, L. 1998. The power of status in transnational social fields. In *Transnationalism from below*, edited by M. P. Smith and L. E. Guarnizo, 165–195. New Brunswick, NJ: Transaction Publishers.

Goldring, L. 2003. Gender, status, and the state in transnational spaces. In *Gender and U.S. immigration: Contemporary trends*, edited by P. Hondagneu-Sotelo, 341–358. Berkeley: University of California Press.

Goodkind, D. 1997. The Vietnamese double marriage squeeze. *International Migration Review* 31: 108–128.

Grasmuck, S., and P. Pessar. 1991. *Between two islands: Dominican international migration*. Berkeley: University of California Press.

Guarnizo, L. E., and M. P. Smith. 1998a. *Transnationalism from below*. New Brunswick, NJ: Transaction Publishers.

Guarnizo, L. E., and M. P. Smith. 1998b. The location of transnationalism. In *Transnationalism from below*, edited by M. P. Smith and L. E. Guarnizo, 3–34. New Brunswick, NJ: Transaction Publishers.

Guttentag, M., and P. F. Secord. 1983. *Too many women?: The sex ratio question*. Beverly Hills, CA: Sage Publications.

Handlin, O. 1951. *The uprooted*. Boston: Little, Brown.

Hardy-Fanta, C. 1993. *Latina politics, Latino politics: Gender, culture, and political participation in Boston*. Philadelphia: Temple University Press.

Hochschild, A. R., with A. Machung. 1989. *The second shift: Working parents and the revolution at home*. New York: Viking.

Hochschild, A. R. 2002. Love and gold. In *Global woman: Nannies, maids, and sex workers in the new economy*, edited by B. Ehrenreich and A. R. Hochschild, 15–30. New York: Metropolitan Books.

Hondagneu-Sotelo, P. 1994. *Gendered transitions: Mexican experiences of immigration*. Berkeley: University of California Press.

Hondagneu-Sotelo, P. 2001. *Domestica: Immigrant workers cleaning and caring in the shadows of affluence.* Berkeley: University of California Press.

Hondagneu-Sotelo, P. 2003. *Gender and U.S. immigration: Contemporary trends.* Berkeley: University of California Press.

Hondagneu-Sotelo, P., and E. Avila. 1997. "I'm here, but I'm there": The meanings of Latina transnational motherhood. *Gender & Society* 11: 548–71.

Houstoun, M. F., R. G. Kramer, and J. Mackin Barrett. 1984. Female predominance in immigration to the United States since 1930s: A first look. *International Migration Review* 18: 908–963.

Howe, I. 1976. *World of our fathers.* New York: Simon & Schuster.

Jones-Correa, M. 1998a. *Between two nations: The political predicament of Latinos in New York City.* Ithaca, NY: Cornell University Press.

Jones-Correa, M. 1998b. Different paths: Gender, immigration and political participation. *International Migration Review* 32: 326–349.

Katrak, K. 1996. South Asian American writers: Geography and memory. *Amerasia Journal* 22: 121–138.

Kibria, N. 1993. *Family tightrope: The changing lives of Vietnamese Americans.* Princeton, NJ: Princeton University Press.

Lee, E. 1966. A theory of migration. *Demography* 3: 47–57.

Lowe, L. 1996. *Immigrant acts: On Asian American cultural politics.* London: Duke University Press.

Mahler, S. J. 1999. Engendering transnational migration: A case study of Salvadorans. *American Behavioral Scientist* 42: 690–719.

Merli, G. M. 1997. *Estimation of international migration for Vietnam 1979–1989.* Seattle: University of Washington Press.

Morley, J. W., and M. Nishihara. 1997. Vietnam joins the world. In *Vietnam joins the world,* edited by J. W. Morley and M. Nishihara, 3–14. Armonk, NY: M. E. Press.

Nguyen Hong 2002. *Viet Kieu* remittances set to top $2 billion target. *Vietnam Investment Review,* December 9, 2002.

Packard, L. A. 1999. Asian American economic engagement: Vietnam case study. In *Across the Pacific: Asian Americans and globalization,* edited by E. Hu-Dehart., 79–108. Philadelphia: Temple University Press.

Parrenas, R. S. 2001a. Mothering from a distance: Emotions, gender, and intergenerational relations in Filipino transnational families. *Feminist Studies* 27: 361–390.

Parrenas, R. S. 2001b. *Servants of globalization: Women, migration, and domestic work.* Stanford, CA: Stanford University Press.

Pedraza, S. 1991. Women and migration: The social consequences of gender. *Annual Review of Sociology* 17: 303–325.

Pessar, P. R. 1999. Engendering migration studies: The case of immigrants in the United States. *American Behavioral Scientist* 42: 577–600.

Phizacklea, A. 1983. *One way ticket: Migration and female labour.* London, Routledge.

Piore, M. J. 1979. *Birds of passage: Migrant labor in industrial society.* Cambridge, U.K.: Cambridge University Press.

Romero, M. 1992. *Maid in the U.S.A.* New York, Routledge.

Schiller, N. G. 2005. Transnational social fields and imperialism. *Identities* 5: 439–461.

Simon, R. J., and C. Brettell. 1986. *International migration: The female experience.* Totowa, NJ: Rowman & Allanheld.

Smith, R. 1998. Transnational localities: Community, technology and politics of membership within the context of Mexico and U.S. migration. In *Transnationalism from below,* edited by M. P. Smith and L. E. Guarnizo, 196–238. New Brunswick, NJ: Transaction Press.

Thai Hung Cam, 2002. Clashing dreams: Highly educated overseas brides and low-wage U.S. husbands. In *Global woman: Nannies, maids and sex workers in the new economy,* edited by B. Ehrenreich and A. R. Hochschild, 230–253. New York: Metropolitan Books.

Thai Hung Cam, 2003. The Vietnamese double gender revolt. *Amerasia Journal* 29: 51–74.

Thai Hung Cam, 2008. *For better or for worse: Vietnamese international marriages in the new global economy.* Rutgers, NJ: Rutgers University Press.

Thomas, M. 1997. Crossing over: The relationship between overseas Vietnamese and their homeland. *Journal of Intercultural Studies* 18: 153–176.

Tran Trong Dang Dan. 1997. *Nguoi Vietnam O Nuoc Ngoai* [Vietnamese people overseas]. Hanoi: National Political Press.

United States Immigration and Naturalization Service (USINS). 2002. *Statistical yearbook of the Immigration and Naturalization Service, 1999.* Washington, DC: U.S. Government Printing Office.

Weber, M. 1978. *Economy and society.* Berkeley: University of California Press.

Whitmore, J. K. 1995. Southeast Asian exodus to the United States. *The Asian American Experience* 5: 1411–1415.

Yamane, L. 2001. The labor market status of foreign born Vietnamese Americans. Unpublished manuscript.

Zavisca, J. 2004. The meaning of consumption in late socialist Russia. Ph.D. Dissertation, Sociology. University of California, Berkeley.

Zhou, M., and C. L. Bankston. 1998. *Growing up American: How Vietnamese children adapt to life in the United States.* New York: Russell Sage Foundation.

PART FOUR

Gender and the Family

Chapter Nine

Daughters, Work, and Families in Globalizing Vietnam

DANIÈLE BÉLANGER AND KATHERINE PENDAKIS

The study of daughters' factory work in Asia has been the subject of much anthropological and sociological inquiry since the 1970s. With the processes of industrialization and globalization creating a need for unskilled and low skilled labor in the region, young women had unprecedented opportunities to work for wages prior to entering marriage. Young women, primarily from rural areas characterized by underemployment and poverty, responded to the pressing demand for millions of single female workers in various areas, such as garment, textiles, and electronics. Construed as being docile, hard working, and free of responsibility (and therefore available to work long hours), these women were often preferred to workers who were older or married. In many countries where this phenomenon occurred, young women's waged work and migration away from home were novelties and represented a significant social change that raised numerous questions regarding gender, family, work, and society. A question at the center of much research has been whether waged factory work has served to empower young women and, if so, to what extent. Another question is whether it has altered gender roles and expectations, particularly within families and kinship systems. These investigations have focused strongly on the empowering possibilities created by wages.

The literature on the "factory daughters" of Asia is extensive and spans over three decades of research on Taiwan (Greenhalgh 1985; Hsiung 1996;

Kung 1983; Mehrotra and Parish 2001; Parish and Willis 1994), Hong Kong (Salaff 1981), Malaysia (Lie and Lund 1994; Ong 1991), Indonesia (Wolf 1990), China (Lee 1998), and Vietnam (Liem 2004; Pendakis and Bélanger 2004). Although diverse in their findings, these studies all focus on women's empowerment, daughters' status, and the meaning of waged work in the specific gender systems of the various countries. In parallel with this literature, extensive published research has emerged that discusses more broadly the relationships between globalization, women's work (for all women and for married women specifically), and processes of empowerment versus exploitation in Asia (see Dong-Sook and Piper 2002; Kaur 2004; Thang and Yu 2004). General considerations as to the impact of labor on Asian women's lives and gender equality prevail in this research. This literature presents a variety of experiences, cases, and arguments. At one end of the spectrum, the processes of exploitation and further patriarchal subordination through work structures are uncovered, while at the other end, the use of negotiation strategies through which women exert agency to enhance their status and better their lives are outlined. Others stress the interplay and connections between exploitation and empowerment.

While the recent literature discusses broad processes pertaining to women workers in general, it does not acknowledge the fundamental differences between married and unmarried women. Indeed, women cannot easily detach from families and kinship systems, particularly in rural areas. A rural woman's marital status generally determines her sphere of belonging: a daughter "belongs" to her natal family until marriage, then, after her marriage, she "belongs" to her husband's family. These spheres of belonging shape women's daily lives and influence how and to whom women channel their time, labor, and earnings. Some would argue that single women enjoy comparatively more freedom than married women who have numerous and specific responsibilities to their husbands, children, in-laws and, sometimes, their natal family as well. Addressing single and married women's potential empowerment through waged work in Asia as distinct processes is important because of the different positions held by these two groups of women in families and society.

Thus, situating the debate of women's work and empowerment within the kinship system is critical to understanding the issue. Within these kinship systems, intergenerational contracts exist that prescribe the roles of children and parents, along with their responsibilities toward one another. These contracts are highly gendered, and they reflect the differential value of sons and daughters. In Vietnam, the contract between generations strongly favors sons over daughters because sons are expected to be responsible for parents in their old age, while daughters—the "children of others"—will move in with their in-laws after marriage and devote themselves to their husbands' parents. In short, parents invest more in sons because they have greater long-term expectations of return (old age security and rituals after one's death). This contract contributes to most couples' strong desire to have a son. At the same time, new migration and work opportunities for young women open new possibilities of exchanges between parents and daughters, which, in turn, may alter the intergenerational contract. Examining family relations and dynamics between female unmarried children and their parents is particularly important because alterations in intergenerational contracts will occur before marriage. Thus, we conceptualize the period between premarital waged work and marriage as being a critical time, given the possibility for change in family relations and exchanges.

In this chapter, we examine the significance of daughters' premarital factory work on their relationships with natal family members and their status within the family. Rather than focusing on the meaning of waged work and economic independence per se, we seek a more comprehensive understanding of women's experiences of leaving and working away from home. More specifically, we are particularly interested in exploring how the experience of migrating, working, and earning "repositions" women toward their parents and siblings and vice versa. To research this topic, we rely here on interview data with single women working in the garment industry who have migrated from rural areas to the city of Hanoi for employment. We document these women's own perceptions of their relationships with family members, specifically with regard to the extent that they have experienced changes. We provide evidence of women's shifting perceptions of themselves as daughters and of their role within the family. We discuss the significance and potential impact of this change on Vietnamese families, gender relations, and work.

We theoretically situate our analysis and discussion in a conceptualization of empowerment as a process, rather than as an outcome. Although empowering daughters is a theme that runs through many studies, the term *empowerment* is not explicitly defined or theorized. Indeed, it has become a "slippery word, a chimera that lets everyone feel comfortable, a motherhood term with a warm, cuddly feeling" (Saunders 2002, 52). Of the attempts made to theorize the concept in other development contexts, there is no consensus regarding whether empowerment refers to an outcome or a process, that is, an achievement or something that is always "in the works." This chapter, however, takes as its premise the perspective that, throughout the life course, individuals experience ebbs and flows of empowerment. In this sense, people are neither empowered nor disempowered in a definitive sense; rather, they are differentially engaged in empowering situations (Rowlands 1996). Conceptualized in this way, empowerment is conceived as situational, contingent, and dynamic. In other words, empowerment is experienced in a variety of ways and at different moments in time. This makes proposing a "theory of empowerment," which can simply be applied to all circumstances, impossible. Nonetheless, it is useful to analyze those conditions that seem to constrain or promote experiences of empowerment.

Pendakis (2004) has explored the empowerment of young Vietnamese women elsewhere. Drawing from previous theoretical contributions by Rowlands (1996), Pendakis examined women's expressions of "personal," "relational," and "collective" empowerment as they became manifest within various domains of women's lives, including the family. Women also discussed other forms of relational empowerment in the context of the workplace, between friends and strangers, and within future marital relationships. In addition, this analysis focused on those elements of the women's environment that served to either inhibit or encourage the process of empowerment.

This chapter, then, focuses specifically on women's experiences of empowerment that shape their relationships within the natal family. We conceptualize expressions of empowerment as an increased capacity to make choices, a sense of having agency or control over one's life and increased powers of negotiation within significant relationships. Contrary to much of the work on empowerment that focuses on measurable outcomes, such as education or health status, we examine empowerment within the family and are interested in more subtle—yet nonetheless significant—manifestations of empowerment. We put forward the notion of "moments of empowerment" to convey the sentiments of women in the examination of their experiences and narratives.

Young Female Factory Workers in Asia

In *The Modern Anthropology of Southeast Asia*, King and Wilder (2003) include a section titled "Factory Girls." For these authors, "factory girls" constitute an important group to study on their own and a group that has generated a number of empirical studies and theories, which have furthered our understanding of gender relations in Asia. One important contribution of this body of literature is that it calls into question sweeping and homogeneous constructions of Asian patriarchy in its subordination of working daughters and the extent to which this patriarchy is the primary factor in unequal industrial relations (Ong 1991). By focusing on this particular group of women and examining the interconnections among ethnicity, class, age, and gender in Asia, it is possible to understand gender relations and inequality more comprehensively.

Research on factory daughters spans the last thirty-five years, testifying to the importance of this research theme in scholarly work on Southeast Asia, as well as East Asia and South Asia. The "dragon economies" of Asia—Taiwan, Hong Kong, and South Korea—were the sites of initial studies. Analyses focusing on factory daughters continued in the 1980s and 1990s; some researchers generally examined countries of Southeast Asia and South Asia, while others revisited the situation in countries examined a few decades earlier.

The studies from the 1970s and 1980s concluded that factory work essentially reproduced existing inequalities and failed to increase daughters' values in families. Greenhalgh (1985) and Kung (1983) independently examined factory daughters in Taiwan in the 1970s. Formulating different research questions and arguments, they nonetheless reached similar conclusions. Greenhalgh (1985) contends that in the early stages of Taiwanese industrial capitalism gender inequalities have increased. Her examination of the status of daughters, relative to sons, reveals how parents strategically educated their daughters in order to "make" them work prior to marriage. This strategy allowed them to pool more family income to invest in their sons' education, marriage, and housing. In a similar vein, Kung argues that "factory work for young women is merely a new opportunity to meet already existing role expectations and that the values on which these role definitions are based have not changed" (1983, xiv). Looking at the situation of young women in the 1970s and early 1980s, these scholars argue that early capitalism and the production of exports led to further female subordination and exploitation. Greenhalgh specifically attributes these negative outcomes of factory work to the patriarchal kinship system and to the reproduction of "sex stratification" by parents through the exploitation of daughters for the benefit of sons.

Also emerging from research is the theme that daughters in families are socialized to experience a feeling of indebtedness toward natal parents. According to some, factory work offers a new way of repaying parents by no longer relying on them and, in the best-case scenario, by contributing to the family income—a difficult thing to do after marriage in a patrilocal kinship system. Salaff's (1981) pioneer study on Hong Kong (which is not restricted to factory workers) stresses the strong sense of filial piety that motivated factory work among young women in the 1970s. Lee (1998), in a more recent study, reaches a similar conclusion for Gangong, China. By giving a voice to young single women, researchers document how women feel obliged to pay their parents back for having raised them. Young women's sense of duty is magnified by the fact that they are born into families that traditionally do not consider them permanent members. In the case of the debt owed by daughters to their parents in Taiwan, Greenhalgh argues: "Although the form of repayment was somewhat flexible, the necessity of repayment was not. Parents enforced this expectation by socializing their daughters to believe that everything they had—their bodies, their upbringing, their schooling—belonged to their parents and had to be paid for" (Greenhalgh 1985, 277).

The common thread connecting the findings of Kung, Salaff, and Greenhalgh is that they all tend to conceptualize waged work as a new way of relieving the sense of debt to parents. Women's control over their wages is, therefore, conceptualized as the ultimate marker of independence and empowerment, while parental control of earnings is seen as disempowering daughters who must labor long hours in difficult conditions to meet parental expectations.

Unlike Kung and Greenhalgh who conclude that premarital waged work serves to reinforce the subordinate position of daughters in Taiwanese families, Lie and Lund (1994) portray Malay women who took part in their research as young agents who are engaged in a reconfiguration of traditional identities. They argue that, while women are becoming increasingly aware of their capacity as economic contributors and are heightening their ambition and social activity with other workers, they are essentially reworking what is appropriate behavior for young, single Malay women. In the same vein, Wolf's (1990) study of female factory workers and their families in Java, Indonesia, is particularly insightful. Wolf attempts to provide a link between the macrophenomenon of globalization and microprocesses by examining what occurs at the intermediary level, namely the dynamics of the family unit. Wolf is concerned with the status of daughters within the family and hypothesizes that employment has the potential of increasing the perceived worth of daughters in the eyes of their parents. Wolf finds that the wages paid to the women interviewed are below subsistence level, which means that some parents must subsidize their daughters' survival by meeting some of their basic financial needs. In those instances where women only have a small surplus after meeting their own costs, they have very little to send home. However, daughters send more money home for parental needs or after a poor harvest. Importantly, there is no evidence that parents encourage their daughters' employment as a strategic move to enhance the family's economic situation.

Wolf further concludes that, "despite the exploitative wages and the need for subsidization, female factory workers in central Java derive both economic and social benefits from factory employment" (Wolf 1990, 42). Although recognizing the contradiction between the women's perception of themselves as privileged and their below-subsistence level wages, Wolf emphasizes the fact that these women do hold somewhat privileged positions in relation to their peers who work in the agricultural sector. Moreover, the women appear to have higher status and have a greater chance of vertical mobility by way of attracting "better-quality" spouses. Similar observations were made in Malaysia by Ong who notes how "the earnings of village daughters helped furnish their parents' houses and improve daily consumption and that the women themselves had discretionary income and could save for their weddings" (1991, 288). Similarly, in Bangladesh, Amin argues that "despite long work hours and harsh working conditions, most workers are able to negotiate within their natal families some independence and autonomy as a result of their earning potential" (Amin et al. 1998, 185).

To summarize, on the one hand, some scholars indicate that waged work is limited in its ability to increase gender equality and foster women's autonomy. As Greenhalgh (1985) argues, daughters' earning potential can further subordinate them to their parents who recognize a new source of family income in their female children. On the other hand, studies done more recently document how factory work can open up new possibilities and offer potential for empowerment. Two factors can explain the different conclusions of the aforementioned studies. First, regarding premarital factory work, the outcomes on family relations and daughters' status depend on the kinship systems that prevail. Taiwan's kinship system is Chinese, thus patrilineal and patriarchal, while Malaysia's and Indonesia's kinship systems are less hierarchical and less oppressive for women. As Ong points out, "bilateral kinship organization and cultural norms exerted fewer claims on daughters than did the patrilineal Chinese system" (1991, 288). This difference also supports Mason's argument, which states that investigators must consider the potential of waged work to empower women within the gender and kinship systems that existed prior to the emergence of new work opportunities for women (Mason 1995). Second, the duration of a country's participation within the global production of labor-intensive sectors, such as the garment industry, will also result in differences. In a recent contribution, Mehrotra and Parish (2001) revisited the situation of unmarried female workers in Taiwan and reexamined the extent to which patriarchal families absorbed their daughters' economic gains. The general conclusions drawn from this study were that, although daughters did not have complete control over their earnings, unmarried daughters did have a greater capacity to manage their income compared to twenty years before. In cases where earnings were passed on to siblings or parents, daughters benefited from their employment in ways not reducible to family economics. For example, the authors argue that even daughters without savings benefited in the long term, since they were able to entice "better quality" spouses; they also had greater chances of maintaining employment after marriage.

Real earnings have increased significantly for women in Taiwan, and women have acquired increasingly greater control over how they spend their income. We suggest that the very pessimistic conclusions for Taiwan coming from the literature on export-led growth may stem from a focus on the early stages of economic growth (Mehrotra and Parish 2001).

This observation raises the question as to whether this pattern will repeat itself in other settings. Perhaps an additional factor accounting for the specific experiences of factory girls in Asia is not only the length of time a country has been in the global network of export-led production, but also the "timing" of a country's entry. Vietnam has recently entered into the export-led garment production, approximately two decades later than neighboring countries. The specificities of Vietnam's kinship system and its trajectory as a participant in the process of global production are also important elements of the discussion.

Vietnamese Daughters in the Asian Context

The kinship system in Vietnam is positioned "between" the Chinese and the Southeast Asian models because it is neither exclusively patrilineal nor bilateral. In rural North Vietnam, sons hold a higher status than daughters, and brides generally move in with the groom's parents for a period of patrilocal co-residence. Residential emancipation occurs for younger sons, while the oldest stays with his parents, since he inherits the parental house. Of course, migration for work leads to adaptations of this ideal model. Despite limited indications of discrimination against female children, as measured by indicators like immunization coverage, duration and intensity of breastfeeding, nutritional status, and mortality differentials, a strong desire to have male children prevails in the region. Fertility and contraceptive use analyses indicate that son preference shapes the family building process (Haughton and Haughton 1995; Johansson 1998). In contrast to China, in India and South Korea there is no evidence of widespread prenatal discrimination through sex-selective abortion, although it appears to exist in Hanoi for the third birth order (Bélanger et al. 2003). In sum, while Vietnam has a similar kinship system as the countries mentioned above, discrimination against female children is not widespread in Vietnamese families.

The renovation, *Doi Moi*, has brought about a return of presocialist funeral and ancestor worship rituals (Kleinen 1999; Luong 1993), which has revived the importance of having a male child. For these rituals to be performed in due form, a male heir is necessary; consequently, the desire to give birth to a son is reinforced. In a more general manner, some scholars have commented on the increasing gender inequalities in the era of postsocialism in Vietnam and other nations experiencing the same process (Fahey 1998; Pelzer 1993; Werner and Bélanger 2002).

Rydstrom's (1998) study of children's socialization vividly illustrates the gendered nature of children's upbringing in Vietnam. Her work shows how different constructions of female and male bodies lead to a significantly different socialization of boys and girls within families and communities. Boys, she argues, hold intrinsic value through their superior, sexed bodies, while girls must acquire a sense of worth and value to their parents and society through socialization. Thus, girls are "blank slates" that have to be shaped through upbringing practices, while boys' inborn value does not call for the same intensity of socialization. Based on ethnographic material, Bélanger (2001) documents how, in the rural North, the presence of male children increases the status of mothers and fathers and provides prestige and legitimacy with their family and community. Sons carry on the family line and perform funeral and cult rituals; they are also responsible for their parents in old age. The findings of past research have led to the argument that the value of daughters to their parents has declined, in fact, over the past decades, especially in rural areas (Bélanger 2002a, 2002b).

Bélanger (2002a) emphasizes the particularly difficult situation faced by daughters born after repeated attempts to produce a son. Given the stopping rule that prevails in the family building process after a son is born, more girls than boys have many siblings and live in large families. Because poverty is more acute in these large families, girls are, therefore, more at risk of living in a household with limited resources. This research demonstrates the importance of the family environment and dynamics for daughters' self-esteem and well-being. Teenage daughters who were interviewed struggled with their families' strong desire to birth and raise a male child; in fact, the family is the first place where girls are can be discriminated against. The family building process and the strong desire to produce sons put female children in a difficult position in the era of low fertility. Teenage daughters carry within them the sense that they are less important than their brothers.

Young single women, as a group, have drawn the attention of research at the intersection of family, migration, and work. A common theme within these studies is the gender ambiguities and tensions arising from women's migration to the city and their participation in the urban workforce. Lien Huong (2004), for instance, discusses how young female garment laborers working in Hanoi negotiate their changing identity and status with their families in their home communities. When returning home for family visits, women experience a tension between their notions of themselves as faithful, hardworking daughters and their parents' perception that they may be too urbanized or worse, sexually "spoiled." In these circumstances, women find themselves having to negotiate pressure to marry as well as parental fears that their daughters' prospects for marriage have been ruined because of their association with the city. The specter of the city as a source of "social evils" is also present in Rydstrom's (2006) research that discusses ways in which young, single, working daughters are subjected to the scrutiny of their family and neighbors during visits home. She argues that, because female sexuality is so closely tied to reproduction, any evidence of premarital sexuality is seen as a form of deviance. Indeed, premarital sex, pornography, drug use, and HIV/AIDS are perceived equally to be "social evils."

Women's agency is present to varying degrees within the analyses of those structuring discourses, practices, and processes that affect young female workers in Vietnam. For example, Thu-huong Nguyen-vo shows how young single women contest the treatment of their bodies as "labouring [. . .], disposable, and not worthy of health protection" under conditions of global capitalism through the consumption and use of products to care for their bodies (Nguyen-vo 2006, 205). In this reading, women are engaging in resistance through these acts of body resignification. Elsewhere, however, Thu-Huong Nguyen-vo argues in an analysis of state discourse on single, female garment workers that the contemporary state "manage(s) women as feminized libidinal subjects who at the same time must work to produce what the local or transnational market demands" (Nguyen-vo 2006, 276). In this manner, state representations of women as laborers and consumers permit the appropriation of women's labor power while reinforcing normative notions of women's femininity.

Moving away from an emphasis on state governance of women to an analysis of women's interventions, Nguyen and Thomas (2004) argue that young women are challenging social norms by "crossing the boundaries of state-sanctioned behavior in relation to sex and family relations." Specifically, they document the ways in which the Internet and communication technologies serve as sites for contesting norms and reimagining new forms of femininity and womanhood.

Women, Migration, and the Vietnam Garment Industry

Since the new work opportunities brought about by the burgeoning manufacturing sector in Vietnam are concentrated in the new economic zones and large urban centers, a large number of workers are also migrants. This is generally the case for unmarried young women who leave their rural villages to establish themselves near the factories where they work. Thus, young female workers often experience being away from home for the first time. Evidence clearly suggests that the jobs offered in manufacturing are prompting important migratory flows of young women between provinces and from rural to urban areas.

The 1999 census data provide evidence of the increasing migration of young women across the country. Given the preference for endogamous marriage and the multiplication of foreign-capital industries, it is reasonable to assume that most of these migrations are work-related. According to the 1999 census data, 4.5 million people (or 6.5% of the total population) had migrated since 1994 (Dang and Tacoli 2003). Over half of these migrants were under the age of twenty-five years, with migration occurring the most frequently among those aged twenty to twenty-four years (Dang and Tacoli 2003). Between the 1980s and 1990s, research reports a reversal of trends by sex among young age groups; while men used to migrate more than females, we see the opposite in recent times. Between 1994 and 1999 for the age group twenty to twenty-four years, only 40 males migrated for every 100 females, partly reflecting the development of new work opportunities for young and, often, unmarried women. An examination of census data by marital status, not surprisingly, indicates that single individuals are more likely to migrate than others, and they are more likely to migrate over longer distances. Among single individuals of all ages, males and females migrated in similar proportions (8 percent). A gender comparison of migrants' work sectors provides evidence of a female advantage in the foreign-capital industrial sector, while women are clearly disadvantaged in other work sectors. Interprovincial migrants tend to work in mixed and foreign sectors, indicating the link between migration and the emerging industrial zones and foreign-capital industries. These sectors have attracted particularly large numbers of women (Dang and Tacoli 2003).

The garment industry in Vietnam provides an interesting site in which to examine the implications of globalization on young women and their family relationships. The garment and textile sector grew substantially between 1995 and 2001, with the number of enterprises increasing eightfold (from approximately 100 to 800) (Mekong Economics 2004). In 2001, estimates were that Vietnam had 1.1 million workers in the garment, textile, and shoe sectors (Mekong Economics 2004). Of this number, nearly 80 percent of the workers were female, and 60 percent of female workers were young and single. Vietnam hosts four different types of enterprises: the state sector, which acts as the largest subcontractor of foreign buyers; the joint ventures; the private Vietnamese enterprises; and the foreign enterprises. In this study, we interviewed women from enterprises belonging to the state sector. In the late 1990s, Vietnam's factory workers in the garment industry received the lowest salaries in the region; consequently, they continued to attract foreign investors (Mekong Economics 2004). Vietnam's garment production ranked third among leading exports after oil and foodstuffs. In 2002, shoe, textile, and garment production together accounted for one-third of Vietnam's total exports in total value.

A recent survey of 1,279 garment workers conducted in Vietnam in 2003 indicates that female garment workers are more often migrants than men

(60 percent against 50 percent) (Mekong Economics 2004). Among all mi-grant workers, more than three-quarters did not have their official residence registration in the place of work. The links between residence and social benefits, such as health and education, make workers more vulnerable due to a lack of social protection. It was more difficult for them to obtain longer contracts and stable positions. This survey showed that a gendered division of labor existed in factories, with women occupying the lower paid, most monotonous jobs. In addition, men enjoy more opportunities for training and promotions. Because women are perceived as having a "natural" ability to do precise, fine work, they are confined to the low end of the job hierar-chy, generally in repetitive sewing and assembling tasks (Tran 2001, 2002).

Garment workers generally obtain a job through family and community networks. Given the demand for work on the part of peasants, enterprises easily find workers whenever they need them. New workers generally have to pay for their training during the first few months of work. They receive a wage only after they have proven themselves satisfactory workers. Employers frequently abuse and exploit workers by making them work long hours with few days off, offering them very low wages and often rendering them vulner-able to dangerous working conditions. Although the labor code in Vietnam provides excellent protection for workers, the growing garment sector does not apply or enforce it.

Fieldwork and Narratives

In this chapter, we use the term *daughters* to describe young single women because young single individuals continue to be "children" until they marry. This manner of conceptualizing adult children is important because it is es-sentially through their relationship with their parents and siblings that un-married adults position themselves socially. This study relies on in-depth in-dividual interviews conducted during the summer of 2003 with twenty-two unmarried daughters (Table 9.1). These women were between the ages of eighteen and twenty-nine years, with education levels ranging from grades nine to twelve. All of the women had migrated from their homes in rural areas to the city to take up employment in one of seven garment factories. At the time of the interviews, the duration of employment varied between six months and five years.

TABLE 9.1
Description of sample.

Name	Age	Education	Factory	Years worked in factory
Sang	19	grade 10	Hanosimex Textile Company	1 year
Mai	22	grade 12	Hanosimex Textile Company	+1 year
Binh	24	grade 10	Hanosimex Textile Company	5 years
Hong	24	grade 12	Northern Textile & Garment General Company	2 years
Van	23	grade 12	Texteco Sewing Company	2 years
Linh	19	grade 9	Hanosimex Textile Company	1 year
Tuyen	27	grade 12	Hacotex Textile Company	5 years
Tam	23	grade 12	Lac Trung Sewing Company	3 years
Cam	21	grade 9	Texteco Sewing Company	2 years
Thuy	22	grade 12	Hanosimex Textile Company	+1 year
Ngu	22	grade 9	Phong Phu Head of Knitting Company	5 years
Kim Cuc	23	grade 12	Phong Phu Head of Knitting Company	3 years
Kieu	23	grade 12	Hanosimex Textile Company	1 year
Viet	20	grade 12	Hanoisimex Textile Company	2 years
Hue	27	grade 12	Thang Long Garment Company	4 years
Chi	25	grade 9	Thang Long Garment Company	1 year
Canh	21	grade 12	Thang Long Garment Company	2 years
Dao	21	grade 12	Thang Long Garment Company	6 months
Tien	21	grade 12	Hanoisimex Textile Company	6 months
Chau	19	grade 9	Northern Textile & Garment General Company	1 year
Hai	20	grade 9	Northern Textile & Garment General Company	6 months

The employees of the Institute for Social Development Studies (ISDS), a Vietnamese nongovernmental research organization located in Hanoi, assisted in the recruitment of participants. Staff of ISDS located a few initial participants through their personal networks, and we obtained the remainder of the sample through a snowball strategy by asking the first respondents to introduce the researchers to more workers. All women who we approached agreed to participate after they were informed of the topic of study and the contents of the interview.

We interviewed all participants outside the workplace at their rented dormitories in a number of locations throughout Hanoi, and no employers were aware that their workers were being interviewed. Interviews varied in length between three-quarters of an hour and two and a half hours, and interviewees received monetary compensation for their participation in the study. The primary goal of the interviews was to understand the subjective and deeply personal worlds of these young women and to capture the per-

ceptions they held of their experiences and circumstances within, and outside, the factory. Interviewees were encouraged to be as descriptive and ex-
pansive as possible. Interviews were tape-recorded and then translated and
transcribed by employees at ISDS.

One focus of the interviews was the women's perceptions of their circumstances in comparison to their rural counterparts. First, questions were
asked about the participants' families: the gender composition, main source
of family income, education of family members, and the degree of closeness
that characterized relationships. Participants' future intentions, with regard
to marriage, family, and work, were determined. Interviewees commented on
the perceived similarities and differences between themselves and their rural
counterparts engaged in agricultural labor on a number of points throughout the interview, including work conditions, status within the family, future
prospects, and perceived level of autonomy and independence.

An important observation that emerged from the study was the great deal
of diversity within the women's accounts. This is especially significant given
that the working lives of these women on the surface appear to be very similar and even seem to mirror one another in their daily routines. The general
daily schedule of these women proceeds as follows. Days begin as early as 6:30
or 7:00 A.M. with a quick breakfast and arrival at the garment factory by 7:00
or 8:00 A.M. Work consists of a particular undifferentiated sewing task, with
a focus on pocket seams, collars, pant legs, belt loops, or the attachment of
manufacturing tags. Each woman focuses on a specific area of the final product, generally shirts or jeans, for five or six hours at a time. The workday is
interrupted by short breaks and a lunch, which is often spent in brief sleep.
During periods of low production, women return home anywhere between
6:00 and 9:00 P.M. During busy stretches they work very late or even throughout the night. Those who are able to return home before nightfall eat dinner,
take a bath, and then go to bed. Sometimes these women do not have a day off
for weeks; however, during less hectic periods they spend every second Sun-
day sleeping, doing chores, and visiting home.

Leaving Home

The transition from one's home to the factory environment and from one's
village to the city of Hanoi represents a major shift in the life course of
young rural women, as none of the women interviewed had ever lived away

from their family before they became factory workers. They offered relatively diverse accounts of the process by which they moved to Hanoi, as well as their motivations for doing so. Women did not speak of a singular impetus for migration; rather, they described a number of factors that they perceived to be significant. We review below the most common processes by which women left the village to enter the city and factory.

THE UNREALIZED DREAM OF EDUCATION

Most women we interviewed intended to pursue university or college studies. In rural Vietnam, higher education is the golden passport to social and economic mobility. All peasants aspire to have at least one successful child in higher education, and some invest substantially in order to achieve this dream. In rural areas of contemporary Vietnam, young men and women who perform well in upper-secondary school are future candidates for the very competitive and difficult university entrance examinations. For a young woman, succeeding in education is a way to demonstrate to one's parents her worth and increase her own family's status in the village. Educational achievements symbolically represent the best way for young women to "pay back" their parents for their care and love; failing to meet parents' expectations and hopes is a source of shame and discouragement. In some cases, the women interviewed tried to enter university for two subsequent years, which represents a substantial investment from parents who usually free daughters up from domestic and agricultural work so they can devote their time to studying. Parents might even pay a private tutor to boost their daughter's probability of success. However, failing the examinations, once or twice, exacerbates the sense of indebtedness toward one's parents.

Confronted with the impossibility of achieving higher education, the women perceived migration to obtain a factory job as an alternate way of demonstrating their ability to learn and be independent. Because factory work is a substitute for education, women's discourse about the nature of their work often stresses its educational value. Therefore, many women view factory work in the garment sector as a potential and real source of learning, in spite of the monotony and repetitive nature of the tasks performed. As Binh (aged twenty-four) reported:

> When I completed secondary school, I took the university entrance examinations. I failed the first time, but my parents encouraged me to try again. When

I failed again, I felt sad that I would not learn anymore and bored because I would have to stay at home. I decided to go to Hanoi as some of my friends had done. When I came to Hanoi and began working, I realized that there were many things to learn . . . I had lessons in the technology of sewing and other specialized kinds of knowledge that are related to my job. I think that these skills are very valuable for the future because I have the ability to go to another factory with these skills or open my own tailor shop. I can also make clothes for my family.

Other women did not reach grade twelve and entered factory work with a grade nine or ten education. It was generally the case that their parents could not afford to see them complete their secondary education, and they, too, felt that they had failed in achieving something valuable in their life.

THE DESIRE FOR EMANCIPATION FROM THE NATAL FAMILY

Women particularly valued the ability to emancipate themselves from their parents by moving to the city. Emancipation (*thoat ly*) from one's family involves both residential and economic dimensions (see the chapter by Xenos et al., this volume for a statistical analysis of home leaving among Vietnamese youth). Residential emancipation generally occurs upon marriage and, for the luckiest ones, through higher education in Hanoi. Leaving home for marriage does not grant the same independence because it involves the transfer of control over women from their natal family to their husband's family. The young women in the study aspired to being independent from one's natal family and, yet, not tied down and responsible for a husband, children, and parents-in-law. Factory work in an urban area, therefore, offered the possibility of carving out for oneself a life course stage of this nature.

A successful emancipation is not only residential, but also economic, and involves no longer being financially dependent upon one's parents. Women who had achieved both residential and financial autonomy following migration expressed pride in no longer being a "burden" to their parents and having demonstrated their ability to stand "on their own feet." Dao, (aged twenty-one) like many others, reflected on her move to the city and the independence that it has afforded her: "I came to Hanoi because I didn't want to be dependent upon my parents any more. I wanted to be an adult with my own wage. I now earn enough to live on . . . and to save a little . . . My parents do not have to shoulder my burden anymore . . . because I can stand on my own two feet. I am bolder now." If the failed attempt to get a postsecondary education represented a push factor for leaving the village, the factory attracted women because it gave them a way to earn an income that would at least be enough to sustain them away from home and, therefore, relieve their sense of burdening their parents.

THE QUEST FOR EXCITEMENT AND DISCOVERY; THE ESCAPE FROM BOREDOM

Intertwined with the desire to become independent was the attraction of the city for its urban culture, excitement, and opportunity to meet people and learn. Women also perceived the city to be a place of adventure, diversity and, most important, a space in which to absorb general knowledge about the world outside the rural community. Women frequently expressed chronic boredom and the feeling that there was "nothing to do at home." Women explained that they had friends who had migrated to the city and the idea of doing the same was "exciting," as it offered an alternative to working on the family's land and just "waiting" to get married. Certainly, the domino effect of having some friends already working in the city played an important role in young women's ability to imagine the possibility of securing a job before leaving. Indeed, women would pass along their experiences to friends at home. The stories were similar in their emphasis on novelty and change. As Hue (aged twenty-seven) said:

> I have certainly learned a lot about society, things that I would never have learned if I had stayed at home with my parents. I have gained so much useful experience for my future life, and I have gained knowledge about many different topics. As a result, I have seen that my perspectives changed . . . they have been expanded . . . I now know about how things happen outside of the country.

Clearly, the opportunity to experience exciting changes of this kind is one significant factor motivating women's migration to the city.

EXERTING AGENCY OVER ONE'S LIFE COURSE

In some analyses of rural women's migration to urban centers for employment, scholars point out that the decision to leave is made primarily by parents, and, similarly, the negotiations for employment are frequently made without reference to the intentions and desires of women themselves. Indeed, some researchers have noted that fathers, uncles, and brothers play a significant role in organizing women's migration and employment, concluding that women are literally "passed" from the men in their family to male employers (Wichterich 2000). Kung (1983) and Greenhalgh (1985), for instance, made this observation for Taiwanese single women in the 1970s. These anthropologists argued that this process perpetuates the very system of patriarchal domination and exploitation that women's employment is allegedly supposed to undermine. In this sense, we consider it integral to our discussion of daughters' empowerment within the family to explore the relational dynamics associated with daughters' migration and subsequent employment.

In contrast to the accounts from other countries and earlier decades, we found that, in the case of the Vietnamese women we interviewed, parents did not take the initiative to "send" them to work. Personal desires and objectives of the women shaped the processes by which they left home; parents and families rarely encouraged daughters to leave. That is, the accounts of daughters did not give the sense that they felt pressured into leaving home in order to obtain a wage or to contribute financially to their families. Although parents had some part in helping their daughters move to the city and secure employment, this only occurred after women expressed a firm desire to leave. Women perceived their parents as being encouraging and helpful during this process, although some women mentioned, in their accounts, that their parents were suspicious about how daughters would function in the city without an extensive network of family and community ties. Canh (aged twenty-one) described how she had to persuade her parents to allow her to move to Hanoi, as they feared that the "social evils" of the city might overwhelm her:

> My parents really did not want me to go to Hanoi. Some people think the city is a dangerous place and worry about drug users and playboys. They wanted me to find work much closer to home. But I said to my parents, "Let me go and learn in the city." I knew that I would learn so much and expand my perspectives. I knew that I would gain so much from working in Hanoi. So once I decided this, no one could discourage me from moving. I even had a boyfriend who asked me to stay home. But I left.

The process of migrating resulted from network connections, and parents were often involved in planning the migration once daughters had demonstrated their eagerness to leave. Some women had a distant relative with whom they could stay when arriving in Hanoi, while others had a sister or a cousin already working in a factory. The migration process was well organized, and women generally secured employment before the move. Only within a certain structure and network would parents permit their daughters' departure from home. The stories of garment workers that we collected illustrate the importance of networks for internal migration in response to work opportunities as described in Luong's analysis (see his chapter in this volume). Moreover, the women themselves took on the role of agents in actively recruiting other young women to the city and the factory. These findings indicate that daughters are not merely "passed" from one patriarchal unit to the next. Indeed, women exerted agency in the process of leaving home and expressed a strong desire to go beyond the idiosyncratic environment of their family, kinship, and village.

Women's agency modifies the "typical" life course of women who do not pursue higher education. The expectation is that these women should marry promptly after leaving school, ideally between the ages of eighteen and twenty-two years. Women's decision to migrate for work thus postponed marriage. Although none of them explicitly articulated the desire to avoid an early marriage, daughters and their parents recognized that migration and premarital work would necessarily delay marriage. Delayed marriage was a source of worry for both daughters and parents who feared that the girls would eventually be "on the shelf" (*e, qua lua*) and difficult to marry. In spite of the risk inherent in their decision, women nonetheless preferred to leave home to work.

It is important to note, as we have attempted to do here, that conceptualizing the changes that have occurred in terms of the life course does not imply that there is a need to obscure or minimize diversity. Indeed, we argue that, although women experience similar motivations to leave their homes to seek work in Hanoi, they experience the move in different ways. The process of leaving home was unique; women were, to varying degrees, engaged in a dialogue with their parents about work, marriage, and the priorities for the future. Some daughters left in order to forget their failure to pursue postsecondary education; others left to remove the financial burden they placed on parents simply by their presence in the household. Other women aspired to a life in the city where they could discover the world outside the village. A common thread to the "home leaving" stories of the women interviewed was an expressed hope for a better life and future.

Working and Earning: Honoring or Redefining the Intergenerational Contract?

While the day-to-day routine of work gave most women a sense of powerlessness and made them feel exhausted, it was also work that provided them with a sense of achievement. In spite of meager wages, most women managed to send remittances back home on a regular basis. Because these amounts were very small, between $5.00 and $20.00 a month, their symbolic value was particularly significant. The mere fact that women lived very simply and did everything to save a portion of their income for their parents spoke of their filial piety and gratitude to their parents. By sending money home, even if the amount was small, women showed that they had accomplished their "home leaving." It is through their independent living away from home and their ability to offer monthly contributions to their parents that women demonstrated their worth and sense of appreciation. The women we interviewed stressed the importance of frequent visits and remittances as forms of support to the older generation; Barbieri's analysis (in this volume) further confirms this.

Research on the implications of daughters' work within the family tends to concentrate on the extent to which they control their wages and the degree of parental influence exerted on decisions pertaining to finances. The extent to which parents urge daughters to send all their income home or "allow" them to keep some of it for themselves cannot be established with our interviews in the case of Vietnam; however, paying attention to the meaning of those remittances is equally, if not more, important. It is particularly important when these remittances are barely sufficient to build up either the daughter's or family's savings; both are poor and can use any extra money to fund immediate needs.

Greenhalgh (1985) explores these "parents-daughters" exchanges in Taiwan. She criticizes the lack of attention paid to the timing and levels of "parents-children" flows. She uses Sahlin's categories of reciprocity—balanced, generalized, and negative—to analyze Chinese "parents-children" flows or exchanges. In the balanced type, exchanges are equivalent in levels and have little delay in timing. In generalized reciprocity, repayments of "gifts" need not be equivalent or immediate. Negative reciprocity involves no return at all. Greenhalgh (1985) argues that balanced reciprocity characterizes "parents-daughters" exchanges. For this reason, daughters feel an urge to give something back to parents as soon as they can. In contrast, "parents-sons" reciprocity is of the generalized type, since sons can pay back parents in old age and beyond through cult rituals. This framework is also very useful for explaining the research that criticizes sons for being more selfish and less filial than daughters (Croll 2000). Since sons do not feel pressed to repay parents in the short term, they could indeed appear less responsible in the short term than daughters. This model fits well when looking at Vietnam because of the gendered constructions of sons and daughters. In our interviews, some women wanted to reciprocate parents for their love and care "as soon as possible," which fits the category of balanced exchange. According to Sang (aged nineteen):

> I could spend all of my salary for myself, like others do, but what I really desire is to save as much as I can and send it back home to my family . . . My mother has worked hard all of her life and I want her now to be able to rest . . . One time, I went home to give my mother all the money I had saved. I did not think though, because I was left with only 15,000 VND [equivalent of 1.50 CAD] and the trip back to the factory on the bus left my pocket completely empty. I [did not tell my mother and instead] asked a friend to borrow a little amount of money until the end of the month.

Even though Sang's mother told her to keep the money for her to buy some "nice things" for herself, she continued to save money to contribute to her family. Sang further expanded on this:

> I think that because I am not married right now that this is the time that I should give as much as possible. If I get married in the future, perhaps my husband will not understand the reason why I want to give so much to my parents, so I want to do the best I can now. My parents raised me and I love them so much . . . this is why I give them as much as I can.

In fact, Sang was so confident in her capacity to be a provider that she later expressed that she did not prefer a son as some other girls did. She further stated that, "everyone wants sons, but the fact is that daughters can give much financial assistance to families." Pointing to the lifestyle of her own brother, she noted: "My brother thinks only about his own needs, as many young men do . . . They always spend what they earn. He might spend all the money he makes in a month in just one day and he sends nothing home." These women wished to alter the symbolic value of daughters, through their financial contribution. When considering their own future family, they strongly voiced the idea that daughters and sons are equal, citing their own lives as examples of the unquestionable value of daughters.

Women elaborated in detail on some of the other ways that their contributions assisted their families. For example, Thuy (aged twenty-two) sent her income home and channeled it directly into the secondary school or university education of other siblings in her family. Some respondents had given up the opportunity to attend school in order to seek employment and fund the educations of their "smarter" or "more capable" siblings. When asked to reflect on their forfeits, however, these few women expressed sadness related to their own loss, along with expressions of pride and contentment in being able to enhance the future prospects of their family members. Any opportunity to act on behalf of a family member or in the family's best interests was extremely significant.

In this sense, we argue that, based on these interviews, despite the disempowering nature of their work, the possibility for women to send remittances to their parents represented an extremely important aspect of their experiences. "Leaving home" was the objective, and factory work represented the means toward achieving this objective. If women could not fulfill the hope of bettering their lives through professional self-advancement due to low wages and harassing working conditions, they were able to fulfill the desire to demonstrate their ability to be independent of parents in most cases. Moreover, these accounts suggest that women redefined the terms of the intergenerational contract through their work by increasing their ability to pay parents back in a timely and satisfactory fashion. Daughters did their best to send money home and felt proud of their contribution. Their accounts provide numerous examples of a conscious attempt to alter their parents' perceptions of their capabilities as female children. Women's agency and sense of empowerment permeate the accounts collected and indicate that migration and work do alter daughters' status within their natal families, at least for the period they are working. Further research will more fully explore the longer-term significance of premarital work for family relations. In the case of the women interviewed here, data suggest that remittances did not simply reinforce the existing intergenerational contract but, in fact, reconfigured it. Daughters focused on paying their parents are also altering their parents' perceptions of their worth and capacities.

Negotiating a New Space Within One's Family

Drawing on the understanding of empowerment as a process, which can manifest itself in multiple domains of everyday life, we argue here that the interviews do provide suggestions that the women have experienced some degree of empowerment within their family relationships. We conceive relational empowerment here as having a sense of oneself within a relationship, as well as the ability to communicate and negotiate with others. This type of empowerment is important for increasing women's self-esteem and sense of themselves in a society where sons generally hold a higher status.

One manifestation of the empowerment and pride expressed by women in narratives is the development of opinions that may or may not be distinct from those held by friends and family. When expressed within relationships, empowerment manifests itself as the ability to formulate opinions and beliefs and express them to others. This capability is an important indication that empowerment is occurring within family relations. Kieu, aged nineteen, for example, provided an example of how her opinions differed strongly from those held by her brother with regard to appropriate dating behaviors.

> I feel very comfortable with myself when expressing my thoughts and opinions now. I have very open conversations with other people. I can speak honestly and confidently about my opinions with my brother who lives in Hanoi even though we have different beliefs. For example, I can explain to him why I think his behavior is not right and why I believe that the pure relationship[1] is better between men and women who are not married.

A theme that arose within the interviews was the women's ability to negotiate the enormous pressure they felt from their family to get married. Linh (aged nineteen), for instance, explained that she felt better equipped to express her real opinions about marriage to her parents who were eager to see her married:

> My mother told me frequently that I should think of getting married soon. She told me how she thinks that I have grown up, and that it is time for me to get married. I know that I am of the age to get married but I don't want to at the moment. So, now I tell her that I don't want to get married yet.

Another indication that empowerment was "in the works" was articulated by women who spoke about having more influence within the family. This entailed vocalizing their personal opinions and believing that their opinions were given more consideration and respect by friends and family. Thuy (aged twenty-three) felt that something of the sort had occurred between herself and her mother. "I definitely feel as though something has changed in my relationship with my mother. I feel that she looks at me as though I am an adult now and as though I have something to offer . . . She seems to ask for my opinions more often and she respects my ideas more." Hai (aged twenty) offered a similar statement about her relationship with those in her rural community generally and with her father more specifically: "It seems as though my father is more concerned about my opinions . . . he often asks what I think when trying to make family decisions . . . I also think that people from my community respect me more since I left."

Further, others noted that, although they had very different opinions than their parents concerning marriage, they believed that their parents would respect their final decision. These narratives corroborate the work of Jayakody and Huy (this volume) on the increasing power of young generations in choosing their own spouse. Kim Cuc (aged twenty-three) described how she and her parents were able to discuss their differences.

> When I told my mother that I wanted to marry a man in the city, she cried at first because she did not want me to marry a man living so far from our hometown.[2] But I was able to persuade her. I told her that transportation is very convenient to travel and visit nowadays. I told her that we could travel by motorbike or bus. My parents respect my wishes, so, in the end, my parents agreed that the most important thing was my happiness, and they agreed to the marriage. They said that they would be unhappy if I were unhappy.

Van (aged twenty-three) further explained that workers, in general, were freer to make decisions regarding marriage compared to those living at home under the supervision of their parents:

> In the city, the decision to marry is made more easily. People are free to choose their partners. At home in the rural areas, women's choice depends on the thoughts and opinions of their parents, close family members and other relatives. Sometimes it even depends on what the neighbors think. When coming

here, it becomes more comfortable to choose for ourselves. If we love someone, we will choose that person despite what others say. In contrast, if we dislike someone, it is our decision to refuse him.

Interestingly, this perceived ability for greater influence within close relationships can affect women's future marital relationships. For example, Tam (aged twenty-three) said that she believed she would defend her own opinions if they contrasted with her future husband's opinions:

Interviewer: When you get married, will you go with your husband back to the countryside?

Tam: No, I won't. I am living here now . . . I have a higher living standard now . . . I don't even know what job I could find in the countryside that is as good as this one.

Interviewer: So what will you do if the man you fall in love with wants to take you to the countryside?

Tam: I tell you that I will not go back. Surely, I will not change my point of view on this issue. I will not change my ideas about this because I want to work here all of my life.

It is, of course, difficult to know whether and to what extent the women interviewed will actually be able to influence decisions made within their future families. Chi's ethnography of Vietnamese families (see her chapter in this volume) suggests that married women who earn an income and have to travel for their job enjoy a favorable position, while struggling with ideals of being a good wife and mother (that is, present at home all the time).

Women's sense of having a voice in their family after becoming workers is significant. For many interviewees, premarital waged work changed their status within the family; they felt as if their families treated them as adults. Marriage, as a rite of passage to adulthood, was, to some extent, substituted by employment and the economic and residential independence it entailed.

Ambiguous Identity and Uncertain Future

Upon becoming "factory girls," women expressed concern over the ambiguity of eventually returning to their village of origin. Ong (1991) explores this ambivalence particularly well in the case of Malaysia. She explains how young single women who leave home for factory work were both a symbol of modernity and independence, as well as a threat to the social norms and expectations of young single women. Fears of premarital sexuality and the consequences of contact with the urban culture represented the major threats for single women without any parental and community supervision. The women we interviewed also expressed an awareness of the ambivalent attitude toward women who followed their path. On the one hand, some felt more respected and esteemed, while, on the other, they feared being labeled "urban girls" (*con gai thanh pho*, a negative connotation) and having difficulties finding a spouse. Partly due to the uncertainty caused by their trajectory, many hoped that they could avoid going back to their village and intended to find a spouse in the city instead. In this sense, women must negotiate these contradictory discourses in such a way as to demonstrate that they are respectable women, a finding which echoes the assertion made by Lie and Lund that "women are now negotiating new female roles and identities within changing social fields and conflicting ideologies" (Lie and Lund 1994, 157). Researchers have further contended that a woman's family could have protected her virtue and honor in the past; however, young migrant workers must now deal with the responsibility of demonstrating this on their own. One woman, Chi (aged twenty-five) noted, for example, that she literally had to alter her behavior when she returned home in order to minimize suspicion: "I dress differently in the city. When I go home to visit my friends and family, I not only have to change some of the things I talk about, but I also have to make sure I don't dress up too much so that I don't stand out." Van (aged twenty-three) expands on her experience of the intersecting rural and urban discourses:

> My way of life in the city is not suitable for country people. I have to completely change my way of life when I visit my home. I have to act differently than I would like to and change the way I communicate and my style of dress. In the countryside people are not skilful or clever when they speak. If I remain speaking as I do in the city, people will comment many negative things about how I am not the same girl as before.

When reading the accounts of the harassing day-to-day lives of many of the women we interviewed, one wonders about the source of motivation for continuing to work in garment factories. In fact, the reason they left home tends to sustain their determination to stay, in spite of the exploitation and exhaustion that many experience. When women return home after a few months they experience shame and are labeled failures. The desire to prove to parents their ability to be independent, coupled with their hope for a better future, makes daughters determined not to return home too soon. Daughters must do factory work for a few years before they can return home with pride. The Asian garment sector's heavy reliance on young single women would probably not have been possible without a very specific form of socialization and "parents-daughter" relations found in many societies of East and Southeast Asia.

Conclusion

In this chapter, we have examined one group of women's perceptions regarding their multiple roles as daughters and workers and the implications that their migration to the city has for their familial relationships. By questioning these women about family dynamics and exchanges in relation to their migration trajectory and work experience, we were able to get some sense of both change and continuity about family relations and women's notion of their responsibilities, roles, and identities as daughters. The theme of negotiation is central to this chapter. Women experienced shifts in their perceptions of themselves as daughters in various ways; they embraced some changes and modified others so that their families would continue to see them as being responsible and "good" daughters. This is a particularly interesting finding and one that should be taken up in further research. It is common within sociological and anthropological research to highlight the family as the primary site in which religious, moral, and ethical traditions are reiterated and inscribed throughout the generations. The above findings raise questions regarding the tensions that emerge in this process, as well as the ways in which normative ideals are negotiated, enacted, and reshaped in various contexts and at different moments of time. One might consider the usefulness of analyses that highlight the performative elements of conduct, for understanding the experiences of young women traveling between the differently coded social spaces of rural home, factory, and city. Certainly, this kind of analysis applied to the contemporary family would challenge the notion of specifically defined "roles" and "functions" and would provide insight into the contingent and performative dimensions of family dynamics. Discourse about the "good woman" also plays a role in women's perception of themselves, as indicated by Scornet's chapter for the case of motherhood (this volume) and research by Nguyen-vo (2002, 2006).

We have argued that there is indication of "moments of empowerment" throughout these accounts. Women discussed the ways in which they had experienced a detachment from their families in terms of dependence, the opinions they held, and their visions of the future. We argue that the opportunity to develop self-awareness, self-confidence, and "relational empowerment" within the family generally arises from interactions within environments that are beyond the scrutiny of parents. Moving to the city created a distance from home that gave women an opportunity to reconsider their role as daughters and to see how their opinions and values differed from those of their parents. The women interviewed describe the ways in which they have begun to establish "new" identities for themselves as increasingly autonomous and financially independent young women who are capable of contributing (albeit very small amounts) to their families, a responsibility that has traditionally fallen to their brothers.

It is important to note that women experienced some changes ambivalently and that there were aspects of their new circumstances that they perceived as troubling and even threatening. There was much discussion about the belief in the "evils" of the city; women reported being aware of them and purposely avoiding them. Women also discussed the ways in which they negotiated certain characteristics and tendencies they had picked up in the city to avoid misperceptions during visits to their rural homes.

We believe that the "moments of empowerment" documented in these women's accounts are potentially significant, given the cultural tendency in Vietnam toward son preference. We can only speculate as to the extent to which women's employment will have lasting implications for women's status within the family. Moreover, the complexity of the question of daughters' empowerment through waged work becomes palpable when we consider the degree of ambivalence that characterizes many of the accounts. To be sure, each of the women interviewed is neither wholly empowered nor disempowered; also, they are not "more" or "less" empowered than one another, such that Tam is "more" empowered than Linh. In this way, we must recognize that women experience migration and employment in varied ways, and their capacity for empowerment will likely be shaped by the particular preexisting family relationships, as well as their unique experiences of factory work and migration.

Notes

Data collection for this chapter was funded by a research grant from the Social Science and Humanities Research Council of Canada. We thank the Institute for Social Development Studies of Hanoi for their assistance with data collection. A preliminary version of this chapter was presented at a seminar of the Laboratoire sur l'Asie du Sud Est et le Monde Austronésien (LASEMA) of CNRS, Paris, France, in May 2005. We thank Nelly Krowolski for organizing this seminar and all participants for their constructive comments and questions, which guided the revision of this chapter.

1. Sexual relationships between unmarried men and women are publicly frowned upon in Vietnamese society. In reality, premarital sex occurs commonly among unmarried youth.

2. Because daughters traditionally move to the area of the groom's family upon marriage, parents of rural women who marry men from the city might view the marriage as a loss, as their daughter will live far from home.

References

Amin, S., I. Diamond, R. T. Naved, and M. Newby. 1998. Transition to adulthood of female garment-factory workers in Bangladesh. *Studies in Family Planning* 29(2): 185–200.

Bélanger, D. 2001. *Son preference and demographic change in Vietnam.* Paper presented at the International Union for the Scientific Study of Population International Conference, Brazil, August 2001.

Bélanger, D. 2002a. Childhood, gender and power in Vietnam. In *Communities in Southeast Asia: Challenges and responses,* edited by H. Lansdowne, P. Dearden, and W. Neilson, 380–402. Victoria, BC, Canada: Center for Asia-Pacific Initiatives.

Bélanger, D. 2002b. Son preference in a rural village in North Vietnam. *Studies in Family Planning* 33(4): 321–334.

Bélanger, D., Khuat T. H. O., J. Liu, Le T. T., and Pham V. T. 2003. Are sex ratios increasing in Vietnam? *Population* 58(2): 231–250.

Croll, E. 2000. *Endangered daughters: Discrimination and development in Asia.* London: Routledge.

Dang Nguyen Anh and C. Tacoli. 2003. Migration in Vietnam. A review of information on current trends and patterns, and their policy implications. Regional Conference on Migration, Development Pro-Poor Policy Choices in Asia, 22–24 June. Dhaka, Bangladesh.

Dong-Sook, G., and N. Piper. 2002. *Women and work in globalizing Asia.* London: Routledge.

Fahey, S. 1998. Vietnam's women in the renovation era. In *Gender and power in affluent Asia,* edited by K. Sen and M. Stevens, 222–249. London: Routledge.

Greenhalgh, S. 1985. Sexual stratification: The other side of "growth with equity" in East Asia. *Population and Development Review* 11(2): 265–314.

Haughton, J., and D. Haughton. 1995. Son preference in Vietnam. *Studies in Family Planning* 26(6): 325–338.

Hsiung, P.-C. 1996. *Living rooms as factories: Class, gender and the satellite factory system in Taiwan.* Philadelphia: Temple University Press.

Johansson, A. 1998. Population policy, son preference and the use of IUDs in North Vietnam. *Reproductive Health Matters* 6(11): 66–76.

Kaur, A., ed. 2004. *Women workers in industrialising Asia: Costed, not valued.* New York: Palgrave Macmillan.

King, V. T., and W. D. Wilder. 2003. *The modern anthropology of Southeast Asia.* London: Routledge.

Kleinen, J. 1999. *Facing the future, reviving the past: A study of social change in a Northern Vietnamese village.* Singapore: Institute of Southeast Asian Studies.

Kung, L. 1983. *Factory women in Taiwan.* Ann Arbor: University of Michigan Research Press.

Lee, C. K. 1998. *Gender and the South China miracle: Two worlds of factory women.* Berkeley: University of California Press.

Lie, M., and R. Lund. 1994. *Renegotiating local values: Working women and factory industry in Malaysia.* Surrey, U.K.: Curzon.

Liem Huong Nghiem. 2004. Female garment workers: The new young volunteers in Vietnam's modernization. In *Social inequality in Vietnam and the challenges of reforms,* edited by P. Taylor, 297–324. Singapore: Institute of Southeast Asian Studies.

Luong, Hy Van. 1993. Economic reforms and the intensification of gender rituals in two North Vietnamese villages, 1980–90. In *The challenge of reforms in Indochina,* edited by Borje Ljunggren, 252–259. Cambridge, MA: Harvard University Press.

Mason, K. O. 1995. *Gender and demographic change: What do we know?* Liege: IUSSP.

Mehrotra, N., and W. L. Parish. 2001. Daughters, parents and globalization: The case of Taiwan. In *Women's working lives in East Asia,* edited by M. C. Brinton, 298–322. Stanford, CA: Stanford University Press.

Mekong Economics. 2004. *Gender in the factory: A study of emerging gender issues in the garment and footwear industries in Viet Nam*, 84. Hanoi: Mekong Economics.

Nguyen Bich Thuan and M. Thomas. 2004. Young women and emergent post-socialist sensibilities in contemporary Vietnam. *Asian Studies Reviews* 28: 133–149.

Nguyen-vo Thu-huong. 2002. Governing sex: Medicine and governmental intervention in prostitution. In *Gender, household, state: Doi Moi in Viet Nam*, edited by J. Werner and D. Bélanger, 129–152. Ithaca, NY: Southeast Asia Program, Cornell University.

Nguyen-vo Thu-huong. 2006. The body wager: Materialist resignification of Vietnamese women workers. *Gender, Place and Culture* 13(3): 267–281.

Ong, A. 1991. The gender and labor politics of postmodernity. *Annual Review of Anthropology* 20: 279–309.

Parish, W. L., and R. J. Willis. 1994. Sons, daughters, and intergenerational support in Taiwan. *American Journal of Sociology* 99(4): 1010–1041.

Pelzer, C. 1993. Socio-cultural dimensions of renovation in Vietnam: *Doi Moi* as dialogue and transformation in gender relations. In *Reinventing Vietnamese socialism: Doi Moi in comparative perspective*, edited by W. S. Turley and M. Selden, 309–336. Boulder, CO: Westview Press.

Pendakis, K. 2004. *Rethinking gender, work and empowerment: A case study of young female, garment workers in globalizing Vietnam*. M.A. Department of Sociology. London: The University of Western Ontario.

Pendakis, K., and D. Bélanger. 2004. *Rethinking empowerment: Globalization, women and work in North Vietnam*. Association for Asian Studies Annual Meeting, San Diego.

Rowlands, J. 1996. *Questioning empowerment*. London: Oxfam.

Rydstrom, H. 1998. Embodying morality: Girls' socialization in a North Vietnamese commune. In *Studies in arts and science*. Linkoping, Sweden: Linkoping University.

Rydstrom, H. 2006. Sexual desires and "social evils": Young women in rural Vietnam. *Gender, place and culture* 13(3): 283–301.

Salaff, J. W. 1981. *Working daughters of Hong Kong: Filial piety or power in the family?* New York: Cambridge University Press.

Saunders, K. 2002. *Feminist development thought*. London: Zed Books.

Thang Leng Leng and W.-H. Yu, eds. 2004. *Old challenges, new strategies: Women, work and family in contemporary Asia*. Leiden: Brill.

Tran, A. N. 2001. Global subcontracting and women workers in comparative perspective. In *Globalization and Third World socialism*, edited by C. Brundenius and J. Weeks, 217–236. New York: Palgrave.

Tran, A. N. 2002. Gender expectations of Vietnamese garment workers: Viet Nam re-integration into the world economy. In *Gender, household, state: Doi Moi in*

Viet Nam, edited by J. Werner and D. Bélanger, 549–571. Ithaca, NY: Cornell University.

Werner, J., and D. Bélanger, eds. 2002. *Gender, household and state: Doi Moi in Viet Nam.* Southeast Asian Series. Ithaca, NY: Cornell University.

Wichterich. C. 2000. *The globalized woman: Reports from a future of inequality.* New York: Zed Books.

Wolf, D. 1990. Linking women's labour with the global economy: Factory workers and their families in rural Java. In *Women workers and global restructuring,* edited by K. Ward, 25–47. Ithaca, NY: Cornell University Press.

Chapter Ten

A Home Divided
Work, Body, and Emotions in the Post-*Doi Moi* Family

TRUONG HUYEN CHI

Recent studies of family changes in post-*Doi Moi* (Reform) Vietnam look at the structure of the household, such as its composition, residential patterns or interhousehold networks (Hirschman and Vu 1996; Krolowski 2002; and see Luong, this volume), discuss the relations between the family and the state (Werner 2002; and see Scornet, this volume), or focus on one or two sets of relations between family members, such as that between husband and wife, children and parents, or between in-laws (Ngo 2004; Pham 1990; Werner 2004; and see Bélanger and Pendakis, this volume). Most research dealing with family issues and gender tends to focus on women (Drummond and Rydstrom 2004; Werner and Bélanger 2002, 23). This chapter contributes to this body of literature by examining family relations and by capturing the different and simultaneous daily life experiences of all family members, without privileging any difference, including gender, at the expense of others (Mohanty 1991; Moore 1994). By expanding a notion of work and its interconnectedness with body and emotions across time, I suggest that a full understanding of experiences of family changes in northern Vietnam since *Doi Moi* requires an understanding of an internally differentiated personhood. Based on ethnographic materials collected in *Dong Vang* village (Red River Delta region) in the late 1990s, this chapter examines how villagers make sense of their embodied experiences of change. I explore how these experiences entail ambiguous emotions because individuals draw on a repertoire of norms and values, images and stories, as well as implicit understanding of expectations of oneself and others. The repertoire of images and ideas that this chapter restitutes is, in short, a social imaginary of the family.

Kinship, Gender, and Personhood

A starting point for conceptualizing this chapter is built on recent critiques of anthropological use of both concepts of gender and kinship. Inasmuch as kinship has to be denaturalized, that is, subject to a scrutiny of how related-ness is socially constructed (Carsten 2004, 82), gender also has to undergo the complications of race, class, sexuality, ethnicity, and other ascriptive identities (Mohanty 1991). Recent feminist critiques of research that favor gender primacy without regard for other forms of difference are particularly illuminating for researchers who seek to understand family changes in post-*Doi Moi* Vietnam. In a context in which every aspect of family life is under-going profound transformations brought about by an increasing availability of economic opportunities, rising consumption options and demands, and an expansion of the state presence, I argue that it is necessary to situate the experience of family subjects in the interconnectedness of crosscutting dif-ferences. These differences are by no means limited to gender, but include, as indicated in *Dong Vang* ethnographic materials, age, place, body, and work among others, but not according to a preconceived hierarchical order. The discussion that follows reveals how experiences of change in the family since *Doi Moi* can be best understood as embodied and materialized in the inter-connected relations that constitute family daily life.

Recognition of a pluralized subject with multiple identities stems from a re-newed interest in the self or personhood in both feminist writing and anthro-pology. Instead of a notion of the unitary and bounded individual prevalent in Western thinking, rich anthropological accounts from Asia attest to a notion of permeable and "dividual" persons composed of social relations that in turn pro-duce, in Strathern's term, a "social microcosm" (Strathern 1988, 13). This alter-native notion of the person is congruent with the attention paid to the body as a site in which societal meanings and moral perceptions are encapsulated and social processes are internalized (Bourdieu 1977; Merleau-Ponty 1995).

I have found this understanding of the plural, composite, society-oriented, and context-laden person that figures in the anthropological literature of Asia pertinent to the well-recorded intricate set of kinship relations of the Viet people living in northern Vietnam (Luong 1989). When a person adopts a pronoun-addressing speech or conducts an act toward another kin, for instance, it is helpful to look beyond the relations directly incurred by that speech or action, to elicit a multilateral frame of reference and the interlocking relations that enfold her. It follows that instead of tracking how a woman switches her roles and/or statuses from mother to wife, and then to daughter or daughter-in-law, it is perhaps more fruitful to try to understand her being all of those *at one and the same time* and, simultaneously and no less importantly, a street vendor, a Mother Goddess worshipper, a member of a marketplace-based credit rotation group, a village *cheo* troupe singer, and whomever else she may identify herself with. Furthermore, if we are to depart from the notion of the woman-individual as a constellation of roles and statuses to reach an understanding of the subject as a locus of differences from within, it is crucial to scrutinize other sources of identity beyond gender and femaleness, such as class, age, work, religion, sexuality, embodied place, and other ascriptive and acquired qualities (Mohanty 1991).

A similar task is required for understanding experiences of changes in the family life for men, children, and the elderly. By juxtaposing discussions on work, body, and emotions of *Dong Vang* children, elderly, women, and men, I aim to achieve more than a complimentary picture of post-*Doi Moi* family life consisting of both gender and intergenerational relations. My discussion on *Dong Vang* men and their engagement in daily discourses and activities is not simply an attempt to reintroduce the other end of the spectrum. In a similar vein, children and elderly are not simply "brought back in" as agents subordinate to the workforce-centered logic. In this chapter, I hope to reach an understanding of intense dialogues among family members employing different, often contrasting, idioms, norms, and values drawn from their local moral worlds. In so doing I hope to elaborate on ambivalent experiences of internally differentiated and multidimensional subjects in their engagement in the market economy via an intensification of relations with their familial others.

Contesting Family Imaginary

I share with the editors and other authors in this volume that despite, and perhaps precisely because of, the resilience of the family in Vietnam, the very concept of the family has to be submitted to critical examination in the first place (see Bélanger and Barbieri, this volume). Among recent trends of inquiry about the family, there is a noticeable shift from focusing on the relations of production to those of reproduction that in turn are linked to larger scale institutions and processes (see Scornet, this volume). This recognition of the importance of the larger political economic context and ideologies in understanding local processes resonates in recent anthropological studies of post-*Doi Moi* Vietnam (Gammeltoft 1999; Luong 1998; Truong 2001). In line with this inquiry of a coexistence and articulation of contrasting ideologies, such as Confucian, non-Confucian, socialist, and market-driven visions in local moral worlds, a more critical treatment of periodization and categorization of these ideological voices is needed for at least two reasons. First, while categories are good to think and, by extension, to write and read with, they ultimately do so to serve researchers and readers of their accounts. In my daily conversations with *Dong Vang* friends, let alone in their interactions among themselves, none of the above categories comes up, and even when they do under different guises their use is far from my abstraction. If we are to truly grasp subjective views and experiences, a different approach should be employed. Second, if our task is to recognize and recover the previously submerged, negated, or dismissed subjectivities, the prior conceptualization of the dominant versus alternative hierarchy prevalent in Vietnam studies should first be extracted (see also Tran and Reid 2006). Where the family and the status of women in contemporary Vietnam is concerned, sociologists and anthropologists seem to be absorbed in the Confucian versus bilateral/indigenous/Southeast Asian debate, either by looking for traits and variations of the former, or by discovering evidences and remnants of the latter (Hirschman and Vu 1996; Krolowski 2002; O'Harrow 1995; Pham 1999). In a recent critique of prevailing paradigms of Vietnamese nationalistic historiography, Tran effectively demystifies the myth of women's equal property rights and thereby a prevalent assumption of the relatively high status of Vietnamese women. In so doing, she posits that an uncritical acceptance of established paradigms would limit genuine attempts at writing women's history from the perspective of their experiences (Tran 2006, 139). Benefiting from these insights, I would add that for social scientists working in and returning from the field, a preconceived Confucian versus non-Confucian, or more broadly, a dominant versus alternative binary, would hinder researchers from recognizing different forms of power at work.

One way to escape this confine is to give way to local employ of norms and values without boxing them into neatly periodized and hierarchically ordered categories. To this end, I find helpful a notion suggested by Charles Taylor, whereby the social imaginary is defined as "the ways people imagine their social existence, how they fit together with others, how things go on between them and their fellows, the expectations that are normally met, and the deeper normative notions and images that underlie these expectations" (C. Taylor 2004, 23). There is nothing unreal, illusionary, or theoretical about this notion. On the contrary, for an anthropologist, social imaginary has the advantage of leading one to take into account "the common understanding that makes possible common practices and a widely shared sense of legitimacy" of the majority of ordinary people in their daily life (C. Taylor 2004, 23). Thus the family as a social imaginary can be extended to include expectations family members have of one another: the kind of images that cause a person to identify with and recognize herself in certain roles, or that lie behind a person's taking up obligations and rights upon herself and assuming the same for others. In the context of this chapter, I ask how the family imaginary enables practices in *Dong Vang* family life by making sense of them; how family norms and ideals constituting this imaginary are sometimes reinforced and sometimes contested in the daily discourse and practice of villagers; how these norms are unevenly shared and variedly invoked by each family member *in* and *for* her actions for, thinking about, feeling toward, and posing claims of her familial others.

In what follows, I examine the ways in which family members—varied in age, gender, self-evaluation of work, embodied place, and so forth—come to terms with their experiences of intensified work as a result of changes in the household division of labor following urban migration. The chapter title suggests not only a geographical spread of a family but also emotional tensions between its members and within each person.[1] Before turning to the daily world of *Dong Vang*, let me provide a brief account of its changes since *Doi Moi*.

"Going Back to the Marketplace"

In 1998, 180 out of 293 households in *Dong Vang* had at least one person engaged in seasonal migration to Hanoi.[2] In describing the major changes since

Doi Moi, Dong Vang villagers often summarize, "We can now return to the marketplace (*di cho*) again." An estimated 40 percent of the *Dong Vang* workforce today takes part in migratory trades and/or wage jobs. Once again, the combination of agriculture and various nonagricultural occupations brings prosperity to *Dong Vang* villagers.

There is insufficient space here to fully discuss the sources and nature of the transformations in *Dong Vang*, but I summarize what occurred in the village through approximately three decades of building socialism and attest to the power of local and daily politics (Kerkvliet 2005; Truong 2001).[3] The transformation in *Dong Vang*, succinctly put in the villagers' own words in the above quotation, has been characterized by a full resurfacing of previously submerged patterns of multiple occupation, migration, and agriculture. The most salient feature is the current migration deeply rooted in the tradition of multiple occupations and gendered images particular to this village. As early as the turn of the twentieth century, when *Dong Vang* economic activities were increasingly diversified, both men and women actively participated in handicraft production and trades: men as silkworm egg producers and merchants and women as paddy processors and traders. Yet these forms of work were deeply gendered: the image of relaxed, generous, intelligent *Dong Vang* craftsmen-merchants directly contrasted with the image of hardworking, thrifty, cunningly smart petty-trading women. Through about three decades under the cooperative system, *Dong Vang* women kept their small trades of agricultural products such as rice, eggs, and shellfish, while silkworm egg production was discontinued. By the end of the 1990s, most of *Dong Vang* seasonal migrants in Hanoi were women, but this gendered pattern of migration may not be representative of the Red River Delta (Dang 2000; cf. Werner 2002). Many men whose wives migrated to trade in Hanoi considered staying in their home village during a transitional period before the prerequisite conditions for them to start making a living in the city were met (see below). In 1998–99, about half the *Dong Vang* women seasonal traders in Hanoi lived with their husbands who worked as wage laborers or joined the service sector in the city. A need for a longitudinal study into the migration strategies of households notwithstanding, the reemergence of the pre-*Doi Moi* trading practices of women in *Dong Vang* offers an interesting case for an inquiry into the impact of female migration, or the diversification of economic activities at large, on the reconfiguration of familial and social relations.

Work or Help, Work as Play? Body and Emotions 1

One of the comments, or complaints, shared by many villagers of different ages and genders on the changes since *Doi Moi* is that life is immensely busier and work is very much harder. The intensification of family labor first includes the self-employment of women in trading, as well as the hiring out of men as wage laborers in the city. This increasing migration of the majority of *Dong Vang*'s workforce has placed a growing burden of household tasks on the shoulders of those remaining, mostly the elderly and young children. Older people in *Dong Vang* increasingly find themselves with more household and interhousehold chores, which means longer working days and a later time of rest. Similarly many children in *Dong Vang* feel that they become adults sooner when they take on many household responsibilities at an earlier age than their schoolmates. Descriptions by both the elderly and the young underscore their embodied experiences of hard work and conflicting emotions: at times stressful, at times rewarding.

"NOWADAYS THE ELDERLY CANNOT REST"

Both Mr. and Mrs. Chien were over seventy years old in 1998. All five of their children—three sons and two daughters—are married and do not live with them in their house in *Dong Vang*. The second and last sons and their families have moved permanently to Ha Dong and Hanoi, respectively, while the first son and the two daughters (numbers 3, 6, and 8 in Figure 10.1) reside in the village with their families. Nevertheless, Mr. and Mrs. Chien's main responsibility is to look after seven out of their eleven grandchildren (numbers 9 to 15), when the parents migrate to Hanoi during the lean seasons.

A typical day for Mr. and Mrs. Chien can be described as follows. At 5 A.M. they both get up and join others to do the 45-minute martial arts exercises at the cooperative ground (*san Hop tac*). Before going home, Mrs. Chien does the grocery shopping for herself, her husband, and three granddaughters ages six to fourteen (numbers 9 to 11 in Figure 10.1), whose parents are both in Hanoi. Mr. Chien goes to his granddaughters' house at the back of the village to make sure that the children wake up on time and have a proper breakfast before going to school. In the midmorning, Van, Mr. Chien's second son-in-law (number 7), drops off his six-month-old baby (number 15) and a ready-cooked meal at Mrs. Chien's house, so she can take care of him for the rest of

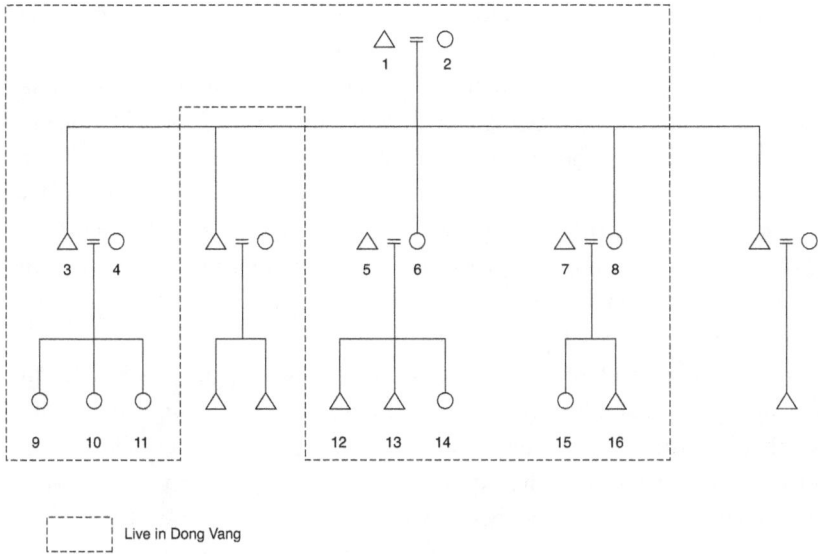

Figure 10.1 Mr. and Mrs. Chien's family.

the day. By noon, the three granddaughters stop by to pick up the groceries. The youngest girl may stay and have lunch with her grandparents. In the afternoon, while the baby is sleeping, Mrs. Chien sifts rice for broken grain to feed the chickens and for rice flour to feed the pigs raised by their children's families. Before cooking dinner, Mrs. Chien checks to see if the eldest granddaughter has fed the pigs properly. At night, the girls and their three cousins (numbers 12 to 14) might come to watch television at their grandparents' house. If they do, Mr. Chien must accompany them home. Otherwise, he drops by their house again to make sure they are at home doing their homework and getting ready for bed.

During the harvest, Mr. and Mrs. Chien's day suddenly becomes hectic, even though their first son and the first son-in-law (numbers 3 and 5) come home from Hanoi to take care of hiring wage laborers to harvest their own paddy. Mrs. Chien now does extra cooking for the hired workers and, after that, feeds the pigs. Mr. Chien spends his day commuting between three different sites and taking on various tasks. Besides working at his own house, Mr. Chien helps his son by sifting the leftover paddy from the straw in the morning, watching the drying paddy for his youngest son-in-law in the afternoon, and collecting and covering the paddy for another son-in-law before it gets dark or rains. Both Mrs. and Mr. Chien make at least five trips every day to their children's houses and back home to share the tasks.

Once or twice a month, Mr. and Mrs. Chien's daughter and daughter-in-law, Dzung and Hoa (numbers 6 and 4), who are both vendors in Hanoi, take an afternoon off from their trades and come home. They bring different kinds of urban-type food delicacies for their children, parents, and parents-in-law. Hoa settles the monthly account with Mrs. Chien and gives her money in advance for the next month's groceries. Every two months on average, Hoa brings ten or fifteen kilograms of rice as her youngest daughter's share of infrequent lunches at her grandparent's home.

This arrangement of intrahousehold tasks and budgets, as well as the sharing of responsibilities between the households of Mr. and Mrs. Chien and their children, is by no means unique in *Dong Vang*. Most of *Dong Vang*'s elderly people, ranging from sixty to eighty years old, are busy orchestrating the numerous daily tasks of their own households and those of their children. These migration strategies of calling upon support within and between households in the community are also found in other parts of the country, characterized by a more or less strong endogamy and inward orientation (see Luong, this volume).

The narratives of the elderly in *Dong Vang* run counter to the assumption of the aged as needy, or as those who are supposed to be recipients of care and support. The *Dong Vang* elderly persistently speak of themselves as active persons who keep working; it is they who continue to provide care and support to their children and grandchildren, but not without a cost, be it physical or in terms of loss of leisure. "Compared to our parents and grandparents," one seventy-year-old woman said, "our life today is harder because it is we who have to go on and take care of ourselves and our grandchildren." In Mrs. Chien's own words, "the elderly today cannot rest." Many of her cohorts complain that the time when they can stop working—sometime around age seventy as they would expect—seems never to come. Working harder and later in life in their home village keeps the elderly from spending time visiting kin and friends nearby or traveling to the city for leisure. In fact, they admit that every time they are invited to the city by their children, it is really to help take care of a newborn child, look after the house, or perform other "small and uncounted jobs" (*giup viec lat vat*). To stay in their home village and attend the Elderly Association's meetings, becomes a truly rare leisure activity. Even though the meetings are often scheduled at the most convenient time of the day, many old women must leave early because they must feed pigs or pick up their grandchildren from kindergarten.

Tiredness and body aches, however, are not the only consequences of this continuous work. What troubles the elderly most is perhaps not the physical cost of their health, but their anxiety when confronted with lazy, unruly grandchildren and ungrateful children. Every time parents in the city learn about conflicts that have erupted between grandparents and grandchildren in the home village, all parties feel guilty and unhappy. This is where one sees the work of the family imaginary: not only does it imply the kind of images compelling the elderly to continue identifying themselves with care providers, it also clearly reflects their expectations of others, in this case a known acknowledgment of debt by their children. "It is so unfair for us," a grandmother sighed, "that they [grandchildren and children] do not acknowledge that we already try our best. Yet, they accuse us of being too old and backward (*lac hau*). If they ever thought of giving up their business in town and coming home to raise their own kids, they would understand what it is all about."

Regardless of this double burden of work and worry, elderly people in *Dong Vang* cite two major reasons for continuing to take on these tasks. First, they do it for the joy of the work itself. Most of the elderly people in *Dong Vang* are proud of themselves for being able to "get [their] bodies moving." At an age when they feel the strength in their various body parts decrease almost daily, they are pleasurably surprised to find themselves able to walk a substantial distance or bend down for a long time. Many of them see these jobs as giving them a physical or fitness exercise (*tap the duc*), which they feel is better than sitting idle doing nothing (*an khong ngoi roi*). As long as they are healthy and physically strong, life for them is worth living. With regards to their health, the elderly most frequently assert that, "I am most afraid of falling sick and not being able to do anything to help myself. As long as I can work I feel fortunate and thankful to God (*may man nho Troi*)." The body here, I suggest, is a focal point where the physical strength and the ability to realize its continuing potential is intrinsically linked to a person's self-worth precisely when the former are challenged or at risk, that is, in the face of the ageing process. The implicit understanding of the family imaginary, again, helps resolve the increasing tension between bodily stress and the sense of self-worth of the aged.

The second idiom used concerning the elderly helping their children's households, is "sacrifice" (*hy sinh*)—a commitment of the elderly toward the future well-being of their offspring. This very notion of generational commitment can be seen as derived from the non-Confucian family-centered (as opposed to lineage-centered) and future-looking (as opposed to ancestor-looking) moral world of *Dong Vang*. But the subtle intricacy between language, thought, and action in daily life requires further examination. In their narrative, the elderly use "work" and "help" interchangeably, as these are at one and the same time meaningful for their own worth and useful in a time of need for others. Even when an elderly couple considers that they have fulfilled their parental duty, for example, in preparing their children to construct their own families (*ra o rieng*), they clearly see the need for giving continued support to their children. Very few of the *Dong Vang* elderly refuse to look after their grandchildren, unless there are serious conflicts between them. Their devotion is driven by their optimism for a better future for their grandchildren. "We already tried hard for the sake of our children, but they still live with difficulties (*con vat va*). If we try harder now, our grandchildren may have a better life," Mrs. Chien explained. For her and her cohorts, sharing the intra- and interhousehold tasks is more than an obligation; it is creating a treasure of good deeds to pass on to their heirs. It is ultimately the satisfaction, even the pleasure, of giving. Nevertheless, it should be stressed that the elderly only consider their labor inputs as a contribution to the maintenance of their children's household(s). Not a single elderly man or woman told me that if she or he decided to quit this supporting role, the household(s) would not function. Conversely, their children, migrant women and men in the city, repeatedly stressed that "without our grandparents' help nothing would work the way it should."

To suggest that the idioms "help" and "sacrifice" are only the postrationalization of the "self-overworking" of the elderly in *Dong Vang* is to miss the subjectivity of the elderly. Because "an agent is one who acts with another [person(s)] in mind" from her own vantage point (Strathern 1988: 272), work, sometimes overwork, is an intersection where the self and the social merge and form one another. Thus, an expanded understanding of work is needed to shed light on the way in which this implicit understanding of the family as a social imaginary is deeply body bound. The notion of a social imaginary is here complementary to Bourdieu's concept of *habitus*. The latter helps to visualize the way in which structuring principles, like parental moral obligations, are internalized through the repetition of hard work and the enactment of embodied distress or satisfaction on the part of the *Dong Vang* elderly. C. Taylor's (2004) notion of social imaginary, likewise, gives way to *inter-*

subjective meanings. In other words, it accommodates the multiple subjectivity in a dialogic fashion joined by the parties involved. It sheds light on the ways in which *Dong Vang* elderly take up obligations and rights upon themselves and assume the same for their children and grandchildren.

The self-work of the elderly in the village is, nevertheless, not without compensation. Invoking expectations of both themselves and their children, the elderly are able to make claims to their migrant children's budget. Limited space here does not allow a full discussion on the budgeting practice and consumption patterns of family members (Truong 2001). Suffice it to say that ritual expenses, including the cost of gifts and banquets for rite-of-life passages, obligatory contributions to various village rituals and public events, and large-scale donations to village religious constructions, which have all increased significantly in recent years in *Dong Vang*, are mostly associated with the elderly family members. It is also important to note that these claims on household and interhousehold budgets vary across gender: while elderly men tend to make known their request of an elaborate banquet for their longevity celebration, elderly women tend to express their wish of a donation to the village temple or having a set of ritual attire of their own with which they can be buried when they die. It is indeed helpful to identify whether such values as filial piety, submission, devotion, care, and love are Confucian or non-Confucian. In the meantime, it is equally important to leave room for the agency of subjects to come to light in the text here as they do in the *Dong Vang* daily life. Moreover, the social imaginary of the family serves as much more than a set, or several interlocking sets, of explicit ideas. It offers the wider grasp that the *Dong Vang* elderly have on the common repertory of visions that incorporate the daily practices commonly shared by themselves and their offspring (C. Taylor 2004, 26).

BEYOND FILIAL PIETY

In *Dong Vang*, the increasing seasonal migration of the majority of the workforce to Hanoi for off-farm income leads to an intensification of work not only for the elderly but also the children. This intensification of children's work in both daily household tasks and agriculture is cast in terms of the joy and pride teenagers take in becoming independent and mature at an early age and their quest for a full understanding of their moral debt, or "filial piety" (*hieu*), toward their parents. The stories below not only illustrate how "filial

piety," central to Confucian values, is understood in the local discourse in
Dong Vang, while being articulated with non-Confucian notions of family
commitment and a future-looking attitude. They also point, yet again, to
a wider grasp of a largely unstructured and inarticulate understanding of
young people in the village, within which an implicit knowledge of a family
imaginary helps them navigate their experience and make sense of the joys
and rewards of their own work contributions (C. Taylor 2004).

   Lua is a fourteen-year-old girl who lives with her nine-year-old brother
Bang, and a sixty-eight-year-old grandfather, while her parents work in Hanoi. She describes her daily routine as follows:

5:30 A.M.: Get up and make the bed.

5:45 A.M.: Wash my clothes and those of my brother and grandfather.

6:15 A.M.: Feed the pigs, wake Bang up, dress him and myself, and check
   bags for school.

6:30 A.M.: Depart for school; stop by the morning market to buy breakfast
   (which is often skipped to save money for "other" purposes). Say goodbye
   to grandfather, who is doing grocery shopping at the marketplace, and
   remind him to take his herbal medicine on time (he has been coughing
   for months).

6:50 A.M.: Arrive at school.

7:00 A.M.–noon: Study at school.

Noon: Come home, feed the pigs, eat lunch (cooked by grandfather) with
   him and Bang, wash the dishes, take a nap.

Afternoon: Work on home assignments, while watching the stewing herbs
   for grandfather.

4:00 P.M.: Collect water spinach from the home garden for cooking and prepare food for the pigs.

4:30 P.M.: Prepare straw for the cooking.

4:45 P.M.: Tidy up the house, collect the dried laundry.

5:00 P.M.: Cook dinner.

6:00 P.M.: Feed the pigs.

6:15 P.M.: Look for Bang (who is playing somewhere in the village), get him
   home, wash him (or supervise him washing himself).

6:30 P.M.: Have dinner with grandfather and Bang, wash the dishes.

7:00 P.M.: Wash myself.

7:30 P.M.: Watch the children's show on TV (sometimes other interesting programs as well)

8:00 P.M.: Revise tomorrow's assignments with some girlfriends.

8:45 P.M.: Check Bang's home assignments, while warming up the medicine for grandfather (he takes medicine three times a day).

9:00 P.M.: Go to bed.

The summer crop of 1999 was the sixth one since Lua started to work in the field. During each harvest, she works for about ten days in the family field, three days in the fields of her two paternal aunts, and another day or two at her close friend's as an exchange. Her school is closed for a week, and, if the break falls at the peak harvest time in her village, she only has to take several days off school. Since fewer days are required for rice transplanting, it does not interfere with Lua's schooling.

As images, stories, and legends are common forms of expression of the family imaginary shared by *Dong Vang* villagers (C. Taylor 2004), Lua is often praised by adults in the village as an exemplar of a young daughter who has matured early to take thorough care of her family. She is, nevertheless, by no means unique among *Dong Vang* teenagers. Parents give different answers when asked about the age at which their children can be left "self-attended." The most common is when they can look after each other, as soon as the youngest child enters the first grade at the age of six and the older children reach advanced grades. *Dong Vang* parents feel relatively comfortable leaving the children on their own or under the supervision of their grandparents. In the eyes of adults, children remain immature as long as their parents need to ask some of their kin, grandparents, or aunts to handle daily cash expenses for them (as in the cases of Mr. and Mrs. Chien and of Lua's grandfather above). Once the children are able to handle money for the household—most often at the age of seventeen or eighteen for both boys and girls—they have reached adulthood.

It is, however, difficult to define when a child really enters agricultural work. Children become "working hands" in the family at the first crop that they are given a sickle. This occurs between the eleventh and fourteenth year of their childhood, but a child can start to work in the field much earlier. Girls can help bring water and meals to workers in the fields, and boys can help their fathers push the paddy cart home. For others, becoming a working hand occurs when a boy is "assigned" a flock of chickens or ducks to tend by himself, or when a girl is "assigned" a pig from the family herd to care for by herself. A good portion of cash from the sale of poultry and pigs, as may be expected, is spent on the herd girl or boy's school needs.

Schoolchildren in *Dong Vang* as elsewhere get excited about their parents' long absence. Notwithstanding the close supervision of their grandparents or other relatives, children often consider themselves to be "taking care of each other." Most of them enjoy being able to organize their lives in a relatively autonomous way, free from the rigid instruction of their parents. If they manage to lead well-organized daily lives, they earn the acknowledgment of their parents and neighbors as being "independent" (*tu lap*), "early mature" (*khon som*), and "early aware" (*nhan thuc som*). Moreover, when parents are absent, brothers and sisters become more dependent on each other for support. My *Dong Vang* teenage friends often tell me that because they have to take care of themselves and each other, they tend to love their sister(s) and/or brother(s) more and take better care of them. It is in this push for early maturity that girls become familiar with their female responsibility of nurture, care, and concession (*nhuong nhin*) for their younger brothers. Similarly, boys learn that sisters are a source of boundless protection and support. Those early days of sibling bonding serve as a base for the natal family bond in the years to come. While the gendering process of children in *Dong Vang* largely supports what Rydstrom describes for *Thinh Tri* commune also in northern Vietnam (Rydstrom 2003), the frequent and long absence of parents peculiar to *Dong Vang* poses a different kind of pressure on its children.

In conflicts with attendant relatives or neighbors, children learn to protect one another. Thus, "sibling's solidarity" is formed among these autonomous children, which is perhaps stronger than that among those who live in a complete family. "Self-attended" children also learn to depend more on their friends: a house without parents often becomes a favorable meeting place for girls and boys. From these groups, they form their first network of helping hands and dating mates. The fact that the life of children and young people in *Dong Vang* whose parents are absent remains full of fun and joy could be surprising to outsiders, but norms and ideals constituting a notion of a good child, ranging from a positive connotation when a working child is described to a much praised image of caring siblings, largely shared by children and parents alike, help children take work and care upon themselves not only for granted by also as a token of pride and self-worth.

Nevertheless, life in the absence of parents may sometimes be tiring and difficult. Girls, like Lua, often complain about the annoyance of repeating the same tasks every day and not having time to go out and play. They are jealous of their younger siblings and those children who can play longer because their parent(s) stay at home and do most of the household chores. Worst of all, verbal conflicts between brothers and sisters occur frequently and are not easily settled. These conflicts result in day-long, sometimes even week-long, tensions between them, as described in their own words:

> Every time my [older] sister and I quarrel, we both cry. Sometimes she yells and threatens to beat me, then she too breaks into tears. Once I refused to eat the whole day, and I told her I would go to Hanoi and look for our parents. At night in my dream I saw my parents coming home and treating me well. I wish we were together all the time. (Tan, an 8-year-old boy)

> I miss my mother a lot and I want her to come home more often. But she told me the bus ticket costs 20,000 *dong*, the money she can make for a whole day selling fruits. She also has terrible car sickness every time she travels. I told her then not to come. I miss our nightlong chats: we talk about everything and laugh and laugh. In the morning, she would make two very neat hair braids for me before catching the bus back to Hanoi. If she comes home I never let her do any washing at all, yet once she is away how much I want her back to give me a hand with this pile of clothes. (with tears in her eyes, Lua, 14 years old, whose routine is reported above)

Hard work, lack of nurturing care, tension, emotional stress, and learning to worry like adults result in an early entrance into adolescence for many *Dong Vang* children. The intensity of physical hardship involved in child work varies significantly; *Dong Vang* children share more or less the same sense of independence and worth with their counterparts in handicraft-producing workshops elsewhere in the region, as described by Nguyen Van Chinh (Nguyen 2001). While this is not the place to engage in a debate on the values and extent of child work, or the differences between child labor and child work, suffice to say here that work, as understood by both children and their parents in *Dong Vang*, is crucial to shaping their experiences growing up in households stretching across geographical space.

When talking about the significance of this transformation, young people often refer to the pitiful love (*thuong*) they feel for their parents. Knowing that their parents are working hard for better days for their family, youths take upon themselves an obligation to share the load. The mutual love, moral indebtedness, willingness to share the hardship, and pay back their debt is strongly felt by *Dong Vang* children and are not simply expressions of filial piety ascribed in a moral model. Rather, these emotions are the moral expectations young people take upon *themselves;* they have, *pace* Bourdieu, been internalized and naturalized. Taylor's concept of social imaginary helps explain the tension between the articulation and materialization of the contrasting experiences of *Dong Vang* children. Their hard work, overwork at times, and feelings toward their parents are consistently cast in overwhelmingly affectionate terms that overshadow any hint of "abuse" (*hanh ha*) or "exploitation" (*boc lot*). These latter words are rarely, if ever, used to describe the parent-children relationship in *Dong Vang*. Nevertheless, I have heard comments about some parents who excessively overworked their children (*qua dang*) while leaving too little cash for their daily expenses. These couples are often criticized for their severity and stinginess, but when I talked with them and their children, both parties insisted that a bright future will come from their hard work and thrift. Both migrant parents and their children share the prospect of having nonagricultural occupations in the future, for example, escaping from agriculture through educational achievements. In other words, in return for their hard work in household chores and in the field, children of migrant families expect to have a better chance of continued schooling and/or vocational training. Parents see their overworking as a "sacrifice for the future generation" and tend to focus on saving for their children's education as a long-term investment. Reciprocity between generations, therefore, makes the notion of "exploitation" unthinkable in *Dong Vang*.

For *Dong Vang* children and their parents, the family imaginary is not a set of ideas, such as, for example, "filial piety" and "sacrifice." Instead, through stories, images, and implicit understanding of each other's expectations, young people in *Dong Vang* come to terms with their experience of work and emotional stress when their families are geographically divided. Anticipating a better future for the family motivates *Dong Vang* children in a daily life that is much more demanding than that of others of their ages. The notion of family as social imaginary proves its usefulness in making visible the multiple subjectivity while not losing sight of the local political economy specific to *Dong Vang*.

Similarly, it is important to consider the elderly as not only objects but also subjects of care and support (see Barbieri in this volume) and to view their work in qualitative terms that incorporate meanings of the self and socially shared values. I have also suggested that age is an indiscernible marker without which an understanding of the richness of experience of family change after *Doi Moi* would be incomplete. In a similar vein, narratives of and about *Dong Vang* children presented in this section allude to something that goes beyond the child-parent construction: the significance of work/play (see Bélanger and Pendakis, this volume), siblingship, and age, all of which, I might suggest, come into play in shaping children's experience of their parents' absence as the latter are engaged full time in the urban market.

Work, Place, and Gender: Body and Emotions 2

After the cooperative's labor control was lifted at the end of the 1980s, *Dong Vang* women's daily trading was no longer labeled as smuggling (Truong 2004). Those who had started by commuting daily began to stay over for longer periods by lodging with relatives in Hanoi, who were also selling rice and eggs on their own. Many *Dong Vang* women started with very little capital. They stayed free of charge with their relatives, took merchandise on credit to resell, and paid at the end of the month until they gradually accumulated enough savings to establish their own independent businesses.

> My two sisters and I stayed at my maternal uncle's place for almost three years. Everyday we took duck eggs from his wife and peddled them on the streets. My brother's wife later joined us in egg selling, but she stayed with her own relatives. In 1992, we [four women] pooled our savings together and purchased this piece of land with a small house on it. We now still sell eggs, but no longer from my uncle's wife. My sisters and I sometimes switch to selling desserts, depending on the season, while my sister-in-law combines rice with egg to sell because her bother sells rice, too. My brother then joins up with his wife. He drives a taxi-motorcycle (*xe om*) everyday. Now we live in our own house, however small, and we do not have to ask for a favor of lodging from our relatives. (Nhan, a 36-year-old duck egg seller)

Women consider these early years the most difficult time in their family life. Today, approximately two hundred *Dong Vang* women, ranging in age from early twenties to late sixties, are trading in Hanoi. More than half of them live with their husbands, while the others are accompanied by one or more female relatives.

Although *Dong Vang* women no longer have to commute every day as they did a decade ago, their jobs in Hanoi involve a significant physical hardship. The day of a female rice retailer starts at five o'clock in the morning and continues until dusk. Every day, the women hurt their backs and arms through the weight of the job as they sift, sort, carry, and lift the heavy sacks of rice up and down and sell it from door to door. However, compared to the daily wage for a nonskilled male worker in the city (15,000 dong, an equivalent of US$1 in 1998) and the income from other merchant trades (20,000 dong in the case of egg or fruit selling), rice trading generates a competitive return (on average 30,000 dong per day, sometimes 50,000).

Despite the different sizes and scope of their trading, *Dong Vang* women traders all agree that their trading in the city is drudgery (*vat va*), mostly because it requires continuity, or in their own words, "having not a single moment of rest" (*khong co luc nao nghi ngoi*). Moreover, by mentioning the word *rest*, women imply not only rest for their tired bodies, but also for their minds. The burden of this trading is increased because of their numerous worries:

> I am very sorry for my daughter. She is entering puberty when she needs her mother most. For several months when I first left her home I could not sleep, thinking and feeling sorry about her. Yet, her younger brother Bang is not a very obedient child; he has not learned to help his sister. I am afraid that they will quarrel. Every time I come home and see how thin my children are and how hard Lua has to work, I have to hold back my tears. I encourage my husband to go home more often every time he does not have a job [as a construction worker in town], but I feel sorry for him too, having to cycle such a distance in this heat. Hopefully, after selling the pigs, we will have enough [money] to buy him a motorbike. But the herbal medicine for grandfather is not cheap. (Sang, 42 years old, mother of Lua, above)

> As soon as I stopped breastfeeding my first child, I started joining my mother in her rice stall in Hanoi. Our mother-in-law offered a helping hand in caring for the baby. Without my help, my mother could not deal with her many customers. My husband was very understanding when he let me leave home. However, I could not stand not being able to cuddle my baby everyday; I missed him terribly. I cried every night, but my mother thought it was because my breasts were too full of milk and were very painful. Perhaps so. I lost a great deal of weight in a week. Finally my husband came and took me home. Now

since my son goes to kindergarten, I continue to work with my mother. Luckily, my husband is willing to take care of our son on his own; in fact he enjoys doing it. However, I try my best to come home as often as I can, not only to caress my son, but also to please (*chieu*) my husband. Otherwise, my mother-in-law would talk badly about my long absence. (Huyen, 28 years old)

Women like Huyen and Sang often see themselves simultaneously in the role of mother and wife (Peletz 1995, 101–10). They emphasize that since they migrated to Hanoi for a longer term, they find themselves caught in a geographical and emotional dilemma, from which they sometimes suffer both physically and mentally. In their own words, "your body is in one place while your mind is in another" (*nguoi mot noi, tam mot neo*). Women traders, in order to build credibility with customers (*giu khach*), must try to maintain active participation in the market. At the same time, as mothers and wives, they struggle with feelings of insecurity and a loss of the chance to fulfill their nurturing and caring responsibilities toward their family members.

The above narratives of Huyen and Sang show how ties that bind can divide and the power of the family as a social imaginary. The risk of having their family, and their social world at large, separated challenges many *Dong Vang* women and stems from their experience as divisible, multiplied subjects. As the fusion of thoughts and feelings or mind and heart in the bodily construct of Vietnamese women has been noted (Gammeltoft 1999, 210), *Dong Vang* women's concerns also spread according to the geographical reach of their households. This is experienced, in their own terms, as dividing their bodies into parts, and this split keeps them in a constant state of anxious body-mind.

Regarding the multiplicity of the internally differentiated self, Huyen is not simply a sum of roles she herself expects, and is expected by others, to perform: daughter, wife, mother, daughter-in-law, street vendor, and so forth. Instead, she operates simultaneously at the intersection of these (and other) social relations that define her; she acts with many if not all of her familial and social others in her mind. That is not to say, however, that these relations compose a frame of reference for Huyen's actions without discrimination. On the contrary, by her single act, Huyen can only act for herself in response to claims from a certain set (or a number of sets) of relations between her and her social others. This, in turn, can only be done at the expense of others, in Strathern's words, "substituting one relationship for another" (Strathern 1988: 327). Huyen's choice of leaving her baby to return to the market calls to different and competing norms. Filial piety toward her own mother and the ideal of help are invoked for her action, that is, motivates her move, while a notion of sacrificing her own motherly love to the responsibility and duties toward her husband and his family are strongly conjured up in her painful undertaking. Understanding Huyen's choice in social imaginary terms reveals the dialogism of the intersubjectivity and multiple subjectivity at best. As "body takes symbols seriously" (Bourdieu 1990, 71), the cost Huyen pays due to her self-chosen priority is as distressing as the pain of her milk-engorged breast. Huyen's anguish compellingly testifies that there is nothing natural about a mother's nurturing: it must instead be socially constructed, contested, instilled in her body through painful enactment, and internalized to the point it becomes natural. Indeed, in this case Huyen's mother response teaches Huyen to take motherly pains naturally. "Social categories [. . .] are," in Moore's words, "most powerful when they appear most natural, most apparent, most taken for granted" (Moore 1994, 99).

We should not, nevertheless, let the centrality of, or perhaps the spectacle of, Huyen's experience as mother-wife complex obscure our sight of her other identities. Being a skillful trader, for instance, requires in Huyen, Sang, and their women counterparts, another set of qualities they would describe as feminine: patience and tactfulness in dealing with customers, being quick- (entrepreneurial-) minded, thrifty, and sometimes, adventurous. These qualities of *Dong Vang* women traders are sometimes articulated to me as a researcher, but most of the time may be observed in the women's daily trade. From my observations, handling the business, or "going to the marketplace," brings *Dong Vang* women as much frustration as joy. This is where, I suppose, focusing primarily on one set (or few certain sets) of relations in a certain context would lead one to consider women's somatic strategies in handling bodily physical symptoms and social stresses in the long term, as a more or less self-defeating endeavor (Gammeltoft 1999, 247). My point is that work identity in the context of the rural-urban social and symbolic construction, whether a factory wage job or self-employed or agricultural work, has formed an indiscernible part of Vietnamese women's experiences since *Doi Moi* (Tran 2002; see Bélanger and Pendakis, this volume; see also McElhinny 1994). The same can be said for their experiences of distance and leisure travel, memberships in both village- and non-village-based religious groups, folk art performance troupes, and so forth—most of these activities occur among same-sex, sometimes nonkin, people—and have only been available to women since the return of the market economy (see also P. Taylor 2004). Again, privileging gender as a primary form of difference would, I suggest, be a serious shortcoming to understanding these women's changing lives.

The increased opportunities for wages in the urban private sector since the early 1990s encourages more and more *Dong Vang* men to join their wives in Hanoi. As soon as the children are believed to be old enough to take care of themselves and the couple has accumulated some funds, the husband takes up a job in the city. After more than three decades of being largely confined to agriculture, *Dong Vang* men do not possess any particular skills to join the better-paid urban workforce; thus, they usually start with piecemeal waged jobs. Wages range from 10,000 to 15,000 dong a day without meals. These types of odd jobs for men, however, are not always available and depend on the network that may be developed. In an unusually lucky construction season in the city, starting from late October through late April, a man can be hired for a maximum of 150 days.

Some *Dong Vang* migrant men have a better start. Those who have a basic means of production, such as a motorbike, can provide a motorcycle taxi (*xe om*) or delivery service (*cho hang*). The services range from cargo transportation to monthly or daily deliveries. A motorcycle driver earns from 20,000 to 50,000 dong a day from which he must cover the fuel cost and his own meals. For many *Dong Vang* men, motorcycle service is seen as a better job, not only because of its relatively higher income compared to waged jobs in construction but also due to the greater flexibility and mobility.

Dong Vang migrant men in Hanoi see themselves working harder than their fellow villagers who remain at home in the lean season and whom they describe as "sitting idle doing nothing but drinking and gambling." Nevertheless, when men compare their jobs to those of their wives, they agree that theirs, except for some demanding periods, are less time and nerve consuming. For wage workers, there are idle between-job periods during which they can gather with relatives and friends, or even sometimes simply street companions, for "some drinks and a card game for fun." For motorcycle drivers, waiting and searching for customers as well as traveling while working can be enjoyable. In sum, due to the specificity of the kinds of jobs *Dong Vang* men do in Hanoi, they often present themselves as more relaxed than their spouses whom they describe as "having a constant headache because of many worries and calculations" (*nhuc dau vi lo lang tinh toan nhieu qua*) (cf. Gammeltoft 1999, 206).

As with *Dong Vang* children, elderly people, and women, work is significant in the ways men identify themselves. While images of work are clearly
gendered, the specific features of the work are also factored into the men's
identity, not only vis-a-vis women but also to differentiate among themselves. This chapter does not permit a full discussion of the significance of
the embodied place for both men and women in *Dong Vang*. Suffice it to say
here that being able to live and work in Hanoi as opposed to remaining in
the village (*o nha que*) not only shapes the visions of mobility for each family
and its members, it also involves forming groups among *Dong Vang* villagers.
In other words, the socially occupied and embodied space has become one
important form of differentiation in post–*Doi Moi* Vietnam.

Men's attitude toward the fact that their wives, mothers, and daughters
are the major source of income for their household is ambiguous. On the
one hand, they acknowledge and show respect toward their women's material
contribution to the household budget. On the other hand, they may ridicule
other men and themselves for being their wives' dependents (*dua vao vo*). In
my more or less formal conversations with *Dong Vang* middle-aged and elderly men, respondents acknowledged women's important role in generating
household income by emphasizing that their contribution was not a just side-
line (*kiem them*) but the major source of income (*thu nhap chinh*).

> Unlike a decade ago when women had to smuggle rice and other agricultural
> products into the Hanoi market, nowadays they are free to trade and earn the
> major household income. *Dong Vang* women have been known through history
> and across this region for being smart and quick-minded in trading and elegant
> and charming in dealing with customers. They use their traditional talents
> (*phat huy truyen thong*). *Dong Vang* women are also known for their diligence
> and endurance (*chiu thuong chiu kho*), and especially their thrift (*tiet kiem*). That
> is why they are successful in trading. (Hach, 51 years old, motorcycle driver)

This explicit commemoration of the "traditional" image of *Dong Vang*
women reveals the extent to which men embrace the state's master narrative of the heroic female model symbolizing the Vietnamese nation (Pettus
2003). The majority of *Dong Vang* men genuinely believe that their mothers,
sisters, wives, and daughters are born to be good market traders and cash
earners. Nevertheless, in their everyday discourse, their unease about this
asymmetry is more often than not hard to conceal.

Dong Vang men find it difficult and confusing to make sense of their own masculine position in the family once it reenters the market economy. To my frustration as a fieldworker, the fact that most *Dong Vang* men do not identify their work with land and agriculture runs counter to my text-bound assumption of the residual "peasant mentality" (*tam ly nong dan*) that honors agriculture (*di nong vi ban*) in the northern Vietnamese countryside. Neither do the men with whom I spoke honor the honesty of menial farming jobs as opposed to the defrauding characteristics of trade—understandable when most of their own female relatives engage in trading activities (cf. Malarney 1998).

Since the conditions necessary to initiate *Dong Vang* men's involvement in the entrepreneurial endeavor have not been met, they stay in the home village, take care of the farming, and keep an eye on their children. Even these hard-working men consider staying in the village as a reluctantly taken option. I heard numerous jokes and anecdotes among young men mocking themselves and men friends for being dependent on their wives.

> *Dong Vang* men today become "wifeless orphans" (*mo coi vo*) too early [sic. and laugh]. The only female feature that we men cannot have is to breast feed our infants; other than that we [men] have taken over everything. *Dong Vang* men have mastered child care (*trong con*). We are also known to be good at pleasing our wife (*chieu vo*), many of us are ready to serve our wives (*phuc vu vo*) in the rice trade. If you don't believe me, just ask any young fellow to sing some lullabies [sings and laughs]. "My baby, my baby, sleep sweetly. Your mother is busy in Hanoi; home has not yet arrived." (Ngoc, 37-year-old man)

Joking is the best possible way in which men, especially young men, deal with their embarrassment—an uncomfortable mixture of feelings that range from owing a material debt to their female relatives on the one hand, and their offended masculinity on the other (Peletz 1995, 100). Faced with a reality in which many of their expectations of themselves and their familial others are seriously challenged, *Dong Vang* men invoke gendered symbols and meanings to negotiate and redefine their masculinity. In an uncontested situation, verbs like *to please* and *to serve* are often used to describe women's acts toward their family and male members. In a normal context, being an "orphan" is considered a matter of misfortune and to say that someone is an orphan does not connote a criticism of the source of the pattern.[4] However, these gender markers, which linguistic anthropologists may identify as indexical, are nonexclusive in meaning and thus contingent upon the intentions of their users (McElhinny 1994).[5] For Ngoc and his male friends, this mocking analogy of "orphans" serves to blame their wives' neglect of their maternal and female duties on the one hand, and to speak sarcastically of their own downgrading to a state of dependence on others. The nurturing quality ascribed here to an exclusively female bodily feature, the breast, is invoked to reinstate the naturalness of a social construct (see above). By using verbs that often describe maternal activities and adjectives that describe feminine characteristics to portray themselves, men both criticize their wives' absence and seek to redefine their masculinity: to be a man in *Dong Vang* must be now understood as being able to rise to the challenge of putting up with female tasks. These are some of a myriad of examples in daily discourse in *Dong Vang* where meanings and symbols are negotiated and constantly remade both to reinforce an existing social order and to make sense of the experiences of change. Ambiguous narratives of *Dong Vang* men clearly demonstrate the power of family imaginary: how expectations of *Dong Vang* men about their own roles and those of their female kin, norms and ideals of masculinity and femininity, and a sense of legitimacy of the unity of the family, underlie the narrators' thinking about and feeling toward their kin. We will continue to see below how these norms are unevenly shared and variedly invoked by different family members.

Since a majority of middle-aged and young men shares similar domestic situations and feelings, common jokes among men about their wives' absence serve as a basis for their grouping, from which they build on their common experience. Husbands of migrant women often tease each other about "missing their wives" (*nho vo*), hinting at their infrequent satisfaction of sexual needs. Men usually comment on the frequency of their wives' visits as an indicator of the couple's affection or attachment and, more importantly, the influence a husband has on his wife. Elderly grandparents echo these criticisms regardless of the fact that their daughters-in-law frequently send home treats and cash to hire laborers for the harvest.

Men and the elderly eventually override the public discourse in *Dong Vang* with a double-sided claim. On the one hand, they can approve of a woman undertaking the hardship of trading in towns since it is driven by her sacrifice for her husband and children. On the other hand, her increased absence from home should be criticized because it means she is behaving improperly (*khong biet dieu*) toward her husband and children, and by extension, her in-laws. This ambivalence toward women reveals the men's paradox: despite their gratefulness for their wives' contributions, they must criticize the women's absence to offset their loss of face or their offended masculinity, as a result of their dependence on their wives' cash income.

Dong Vang women, however, are not subsumed entirely to the male-dominated discourse. Women traders have their own way of appropriating the same language of endurance and sacrifice. While telling their versions of stories, *Dong Vang* women usually highlight their role as the central pillar (*tru cot*) of the family life in both material and emotional terms, not simply in budgetary terms. Besides, several large-scale rice traders have adopted the language of their profit-making pursuit that emerged from the market. A woman owner of a large store emphasized that every member in her household is required to work harder during her absence because she is the only person who can calculate and make a profit in the urban market.

Furthermore, *Dong Vang* women have their own ways of posing counter-claims of their husbands and male relatives. They tend to highlight the responsibility (*trach nhiem*) and commitment required of men to their family. Those men who do not actively participate in livelihood activities are accused by their female counterparts of being lazy (*luoi bieng*), playful (*ham choi*), not serious about their self-teaching (*khong tu than*), and not caring about their wives and children (*khong biet lo cho vo con*). Clearly, the women's counterclaims stem from their expectations that men should contribute to their common family project. While one can point out that these expectations could be based on both the Confucian ideal of the self (male) and the conjugal bond, the fact that women can and do invoke these idioms from the shared family imaginary for their own cause, reveals the intersubjectivity of culture and attests to women's agency.

Conclusion

By the late 1990s, the return to the free market brought significant changes to *Dong Vang* families. Some of these are observable: a greater participation to the workforce in the city, increased interhousehold arrangements of labor and budget in the home village, and intensified use of family labor through the work of children and the elderly. Some changes, however, are less visible yet still communicable and much more ambivalent. Hard work brings joy but also takes its toll on the body. Every person's ordinary day seems to be filled with ambiguous emotions ranging from pride and fulfillment to anguish and distress. The daily practice and discourse enriched with meanings and interpretations makes it impossible to identify losers and winners. Rather, it is precisely the shared family imaginary—a common repertory of norms and values, images and stories, and implicit understanding of what to expect and how to lay claims on oneself and familial others—that enables day-to-day practice in *Dong Vang*. In so doing it confers a strong sense of legitimacy within which even the most contrasting experiences and conflicting emotions appeal to actors and audience alike.

Dong Vang stories compel one to find ways to grasp the fullness of life experience during the transformations. One way that I have attempted is to situate individual and familial experiences at the intersection of multiple forms of difference, among which gender at times is most salient, at times gives way to age, work, an embodied sense of place, and possibly other ascriptive and acquired identities. *Dong Vang* accounts suggest the importance of an expanded and qualitative understanding of work as it is experienced bodily and its values are understood and articulated by not only those of the main workforce but also the young and the old. Age, by the same token, is an indiscernible marker that inherently connects with both physical health and a sense of one's self-worth. Even when gender reigns, that is, not only is it most salient to the eyes and ears of researchers but effectively forms the central axis against which lives are lived, it is important to reach an understanding of how this has become the case: how certain idioms have been given unshakable priority, how certain norms have been unquestionably taken for granted. Moreover, as seen in the ways *Dong Vang* men attempt to negotiate and redefine their masculinity, it is just as important to look for ways of marking both sameness and difference among the same sex and the nonkin.

This multiplicity of internal differences of the person, as I believe I have demonstrated, lies at the heart of the tension that endangers the binding family ties with the possibility of division. Following Strathern, since an act endorsing a certain identity of a person and thereby performing a certain set of relations necessarily substitutes one relationship for another, a home has indeed never been united. It is our task then to ask whether the transformation since *Doi Moi* entails bringing these dividing potentials to the fore and, if so, then how the family successfully maintains its remarkable resilience (see Bélanger and Barbieri, this volume). To this end, thinking of the *Dong Vang* local moral worlds in social imaginary terms helps shed light not only on the resilience of the family but also on the tension between articulation and realization of contrasting experiences of various family members, men and women, the aged and the young in *Dong Vang*. The family imaginary lens makes visible *inter*subjective meanings which, as ethnographic examples from *Dong Vang* presented in this chapter attest, are profoundly historically and culturally grounded. The notion of social imaginary proves a powerful conceptual tool that accommodates the multiple subjectivity constituted through diverse positions while not losing sight of the historical depth of the local political economy.

My accounts of family changes for *Dong Vang* villagers as presented in this chapter are by no means exhaustive. Consumption, reinvestment, education, leisure, religion, and so forth (again not in any preconceived hierarchical order), in other words, the reproduction of family members as certain kinds of people for a certain kind of society are left out because of the selectivity required for this particular intellectual assignment, but not because they are negated in the life of *Dong Vang* (Truong 2001). Being aware of these features, not only as aspects constituting family life but also as yet another set of socially acquired markers of difference within and among family members and families, allows us to recognize the limits and potential of our understanding of the richness of experience of the ongoing transformations in Vietnam.

Notes

I would like to thank Danièle Bélanger, Magali Barbieri, and the anonymous reviewers for their comments on the earlier drafts of this chapter. The research on which this chapter is based was funded by the Wenner-Gren Foundation for Anthropological Research, Harvard-Yenching Institute, and a travel grant from the University of Toronto, 1996–2001.
   1. I have deliberately borrowed this phrase from the title of a volume edited by D. Dwyer and J. Bruce, *A Home Divided: Women and Income in the Third World*, Stanford: Stanford University Press, 1988.
   2. *Dong Vang* is located less than 30 kilometers from the city of Hanoi and the town of Ha Dong, and had 1,197 inhabitants in 1998 (Truong 2001, 2004).
   3. Elsewhere I discuss in detail how the ethnography of *Dong Vang* contributes to the body of work on "transitional" societies (Truong 2001). By showing the viability of the simple commodity-producing enterprise in *Dong Vang* as it engaged in the socialist market economy of the 1990s in northern Vietnam, I argue that

this period is not a transitional period between a noncapitalist and capitalist social formation, but rather "a function of its relations to large-scale capital on the one hand, and the use it makes of pre-existing relations of production on the other" (Smith 1989, 161).

4. I would like to thank Hy Van Luong for his help in refining this point.

5. In contrast with indexical markers that are contingent, "referential markers of gender are unequivocal, unambiguous, categorical symbols of gender" (McElhinny 1994, 167). Examples of referential markers in the Vietnamese language are terms such as *ba* (grandmother, Mrs.) and *co* (aunt, Ms.) that reference female entity.

References

Bourdieu, P. 1977. *Outline of a theory of practice.* Cambridge, U.K.: Cambridge University Press.

Bourdieu, P. 1990. *The logic of practice.* Cambridge, U.K.: Cambridge University Press.

Carsten, J. 2004. *After kinship.* Cambridge, U.K.: Cambridge University Press.

Dang Nguyen Anh. 2000. Women's migration and urban integration in the context of *Doi Moi. Viet Nam's Socio-Economic Development: A Quarterly Review,* 23: 66–80.

Drummond, L., and H. Rydstrom, eds. 2004. *Gender practices in contemporary Vietnam.* Singapore: Singapore University Press.

Gammeltoft, T. 1999. *Women's bodies, women's worries: Health and family planning in a Vietnamese rural community.* Richmond: Curzon Press.

Hirschman, C., and M. L. Vu. 1996. Family and household structure in Vietnam: Some glimpses from a recent survey. *Pacific Affairs,* 69: 226–249.

Kerkvliet, B. T. 2005. *The power of everyday politics: How Vietnamese peasants transformed national policy.* Ithaca, NY: Cornell University Press.

Krolowski, N. 2002. Village households in the Red River Delta: The case of Ta Thanh Oai, on the outskirts of the capital city, Hanoi. In *Gender, household, state:* Doi Moi *in Viet Nam,* edited by J. Werner and D. Bélanger, 73–88. Ithaca, NY: Cornell University Southeast Asia Program Publications.

Luong, Hy Van. 1989. Vietnamese kinship: Structural principles and the socialist transformation in northern Vietnam. *Journal of Asian Studies,* 48(4): 741–756.

Luong, Hy Van. 1998. Engendered entrepreneurship: Ideologies and political-economic transformation in a northern Vietnamese center of ceramic production. In *Market cultures: Society and morality in new Asian capitalisms,* edited by R. Hefner, 290–314. Boulder, CO: Westview Press.

Malarney, S. K. 1998. State stigma, family prestige and the development and commerce in the Red River Delta of Vietnam. In *Market cultures: Society and morality in new Asian capitalisms*, edited by R. Hefner, 268–289. Boulder, CO: Westview Press.

McElhinny, B. 1994. An economy of affect: Objectivity, masculinity and the gendering of police work. In *Dislocating masculinity: Comparative ethnographies*, edited by A. Cornwall and N. Lindsfarne, 159–171. London: Routledge.

Merleau-Ponty, M. 1995 [1962]. *The phenomenology of perception*. New York: Routledge.

Mohanty, C. T. 1991. Under Western eyes: Feminist scholarship and colonial discourses. In *Third World women and the politics of feminism*, edited by C. T. Mohanty, A. Russo and L. Torres, 51–80. Indianapolis: Indiana University Press.

Moore, H. 1994. *A passion for difference*. Cambridge, U.K.: Polity Press.

Ngo Thi Nhan Binh. 2004. The Confucian four feminine virtues (*tu duc*): The old versus the new—*Ke thua* versus *Phat huy*. In *Gender practices in contemporary Vietnam*, edited by L. Drummond and H. Rydstrom, 47–73. Singapore: Singapore University Press.

Nguyen Van Chinh. 2001. *Work without name: Changing patterns of children work in a northern Vietnamese Village*. Unpublished Ph.D. dissertation. Amsterdam: University of Amsterdam.

O'Harrow, S. 1995. Vietnamese women and Confucianism: Creating spaces from patriarchy. In *"Male" and "female" in developing Southeast Asia*, edited by W. Karim, 161–180. Washington, DC: Berg.

Peletz, M. 1995. Neither reasonable nor responsible: Contrasting representations of masculinity in a Malay society. In *Bewitching women, pious men: Gender and body politics in Southeast Asia*, edited by A. Ong and M. Peletz, 76–123. Berkeley: University of California Press.

Pettus, A. 2003. *Between sacrifice and desire: National identity and the governing of femininity in Vietnam*. New York: Routledge.

Pham Van Bich. 1999. *The Vietnamese family in change: The case of the Red River Delta*. Richmond: Curzon Press.

Rydstrom, H. 2003. *Embodying morality: Growing up in northern rural Vietnam*. Honolulu: University of Hawaii Press.

Smith, G. A. 1989. *Livelihood and resistance*. Berkeley: University of California Press.

Strathern, M. 1988. *The gender of the gift*. Berkeley: University of California Press.

Taylor, C. 2004. *Modern social imaginaries*. Durham, NC: Duke University Press.

Taylor, P. 2004. *Goddess on the rise: Pilgrimage and popular religion in Vietnam*. Honolulu: University of Hawaii Press.

Tran, A. N. 2002. Gender expectations of Vietnamese garment workers: Viet Nam's re-integration into the world economy. In *Gender, household, state: Doi Moi in Viet Nam*, edited by J. Werner and D. Bélanger, 49–72. Ithaca, NY: Cornell University Southeast Asia Program Publications.

Tran Tuyet Nhung and A. Reid. 2006. Introduction: The construction of historical Vietnamese identities. In *Viet Nam: Borderless histories*, edited by N. T. Tran
and A. Reid, 1–22. Madison: University of Wisconsin Press.

Tran Tuyet Nhung. 2006. Beyond the myth of equality: Daughters' inheritance
rights in the Le code. In *Viet Nam: Borderless histories*, edited by N. T. Tran and
A. Reid, 121–144. Madison: University of Wisconsin Press.

Truong Huyen Chi. 2001. *Changing processes of social reproduction in the northern
Vietnamese countryside: An ethnographic study of Dong Van Village (Red River
Delta)*. Unpublished Ph.D. dissertation, University of Toronto.

Truong Huyen Chi. 2004. Winter crop and spring festival: The contestations
of local government in a Red River Delta commune. In *Beyond Hanoi: Local
government in Vietnam*, edited by B. T. Kerkvliet and D. Marr, 110–136. Singapore: Institute of Southeast Asian Studies Press.

Werner, J. 2002. Gender, household, and the state. Renovation (Doi Moi) as social
process in Viet Nam. In *Gender, household, state: Doi Moi in Viet Nam*, edited
by J. Werner and D. Bélanger, 29–48. Ithaca, NY: Cornell University Southeast Asia Program Publications.

Werner, J. 2004. Managing womanhoods in the family: Gendered subjectivities
and the state in the Red River Delta in Vietnam. In *Gender practices in contemporary Vietnam*, edited by L. Drummond and H. Rydstrom, 26–46. Singapore:
Singapore University Press.

Werner J., and D. Bélanger. 2002. Introduction. In *Gender, household, state: Doi
Moi in Viet Nam*, edited by J. Werner and D. Bélanger, 13–18. Ithaca, NY:
Cornell University Southeast Asia Program Publications.

Chapter Eleven

Household Headship in the Red River Delta, Vietnam

The Political Construction of the Family

BUSSARAWAN TEERAWICHITCHAINAN

It is widely assumed in social science research that a woman becomes household head when there is no adult man in the household. Prior studies in many developing countries have found that the rising levels of female-headed households correspond to demographic events that lead to male absence, such as increased rates of divorce, out-of-wedlock pregnancies, and male out-migration (Buvinic and Youssef 1978; Lloyd and Gage-Brandon 1994). In these countries, the overwhelming majority of female heads are single mothers who live with their children and often experience chronic poverty. Evidence from Vietnam, however, tells a different story. Female-headed households are common, particularly in urban areas. Unlike most other societies where female heads are usually divorced, widowed, or deserted by their husbands, a substantial number of Vietnamese female heads are actually married and reportedly living in the same household as their spouse (Bélanger 2000; Vu 1994).

Why many married Vietnamese women become household heads despite the presence of their husbands has not yet been fully understood. If the traditional-Confucian Vietnamese family model, which idealizes patrilineality, virilocality, and patriarchy, were strictly upheld, the high prevalence of female headship would appear as a surprise. However, historical evidence shows a complex picture of the Vietnamese family system and women's status departing from the Confucian ideals (see Bélanger and Barbieri, this volume). Further, during the latter half of the twentieth century, Vietnam underwent two of the world's most pervasive social experimentations, under the socialist revolution in the 1950s and the *Doi Moi* reforms in the late 1980s. The country also experienced repeated warfare and military mobilization from the 1940s to the 1980s. A consideration of these historical events and associated socioeconomic change may help understand what household headship—female headship in particular—means in the contemporary Vietnamese context. Several questions need to be addressed, including:

1. How useful is the "traditional-Confucian" model in explaining the prevalence of female-headed households in Vietnam?
2. Did the decades of war mobilization force married men to leave home and impose the role of household head on their wives?
3. Did state policies, such as the implementation of the household registration system in the 1950s, change how headship is perceived and how it is assigned to a family member?
4. Could female headship in Vietnam be explained by the socialist revolution that attempted to promote gender egalitarianism, or by the more recent *Doi Moi* reforms that may have created more educational and economic opportunities for women?

Based on the 1995 Vietnam Longitudinal Survey (VLS), this study attempts to shed some light on these questions by examining the patterns and determinants of female headship in the Red River Delta in northern Vietnam. I find that in Vietnam, as elsewhere, the absence of men makes women more likely to be household heads, but it does not fully explain the incidence of female headship. Female heads of households interviewed in the VLS represent a diverse group of women with a large range of characteristics and backgrounds—contrary to the conventional model that simply presents female heads as being widows, divorcees, or those experiencing separation from spouses. Many married women in the Red River Delta take on the title of household head despite the presence of their spouse in the household. I find that a variety of factors account for this phenomenon. Women's individual attributes, such as age, marital status, education, and place of residence, determine their likelihood of becoming household heads. I also find that state policies, such as mass mobilization into the military during the American war and the *ho khau* household registration policies, contribute significantly to the incidence of female headship. The *ho khau* registration system appears to have created an administrative meaning to the concept of household headship, adding to the already complex notions constructed by the patriarchal ideology, and perhaps influenced by women's increased educational attainment and enhanced roles as economic providers.

Background

THE CONVENTIONAL MODEL OF FEMALE HEADSHIP IN COMPARATIVE PERSPECTIVE

In many settings around the world, it is commonly assumed that women become household heads only when adult men, particularly husbands, are absent. Researchers distinguish between de jure and de facto female-headed households (Chant 1997). The former refers to female heads who are widowed or legally separated, while the latter refers to instances in which husbands are away from the household (usually for work). Underlying both circumstances is the notion that male absence is a default for female headship.

Evidence from various societies suggests that marital dissolution and migration are the two major reasons for the absence of men from a household. Marital dissolution through widowhood and divorce leads to spousal absence and, consequently, to women becoming household heads. In the United States, for example, the incidence of female-headed households is accounted for mainly by divorce, separation, widowhood, and nonmarital childbearing (Cherlin 1992; Wojtkiewicz, McLanahan, and Garfinkel 1990). Mobility and migration are other important factors explaining male absence, particularly in less developed countries (Population Council/International Center for Research on Women [ICRW] 1988). In rural Africa, for instance, a large number of women are household heads because they are left behind by their husbands who migrate to the cities. Another example is found in many Latin American countries, where female heads of households are mostly women who migrate from the countryside and set up their households in the cities.

One of the most important characteristics of female-headed households is the relationship between female headship and poverty. Evidence from both developed and less developed countries shows that female-headed households are disproportionately overrepresented among the poor. Female-headed households tend to carry higher dependency ratios (for example, they have a greater number of nonworkers than workers), and women are more likely to experience discrimination in the labor market. For these reasons, households with female heads are believed to be economically vulnerable (Buvinic and Gupta 1997). As the number of female-headed households continues to rise worldwide, the relationship between female headship and poverty has drawn considerable attention from researchers and policy makers. There has been a growing debate over whether female-headed households are poverty prone and whether female headship is a helpful concept to identify the poorest of the poor (Kibreab 2003; Rogers 1995).

THE UNUSUAL CASE OF VIETNAMESE FEMALE HEADSHIP

Censuses and surveys suggest that female-headed households are not uncommon in Vietnam. A cross-national study ranks Vietnam as potentially having a "high-medium" level of female-headed households among seventy-three less developed countries (Buvinic and Youssef 1978, 39, 86). The 1989 census showed that female-headed households represented 36 percent of all households in Vietnam, and 39 percent in the Red River Delta (Vu 1994). Further, the more recent census, conducted in 1999, suggests a consistent, yet declining, pattern of female-headed households. In 1999, the nationwide proportion of female-headed households was 29 percent—a level similar to that estimated for the Red River Delta. The relatively high prevalence of female-headed households, as well as its recent decline, have not yet been explained in the literature.

The characteristics of female-headed households in Vietnam are very striking. First, it is common for Vietnamese female heads to be married and to live with their spouses. According to the 1992–93 Vietnam Living Standards Survey, one-third of female heads live in the same household as their spouses (Bélanger 2000). Further, study after study consistently finds that female-headed households in Vietnam are, on average, better off economically than their male-headed counterparts (Desai 2000; Haughton, Haughton, and Nguyen 2001; Vu 1994). Even after excluding female-headed households with resident males, mean per capita household expenditure is still higher for female-headed than for male-headed households (World Bank 1999).

These characteristics of Vietnamese female-headed households are incongruent with the conventional model of female headship, observed internationally. Recent studies focus on the heterogeneity of Vietnamese female-headed households (Luong 2003; Scott 2003). Female-headed households may vary by their size and composition, and these factors may be important in understanding their economic well-being. Nonetheless, there is still a lack of empirically supported explanations for why many Vietnamese wives become household heads even when their husbands are present. The conventional model, which treats male absence as a default for female headship, fails to fully explain the phenomenon observed in Vietnam. An alternative analytical approach is needed. A consideration of the sociohistorical contexts that shape the Vietnamese family system, including three decades of war, a socialist revolution, and market reforms, may shed light on how household headship is assigned and what the concept really means in Vietnam.

THE CULTURALLY CONSTRUCTED NOTION OF HOUSEHOLD HEADSHIP

The "traditional-Confucian" Vietnamese family structure is characterized by a strictly defined hierarchy among family members (Pham 1999). According to traditional ideals, everyone in a household occupies a certain position based on generation, age, and gender. The position of household head—or *chu ho* in Vietnamese—is attributed to an adult, whose duties include making major decisions, representing the family in the outside world, and supporting other members morally and financially (Tran 1991). Ideally, household headship is a position reserved for the eldest man in the family (typically the husband or father) and usually transferred from a man to his eldest son who inherits the land after his father dies. In a very strict sense, the traditional model offers Vietnamese women few opportunities to become household heads.

However, evidence clearly indicates that local practices are a far cry from this model of family hierarchy and gender relations (Bélanger 2000; Hirschman and Vu 1996; see Luong, this volume). While Vietnamese and non-Vietnamese researchers had a tendency to inflate the influence of Confucianism on the Vietnamese family system, research over the last ten years has consistently demonstrated the truly mixed influences shaping traditional Vietnamese culture, particularly those pertaining to women's position within the family (see Bélanger and Barbieri, this volume). The Confucian model of women's status observed in China is partly counterbalanced by the more egalitarian Southeast Asian culture.

Illustrations of such mixed influences are ample. During the presocialist era, Vietnamese wives, like women in other Southeast Asian societies, were known for being active in productive roles and in petty trading, for being in charge of managing the household and for holding the household purse strings (Keyes 1995). Further, in extended households comprising two or more generations, a Vietnamese widow usually held some authority over her married son and served as a matriarch for the household after her husband's death. Vietnamese women's dominant roles in household financial management and the headship of elderly widows call into question the validity of the Confucian stereotype of household headship. Rather than an oversimplified version that asserts that women should never be household heads, evidence points to the complex notion of headship in Vietnam. There are clearly diverse cultural practices regarding the household division of labor and the role of the household head and his or her spouse in the public as well as in the domestic spheres.

DECADES OF WAR AND MILITARY MOBILIZATION

From the 1940s to the 1970s, Vietnam was the theatre of practically continuous military conflict. The universal draft law requiring every eligible Vietnamese man to serve in the military was implemented in 1960 in northern Vietnam. In the Red River Delta region, at least 70 percent of the men who entered adulthood during the armed conflict between Vietnam and the United States (1965–75) were inducted into the military (Teerawichitchainan 2005). In addition to the massive military mobilization from the American War of the 1960s to the Cambodian War of the 1980s, the conflicts inflicted a heavy death toll, particularly among young men (Hirschman, Preston, and Vu 1995; Merli 2000).

Recent empirical studies show that excess male mortality during wartime and mass mobilization into the military affected patterns of marriage and family formation in Vietnam (Goodkind 1995; Nguyen 1998; Teerawichitchainan 2005). Excess male casualties during the war left many Vietnamese wives widowed. Moreover, an imbalance in the sex ratio as a result of war mortality produced a marriage squeeze and forced a significant number of young Vietnamese women to remain unmarried in the 1970s and 1980s (Goodkind 1997). The lives of war spinsters are discussed in recent ethnographic studies (Bélanger and Khuat 2002; Phinney 2002). Further, protracted war years leading to extended military service caused long separations for many couples

(Pham 1999). With their husbands away, wives were often required to take full responsibility for managing the household.

Changes in marriage and family living arrangements caused by the war further contributed to a particular household pattern, characterized by a high prevalence of female headship (see Haines 2006 for a discussion of the phenomenon in southern Vietnam in 1954–75). War widows, never-married mothers, and wives whose husbands were away for military duties were likely candidates for the position of household head. Nonetheless, the likelihood of female headship also depended on other factors, such as remarriage rates and postmarital living arrangements. For example, if remarriage had been common and Vietnamese widows had usually remarried quickly after the death of their husbands, female headship of war widows might have been short-lived. The lack of marriageable men during the war would however operate against rapid remarriage of widows. Additionally, if newlyweds had typically lived with their parents' families after marriage (either on the groom's or bride's side) (Hirschman and Nguyen 2002), young wives would have been less likely to become household heads when their husbands were away for military service over an extended period of time.

THE TRANSITION FROM SOCIALISM AND IMPLICATIONS FOR WOMEN'S STATUS

The highest female labor force participation rates in the Southeast Asian region are found among women in Vietnam (Korinek 2004). Approximately 80 percent of women are economically active. Vietnamese women also tend to continue working throughout the life course without interruption for child-bearing. Inspired by the Leninist doctrine, the integration of women in the labor force and in public social roles is a legacy of the socialist regime's attempts to promote gender egalitarianism in education and employment outside the home (Le 1995). The socialist regime had an explicit interest in abolishing what was perceived to be the Confucian and feudal model of the Vietnamese family by creating gender equality and promoting gender empowerment (see Bélanger and Barbieri, this volume). Many studies suggest, however, that Vietnamese women were exhausted rather than emancipated by these policies (Gammeltoft 2001). Women's gains in public spheres were achieved by overloading them with the burdens of the household, private production, and state sector work (Pham 1999). Some scholars further claim that the socialist commitment to women's status was short-lived and waned in the mid-1970s soon after the men returned from the American war (Luong 2003).

During the transition to a market economy, Vietnam witnessed a dismantling of the collective structure and subsidization system. Working women were disproportionately affected by the state sector cutbacks. Through state-sponsored campaigns, the socialist government renewed its emphasis on women's motherhood responsibilities (Gammeltoft 2001). Studies also show that gender disparities in the household division of labor have either remained unchanged or have increased in postsocialist Vietnam (Knodel et al. 2004; Luong 2003), partly as a result of reemerging male-centered kin and family relations. Women carry out more household duties and work for long hours in multiple jobs (Korinek 2004).

The culturally constructed notion of household headship may be affected by Vietnamese women's increased educational opportunities and access to employment outside the home and agriculture sector. For example, women's enhanced capability to provide economic support to their families might improve their position within the household hierarchy and increase their likelihood of becoming household head. However, as other scholars caution, women's economic contribution may not necessarily translate into an enhanced status within the household and reduced disparities in the household division of labor. Therefore, if positive changes in women's socioeconomic characteristics do not increase their likelihood of becoming female household heads, the observed high levels of female headship in Vietnam might then have to be explained by factors other than women's empowerment.

STATE POLICIES AND HOUSEHOLD HEADSHIP

The influence of state policies, particularly the household registration (*ho khau*) requirement, on the assignment of household headship has not been discussed in prior studies (for an exception, see Vu 1994). The current household registration system was introduced in Vietnam by the socialist regime in 1954 following the *hukou* system in China. The Vietnamese *ho khau* system required each citizen to legally register in one, and only one, permanent residential location in either an urban or a rural area. The system also required residents to specify their status as agricultural or nonagricultural (Le 2004).

Prior to market reforms, *ho khau* was vitally important because residential location and agricultural status were linked to the supply of food, housing, jobs, and other welfare benefits by the government (Le 1998). Urban residents, particularly state employees, received more benefits than rural residents with agricultural status. Like centrally planned China, Vietnam's socialist regime disproportionately invested in heavy industry to speed up its economic modernization. To achieve the goal of socialist industrialization, the regime channeled greater resources to the priority urban-industrial sector while providing fewer resources to the rural-agriculture sector, which accounted for a majority of the Vietnamese population (Hardy 2001). The *ho khau* system was one of the mechanisms used to maintain this unequal resource distribution and to control mobility and migration between industry and agriculture and between cities and the countryside (Le 2004).

There are two types of *ho khau:* family and collective (Hardy 2001). A family *ho khau* is closely tied to a residential location. Families in urban areas keep their own *ho khau* book (called *so ho tich* in Vietnamese), while the *ho khau* books of families in rural areas are maintained by village authorities. A member of the family *ho khau* is designated as the household head with the civil duty to represent the household in external relations, such as declaring the household members' births and deaths to local authorities and attending commune meetings (Vu 1994). Examples of collective *ho khau* include state factories and other enterprises, hospitals, military units, and forestry enterprises (Hardy 2001). Each of these collective *ho khau* maintains a single *ho khau* book for its member workers. In other words, Vietnamese who work for these sectors register in the collective *ho khau* of their workplace. Only the workers themselves, not their immediate families, are allowed to register in a collective *ho khau*.

Since each citizen is required to register in only one location, it is common to observe that state workers register in their collective *ho khau*, instead of in their family *ho khau*, where their parents, husbands, wives, or children reside. Prior to market reforms, collective *ho khau* and family *ho khau* in urban settlements were generally favored over the rural *ho khau* because members in the former types of *ho khau* were entitled to greater welfare benefits (Hardy 2001). This preference might have had implications for the assignment of household headship, particularly when a couple worked in different economic sectors. For example, if the husband worked for a state factory and his wife was a farmer working in a rural commune, the husband would register (and prefer to register) in the collective *ho khau*, while his wife remained in a family *ho khau* in the countryside. In such a situation, women were more likely to hold the position of household head in the *ho khau* registration system.

Besides the *ho khau* policy, other state policies may also have determined the gender assignment of household headship. For example, between 1976 and 1986, the socialist regime gave preference for subsidized housing in urban areas to female state employees (Hoang 1999, 80). Those in favor included female workers who had children and whose husbands' workplace did not provide subsidized housing, or whose husbands lived somewhere else for professional reasons. Since these women had the right to be allocated land, they may also have been recognized as household heads on the *ho khau* registry. Note that there has not yet been any documentation of how many Vietnamese women actually benefited from the land policy.

The *ho khau* system appears to have created an administrative meaning to the concept of household headship, in addition to the notion culturally constructed by the traditional Confucian model of the family and perhaps influenced by women's increased roles in public spheres, especially after the socialist revolution. This administrative concept may or may not correspond to other notions of household headship. For example, a person who registers as the household head in the *ho khau* system may or may not be the main family breadwinner and may or may not hold the decision-making power. This discrepancy reveals the need to distinguish the legal or administrative meaning of household headship from other possible meanings, and to understand how these differences might affect the way researchers measure trends in female household headship in Vietnam.

Data, Measures, and Analytical Approach

An informed analysis of female-headed households in Vietnam should take the Vietnamese cultural and sociohistorical context into account, particularly the influence of state policies, such as the *ho khau* registration system. In this study, I extend the conventional model of female headship, which narrowly treats male absence as a default for female headship, to encompass several other factors that may influence female headship. These factors are women's individual attributes, measures of power relations within the household, and proxies for the effect of state policies. The measure of household headship used in this study is commonly found in censuses and surveys.

I analyze cross-sectional data from the 1995 round of the VLS. The VLS is one of the first social surveys designed to document social change in Vietnam, including the transformation of families and households under *Doi Moi* (Renovation). The survey was first conducted in 1995 in Ha Nam Ninh,[1] a core province of northern Vietnam's Red River Delta region. Located about 90 kilometers from Hanoi, Ha Nam Ninh is a densely settled, heavily cultivated province. Farming households cultivate rice, commonly grow horticultural crops, and raise livestock for household consumption and sale in local markets. While there was a decline in state-sector employment in the late 1980s, a number of state-run enterprises continue to operate in the province and provide many of the formal-sector jobs to the local population (Korinek 2004).

The VLS used a stratified random sampling design. Ten communes/districts were randomly selected from the study area, yielding a total of 1,855 households and 5,255 eligible adult members in these households. VLS interviewers successfully interviewed 4,465 individuals aged fifteen to sixty-five years. The analytical sample in this study consists of adult women aged twenty to sixty-five years interviewed in the 1995 VLS. Female headship is measured by the sex of the household head reported in the VLS household rosters. VLS interviewers asked household informants at the beginning of each interview: "Please give me the names of persons who usually live in your household and guests of the household who stayed here last night, starting with the head of the household." The individual defined as the head of the household was then recorded on the first line of the household roster. Household headship reported in the VLS usually agrees with the *ho khau* registration records provided by local authorities for the random selection of the VLS sample. The measure of headship in VLS most likely refers to the administrative meaning of household headship, which may or may not be consistent with other notions that assume that the household head is the main economic provider, household manager, or decision maker. In this study, a dummy variable indicates whether the woman interviewed is the household head.

While this study focuses on the pattern of female headship in the Red River Delta, a preliminary analysis of Vietnam censuses (not shown here) suggests that the proportion of female-headed households in the region is comparable to that of the country as a whole, as well as to other regions. Further, the urban and rural patterns of the Red River Delta were also consistent with the respective national patterns. Gaining an understanding of female headship in the Red River Delta may help comprehend the high levels of female headship observed throughout Vietnam.

Individual characteristics such as age, marital status, educational attainment, and employment type are included in the analytical model as covariates that influence the incidence of female headship. In the Vietnamese cultural context, *age* is an important indicator of seniority and maturity (Pham 1999). Therefore, it is a significant criterion for considering whether a woman is qualified to be household head. It is expected that older women are more likely to serve as household heads than their younger counterparts. *Marital status* is measured by a categorical variable indicating whether an individual is married, never married, or widowed/divorced at the time of the survey. Since divorce rates are reportedly low in Vietnam (Nguyen 1998), women represented in the last category are mostly widows. Marital status is widely used as a proxy for male absence, although it should be noted that, in Vietnam, it is common for elderly parents to live with their married children. Widowhood in Vietnam may not necessarily involve an absence of adult men from the household.

Women's education and employment type are indicators of their potential economic contribution to the household. For *education*, I incorporate a categorical variable indicating whether the respondent completed zero to five years of schooling (none or primary education), six to nine years (lower secondary level), or ten or more years (upper secondary or higher). To measure the effects of *employment type*, I use a categorical variable indicating whether the individual works in the agricultural sector, nonagricultural private sector, government sector, or not outside the home. In general, women who are well educated and those working in the nonagricultural private sector are able to make a significant financial contribution to the household income, and this may qualify them to be household heads. Nonetheless, it is also possible that these modern characteristics have no effect on the likelihood of female headship. Scholars are skeptical as to whether the status of Vietnamese women within the household is enhanced by their increased economic roles and contribution to the household (Korinek 2004; Luong 2003).

Two variables measured at the household level—respondent household location and presence of married adult men—are included in the analytical model. *Rural-urban location* is measured by a dummy variable indicating whether the woman lives in an urban district or a rural commune. Census and survey data indicate that female-headed households are more common in cities than in the countryside (Desai 2000; Vu 1994). This finding could arise from a composition effect, whereby women with individual characteristics conducive to female headship would be disproportionately represented in the cities. Alternatively, urban living could be independently associated with a relative preference for female headship. For example, female headship might be considered unconventional and people in urban areas are perhaps more receptive to this nontraditional phenomenon. Also, the subsidized housing programs, such as those existing in Hanoi during the mid-1970s to 1980s, may have increased female land ownership (Hoang 1999) and, subsequently, female headship in the urban areas of Vietnam. The *presence of adult men* is measured as a dummy variable indicating whether the respondent lives in a household with at least one adult man. An adult man is defined as an ever-married male over twenty years. Marriage is an important indicator for young Vietnamese to be fully considered as adults (Bélanger 2000). The presence of an adult man in the respondent's household is expected to limit the opportunity for a woman to become household head.

In addition to women's individual attributes and to the household variables, I incorporate the characteristics of their spouse in assessing their likelihood of being household head. These characteristics include age, education, military experience, and employment type. *Husband's age* and *education* are measured relative to his wife's attributes. Women who are younger and less educated than their spouse are expected to be in a position of subordination within the household, which would then lower their chances of becoming household heads (England and Farkas 1986). *Husband's military experience* is measured as a categorical variable indicating whether the respondent's husband had served in the military and, if so, for how long. In this study, military service is considered short term if three years or less; medium term if four to six years; and long term if seven or more years. Long-term service was very common during the Vietnam-American conflict. Spousal absence due to long-term military service is expected to increase the probability that women become household heads.

The *husband's type of employment* is measured as a categorical variable indicating whether the respondent's spouse works in the farm sector, in the nonfarm private sector, in a state enterprise or public sector, or if he does not work outside the home. In this study, the respondent's and her husband's employment in the government sector are used as a proxy for documenting the influence of state policies, such as the *ho khau* registration system, on the incidence of female headship. Prior to market reforms, state employees were likely to register in the collective *ho khau* of their work unit instead of registering in their family *ho khau* due to associated benefits. For this reason, female state employees were presumably less likely to become official household heads. For the same reason, when a man is employed in the state sector, his wife is more likely to be the official household head than when the husband works in other sectors. Statistical analyses were complemented by qualitative information collected during a follow-up study conducted by the author in selected VLS communes in Ha Nam, Nam Dinh, and Ninh Binh Provinces in 2002.

Results

DESCRIPTIVE ANALYSES: WHO ARE FEMALE HOUSEHOLD HEADS IN VIETNAM?

I used two approaches to describe the pattern of female household headship. The first analysis presented in Table 11.1 examines the incidence of female headship among all adult women in the sample (N = 2,086) based on their age and marital status. In other words, I want to determine whether Vietnamese women of a certain age and marital status are more likely to be household heads. The second approach, presented in Figure 11.1, focuses on the population of female heads only (N = 360) and describes their characteristics, such as their marital status and the presence or absence of a spouse.

The results presented in the topmost panel of Table 11.1 suggest that the incidence of female headship varies by the woman's age and marital status. Middle-aged women are in a favorable position to be household heads. Thirty percent of women aged fifty to sixty-five years serve as household heads, whereas only 14 percent of their younger counterparts, aged twenty to forty-nine years, do so. Age and marital status are highly correlated. Women in older and younger age brackets are at different stages of their family life course and, therefore, might be subject to different demographic and socioeconomic influences. Older women are expected to experience a greater likelihood of widowhood, while their younger counterparts are more likely to be single. The descriptive analyses show that, regardless of age, Vietnamese women who are widowed or divorced have a greater likelihood of becoming household heads. Approximately four out of every five widows/divorcees in-

TABLE 11.1
Number of adult women, number of female household heads,
and percentage of female household heads by marital status, 1995 VLS

	Number of adult women		
	All	Age 20–49	Age 50–65
All marital statuses	2,086	1,699	387
Never married	171	168	3
Currently married	1,769	1,499	297
Widowed/Divorced	119	32	87
	Number of household heads		
	All	Age 20–49	Age 50–65
All marital statuses	360	244	116
Never married	8	7	1
Currently married	256	209	47
Widowed/Divorced	96	28	68
	Percent household heads		
	All	Age 20–49	Age 50–65
All marital statuses	17%	14%	30%
Never married	6%	4%	—
Currently married	14%	14%	16%
Widowed/Divorced	81%	88%	78%

SOURCE: Vietnam Longitudinal Survey 1995.
NOTE: — denotes percentage not reported due to the small number of observations (less than 5).

terviewed in the VLS are household heads. Evidence also suggests that it is not uncommon for married women to serve as household heads—in both the younger and the older age groups. About 14 percent of them do so. However, very few never-married women become household heads (6 percent only). Descriptive analyses of the incidence of female headship presented in Table 11.1 are consistent with the hypothesis regarding the positive association between female headship and marital dissolution. This suggests that male/spousal absence is one of the major determinants of female headship in Vietnam.

Figure 11.1 describes the marital status of female heads in the Red River Delta. The analysis is restricted to women who are heads of the household. While findings from Table 11.1 show that Vietnamese widows and divorcees are more likely to become household heads than married and never-married

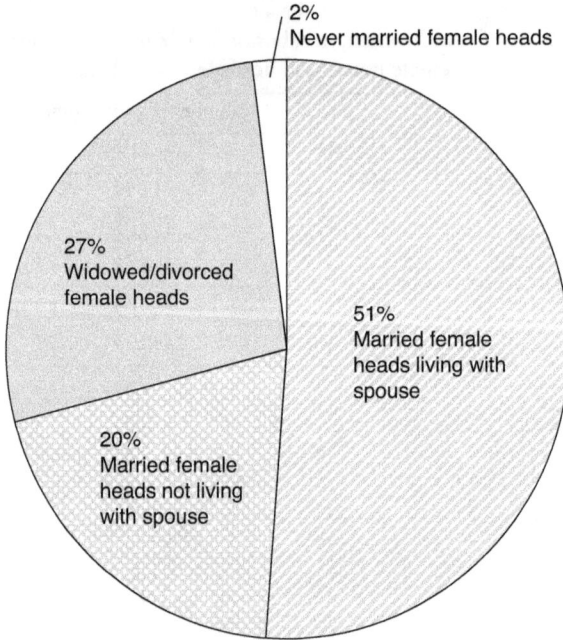

Figure 11.1   Proportions of Female Heads in the Red River Delta by Marital Status and Presence of Spouse (N = 360).
   SOURCE: Vietnam Longitudinal Survey, 1995

women, Figure 11.1 suggests that they account for only a small proportion of all female heads in the Red River Delta. Only one out of every four female heads is widowed or divorced. The proportion of female heads who were never married is also very small (only 2 percent).

The results presented in Figure 11.1 indicate that a majority of female heads in the Red River Delta are married (71 percent). Further, most of them reportedly live with their spouse on a regular basis,[2] confirming that, by contrast with findings from studies in other countries, the absence of a spouse is not the only factor explaining female headship in the region, and probably in Vietnam as a whole, as the overall pattern and characteristics of female-headed households in the Red River Delta are similar to those revealed by other sources of data (Bélanger 2000; Desai 2000; Vu 1994).

MULTIVARIATE ANALYSES:
DETERMINANTS OF FEMALE HEADSHIP

Spousal absence is important in explaining the incidence of female headship; yet, we must keep in mind that a majority of female household heads in the Red River Delta are married and live with their spouse. Findings from descriptive analyses suggest that other influences also account for the uncommonly widespread female headship in Vietnam. Multivariate analyses are useful to delineate the relationship between female headship, spousal absence, and other possible factors. In this study, I carried out two separate sets of multivariate analyses. The first set, with results in Table 11.2, examines the determinants of female headship among all adult women, with a focus on the net effect of male absence. The second set, shown in Table 11.3, addresses why many married women in the Red River Delta become household heads, despite the presence of their husbands. This analysis is restricted to married women living with their spouses.

Table 11.2 presents results from a series of binary logistic regressions on the incidence of female headship among all adult women (N = 2,086). The analysis consists of four additive models attempting to document various sets of influences on female headship. The first model measures female headship as a function of an absence of adult males in the respondent's household; Model 2 adds the respondent's age and marital status; Model 3 incorporates the respondent's level of education and type of employment as covariates; and Model 4 includes the respondent's household location. The exponential coefficients reported in Table 11.2 are expressed as the ratio of the odds of being household head (versus not being household head) for each category, relative to the comparable odds of the omitted category for each covariate. For example, in Model 2, the omitted category of women aged 56–65 years has a standard odds ratio of 1.00. Keeping other characteristics equal, women aged 20–25 years have an odds ratio of 0.31, implying that they have a much lower risk of being household heads than women aged 56–65 years. By contrast, women aged 46–56 years have an odds ratio of 1.52, indicating that they are at a higher risk of being household heads than their older counterparts.

One of the most striking results in Table 11.2, which is consistent with the conventional model of female headship, is that male absence is the single most important predictor of female headship in the Red River Delta. Women

TABLE 11.2
Binary logistic regression analysis—Determinants of female headship among adult women

	Model 1		Model 2		Model 3		Model 4		
	Odds Ratio	Std Error	Odds Ratio	Std Error	Odds Ratio	Std Error	Odds Ratio	Std Error	n
Presence of married adult men									
None	22.28***	0.21	33.97***	0.35	33.17***	0.35	43.22***	0.36	142
At least one married man[1]	1.00	—	1.00	—	1.00	—	1.00	—	1944
Respondent age in years									
20–25			0.31***	0.36	0.15***	0.41	0.22***	0.41	344
26–35			0.65^	0.26	0.33***	0.32	0.47*	0.32	633
36–45			1.54^	0.25	0.86	0.30	1.08	0.30	587
46–55			1.52^	0.26	1.08	0.28	1.07	0.29	303
56–65[1]			1.00	—	1.00	—	1.00	—	219
Respondent marital status									
Currently married[1]			1.00	—	1.00	—	1.00	—	1796
Never married			0.10***	0.50	0.10***	0.50	0.11***	0.50	171
Widowed/Divorced			8.90***	0.31	9.22***	0.32	11.14***	0.33	119
Respondent education									
0–5 years[1]					1.00		1.00		500
6–9 years					1.75*	0.22	1.37	0.22	1202
10 years and higher					3.02***	0.27	1.89*	0.28	384
Respondent employment type									
Agriculture[1]					1.00		1.00		1188
Nonagriculture, private sector					1.86***	0.18	0.85	0.22	397
Government sector					1.62*	0.23	0.64^	0.27	219
Does not work outside home					1.26	0.22	0.78	0.24	282
Respondent household location									
Rural[1]							1.00		1694
Urban							4.81***	0.21	392
–2 Loglikelihood	1649.69		1440.65		1395.45		1334.01		
Degrees of freedom	1		7		12		13		
N	2086		2086		2086		2086		2086

SOURCE: Vietnam Longitudinal Survey 1995.

NOTE: ^Statistically significant at p ≤ .1, *p ≤ .05, **p ≤ .01, ***p ≤ .001

[1]Omitted

living in a household without an adult man are much more likely to experience female headship than others. Model 1 indicates that the odds of headship for women in such living arrangements are twenty-two times greater than those for women living with at least one adult man. The net effect of male absence becomes even stronger after we introduce the other covariates in the models. In the saturated model (Model 4), all other characteristics being equal, the odds of female headship when no adult man lives in the household are forty-three times higher than in the opposite situation.

The quantitative evidence is consistent with findings from the qualitative interviews. In the interviews, adult men and women usually emphasized that the *chu ho* (household head) should be a man. They often associated the status of *chu ho* with the ability to be "the family breadwinner," "the leader," and to be in charge of "tough jobs." The underlying impression was that it was "more appropriate" for men to assume these roles. However, the participants did recognize that it was not uncommon for women to take on the role of household head. Male absence was cited as one of the most common circumstances that inevitably lead to women becoming household heads. Mai, a divorced mother in her late forties, articulated her experience as follows: "Had my husband not deserted me, I would not have been *chu ho*. I think every household should have a man. He can help take care of many difficulties. Things would have been so much easier for me if I had had a husband."

While male absence is the main predictor for female headship, results presented in Table 11.2 indicate that a variety of women's individual attributes constitute important determinants of female headship, independently from the presence or absence of adult men. Age is a particularly strong determinant of female headship, as young women in their twenties and early thirties are clearly less likely than older women to experience household headship. The relationship between women's age and female headship appears to be linear. All other attributes being equal, the lower a woman's age, the less likely she is to be head of her household. Marital status is another significant determinant of female headship. Consistent with the descriptive analyses presented in Table 11.1, very few never-married women serve as household heads. Results show that the odds of single women being household heads are about 90 percent lower than those of married women. This finding is consistent with the importance of marriage as a life-course marker of adulthood. Adult children usually gain autonomy from their parents upon getting married (Bélanger and Khuat 2002; Goodkind 1995). Despite their increasing level of education and earnings in recent years, never-married women are still considered not mature enough to take on the responsibilities that come with the position of household headship. Vietnamese widows and divorcees, however, experience the opposite. Even in the presence of other adult men, they are much more likely than those who are either married or have never been married to become household heads. Results presented in Table 11.2 suggest that after controlling for other characteristics, the odds of household headship for widows and divorcees are about ten times higher than those for married women. It is common in Vietnam for a widow to assume the role of a matriarch after the death of her husband, even when she lives with her married son and his family.

Education appears to increase women's likelihood of female headship. Better-educated women are in a more favorable position to become household heads. Note that women's education is highly correlated with their place of residence. Women in urban areas have generally attained a higher level of education than those in the countryside. Nonetheless, women's education retains a statistical significance effect even after controlling for their area of residence. According to Model 4, the odds of household headship for women with at least ten years of schooling are about 90 percent higher than those for women with less than six years of education. This result lends some support to the hypotheses that women's education is an important indicator of their position within the household and that the better educated they are the more likely they are to take on the roles and responsibilities of a household head.

Like education, women's employment is closely associated with their household location. According to Model 3, women's employment outside the agricultural sector has an independent positive effect on female headship. However, once the area of residence (urban vs. rural) is taken into consideration, the employment effect almost disappears (Model 4). In Model 4, women's employment in the nonagricultural private sector has no independent effects on the probability of becoming a household head. Interestingly, the net effect of women's employment in the government sector switches from being positive in Model 3 to being negative in Model 4. The odds of being household head for female state employees are nearly 40 percent lower than those of women in farming households once we control for the household characteristics and for the husbands' attributes.

The negative effect of state employment could be explained partly by the *ho khau* registration system since, as previously discussed, incentives to register in a collective *ho khau* were stronger for state employees than for other workers. Female state employees were consequently less likely than other women to become household heads.

The multivariate analyses presented in Table 11.2 further suggest that women's household location is a strong determinant of female headship. Other characteristics held equal, the odds of household headship for women in urban areas are nearly five times higher than those for women in the countryside. This evidence is consistent with the pattern of female headship revealed by previous studies, which found that the prevalence of female headship is higher in urban than in rural areas (Desai 2000; Vu 1994). As mentioned, it is possible that people in urban areas are more receptive to the idea of female heads of households. The following comment by Tien, a fifty-year-old male head of household in an urban setting in Ninh Binh Province, is typical: "Either men or women can be *chu ho*. According to our law, there is no such restriction for women. In my family, it doesn't matter who is the head of the household."

This middle-aged man and a few other male and female respondents in my follow-up interviews clearly regarded household headship as a matter of formality and bureaucracy. That is, the assignment of household headship was imposed on them by the state. Some of them articulated that the title of household head had little to do with the actual household division of labor in their daily life. Regardless of who the head of the household was, respondents considered that, ideally, husbands and wives shared important decisions regarding their family. Such decisions included the type of income-generating activities they should pursue and how much should be spent on some household assets such as motorcycles or refrigerators.

My follow-up interviews supported other research results, such as those of Truong Huyen Chi (this volume), according to whom male villagers who depended on the income earned by their wives working in Hanoi felt uncomfortable about not being the main breadwinners in the family. In my study, men whose wives were household heads tended to minimize the meaning of such a status. These men often claimed that they were as active and influential as their wives in many of the household activities, including income provision. Likewise, women heads of households were often humble about their roles and contributions to the family. Some defended their husbands' masculinity by giving them credits for being the major decision maker and representative of the family in the public sphere.

Multivariate analysis confirms that in the Red River Delta, as elsewhere, male absence increases the likelihood of women becoming household heads. While the evidence suggests that male absence is the single most important factor in female headship, women's individual characteristics, including age, marital status, education, employment, and their place of residence, are statistically significant in determining their likelihood of becoming household heads. The analysis shown in Table 11.3 presents a robust model for explaining the general pattern of female headship among married Vietnamese women. The analysis focuses on women in the VLS sample who are currently married and who report living with their spouse on a regular basis (N = 1,579). The women's characteristics included in this analysis are similar to those in the analysis presented in the previous table (Table 11.2). There are a few exceptions. The main difference is that I included information on the women's marriage cohort to estimate change in the prevalence of female headship among women who were married in different historical periods. In particular, I am interested in assessing whether women who married after the onset of reforms were less likely to become household heads than those in earlier marriage cohorts as suggested by census results. The marriage cohort is identified as a categorical variable indicating whether the respondent was married before the end of the Vietnam-American conflict (prior to 1976), during the reunification period (1976–85), or after *Doi Moi* was initiated (from 1986 onward). I expected women in the first cohort to have experienced a greater likelihood of household headship than those in subsequent cohorts, particularly the *Doi Moi* cohort. In addition to women's marriage cohorts, I introduced the information on the husband's age, level of education, military experience, and type of employment.

The analysis includes five nested logistic models. Model 1 measures female headship as a function of the women's marriage cohorts, educational attainment, and employment; Model 2 adds the respondent's place of residence as a covariate; Model 3 also includes the husband's age and level of education, relative to his wife's, to estimate the effects of marital dynamics; Model 4 introduces the spouse's military experience; and Model 5 includes the spouse's type of employment.

The results presented in Table 11.3 suggest that a woman's marriage cohort is a significant determinant of household headship. Model 1 indicates that the odds of being household head for women who married during *Doi Moi* are about 50 percent lower than those for women in the other two cohorts, with no significant difference between women who married during the war of female headship among married women with husband present

	Model 1 Odds Ratio	Model 1 Std Error	Model 2 Odds Ratio	Model 2 Std Error	Model 3 Odds Ratio	Model 3 Std Error	Model 4 Odds Ratio	Model 4 Std Error	Model 5 Odds Ratio	Model 5 Std Error	Number
Marriage cohorts											
Wartime or before (omitted)	1.00	—	1.00	—	1.00	—	1.00	—	1.00	—	528
Reunification	0.85	0.20	0.98	0.21	0.98	0.21	0.99	0.21	1.00	0.21	564
Doi Moi	0.46***	0.23	0.61*	0.24	0.60*	0.24	0.71	0.25	0.72	0.25	487
Respondent education											
0–5 years (omitted)	1.00	—	1.00	—	1.00	—	1.00	—	1.00	—	331
6–9 years	1.44	0.24	1.22	0.25	1.23	0.25	1.18	0.25	1.15	0.25	963
10 and higher	2.52***	0.30	1.59^	0.31	1.60	0.33	1.55	0.33	1.47	0.34	291
Respondent employment type											
Agriculture (omitted)	1.00	—	1.00	—	1.00	—	1.00	—	1.00	—	923
Non-agriculture, private sector	2.11***	0.20	0.74	0.26	0.74	0.26	0.73	0.27	0.68	0.28	292
Government sector	1.71*	0.26	0.50*	0.33	0.50*	0.33	0.49*	0.33	0.43^	0.34	160
Does not work outside home	1.38	0.25	0.69	0.29	0.69	0.29	0.68	0.29	0.63	0.31	204
Respondent household location											
Rural (omitted)			1.00	—	1.00	—	1.00	—	1.00	—	1287
Urban			6.78***	0.24	6.77***	0.24	6.50***	0.25	5.94***	0.25	298
Spouse age											
Spouse older (omitted)					1.00	—	1.00	—	1.00	—	1501
Spouse same age or younger					1.15	0.36	1.19	0.37	1.22	0.37	84
Spouse education											
Spouse having equal/higher education (omitted)					1.00	—	1.00	—	1.00	—	1278
Spouse having lower education					1.01	0.23	1.00	0.23	1.03	0.23	307
Spouse military experience											
Never served							1.52^	0.25	1.51^	0.25	617
Served less than 3 years (omitted)							1.00	—	1.00	—	386
Served 4–6 years							1.58^	0.28	1.56^	0.28	297
Served 7+ years							2.04**	0.28	2.10**	0.28	279
Spouse employment type											
Agriculture (omitted)									1.00	—	796
Non-agriculture, private sector									1.23	0.24	432
Government sector									1.53^	0.30	174
Does not work outside home									1.22	0.30	177
-2 Loglikelihood	1092.50		1022.43		1022.29		1015.28		1013.25		
Degrees of freedom	7		8		10		13		16		
N	1579		1579		1579		1579		1579		1579

SOURCE: Vietnam Longitudinal Survey 1995.

NOTE: Statistically significant at *$p \le .05$, **$p \le .01$, ***$p \le .001$

and those who married during reunification. This finding confirms that female headship is less prevalent among those who married during renovation. However, the effect of the marriage cohort wanes as other covariates are successively introduced into the model, eventually disappearing in Model 4 and Model 5, which included the effect of the husband's characteristics (military experience and type of employment). This finding tends to suggest that the declining prevalence of female-headed households during the 1989–99 intercensal period results from a change in the characteristics of the population rather than from a change in female headship within each population subgroup. More specifically, female headship appears to have declined between the 1989 and the 1999 census because the proportion of women whose husbands served in the military for an extended period (introduced in Model 4) and the proportion of women whose husbands worked in the state sector (introduced in Model 5) have fallen since the implementation of the economic reforms. Because, as discussed earlier, women in these situations are more likely to be household heads than other women, the change was logically associated with a decline in female headship.

The results also suggest that women's education has a weak positive effect on female headship. In situations where married women co-reside with their husbands, better-educated wives have a higher probability of female headship (OR = 2.52 in Model 1 and OR = 1.59 in Model 2) than those with less education. However, the effect of education disappears once the husband's characteristics are controlled for (Models 3–5). Consistent with results presented in the previous set of analyses, the odds of headship for women working in the government sector are significantly lower than those for other women when the place of residence (urban vs. rural) is taken into account (OR = 0.5 in Models 2–5). As previously suggested, this negative effect is likely an outcome of the *ho khau* registration system. There are no significant differences in the odds of household headship among women in other types of employment and nonworking women.

The place of residence is the strongest predictor of women's probability of household headship. Among all married women, the odds of being household head are six to seven times higher for those living in urban areas than for those living in rural areas, and the strength of the effect remains basically the same in every model, that is, the effect of this variable is independent from that of all the other factors taken into account. This observation might be explained by mechanisms associated with urban life and urbanization.

One possible, yet limited, explanation is related to the state housing policy during the mid-1970s and the 1980s, which favored female state workers in urban areas (Hoang 1999; Vu 1994). While the extent of this policy coverage was likely restricted to a small number of women during the subsidy period, it is possible that the housing program increased land ownership and, subsequently, female household headship in this group of women. During a follow-up interview I conducted in a town of Ninh Binh Province, a comment by Hoa, a married female head who lives with her husband, supported this hypothesis: "I used to work for the state railway department until I retired in 1990. When I worked there, I received this piece of land [where my house is located] from my office. So that's why I have become *chu ho*. My husband's office did not grant him any land."

Right after *Doi Moi*, state employment cutbacks hit Hoa's company, forcing her to retire early. While the state now provides fewer social security and other benefits, such as those related to health and education (see Oudin, this volume), in the case of Hoa the policy change did not affect the ownership of the land previously granted by the government. After retiring, Hoa was allowed to keep the land and continued to be designated as the household head. Like many people I interviewed, the headship on the *ho khau* had only an administrative meaning for Hoa. At the time of the interview, she did not designate her husband as the household head though she implied that what mattered was the respect she expressed to her husband in their daily interactions.

Results further indicate that in addition to the wife's characteristics, several of the husband's attributes have an independent effect on the likelihood of a married woman becoming household head. Husband's age and education are measured, relative to his wife's, in order to estimate the effects of marital dynamics on the incidence of female headship. Wives older or more educated than their husbands might be in a better position to negotiate important decisions with their spouses. It might also help them become household heads. However, the analysis does not support this hypothesis. Results suggest that the effects of the husband's relative age and level of education do not have any statistically significant effect on household headship.

By contrast, a husband's long-term military service increases the likelihood of his wife being the household head (Table 11.3). Holding all other characteristics constant, the odds of being the household head for a woman whose husband served in the military for at least seven years are twice as high as those of a woman whose husband served for less than three years. During the follow-up study, a comment by Huu, a fifty-year-old man, about his military experience reflects this particular circumstance: "Vietnam experienced several decades of war. During the war, men were called to serve in the front. We had to leave our wives and families behind. In such cases, women had to take care of their families. They automatically became household head."

In addition to extended military experience, results from the quantitative analysis suggest that husband's employment in the government sector increases the probability of his wife becoming household head. For wives whose husbands are state employees, the odds of becoming the household head increase by 53 percent compared to those of women with husbands working in agriculture. The net positive effects of a husband's government employment are consistent with earlier findings for female state employees. Again, this might be interpreted as a result of the *ho khau* system. On the one hand, when a wife works for the state, she tends to register in the collective *ho khau* of her enterprise or administrative office and, thus, is less likely to be the household head in her family *ho khau*. On the other hand, when a husband is a state employee, he registers at his office's collective *ho khau*, so his wife is more likely to become the household head in their family *ho khau*.

During the follow-up study, I interviewed eight female heads of households and encountered two female heads in rural communes who became household heads because of the *ho khau* registration policy. One of them was Lan, a forty-year-old farmer. Lan, whose husband worked as a medical assistant at the district hospital, explained: "In our family *ho khau* records, I am the *chu ho*. My husband works for a public hospital. He is listed there—in the *ho khau* of the hospital he works for."

During the interview, Lan commented that her husband had always been living at home and commuted to work daily. Her story illustrates how Vietnamese female heads might be considered "household heads" on the official record of the *ho khau* registry. Her role as *chu ho* included attending commune meetings and visiting local authorities when needed. Lan however pointed out that her husband attended these functions on her behalf when she was busy. She credited her husband for providing economic support to the family and making major decisions in the household. While Lan's case might not be generalizeable, it reminds us that the administrative meaning of household headship may not always be congruent with the conventional concept of headship.

To summarize, the results presented in Table 11.3 suggest that several factors are important in explaining the incidence of female headship among married women in the Red River Delta. Evidence shows that the major determinants of female headship include a woman's urban residence, her husband's extended military service, and the couple's employment in the public sector. In this study, I use employment in the state sector as a proxy for estimating the impact of the *ho khau* registration system. A consideration of the impact of the *ho khau* registration system has not yet been discussed in previous studies. Results presented here suggest that the *ho khau* system appears to be one of the factors to explain the high incidence of female headship in Vietnam.

Prior to the *Doi Moi* reforms, women became household heads when their husbands registered in a collective *ho khau*, as part of a rational economic strategy to maximize the household resources and access to social security in a context of widespread poverty and a stagnating economy. Previous studies indicate that urban and collective *ho khau* were preferred over rural *ho khau* because members of urban and collective *ho khau* were entitled to greater welfare benefits (Hardy 2001; Le 1998). For these reasons, rural households in which one member—either the husband or the wife—worked for the government preferred to have that particular member register in a collective *ho khau*. Such a strategy allowed rural households to benefit from the resource discrepancy created by the *ho khau* system. After *Doi Moi*, state subsidies were substantially reduced, particularly those related to health and education, thereby weakening the incentive for registering in a collective *ho khau* (Hardy 2001). Furthermore, according to a recent World Bank report,[3] Vietnam has been experiencing a major downsizing of its public sector, and a total of nearly 1.7 million workers, accounting for about 5 percent of the country labor force, could lose their jobs. Considering the relationship between state employment (of men) and women's household headship indicated by my study, this phenomenon could explain the decline in the prevalence of female headship observed during the 1989–99 intercensal period, a decline that could accelerate in the future. Data used in this study were collected in 1995—after about a decade of *Doi Moi*. The declining trend and recent pattern of female household headship deserve further investigation using more recent sources of information.

Discussion

This study has discussed empirically supported explanations for the widespread phenomenon of female household headship in Vietnam. Past studies have shown that female-headed households are common, particularly in the urban areas of Vietnam. While women are most likely to become household heads when adult men are absent from the family, many Vietnamese females become heads in the presence of adult males in their family. In this study, I have analyzed data from the 1995 round of the Vietnam Longitudinal Survey. I have found that over half of all female household heads in the Red River Delta area under investigation are married and reportedly living with their spouses. Complementing the statistical information with more qualitative documentation, I also have shown that a variety of factors—reflecting both continuity and change—account for the pattern of female headship in Vietnam.

On the one hand, my findings suggest that the patriarchal model of the family typical of northern Vietnam continues to assert its influences on how people think about household headship and the role of household heads. To a certain extent, these influences translate into actual behaviors. Of all factors, male absence is the single most important determinant of female headship. This suggests a persisting belief that it is more culturally appropriate for a man to be the household head. In addition, I find that the assignment of household headship in Vietnam is affected by individual circumstances, such as the age and marital status of the household members, so that young unmarried women are unlikely to become household heads. Widows and divorcees, by contrast, experience a considerably greater probability of household headship. This is consistent with the Vietnamese tradition that elderly widows serve as matriarchs in their families.

On the other hand, results indicate that change might be under way. Some recent trends appear favorable to female headship in Vietnam. For instance, women's overall level of education tends to increase, and this has a positive effect on the likelihood of female headship in my statistical analysis. In reformed Vietnam, education improves women's abilities to work in the wage labor force and to become significant contributors to their household income. This situation may favorably alter their position in the household hierarchy—making it more likely for them to become household heads. Other factors operate in the opposite direction. My study suggests that the unusual prevalence of female headship in Vietnam is partly explained by policies implemented by the state, both in the past and currently, ranging from the household registration system to housing subsidies, land ownership, and mass mobilization. Massive drafting into the military during the extended war required many husbands to leave their wives and families behind. Women became household heads for practical reasons but maintained their status after the return of their husbands, so that my logistic regression results show a statistical association between a husband's extended military service and his wife's likelihood of being the household head. The *ho khau* registration system is another contextual factor with a significant impact on the incidence of female headship. Results indicate that the *ho khau* system might explain why many Vietnamese wives become household heads though living with their husbands. This is particularly true for wives whose husbands are state employees. Further, limited evidence points to the effects of the housing policy that granted land, in rural areas, or lodging, in urban areas, to women rather than to men.

This study shows that female household heads in Vietnam represent a heterogeneous group. The stereotypical depiction of female heads as being those who experience male/spousal absence fails to fully explain the patterns of female headship in Vietnam. It is certainly the case that the likelihood of women being household heads is high among widows as well as among divorced women living with their children, but one also finds household heads among women who are the main family breadwinners and among wives assigned as such by the *ho khau* registration system. While this is by no means an exhaustive list of archetypical female heads in the Red River Delta, evidence suggests that future studies of household headship in Vietnam should consider the interplay and discrepancies between the administrative meaning, the culturally constructed notion, and other possible concepts of household headship. A parallel study would be worth conducting in other areas of Vietnam, particularly in the South where traditional family patterns have been shown to significantly differ from those in the North (Haines 2006; Luong 2003).

The issue of female-headed households is an interesting area of research that questions the traditional model of patriarchy in the literature on the Vietnamese family. It provides an opportunity to further investigate changing gender relations within the household, the household division of labor, and men's roles in the Vietnamese family. To assess the trends in the national and regional prevalence of female-headed households in Vietnam, particularly after *Doi Moi* reforms, future studies may benefit from taking the declining significance of the *ho khau* system into account (Hardy 2001). Note, however, that female household headship does not necessarily imply gender equality in the household division of labor and balance of power. The duties associated with household headship, such as dealing with the outside world and representing the family for administrative purposes, may in fact have added to the heavy burden supported by women in their already busy domestic and productive lives, and further investigation into the actual meaning of female household headship for both men and women would greatly improve our understanding of gender relations and the household power hierarchy in Vietnam.

Notes

I thank Charles Hirschman, Le Thanh Sang, Vu Manh Loi, Danièle Bélanger, Magali Barbieri, Dang Bao Khanh, and Patty Glynn for their helpful comments and research assistance on earlier drafts of this chapter. The Social Science Research Council's International Pre-Dissertation Program provided funding to conduct field research for this study.

1. Subsequent to the VLS baseline survey in 1995, Ha Nam Ninh was subdivided into three provinces (Ha Nam, Nam Dinh, and Ninh Binh). According to the 1999 census, the population of these three provinces combined was 3.2 million, while the total population for the Red River Delta region was 14.8 million—accounting for approximately 19 percent of Vietnam's population.

2. The VLS documents whether a household member is a regular resident of the household by asking, "Does (NAME) usually live here or is s/he a temporary visitor?" This information allows for a precise measurement of the regular presence of spouses.

3. http://lnweb18.worldbank.org/ESSD/sdvext.nsf/PrintFriendly/ 1458A52CC16A4EB285256DD7005F04EF? Open document, downloaded on June 18, 2007.

References

Bélanger, D. 2000. Regional differences in household composition and family formation patterns in Vietnam. *Journal of Comparative Family Studies*, 31(2): 171–189.

Bélanger, D., and Khuat T. H. 2002. Too late to marry: Failure, fate, or fortune? Female singlehood in rural North Viet Nam. In *Gender, household, state: Doi Moi in Viet Nam*, edited by J. Werner and D. Bélanger, 89–110. Ithaca, NY: Cornell University.

Buvinic, M., and G. Rao Gupta. 1997. Female-headed households and female-maintained families: Are they worth targeting to reduce poverty in developing countries? *Economic Development and Cultural Change*, 45(2): 259–280.

Buvinic, M., and N. Youssef. 1978. *Women-headed households: The ignored factor in development planning*. Report submitted to the Office of Women in Development, U.S. Agency for International Development. Washington, DC: International Center for Research for Women.

Chant, S. 1997. Women-headed households: Poorest of the poor? Perspectives from Mexico, Costa Rica, and the Philippines. *IDS Bulletin*, 28(3): 26–48.

Cherlin, A. J. 1992. *Marriage, divorce, remarriage* (Revised edition). Cambridge, MA: Harvard University Press.

Desai, J. 2000. *Vietnam through the lens of gender: Five years later.* Report prepared for the Food and Agriculture Organization of the United Nations, Regional Office for Asia and the Pacific.

England, P., and G. Farkas. 1986. *Households, employment, and gender: A social, economic, and demographic view.* New York: Aldine.

Gammeltoft, T. 2001. Faithful, heroic, resourceful: Changing images of women in Vietnam. In *Vietnamese society in transition: The daily politics of reform and change*, edited by J. Kleinen, 265–280. Amsterdam: Het Spinhuis.

Goodkind, D. 1995. *Marriage style, development, and spousal distances: Sex and the transition to parenthood in a province of northern Vietnam, 1948–93*, 33. Ann Arbor: Population Studies Center, University of Michigan.

Goodkind, D. 1997. The Vietnamese double marriage squeeze. *International Migration Review*, 31(1): 108–127.

Haines, D. W. 2006. *The limits of kinship: South Vietnamese households 1954–1975.* De Kalb: Southeast Asia Publications, Center for Southeast Asian Studies, Northern Illinois University.

Hardy, A. 2001. Rules and resources: Negotiating the household registration system in Vietnam under reform. *SOJOURN: Journal of Social Issues in Southeast Asia*, 16(2): 187–212.

Haughton, D., J. Haughton, and Nguyen P., eds. 2001. *Living standards during an economic boom: The case of Vietnam.* Hanoi: Statistical Publishing House.

Hirschman, C., S. Preston, and Vu M. L. 1995. Vietnamese casualties during the American War: A new estimate. *Population and Development Review*, 21(4): 783–812.

Hirschman, C., and Nguyen H. M. 2002. Tradition and change in Vietnamese family structure in the Red River Delta. *Journal of Marriage and Family*, 64 (November): 1063–1079.

Hirschman, C., and Vu M. L. 1996. Family and household structure in Vietnam: Some glimpses from a recent survey. *Pacific Affairs*, 69 (Summer): 229–249.

Hoang Thi Lich. 1999. Women's access to housing in Hanoi. In *Women's right to house and land: China, Laos, Vietnam*, edited by I. Tinker and G. Summerfield, 77–94. Boulder, CO, and London: Lynne Rienner Publishers.

Keyes, C. 1995. *The Golden Peninsula: Culture and adaptation in mainland Southeast Asia.* New York: Macmillan (1977). Reprinted, Honolulu: University of Hawaii Press.

Kibreab, G. 2003. Rethinking household headship among Eritrean refugees and returnees. *Development and Change*, 34(2): 311–337.

Knodel, J., Vu M. L., R. Jayakody, and Vu T. H. 2004. *Gender roles in the family: Change and stability in Vietnam*. Ann Arbor: Population Studies Center, University of Michigan.

Korinek, K. 2004. Maternal employment during Northern Vietnam's era of market reform. *Social Forces*, 83(2): 791–822.

Le Bach Duong. 1998. *State, economic development, and internal migration in Vietnam*. Ph.D. dissertation, State University of New York, Binghamton.

Le Thanh Sang. 2004. *Urbanization and urban areas in Viet Nam in pre- and post-reform eras: 1979–1989 and 1989–1999*. Ph.D. dissertation, University of Washington, Seattle.

Le Thi. 1995. Women's labor and socio-economic status in a market-oriented economy. In *Vietnam in a changing world*, edited by I. Norland, C. L. Gates and Vu Cao Dam, 207–218. Surrey, U.K.: Curzon Press.

Lloyd, C., and A. Gage-Brandon. 1994. High fertility and children's schooling in Ghana: Sex differences in parental contributions and educational outcomes. *Population Studies*, 48 (2): 293–306.

Luong, Hy Van. 2003. Gender relations: Ideologies, kinship practices, and political economy. In *Post-War Vietnam: Dynamics of a transforming society*, edited by Hy Van Luong, 201–224. Lanham, MD: Rowman & Littlefield.

Merli, M. G. 2000. Socioeconomic background and war mortality during Vietnam's wars. *Demography*, 37(1): 1–15.

Nguyen Huu Minh. 1998. *Tradition and change in Vietnamese marriage patterns in the Red River Delta*. Seattle: Department of Sociology, University of Washington.

Pham Van Bich. 1999. *The Vietnamese family in change: The case of the Red River Delta*. Surrey, UK: Curzon.

Phinney, H. M. 2002. *Asking for the essential child: Revolutionary transformations in reproductive space in northern Viet Nam*. Ph.D. dissertation, University of Washington, Seattle.

Population Council/International Center for Research on Women. 1988. *The determinants and consequences of female-headed households*. Washington, DC: Population Council.

Rogers, B. L. 1995. Alternative definitions of female headship in the Dominican Republic. *World Development*, 23(12): 2033–2039.

Scott, S. 2003. Gender, household headship and entitlements to land: New vulnerabilities in Vietnam's decollectivization. *Gender, Technology and Development*, 7(2): 233–263.

Teerawichitchainan, B. 2005. *Impact of war and military service on the transition to adulthood and long-term socioeconomic achievement in northern Vietnam*. Ph.D. dissertation, University of Washington, Seattle.

Tran Dinh Huou. 1991. Traditional families in Vietnam and the influence of Confucianism. In *Sociological studies on the Vietnamese family*, edited by R. Liljestrom and Tuong Lai. Hanoi: Social Sciences Publishing House.

Vu Manh Loi. 1994. *Female-headed households in Vietnam*. Paper prepared for the 6th Conference of the Northwest Regional Consortium for Southeast Asian Studies, Seattle, WA, November 4–6, 1994.

Wojtkiewicz, R. A., S. S. McLanahan, and I. Garfinkel. 1990. The growth of families headed by women: 1950–1980. *Demography*, 27(1): 19–30.

World Bank. 1999. *Vietnam: Attacking poverty. Vietnam development report 2000*, Joint Report of the Government of Vietnam-Donor-NGO Poverty Working Group. Consultative Group Meeting for Vietnam, 14–15 December 1999, World Bank, Hanoi.

PART FIVE

Family Livelihood Strategies

Chapter Twelve

Household Structure and Employment Strategies in a Changing Economy

XAVIER OUDIN

The *Doi Moi* reforms, gradually implemented after the sixth Congress of the Communist Party of Vietnam in December 1986, have ended the virtual monopoly held by the state and the cooperatives over the economy. By allowing private enterprise and investment, the new policy has radically changed the conditions under which a majority of people work and earn their living. In particular, the breakdown of the economically active population by sector has changed very quickly. Whereas over three-quarters of those who worked were employed in the public sector and cooperatives before *Doi Moi*, there have been massive reductions in state-owned companies and the civil service, and the cooperatives have virtually disappeared. Farming excluded, only a quarter of the working population now works in the public sector compared to half before *Doi Moi*. The number of nonfarm jobs has doubled in fifteen years, and this growth has mainly been in the nonwage sector, consisting of small family businesses, self-employed workers, and small-scale trade.[1]

As the state no longer provides social security and free education, forms of social solidarity, which are inseparable from forms of employment, are taking on a new shape. The family has become the main channel for solidarity, and households contribute a growing share of their members' health and education expenses (for references to this issue, see Bélanger and Barbieri's Chapter 1, this volume).

Thus, the changes under way in Vietnam simultaneously affect forms of employment and solidarity systems. As we investigate to what extent these changes affect the institution of the family, we will attempt to find a correlation between forms of employment and solidarity, on the one hand, and types of family, on the other. This requires an examination of forms of employment and the types of solidarity they generate, along with a sociological analysis of the family, to identify links between the household types generally used for family studies in demography and types of employment. In short, our aim is to compare household types with the occupational profile of these households.

In the first section, I describe the problems of solidarity in the particular case of Vietnam in recent years. In the second section, I use survey data to analyze links between types of family, forms of employment, and modes of provision for the economically inactive.

Work and Family Solidarity

SOLIDARITY AND POPULATION

All societies are organized in such a way as to ensure their reproduction and the well-being, or at least survival, of their members. Economic and political systems are forms of organization for solving that problem. As a significant proportion of people cannot provide for their own subsistence, various institutions are established to provide for those who are not economically active. The production system (and hence work relations) that produces and distributes resources and the solidarity system that covers the needs of those who are not economically active are interlinked, and it is not possible to understand one without examining the other. As the family is both one of the main institutions through which solidarity functions and the basic economic unit, especially for resource allocation, it is reasonable to look for links between family structures and forms of work.

Solidarity can be understood as a set of mechanisms that provide for members of society who are unable to provide for their own subsistence; that is, those who are in work and earning (excluding the unemployed)[2] provide for the economically inactive, which includes small children, schoolchildren, students, nonworking adults (the unemployed and other adults at home), and the elderly. These people cannot work because they are too young or too old, they are sick or disabled, they are studying, they cannot find a job, or they are fully occupied by their domestic responsibilities.

How do solidarity mechanisms operate and how are they financed? The answers to these questions depend on the economic and political systems. Societies with a wage economy have developed various social security institutions, a health system, and an education system that are, in principle, accessible to virtually the whole population. The history of capitalism in the West coincides with the development of solidarity institutions, from social security and protection of mothers and children to pensions (see Castel 1995). Gradually, institutions outside the family took whole categories of solidarity in hand. The state covers a large part of the costs of these institutions, but families must still pay a portion, either directly or through insurance or private institutions. In industrialized countries, solidarity is expressed through taxation and welfare contributions paid by workers, employers, and the self-employed, and it operates through systems of redistribution by the state or welfare institutions, such as mutual funds. Welfare insurance, free education, and sufficient old age pensions have become citizens' rights. As a rule, access to welfare benefits coincides with a person's past or present work or the work of another household member.

In communist countries, the state plays a greater role in these areas. In principle, citizens receive free education and complete health care coverage. In the past, Vietnam set up a completely free education and health care system even though, given the country's poverty, the quality of provision may have been inadequate. With the *Doi Moi* reforms, the state required that citizens pay an increasing contribution to costs, and private institutions, private medical practices, and private education were allowed to develop. In the span of a few years, education and health became major items in household budgets and a constant preoccupation for families. Between 1992–93 and 1997–98, although average incomes were rising quickly, spending on children's education rose even more quickly from an average of 3.8 percent of the family budget to 7.4 percent. Health expenditures were more stable, at about 4.5 percent (General Statistics Office 2000). These statistics are averages for all households, whether or not they include children of school age. Many families spend more than 20 percent of their budgets on children's education. The high cost of secondary and higher education actually caused a brief reduction in school attendance in the early 1990s (World Bank 1996).

The changes introduced under *Doi Moi* in the systems for financing education and health profoundly affect the lives and finances of families. Household costs obviously vary according to the number and ages of the children and the number of sick or elderly people unable to provide for their own needs. The presence of able-bodied adults who can take care of children and domestic tasks is another important factor. These characteristics depend on family type.

In both a family and a country, the ratio of economically active to inactive persons is a key to understanding the terms in which the question of solidarity is posed. Understanding solidarity depends on the institutions set up for that purpose, on health and education policies, and on the roles played by nonprofit organizations, churches, and other social groups. However, it is in the family that solidarity mainly operates, and it does so in different ways, depending on its structure, whether intergenerational or extended.

The ratio of economically active to inactive persons is one way of examining the question of solidarity, though solidarity cannot be reduced to this ratio. Although it is a useful indicator at the macroeconomic level and easily measurable over time and space, it does not account for some major alternatives, such as the role of migrant workers in providing for inactive family members at home.

For a household, the ratio of active to inactive members is even more simplistic. Many solidarity mechanisms reach beyond the household. For example, a couple may look after the parents of either spouse, even though they are not living with them and are not part of their household (see Barbieri, this volume). More generally, providing for household members involves many kinds of transfers. A 1996 MOLISA-ORSTROM[3] survey showed that 11 percent of total nonfarm household income was received as transfers, including retirement pensions, gifts, and money from abroad, and 18 percent was sent to nonresident family members (typically children away from home and parents) (MOLISA/ORSTROM 1998).

Though I recognize its limitations, this chapter only addresses the ratio of economically active to inactive household members as a measure of intrafamily solidarity. This ratio depends largely on the population age structure. Because periods of economic activity versus inactivity depend on age, the demographic literature defines this ratio in terms of an indicator of the population's age structure—the "dependency ratio." Generally, the economically active age bracket extends from fifteen to sixty-four years, but Vietnamese statistics take fifty-nine years as the ceiling, given that the legal retirement age is sixty.[4] The dependency ratio is the total number of people under fifteen years and over sixty (or sixty-five) years expressed as a percentage of those aged fifteen to fifty-nine (or sixty-four as the case may be).

This indicator is of particular importance in a period of demographic transition, when the population's age structure is changing rapidly. In particular, when fertility declines, the proportion of children in the population shrinks and the proportion of the economically active increases. Falling mortality rates and an extension of life expectancy to the end of the economically active period accentuates this trend to some extent.[5]

In East and Southeast Asia, where fertility rates have fallen rapidly, dependency ratios have also fallen sharply. This means that the burden of providing for children and the elderly has declined both at the national level and, on average, in families. In Vietnam, the demographic dependency ratio was stable until 1935. In the period of war and famine between 1935 and 1948, fertility dropped, leading to a decline in the proportion of the population under fifteen years old and, hence, in the dependency ratio. After 1948, increasing fertility pushed up the dependency ratio again until 1970. Since 1970, fertility has gradually declined, especially over the past twenty years, so the decrease in the dependency ratio has accelerated recently[6] (Figure 12.1).

The drop in the dependency ratio seems to have a major impact on economic growth (Bloom and Williamson 1998). It also reduces the per capita burden of education and health spending borne by the working-age population, which makes it easier to cope with this type of expenditure. It then becomes possible to extend school enrollment or prolong education, as has happened in Vietnam over the past ten years. The relative increase in the working-age population also encourages both savings and consumption, which stimulates economic growth (Williamson 1993). With fewer inactive dependents relative to each economically active person, living standards rise even if income does not. This explains why, in many East and Southeast Asian countries, living standards and infrastructure quality have risen considerably, even though family incomes remain low. A lower number of dependent persons for each wage earner and rising levels of consumption meant that low-wage policies were more readily accepted.[7] Consequently, these countries have become more attractive to foreign investors thanks to their abundant supply of cheap labor. In short, it can be said that the drop in the dependency ratio fosters a virtuous circle of growth, which the United Nations Population Fund (UNFPA) calls the "demographic window." The economic and social advantages resulting from a drop in the dependency ratio constitute a "demographic bonus" (UNFPA 2002).

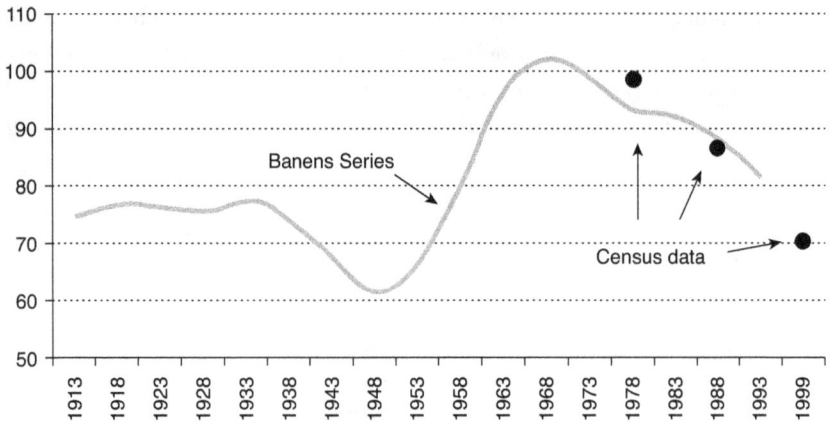

Figure 12.1   Dependency ratio: Population under 15 and over 60 per 100 persons 15 to 59, 1913–1999, Vietnam.

SOURCE: Banens series (Banens 1998); Censuses 1979–89–99 (Banister 1994; GSO 1992, 2000).

This theory is based solely on the population's age structure. It uses the working-age population as a proxy for the population that is actually working and earning an income. The basic assumption is that the rapid increase in the working-age population, as children born during the high-fertility period reach working age, is reflected in an equivalent increase in actual labor.

However, this is by no means certain. On the contrary, an abundant labor supply may result in increased unemployment and economic inactivity. Low wages can also leave large sections of the population in extreme poverty. In Vietnam, employment rates are declining as large cohorts reach working age. More years of schooling, the withdrawal of many women from the labor market, and a persistent unemployment rate of 7 percent of the active population may be signs of difficulty in managing the labor market.

A growing active population and, hence, an increasing supply of labor do not only depend on new cohorts joining the labor market and, therefore, on the previous generation's fertility, but also on changes in attitudes toward work. Institutional characteristics, such as labor demand and economic policy, also affect the volume and quality of the labor supply at a given moment, either delaying or amplifying the effects of demography. Social phenomena, such as an increase or decrease in female economic activity, increased years of schooling and urbanization, changes of behavior toward labor, money, and leisure (see Xenos et al., this volume), can have a lasting impact on the labor supply.

For these reasons, the simple ratio between age groups does not provide an accurate picture of the dependency burden. I prefer to consider a real dependency ratio by comparing the ratio of persons not actually participating in work to those who are working, in other words, the number of dependents per 100 persons with a job and an income. Given that economic activity is recorded in the available statistics only for those over twelve years of age and that the unemployed are counted as economically active, even though they are dependent on society as a whole, I define real dependency as follows:

$$\frac{\text{Population} < 13 \text{ yrs} + \text{economically inactive population}^8 + \text{unemployed}}{\text{Population in the labor force (economically active population)} - \text{unemployed}} \times 100$$

Defined in this way, the dependency ratio measures the actual burden borne by the population in the labor force in providing for the inactive population. It can be measured at the macrosocial level and at the family level. In Vietnam, the dependency ratio has fallen from 170 inactive per 100 who are working in 1977 to fewer than 100 in 2002 (Oudin 2003). The real dependency ratio depends not only on the age structure, but also on the economic, social, and even cultural conditions under which people find work. This calls for a more detailed analysis of labor supply.

LABOR SUPPLY AND FORMS OF EMPLOYMENT

The decision to work is generally not an individual decision, since it depends on the demand for income, on the number of people who need support and on the constraints of domestic tasks in the family. Therefore, it represents a compromise between individuals of working age and between working time, domestic tasks, and leisure time for each individual. However, microeconomic theory on labor supply assumes it a matter of individual preference. In choosing between economic activity and inactivity, an individual is assumed to optimize the balance between work and leisure under the constraints of available time and budget (Becker 1965). This takes place in the context of a labor market where the wages offered depend on supply and demand.

Applied in the family context, this theory requires that other factors be taken into account. The decision to work depends on the spouse's situation, domestic burdens, and many other elements. Economic theory tries to integrate these through the opportunity costs and the reserve wage. It may be an individual decision or a collective family decision, but the criteria applied— "preferences"—are not individually determined (Chiappori 1998).

Economic theory usually refers to the situation in Western countries where wage employment is the predominant form of labor. There is no compromise solution between productive labor and leisure time or time spent on domestic tasks: one either works or does not work. Although, in reality, compromises are possible in many employment situations, wage labor usually involves opportunity costs for this reason. The most common example is the matter of childcare costs when both spouses work. Although working at home (in a family business or a small shop) brings in less income than wage labor, it involves much lower opportunity costs.

Nevertheless, wage labor provides theoretically a guaranteed income (the wage), plus the social benefits granted under the national welfare policy, national collective agreements, or simply an arrangement with the employer. The security of a wage and attendant social benefits presents an advantage over self-employment because it offers better social protection. More precisely, different types of wage employment offer different guarantees. In the following paragraphs, I draw up a scale of various types of employment for Vietnam, which I then apply to the survey data.

Security of employment depends on the type of contract between employee and employer. In general, and this is also the case in Vietnam, employment in the public sector, especially the civil service, offers the best job security. Public servants cannot be dismissed, have a guaranteed wage at the end of the month, and enjoy a number of welfare benefits, including a retirement pension. Although civil service wages, pensions, and social security benefits are low, the Vietnamese generally appreciate the security. Few civil servants resign to start a new career; if they are able to work privately, they arrange to keep their civil service position and the attendant advantages.[9]

Employment in state-owned companies used to provide the same guarantees, but this changed with *Doi Moi*. These companies now have the right to dismiss workers, and welfare benefits (particularly housing) are no longer systematically granted. Moreover, many state-owned companies now employ staff under fixed-term contracts or use subcontractors. Although conditions vary (provincial companies do not provide the same advantages as national companies), a job in a state-owned company still has the advantage of providing some degree of job security. Likewise, public sector employment brings people closer to decision centers and confers an appreciable social status. This social capital can be a valuable asset in getting things done on a day-to-day basis.

Despite sophisticated labor regulations, there is little long-term job security in the private sector, though the situation differs between multinational companies and small, local firms. Security lies in the wage at the end of the month, sometimes in welfare benefits (welfare insurance in particular), but scarcely more. There is nothing to prevent an employer from dismissing workers when business slumps. Small and medium-sized firms largely ignore the labor regulations and exploit their workers at will. Danièle Bélanger and Katherine Pendakis's chapter in this volume provides some vivid examples of such exploitation of young women in the garment and textile sectors.

All wage earners, in the public and private sectors alike, have the guarantee of a wage at month's end. This is not the case for the self-employed, who constitute the majority of the active population in Vietnam. Aside from agriculture, the income from a family business is comparable to a private sector wage or higher (General Statistics Office 2000), but the income is less regular. What is important here is that the self-employed have less security, of employment and of income. Not only are they heavily dependent on the state of the business cycle, with incomes fluctuating considerably, they are also exposed to the risk of accident or illness that may endanger their income and that of their family.

In this chapter I distinguish between self-employed workers, including those working in family businesses in the production sector and small-scale trade, either well-established family shops or street and market vending. Then, I use survey data to define another category of workers with no job security, that is, casual laborers, called *lam thue*, who are hired on a daily basis with no guarantee of work the next day. They can be found everywhere in South Vietnam. They are at the bottom of the scale for both job security and income.

Thus, forms of work and family structure define the security and solidarity of the population. In most cases, participation in the wage labor sector is a collective family decision, and, leaving aside the constraints of the demand for labor in the economy, it depends on the number of dependents in the household, the number of adults already working, and the number of adults (or their time) available for domestic duties.

Family and Work

I discuss the possible relations between household structure and type of employment. First, the different types of household structure are examined, then their respective dependency ratios are considered, and, finally, correlations with the employment typology are appraised.

The main source of data is the 1996 MOLISA-ORSTROM survey. The survey was conducted among 1,950 nonfarm households, defined in Vietnam as households where the main economic activity of the head is a nonfarm activity. At the time, this concept was relatively clear, since the commune household lists included the information. The main purpose of the survey was to discern changes in the labor market following the introduction of *Doi Moi*. Only nonfarm households were included because most mobility was expected to occur either in nonfarm sectors or from the farm sector to other sectors.

The survey was carried out in twelve provinces, scattered across the country. A third of the questionnaires were administered in rural areas, with the other two-thirds in urban areas. The survey was constructed by using area sampling and then, in the selected areas, random sampling of households from the commune lists. This method excluded any household not on the lists. Such households were mainly households of "illegal" migrants which were growing in number, as people rarely applied for residence certificates at the time when the survey was conducted.[10]

HOUSEHOLD TYPOLOGY AND DEPENDENCY RATIOS

I adopted the household typology used by Bélanger (1997) and originally drawn from Laslett (1972), which centers on the notion of the family nucleus and the reconstitution of the nuclei in the household. It is a typology of households in the statistical sense, with the household defined as the residential unit. A typology based on the concept of family nucleus is particularly well suited to this topic because it is in the family nucleus, more than in the household per se, that most relations of solidarity and dependence operate. The family nucleus is the basic economic unit: a unit of income and expenditure, a unit of commensality (*an chung*).[11]

I have simplified the typology, mainly because the data (and the number of households involved) in the MOLISA-ORSTOM survey were not sufficient to establish a detailed typology. In addition, detailed family types were not necessary for my purpose. As an example, I classified all family nuclei (couples with children), with or without unrelated additional members, in the same group (that of "extended families"), regardless of the type of relationship with the additional person or persons (i.e., whether the additional individuals were biologically related to the main nucleus).

Further, I do not place too much emphasis on the notion of household head. Though Teerawichitchainan's findings in this volume suggest otherwise in a more official context, I believe that, in this survey, the person designated to the interviewer as the "household head" was often the adult most available to talk to the interviewer, so, for this study, I consider the wife to be the household head if the husband is absent. With multinuclear families, any adult couple qualifies as the main nucleus, the others being classified as secondary nuclei, depending on who is regarded as the household head. I could have constructed a formal definition to identify the "household head" using a precise criteria (for example, primarily a married adult male with unmarried children), but this did not seem necessary for my purpose, except when the family definition may otherwise have been distorted.[12] In sum, the status of the adult designated as the "household head," though sociologically significant, was not expected to influence the findings of the study.

Households with no economically active members were not included in the survey, but there are very few of them (households of elderly people). For the others, I have simplified Bélanger's typology by merging some categories to produce five household types, namely: unrelated adults without children, couples with children, lone parents with children, extended mononuclear families, and multinuclear families.

Category 1 consists of all households with adults and no children and includes one-person adult households (thirty-eight cases) as well as adults living in nonfamily households (three cases). Category 2 contains households with one couple and their children, as well as childless couples (thirty-five cases) because they form a nucleus. Category 3 is made up of lone parents and their children. Category 4 includes all families with a father and/or mother, their children and an ascendant, descendant, or lateral relative. Also included are families with one additional, but unrelated, person (nineteen cases). Category 5 covers all households with more than one nucleus. Table 12.1 displays the distribution of the survey's 1,914 households.

The nuclear family (categories 2 and 3) is predominant and represents two-thirds of the households in the survey; 12.2 percent of them are lone-parent

TABLE 12.1

Distribution of households by type and by region, 1996, Vietnam
(nonfarm households)

	North	Centre	South	Total	Number of households	Number of persons	Average size
Adults without children	3.3	4.3	4.1	3.9	75	138	1.8
Simple nuclear family	69.6	55.3	51.9	57.7	1105	4725	4.3
Lone parent with children	5.2	8.7	9.4	8.0	154	479	3.1
Extended nuclear family	15.7	24.5	28.3	23.8	456	2366	5.2
Multinuclear family	6.3	7.2	6.3	6.5	124	904	7.3
N	542	461	911	1914	1914	8612	4.5

households (8 percent of all households). These results, and the results for one-person and nonfamily households, are very similar to those reported by Bélanger from the 1992–93 Vietnam Living Standard Survey (VLSS) (Bélanger 1997).[13] However, there are significant differences for extended and multinuclear families. In the VLSS survey, only 12.7 percent of households are extended family households (extended simple nuclear family households), and 12.1 percent are multinuclear family households, compared to 23.8 and only 6.5 percent, respectively, in my study. I may have underestimated multinuclear families in this survey or not identified all additional nuclei in some households. I cannot easily reconstitute the nuclei, and I have counted only those families with at least two married couples. However, the most likely hypothesis is that multinuclear families are most frequent in farm households, which are not included in this sample.

There are marked differences between regions, particularly the North on the one hand and the Center and South on the other. In the North, the simple nuclear family clearly predominates, accounting for nearly seven cases in ten, whereas in the South, this family type represents half the total. Extended families are more frequent in the South, as are lone parents with children. There are no significant regional differences in the proportion of multinuclear families.

Family size also varies between regions. The average nuclear family in the North consists of two parents and two children. In the South, the average nuclear family has 2.5 children. The contrast is even more marked for extended families and, above all, for multinuclear families, which have, on average, eight members in the South, compared to six in the North.

These regional variations in family size and structure are similar to those found in the VLSS surveys. Next, household characteristics are examined in detail to include the employment and solidarity aspects.

DEPENDENCY RATIOS IN VIETNAM

Before examining dependency ratios by family type, it is useful to look at dependency ratios at the national level and time trends—information that this survey could not provide but that is readily available in censuses. In 1976, real dependency ratios in Vietnam were extremely high due to high fertility. The fact that many young men were in the army or disabled and many people were without work aggravated this situation. There was also considerable emigration of working-age people (the boat people). Nearly two-thirds of those aged over fifteen years were not in work, whereas, today, the proportion is one-half (Oudin 2003).

Thus, the dependent population has declined considerably in relative terms, and its composition has changed, which reflects the fundamental social changes that accompany the demographic transition. The composition of the dependent population is important because it is a direct determinant of the economic burden borne by society to fulfill the needs of young children, schoolchildren, the unemployed and the elderly. Shifts in this population between the 1989 and 1999 censuses illustrate the changes that occurred over that period (Figure 12.2).

Within the dependent population, the number of schoolchildren and students aged twelve to twenty-four years has risen quite quickly. This increase compensates for the drop in the number of small children, which is a consequence of the decline in fertility. Although Vietnamese families now have fewer children, their average dependency burden has remained the same or has even increased because, on average, children's education lasts longer. This compensation effect reflects a major change: families spend more of their resources on children's education, which has become possible even without rising incomes because there are fewer children. Quality is now stressed rather than quantity.

The proportion of economically inactive adult women in the dependent population increased between 1989 and 1999, while the proportion of inactive

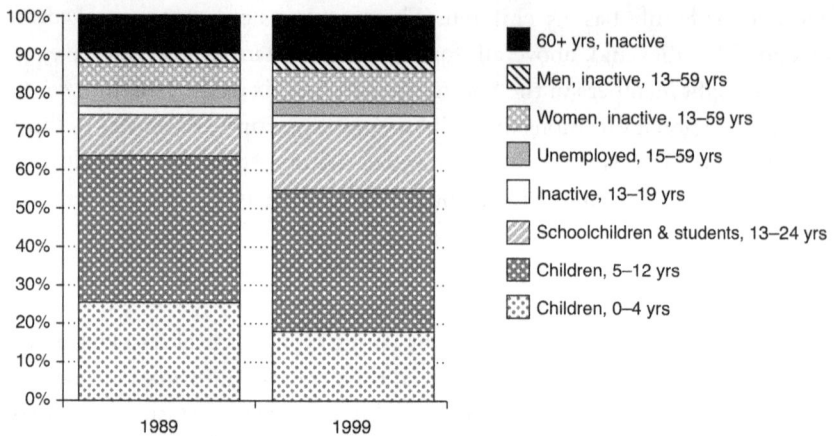

Figure 12.2   Distribution of the dependent population by age, sex, and employment status, 1989 and 1999, Vietnam.

men declined. For women, this results from a return to the home, the sign of a profound change in women's status and, probably, the value system overall (see Bélanger and Oudin 2007). The decline in women's economic activity is a mechanism of regulation of the labor supply, particularly in urban areas of Vietnam. When there are job shortages, women typically suffer more than men do; for example, employers hire men more readily for jobs suitable for either men or women. Further, some women decide to stay at home and look after the children because childcare costs are too high. This drop in women's economic activity is exceptional, because the world trend is for more women to join the workforce as fertility declines. It is true that, in the past, particularly during the American war, women's participation rates in the labor force were very high. The drop recorded since *Doi Moi* is slight, but symptomatic.

The unemployed constitute only a small proportion of dependents, which remained stable between the 1989 and the 1999 census. Although unemployment is high in some population groups, such as urban youth, there was no major change on a countrywide scale. Before 1989, unemployment was not officially recognized; those who did not have a "position" under cooperative or public sector control were characterized as being economically inactive. In reality, even before 1976 in the North and, to a significant degree, after 1976 in the South, unregulated work in the informal sector continued or increased (Oudin 2003; Vo 1992). For the Vietnamese government to admit the existence of unemployment was to acknowledge the difficulty of providing work for everyone who reached working age or had lost his or her job through public sector restructuring. Since 1989, unemployment statistics have been recorded (and become an increasingly meaningful economic indicator) in Vietnam, which clearly illustrates the change in the state's position with respect to the labor market. The state is no longer responsible, as it once was, for providing work to the population.

In household surveys, particularly the MOLISA employment survey, respondents' statements document unemployment. Those who say they have no work and are available for work are counted as "unemployed." I used the same methodology for this survey, and the results are similar to those published by the General Statistics Office.

Finally, the population over sixty years of age is still small: 7 percent of the total population in 1979 (Banister 1994) and 8 percent in 1999 (General Statistics Office 2001). Further, in 1999, a quarter of those over sixty years were working (one-third of the men, one-fifth of the women). These people were, therefore, included in the economically active population. Thus, changes in the structure of the dependent population reflect changes in the age structure of the general population due equally to the demographic transition and to socioeconomic change.

Dependency ratios are usually studied at the macrosocial level for the whole country. However, the family provides for its members' health care and children's education on a daily basis, so it is useful to examine the composition of the dependent population and the ratio of economically active to inactive members at family level. Dependency ratios do not differ greatly between family types, except in households without children. By contrast, the composition of the dependent population does vary according to family type (Figures 12.3 and 12.4).

For the entire sample, the real dependency ratio is 138 inactive persons per 100 economically active. It is significantly lower for nonfamily households, lone parents with children, and adults without children, because of the small number of dependent children. The lowest dependency rate is found in the adults without children category (41). Among lone parents with unmarried children, a significant proportion has older economically active children. Of 154 lone-parent families in the sample, 49 had economically active members other than the household head. The number of inactive children in these households was below average, resulting in a dependency ratio of 114.

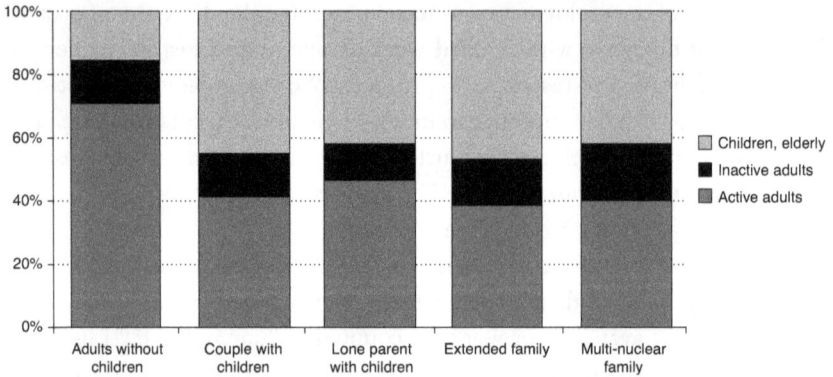

Figure 12.3 Distribution of economically active and inactive persons, by family type, 1996, Vietnam (nonfarm households).

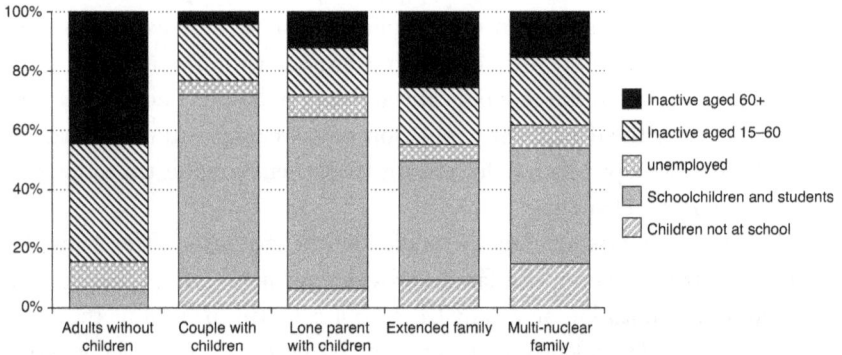

Figure 12.4 Distribution of dependent population by family type, 1996, Vietnam (nonfarm households).

Dependency ratios were highest for extended families and multinuclear families at 154 and 144, respectively.

Both simple nuclear families and lone parents with children had to provide for a particularly high proportion of children in school—two-thirds of the dependent population in these families. In addition, since I have excluded retired couples and lone elderly people from the sample, nearly all the inactive elderly people are in extended nuclear families or multinuclear families. Therefore, the prevalence of these family types provides us with a measure of family support for the elderly.

Few elderly people in Vietnam receive old-age pensions, and pensions are pitifully small.[14] Hence, family solidarity is essential, although recording the number of extended family households that include elderly people may not measure it adequately. People may make transfers to provide for elderly parents who do not live in the same household, as indicated in Barbieri's contribution to this volume.

To sum up, the family types most represented in the sample have similar dependency ratios, but different types of solidarity as expressed in the composition of their dependent populations.

ECONOMICALLY ACTIVE PERSONS PER HOUSEHOLD

The number of economically active people in the family is the prime determinant of the level of dependency ratios. Obviously, as the number of working family members increases, the burden of providing for the inactive decreases. This raises the issue of women's economic activity, especially in simple nuclear families. In nearly 40 percent of these families, there is only one economically active person in the household, and, in about the same number of cases, both spouses are economically active (Figure 12.5).

The dependency ratio is extremely sensitive to variations in the number of economically active people. In simple nuclear families with only one active person, an average of four economically inactive persons is found; in families with two active persons, there are, on average, two economically inactive people; and in families with four or more active persons, there is only one economically inactive person. In extended and multinuclear families, dependency ratios are even higher for families with few economically active members, but these represent a very small proportion of the sample.

Although the composition of the dependent population differs according to family type, the most sharply distinguishing factor for dependency ratios is the number of economically active family members, rather than the family type. Age characteristics are clearly relevant as families with young children are disadvantaged when compared with families with working-age children.

The ratio of economically inactive persons to active persons is an imperfect indicator of the dependency burden supported by families. In some families, the presence of only one economically active member (usually the father) tends to reflect a relatively good standard of living, with a high salary and a spouse who is not seeking paid work. Conversely, the fact that many household members are economically active and contribute to the household income may be a sign of poverty, where each of them is earning barely enough.

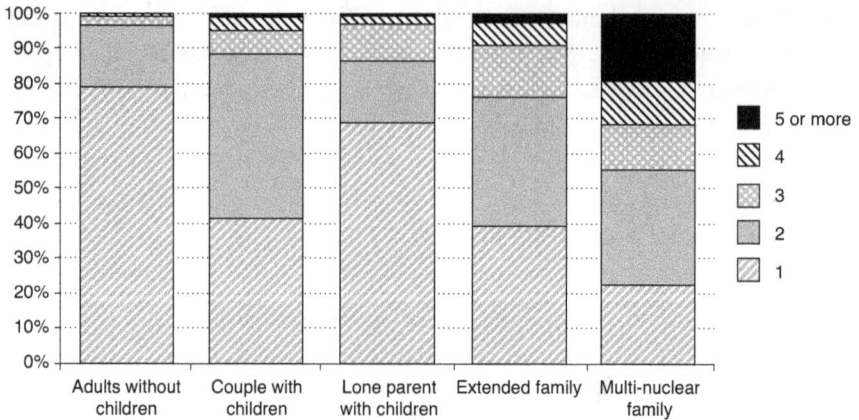

Figure 12.5 Distribution of economically active persons by family type, 1996, Vietnam (nonfarm households).

HOUSEHOLD INCOME AND DEPENDENCY BURDEN

We can check these hypotheses by considering household income by the ratio of active members to the number of dependents. In this way, we can calculate both income per active person and income per household member. Although I took care in this survey to consider all possible sources of income, including transfers, and to enumerate expenditures accurately, it is difficult to assess income in Vietnam. Nominal wages are paltry, and most income from work consists of bonuses or illicit payments. It is equally difficult to estimate self-employed workers' incomes, as most of them keep no accounts and make no distinction between personal and professional expenditure. Where it was not possible to estimate a household's income, I focused on expenditures and assumed that the theoretical income level is at least equal to expenditure (other than exceptional expenses). Despite the two-pronged approach, estimations of income are uncertain.

For all households, three types of income can be distinguished: wages (including bonuses), business income (all income from the sale of goods or services produced or sold by self-employed workers or those working in the family business), and other income (including transfers).

The average monthly household income in my sample is 1.9 million dongs.[15] It varies with the household type. Variation is smaller if we consider per capita income. More importantly, there is a reversal of hierarchical order. Households consisting entirely of adults have the lowest total income, but the highest per capita income, while in multinuclear families, per capita

TABLE 12.2

Average monthly income (thousands of dongs) by family type, 1996, Vietnam (nonfarm households)

	Adult without children	Couple with children	Lone parent with children	Extended family	Multi-nuclear family	Total
Total income	1124	1910	1276	2059	2478	1890
Per capita income	594	439	410	401	346	420

income is lower and dependency ratios are high. A few adults who can earn high incomes provide for parents or collaterals, as well as for their own children. Other extended families have a high number of economically active members (hence a low dependency ratio), but the active members' average incomes are low. In both cases, living in the same household reflects solidarity reaching beyond the family nucleus. (Table 12.2)

Despite a close correlation between the two, family size was more significant than family type when considering income. One-person households consisting of one economically active person were a rare exception, and these people had very high income on average. Two-person households had an average income of 500,000 dongs for one economically active person and 640,000 for two, indicating that the marginal income brought in by the second active household member is fairly low. This finding applies to all families. In families of four to five people, which amounted to half the sample, the monthly income of a primary economically active member was 1.6 million dongs, and the income provided by each additional active member was, on average, only 300,000 dongs (Figure 12.6). Therefore, we can assume that the need to supplement the income of the family's first economically active member determines the spouse's decision to work. When one income is sufficient, spouses prefer to stay at home and look after children. The hypothesis that the number of active members increases to make up for the lack of an adequate income appears to be validated.

This finding sheds a different light, expressing dependency ratios as the ratio of active to inactive people in the family. Average per capita income differs less between family types than do dependency ratios. This finding also sheds an interesting (though not new) light on the working-age household members' decision to work for pay or not. It suggests that the drop in economic activity among women in urban areas and the increase in the duration of schooling results from the increase in the average family income.

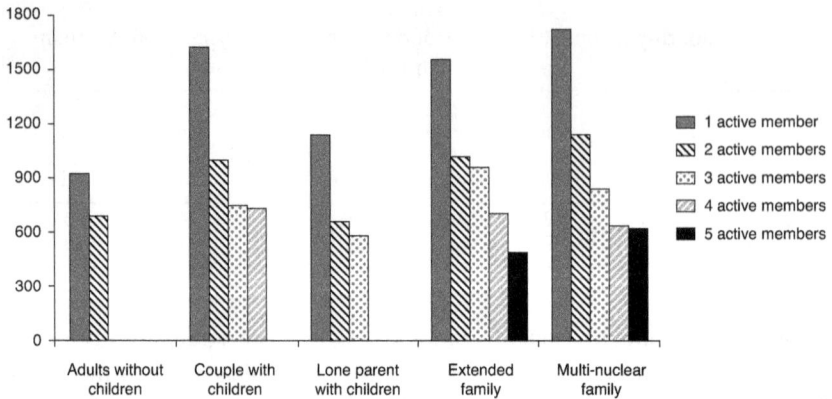

Figure 12.6   Average per capita income (thousands of dongs per month) by family type and number of economically active persons in the family, 1996, Vietnam (nonfarm households).

TYPES OF EMPLOYMENT AND TYPES OF HOUSEHOLD

Household strategies, regarding employment, vary according to the family members' situations and income level, and they probably do not operate in the same way for all family types.[16] Next, I consider the nature of employment in the survey families and attempt to identify a correlation between employment and family type.

As described earlier, the categories for employment are civil servant, state-owned company employee, private enterprise employee, self-employed worker (in a family enterprise), small-scale trade, and day laborer. We may assume that, in general, these categories can be ranked in this order in terms of job security, with civil servants at the top of the list.

The distribution of economically active persons, by type of employment and family structure, is moderately heterogeneous (Figure 12.7). Nuclear families are characterized by the highest proportion of civil servants and public sector employees, with one-third of economically active persons in these families working in those sectors. However, the corresponding figures for other family types, that is, between 20 and 30 percent, are quite similar.

Private sector employment is more common among extended families, primarily due to the higher frequency of such families in the South where more people work in the private sector. Nearly 40 percent of economically active persons in lone-parent families or families without children work in

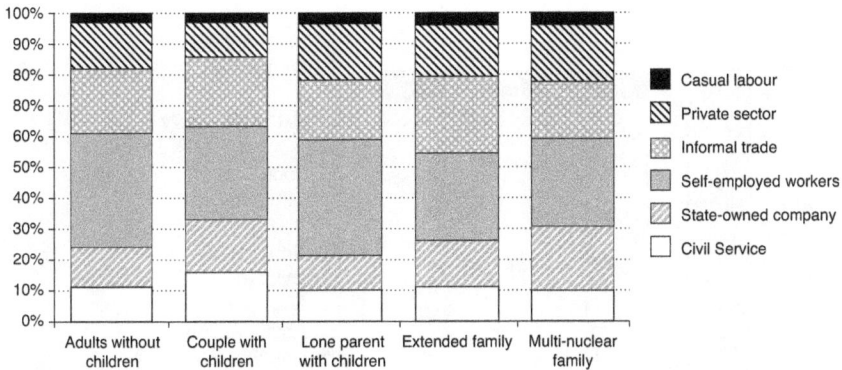

Figure 12.7 Distribution of forms of work by family type, 1996, Vietnam (non-farm households).

the informal trade sector. However, this proportion is also high (30 percent) in other family types.

Although there are differences in the pattern of work according to family type, overall, it does not seem possible to link family structure, as such, with the type of employment, waged or otherwise. Regional variations help explain some of the differences. In the North, half of all economically active members in nuclear families work in the public sector, compared to one-third in other family types, while in nuclear families in the Center and South, the proportion is one-quarter. In the North, three-quarters of civil servants live in nuclear families, compared to a little over half in the South (Figure 12.8).

The only significant factor that links type of work and family structure is found in the North: it is the breakdown of civil servants and, to a lesser extent, state-owned company employees by family type. Civil servants are more likely to live in nuclear families. This trend is strengthened by the fact that there are many nuclear families in which both partners are state employees, and very few such couples in other family types. In nuclear families, almost 44 percent of male household heads who work for the state have a wife who also works for the state, while the proportion is only 3.5 percent in other family types.

The question that arises is whether this is a legacy from the communist period, when government policy encouraged social homogamy (see Bélanger and Khuat 1996), or whether it is a new trend. I am inclined to think it is a legacy from communism, but do not have the retrospective data to check this hypothesis.

North

Multi-nuclear family

Extended family

Lone parent with children

Couple with children

Adults without children

South

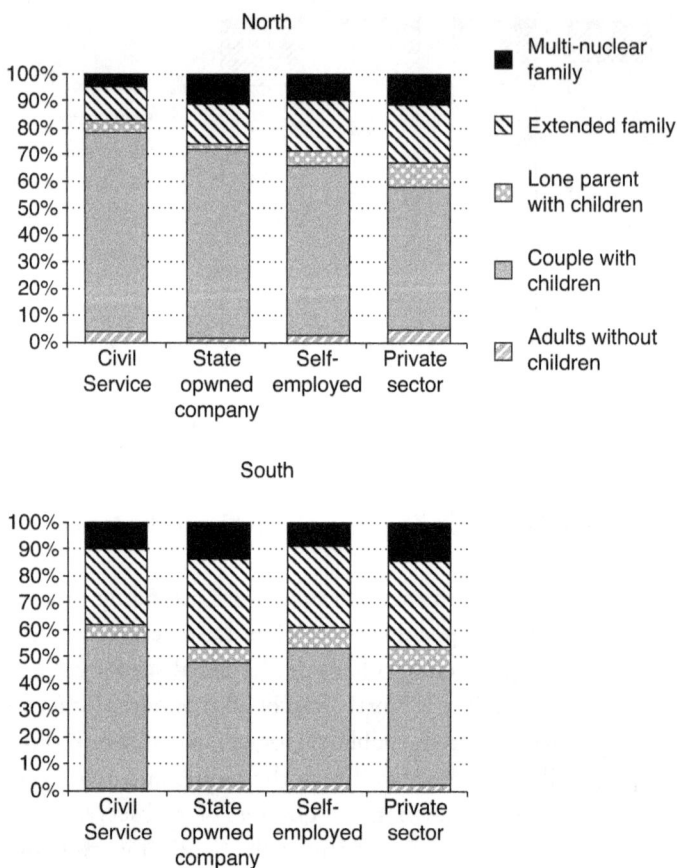

Figure 12.8 Distribution of family types by forms of work and region, 1996, Vietnam (nonfarm households).

Conclusion

Overall, the hypothesis of a link between the form of employment and family structure does not seem to be valid for modern-day Vietnam, although there are some connections. The wage-earning family has only really developed among civil servants in the North and does not yet exist on a large scale in Vietnam.

Several factors may explain this. First, *Doi Moi* is a process of state withdrawal from the labor market (and from the domestic sphere to some extent) that has resulted in the rapid expansion of nonwage labor. This process, though successful in terms of its consequences for economic growth, runs counter to the trends currently found in many countries, including industrialized ones. Quite clearly, there has been a reduction in "protected" employment, for example secure tenure with welfare benefits and guarantees on working conditions and wages. The same applies to the state solidarity system. As a result, the Vietnamese have seen their living standards rise considerably over the past fifteen years, but economic insecurity has also increased. The quality of health and education services has undoubtedly improved, but both are now costly. Today, the Vietnamese experience the fear that an illness could lead to increased expenses, job loss, and financial difficulties, which might prevent them from sending their children to an expensive school. In contrast, twenty years ago they were primarily concerned about providing enough food for family and other close relatives.[17]

This certainly encourages people to reinforce family ties, but the development of new, or the revival of old, forms of mutual aid does not necessarily have an impact on family structure. These changes can occur without altering the basis of the family institution in any fundamental way. Although the economy is undergoing rapid transformation, we cannot expect to see long-established family structures adapt to forms of work, which, for their part, are highly volatile, over such a short period of time. The complexity of the social changes currently under way in Vietnam is a warning against an overlinear, evolutionist view of history.

Vietnam is not the only country where the solidarity structures set up by the state are crumbling. With the current process of globalization and the introduction of free market policies, there has been a cutback in many national solidarity systems (see Bélanger and Barbieri's chapter, this volume). The same is happening with forms of employment. Under so-called "flexibility" policies, employment security has declined, even in Western countries. In Vietnam, this process is a direct consequence of the country's integration into the global economy. Competition among Southeast Asian countries to attract foreign investment puts pressure on labor costs and flexibility. By reducing welfare benefits and allowing unprotected labor to proliferate, the Vietnamese government is only following a virtually universal trend, which is affecting industrialized countries as well. It is therefore possible that Vietnam is simply going through the same changes as those affecting the world as a whole. The question of how these changes will affect families over the long run remains to be answered.

Notes

1. The statistical data are drawn from a series established by the author based on General Statistics Office yearbooks.

2. Although ILO statistics include the unemployed in the economically active population, in this study we include them among the economically inactive, since they depend on the solidarity of institutions or other individuals for their survival.

3. ORSTOM (now IRD, *Institut de recherche pour le développement*) is a French Government institute for research in and with developing countries. MOLISA is the Vietnamese Ministry of Labor, Invalids and Social Affairs, commonly referred to by the English abbreviation MOLISA.

4. The legal age for retirement is sixty for men and fifty-five for women. This provision of the labor code applies only to workers in the public sector, who represent less than 20 percent of the total labor force.

5. Conversely, the rise in life expectancy and the drop in mortality beyond age sixty increase the number of elderly and push up the dependency ratio.

6. The fertility decline, changes in the age structure, and life expectancy increase in Vietnam are detailed in Catherine Scornet's and Magali Barbieri's chapters in this volume.

7. This also explains the spectacular increase in savings in East and Southeast Asian countries.

8. Schoolchildren, students, homemakers, the disabled, retirees, and others aged thirteen and over.

9. In the early 1990s, redundancies from the public sector were voluntary. Early retirement or redundancy payments were offered. At the time, salaries were so low that many workers preferred to set up on their own account.

10. (MOLISA/ORSTOM, 1998). For the purpose of this study, we made original (unpublished) analyses of the data.

11. For a detailed discussion of the family as approached by household level data, see Haines 2006, chapter 2.

12. For example, a family consisting of two parents of working age and unmarried children, with the eldest in employment and identified as the household head, constitutes a nuclear family, but the fact that the household head is one of the children and, therefore, reports both ascendant and lateral relatives may result in inaccurately classifying the family. Such cases are fortunately rare.

13. The VLSSs were jointly conducted by the Vietnamese General Statistics Office and the World Bank, first in 1992–93 and again in 1997–98. These panel surveys provide the most useful basic data on household structure, consumption, and expenditure over that period (General Statistics Office 2001; General Statistics Office State Planning Committee 1994). See Barbieri's chapter in this volume

for more details on the VLSSs and their usefulness in documenting family structure and organization.

14. The Vietnamese press often mentions the difficult situation of army veterans ending their days in extreme poverty.

15. At the time of the survey (1996), the exchange rate was 12,000 dongs to US$1.

16. See Hy Van Luong's chapter in this volume for more analyses on employment and migration by family type.

17. Sélim (2003) addresses anxiety about illness and other setbacks in greater depth.

References

Banens, M. (1998). Estimating population and labour force in Vietnam under French rule (1900–1954). Asian Historical Statistics Project (AHSTAT-COE Project), Vietnam 1895–1954 Research Group (VN98-2), Paul Valéry University, Montpellier. http://www.ier.hit-u.ac.jp/COE/Japanese/discussionpapers/DP98.7/Append2.htm

Banister, J. 1994. *Vietnam population dynamics and prospects.* Berkeley: Institute of East Asian Studies, University of California.

Becker, G. 1965. A theory of the allocation of time. *Economic Journal,* 75: 493–517.

Bélanger, D. 1997. *Rapport intergénérationnel et rapport hommes-femmes dans la transition démographique au Vietnam, de 1930 à 1990.* Doctoral thesis, Department of Demography, University of Montréal.

Bélanger, D., and Khuat T. H. 1996. Marriage and the family in urban North Vietnam, 1965–1993. *Journal of Population,* 2–1: 83–112.

Bélanger, D., and X. Oudin. 2007. For better or worse? Working and mothering in late Vietnamese socialism. In *Working mothers of Asia,* edited by T. Devashayam and B. Yeoh, 106–110. Singapore: Singapore University Press.

Bloom, D., and J. Williamson. 1998. Demographic transitions and economic miracles in emerging Asia. *The World Bank Economic Review,* 12(3): 419–445.

Castel R. 1995. *Les métamorphoses de la question sociale. Une chronique du salariat.* Paris: Fayard.

Chiappori, P. A. 1998. Rational household labour supply. *Econometrica,* 56(1): 63–89.

General Statistics Office. 1992. *Vietnam population census—1989. Completed census results.* Hanoi: Statistical Publishing House.

General Statistics Office. 2000. *Viet Nam living standards survey 1997–1998.* Hanoi: Statistical Publishing House.

General Statistics Office. 2001. *Population and housing census Vietnam 1999, Completed census results.* Hanoi: Statistical Publishing House.

General Statistics Office State Planning Committee. 1994. *Viet Nam living standards survey 1992–1993*. Hanoi: Statistical Publishing House.

Haines, D. 2006. *The limits of kinship: South Vietnamese households 1954–1975*. De Kalb: Southeast Asia Publications, Northern Illinois University.

Laslett, P. 1972. La famille et le ménage: Approches historiques. *Annales Economie, Sociétés, Civilisations*, 4(5): 847–872.

MOLISA/ORSTOM. 1998. *Observatory system of employment and human resources, Vietnam: Report on the first round survey, 1996*. Hanoi: MOLISA.

Oudin, X. 2003. La mobilisation de la main-d'œuvre au Vietnam. In *La mobilisation de la main-d'œuvre*, edited by S. Michel and X. Oudin, 69–94. Collection "Travail et Mondialisation." Paris: L'Harmattan.

Sélim, M. 2003. *Pouvoirs et marché au Vietnam*. Paris: L'Harmattan.

UNFPA. 2002. *Population report 2002. People, poverty and possibilities*. New York: UNFPA.

Vo Nhan Tri. 1992. *Vietnam's economic policy since 1975*. Singapore: Institute of Southeast Asian Studies.

Williamson, J. G. 1993. Human capital deepening, inequality, and demographic events along the Asia-Pacific Rim. In *Human resources in development along the Asia-Pacific Rim*, edited by N. Ogawa, G. W. Jones, and J. G. Williamson, 129–158. Singapore: Oxford University Press.

World Bank. 1996. *Vietnam education financing sector study*. Report No.15925-VN. Washington: The World Bank.

Chapter Thirteen

Rural-to-Urban Migration in Vietnam
A Tale of Three Regions

HY VAN LUONG

A major question in the study of Vietnamese households and kinship involves the extent to which they are male centered (patrilineal, patrilocal,
and patriarchal), presumably under Chinese influence, and the degree to
which they vary across different regions and over time (Haines 1984; Hickey
1958; Hirschman and Nguyen 2002; Hirschman and Vu 1996; Luong 1989;
Nguyen 1998). Analyses of regional variations have focused on the Red River
Delta in the North and the Mekong Delta in the South, and on the dominant
thesis that southern households and kinship systems are less male centered
than northern ones.

Based on survey and interview data in five Vietnamese rural communities
in 2000, this chapter examines the variation in Vietnamese household structure in the three main regions of the Vietnamese lowlands, as well as spatial
and temporal variations in the community-mediated process of household
formation. My data indicate that the variation in household structure in the
Doi Moi era is insignificant across three main regions of the Vietnamese lowlands. However, as mediated by community structure and interhousehold
networks, more specifically by the stronger centripetal forces of local communities in the North and the Center than in the South, household structure
and postmarital residence pattern relate fairly systematically to the migration in and out of the studied communities in different regions of Vietnam.
I would suggest that studies of migration would be considerably enriched by
greater attention to local sociocultural dynamics.

Background on Five Studied Rural Communities

The two studied communities in the Mekong Delta of the South are both located in the district of Can Duoc, Long An province, and situated at about 30 kilometers from downtown Ho Chi Minh City. The studied community in the North, in the province of Bac Ninh, is similarly located at about 30 kilometers from downtown Hanoi. The two central Vietnamese communities, both in the coastal district of Son Tinh in Quang Ngai province, are situated at about 20 kilometers from the provincial capital, about 800 kilometers north of Ho Chi Minh City, and about 1,000 kilometers south of Hanoi.[1] Long An and Quang Ngai were chosen because they sent the largest number of migrants to Ho Chi Minh City from the Mekong Delta and Central Vietnam in the 1994–99 period, according to a block-by-block census of migrants in three sites in Ho Chi Minh City in 1999 and the 1999 national census (Population and Housing Census Steering Committee 2000).[2] One commune in Long An and another in Quang Ngai were chosen from a list of communes sending the largest number of migrants to those three sites. In addition, another commune in the same district as the major migrant-sending commune represents a wider spectrum of communities in prospective sending areas (see Luong 2005 and Nguyen et al. 2005). I have added the northern village, from an earlier study of mine from the early 1990s on sociocultural transformation in rural Vietnam, to my analysis in this chapter for three reasons:

1.   It has sent a good number of migrants to Hanoi.
2.   It is located at about the same distance to Hanoi as the two communities in Long An province are to Ho Chi Minh City.
3.   It was studied with the same research instruments at about the same time as the four communities in Long An and Quang Ngai.

The research in all five communities in 2000 relied on both survey and interview methods. In the village in the North, the survey on socioeconomic conditions at the household level was conducted in all of its 208 households due to the small village population (955). In the four remaining communities in the Center and the South, the survey consisted of a random probability sample of 150 households in each. The household survey was complemented by in-depth interviews with 35 households in each village and with

72 migrants from the surveyed households in Long An and Quang Ngai who could be found in Ho Chi Minh City.[3]

The following analysis of household formation and migration in three main regions of Vietnam relies mainly on survey data. The first question under focus is whether northern rural households and, to a lesser extent, central Vietnamese ones, tend to be more male centered than their southern counterparts. In an earlier work, I have suggested that household formation in Vietnam is embedded in the general principles of Vietnamese kinship and that Vietnamese kinship is underlain by the structural opposition between a male-oriented model and a non-male-oriented one. In the former, descent is traced through men (patrilineal); postmarital residence is with the husband's parents (patrilocal); and authority is vested in men (patriarchical). The male-oriented model emphasizes the male-centered continuity of the family, to which polygyny potentially contributes. In the pre-1954 period, among Confucian elite, the ideal household is a patrilineally joint or extended household with many generations under one roof. It has been hypothesized that northern Vietnamese kinship and household are more strongly male oriented, partly under Confucian influence, than southern ones (Hickey 1958; see Do 1991). In the *Doi Moi* era, it is in northern Vietnam and many parts of central Vietnam that patrilineages have been revitalized. In their analysis of longitudinal data from thirteen localities in the Ha Nam Ninh region of the Red River Delta in northern Vietnam, Hirschman and Nguyen Huu Minh have also discovered that the percentage of men residing with parents after marriage increased steadily from 71.5 percent among those married in the 1956–65 period to 83.4 percent among those getting married from 1986 to 1995; and that the percentage of women residing with husbands' parents after marriage similarly increased from 70.5 percent among those married in 1956–65 to 80.5 percent among those married in 1986–95 (Hirschman and Nguyen 2002, 1067; Nguyen 1998, 223). In examining the hypothesis on the stronger male orientation in the North and possibly the Center than in the South, I focus not on authority relations within the household, but on household form and postmarital residence pattern. In the context of the significant increase in spontaneous migration in the *Doi Moi* period, I also examine whether and how household structure and postmarital residence pattern might relate to the migration flows in different regions of Vietnam. In the following analysis, I consider as a migrant any long-term resident of a studied community who has lived outside his or her commune/village for at least one month, except for hospitalization and being drafted into the armed forces. I conduct the analysis of the relation of household structure and postmarital residence pattern to migration with the hypothesis that this relation is mediated by community dynamics, specifically by stronger centripetal community forces in the rural North and Center than in the rural South of Vietnam. These forces are reflected in intracommunity mutual assistance and villagers' preference for community endogamy, which is closely intertwined with their social networks within and beyond their community.

The relation between household structure and migration is also examined through a multiple-regression analysis in which the dependent variable is the number of migrants from each household, and in which household structure is only one of the numerous independent variables (Table 13.1). The dependent variable is the number of migrants from each household (from 0 to 4) in the six months preceding the survey in 2000, including migrations for reasons of marriage and family reunions but excluding hospitalizations elsewhere and the involuntary departures into armed services. Migrations before 2000 are excluded from the analysis because of missing information on some major independent variables. For example, although migrants' individual characteristics at the time of migration are known, household conditions (demographic composition and particularly household wealth, household debts, and amount of land per capita) as well as many of the nonmigrants' individual characteristics (for example, level of education) could not be reliably reconstructed for each of the years in the 1986–99 period. In contrast, we have good data on household income, land ownership, and debt levels for 2000 as prospective migrants faced the decisions whether to migrate or not. In my statistical analyses, I only include villagers above the age of fifteen. I hypothesize that migration decisions may be influenced by the following factors at the household level: the number of household members migrating before the year 2000 and household members' social networks in the possible destination areas;[4] household structure and the dependent care burden (number of young children below the age of eleven and elderly at the age of seventy-five or above);[5] cultivable land per capita, household income per capita, transfers (from other households) and remittances (from household members away from home) received per capita, and the level of household debts. However, in the larger sample of 600 households in Long An and Quang Ngai, due to the time-consuming nature of detailed network data collection, network data are available only for households with migrants and

TABLE 13.1

Five sending communities: Basic demographic and economic information

| Community | Entire community | | Surveyed households in each community in 2000 | | | |
	Cultivated acreage (hectare)	Population (1999)	Population	Population in residence*	Migrants*	Per capita income (000d)
Northern						
Bac Ninh	44	955	955	895	60	2,481
Central						1,514
Quang Ngai 1	404	6,435	712	661	51	1,628
Quang Ngai 2	947	11,206	740	655	85	1,409
Southern						2,649
Long An 1	1,159	11,036	721	633	88	2,488
Long An 2	934	8,037	736	626	110	2,838

*in whole-year equivalent (a five-person household with two members migrating for half a year each is considered to have the equivalent of four whole-year residents and one whole-year migrant).

not for others.[6] This variable of social networks was dropped from multiple-regression analyses, although it is examined through a qualitative analysis of interview data.

At the time of research in 2000, the two southern communes and the northern village, being close respectively to Ho Chi Minh City and Hanoi, enjoyed higher per capita incomes than those in the center of the country.

The economies of all five studied communities had become strongly diversified from their agricultural bases. In the two Long An communities and the Bac Ninh village, given their proximity to major urban centers, non-agricultural earnings amounted to at least 140 percent of agricultural incomes (Table 13.2). In Quang Ngai 1 commune, with its strong metal casting tradition and its metal products distributed throughout the southern part of Vietnam, nonagricultural earnings remained more significant than agricultural incomes. Only in the second Quang Ngai field site, a community without a strong handicraft and commerce tradition, did agricultural incomes exceed nonagricultural ones among the study households.

Cashing in on its century-old fame for rice and rice wine, many residents of the first southern commune (Long An 1) engaged in trading these well-known local products. Almost half of its sampled residents with significant nonagricultural incomes derived their earnings from commerce. With its fame in straw-mat production, the second southern commune (Long An 2)

TABLE 13.2
Annual income sources of all households (in million dongs)

	Agriculture (net)	Non-agriculture	Government assistance	Transfers from other households	Remittances from the household's migrants	Total income in million dongs
Northern						
Bac Ninh	38%	56%	0.1%	1%	5%	2226
Central						
Quang Ngai 1	41%	48%	1%	1%	8%	1075
Quang Ngai 2	43%	33%	2%	1%	21%	923
Southern						
Long An 1	27%	52%	0.0%	8%	13%	1575
Long An 2	30%	54%	0.3%	6%	9%	1777

had two medium-size straw mat factories, employing 116 workers in 2000. They exported their products to Eastern Europe in the 1980s and to South Korea since then. This southern commune (Long An 2) also had many small workshops serving local and district economies: nine rice mills, ten flour-producing workshops, eight alcohol-distilling households, five wood factories, and forty motorcycle and bicycle-repair shops. While the studied northern village did not have any major handicraft tradition, many of its villagers commuted to Hanoi for the alcohol and hog trade: this number had increased from about 80 in 1990 to 141 a decade later. Forty-five villagers also commuted to urban and surrounding rural areas in Bac Ninh province (north of Hanoi) to work as construction workers. The first studied central commune (Quang Ngai 1) is well known for its foundries, whose main products are knives, scissors, and plows, among others. Its sixty-five foundries employed about 330 workers in 2000. A small number of workers were also employed in the commune's nineteen rice mills, nine wood-processing workshops, and three brick kilns. The second central commune (Quang Ngai 2), alone among the five studied communities, had no special trades or handicrafts, leading to the lowest percentage of nonagricultural income and the lowest number of villagers with primarily nonagricultural occupations (Table 13.2).

The five studied communities in the three lowland regions of Vietnam differed not only in wealth but also in their centripetal forces, measured in terms of intracommunity mutual assistance and villagers' preference for community endogamy/exogamy which is closely intertwined with their social networks within and beyond their community. It has long been observed that southern communities, especially in the Mekong Delta, have physically and socially more open landscapes and lesser centripetal forces than northern and central ones.

In terms of the physical landscape, human settlements in the two southern communes (Long An 1 and 2) were strung along the main roads, while that in the northern village in Bac Ninh province were highly nucleated; those in the first Quang Ngai commune were strongly clustered near the Tra Khuc River; and those in the second Quang Ngai commune had a few major clusters. They reflect the more open landscape of the relatively flat Mekong Delta, and the more nucleated settlement pattern in northern and central coastal Vietnamese villages. The differences in residential settlements also relate to the social landscapes of the five villages: northern and central coastal villages were more centripetal, with more tightly knit social and kinship networks within the villages and more intracommunity mutual assistance. Northern and central Vietnamese communities, respectively in Bac Ninh and Quang Ngai, had higher rates of village endogamy than the studied southern villages in Long An (to be further discussed). Patrilineages also played an important role in the social lives of Bac Ninh and Quang Ngai villagers, while they were seldom found in the Mekong Delta. The stronger mutual assistance is reflected in credit sources of sampled central and northern villagers. Twenty-eight percent of the credit amounts received by northern households and 41 to 57 percent of that received by central coastal households took the form of interest-free loans, while the percentage is only 12 to 17 percent in the two studied southern villages (Table 13.3).

Household Structure and Household Formation Process

The household is defined here as a residential unit with significant budgetary sharing. A household includes the migrants who are still considered an integral part of the unit by other members and who normally contribute to the household budget through remittances. Clusters of close relatives in the same house who eat separately and who have different budgets are considered in my analysis to have formed separate households. Most households with only one person each involve a co-residence of this person with other close relatives under the same roof or in the same housing compound.

TABLE 13.3
Credit (in thousand dongs)

	Outstanding loans		
	Interest-free	With interest	Total (thousands of dongs)
Northern			
Bac Ninh	28%	72%	405,348
Central			
Quang Ngai 1	41%	59%	229,346
Quang Ngai 2	57%	43%	185,070
Southern			
Long An 1	12%	88%	289,380
Long An 2	17%	83%	472,035

TABLE 13.4
Percent distribution of households by structure
in five studied sites in three regions (%)

	North	Central	South
No nuclear family base	3.4	5.3	3.0
Single alone	2.9	4.3	2.3
With other relatives	0.5	1.0	0.7
Nuclear family	69.0	64.0	62.7
Husband & wife	5.4	2.3	3.0
Husband, wife & children	56.1	50.7	52.7
Disintegrated-male headed	0.5	0.7	0.7
Disintegrated-female headed	7.3	10.3	6.3
Extended family	10.0	17.0	17.0
Joint family	17.6	13.6	17.3
All	100.0	100.0	100.0
Number of households	208	300	300

Despite variations in wealth, there were little regional differences among the studied communities in the three regions in the distribution of household forms or in postmarital residence pattern. Of the households in the studied sites, 60 to 70 percent in each region are nuclear families, while 28 to 34 percent are extended or joint families (Table 13.4).[7] The slightly higher percent-

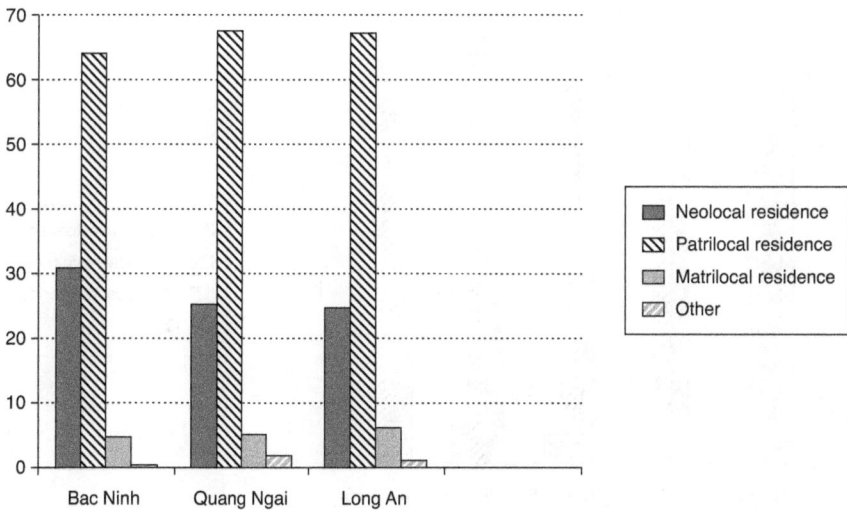

Figure 13.1   Postmarital residence pattern in three regions (percent of total cases in each region).

age of nuclear family households in the studied northern village than in the central and southern ones is in the same direction as Bélanger's findings on the basis of the 1992–93 Vietnam Living Standard Survey data: the percentages of nuclear, extended, and joint family households were 75 percent, 11 percent, and 7 percent, respectively, in the Red River Delta; 64 percent, 15 percent, and 14 percent, respectively, in the South Central Coast (including Quang Ngai province); and 63 percent, 14 percent, and 15 percent, respectively, in the Mekong Delta (Bélanger 1997, 98).[8] It remains an open question why the Red River Delta in the North had a higher percentage of nuclear families and a lower percentage of extended/jointed families than the South Central Coast or the Mekong Delta in the South.[9]

Similarly, although the postmarital residence pattern in the Mekong Delta of southern Vietnam has been hypothesized to be less male centered, there was no significant difference in the aggregate in the postmarital residential pattern among the three regions (Figure 13.1). Approximately two-thirds of the couples in all three regions lived for a period with the husbands' parents upon marriage; and between 25 to 30 percent established their own households at the time of marriage.[10] However, many young married couples lived with the husbands' parents only for a few years before establishing their own

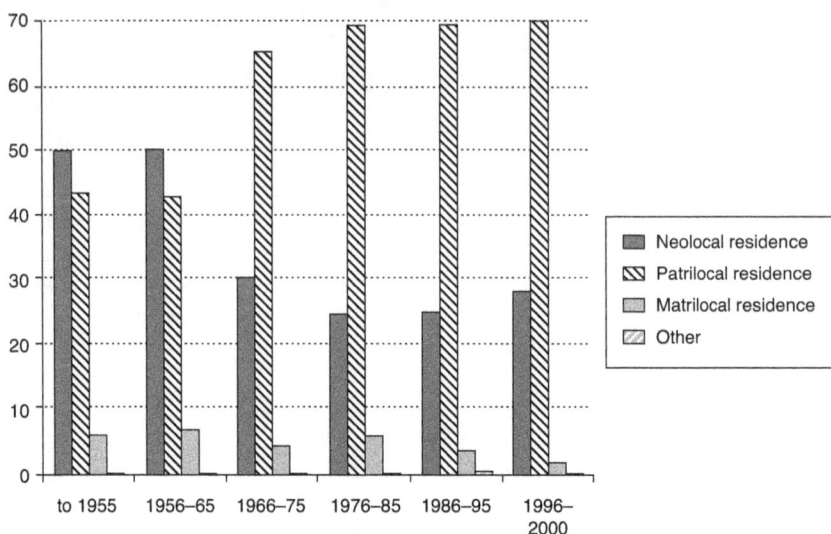

Figure 13.2   Postmarital residence pattern in the northern village (*Bac Ninh* province) over time.

households, leading to a relatively high percentage of nuclear family households (63 to 69 percent) in all three regions.

From a diachronic perspective, in the northern village of Bac Ninh province, the proportion of couples adopting a patrilocal residence actually increased from 40 percent before 1966 to 65 to 70 percent in the following thirty-five years (cf. Hirschman and Nguyen 2002, 1067). The proportion of couples establishing their own households upon marriage dropped from 50 percent before 1966 to 25 to 30 percent in 1966–2000. In the 1966–2000 period, in the studied northern village, there are no significant differences before and after *Doi Moi* (1986) (Figure 13.2; cf. Nguyen 1998, 176–235). In the central province of Quang Ngai and the southern one of Long An, within the 1966–2000 period, the percentage of couples choosing a matrilocal residence increased at the expense of those with a neolocal residence (Figures 13.3 and 13.4). Whether this phenomenon reflects the declining birthrate and the lack of sons or their migration in Quang Ngai and Long An, leading to a pragmatic acceptance of matrilocal residence by sons-in-law, remains an open question (see Barbieri's chapter, this volume).

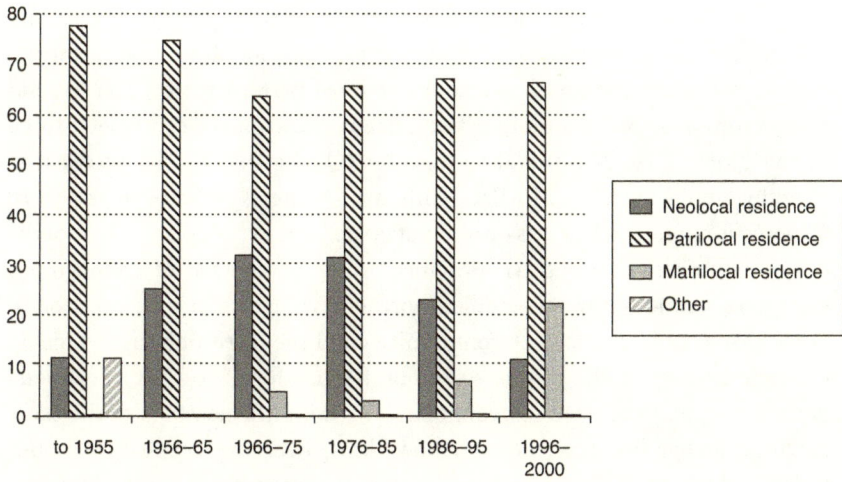

Figure 13.3   Postmarital residence pattern in two central Vietnamese communes over time.

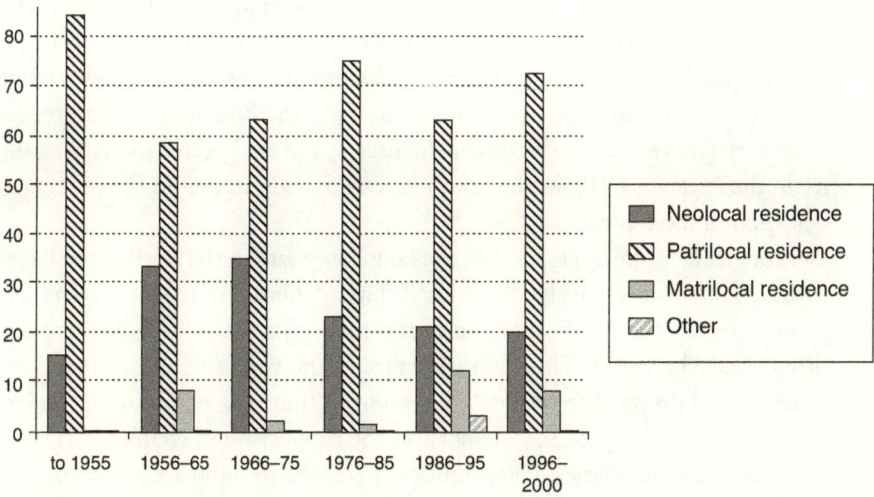

Figure 13.4   Postmarital residence pattern in two southern Vietnamese communes over time.

If household structure and the household formation process as partially reflected in the postmarital residence pattern do not show significant regional variations, the interhousehold relational pattern within and beyond each community reflects more systematically the stronger centripetal force in the North (Bac Ninh) and the Center (Quang Ngai). The proportion of endogamous marriages in Bac Ninh and Quang Ngai were in the 50 to 65 percent range, while it was only about 40 percent in the two studied southern communities in Long An province.[11] The percentage of endogamous marriages was lower in the studied northern village than in central ones. Some residents in the former community cited the intricately tight kinship network in a small village due to the preference for endogamy over many generations, and the need to avoid marrying not only members of the same patrilineage but also many nonpatrilineal kin. Given the fact that the population of each studied community in central Vietnam was 6.5 to 11 times bigger than that in the northern village under focus, it was more feasible to marry within the community in either Quang Ngai commune *and* to avoid marrying patrilineal kin and many nonpatrilineal ones. The percentage of couples born entirely outside the studied communities exceeded 10 percent in Long An, while it is insignificant in Quang Ngai and nonexistent in Bac Ninh (Figure 13.5). The percentage of community-exogamous marriages with the husbands moving to their wives' communities was also more than twice as high in the South as in the Center and the North. This difference reflects the more open sociocultural landscape and the greater spatial mobility in the Mekong Delta in the South, in comparison to that in the northern delta and in the central coast.

From a diachronic perspective, the endogamy rate in the northern village in Bac Ninh was relatively stable for different cohorts over the past eighty years, except for a significant drop in the 1966–75 period due to the impact of war (see Mai 2004). The endogamy rate in the two central communes in Quang Ngai dropped from over 60 percent in the 1956–95 period to under 30 percent for the 1996–2000 cohort, as the proportion of couples born entirely outside the studied communities increased to almost 20 percent for this young cohort. Similarly, in the two southern communities in Long An province, the endogamy rate dropped from about 40 percent in 1956–95 to 20 percent in 1996–2000, as the proportion of couples born entirely outside the studied community also reached almost 20 percent.

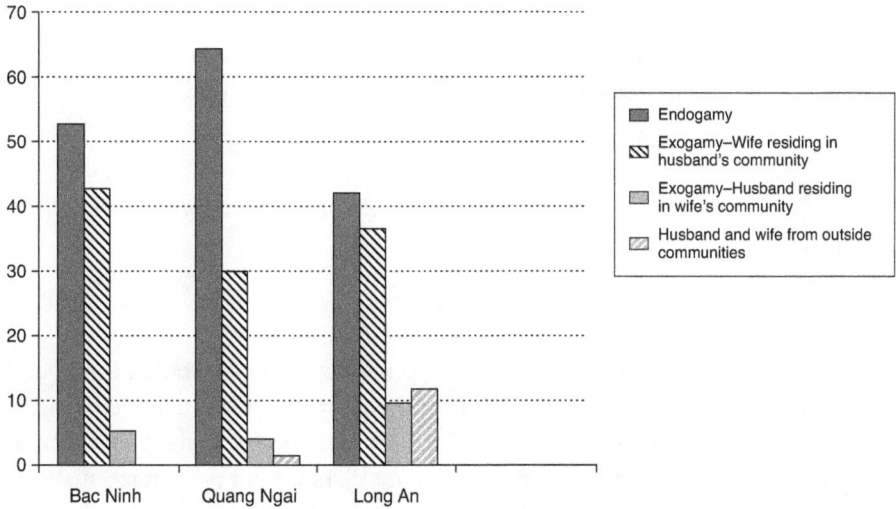

Figure 13.5 Community endogamy and exogamy in three regions (%).

Although household structure and postmarital residence were not significantly different across the three main regions of the Vietnamese lowlands, in the context of the significant regional variation in community exogamy, *intrahousehold* heterogeneity in members' birthplaces was generally greater in the rural South than in the countryside of the Center and the North. Given household members' greater birthplace diversity, the *interhousehold* networks of individual households in the South also more likely extended beyond local communities, in comparison to those in the Center and the North. The considerably higher interhousehold income transfers[12] in the two studied southern communities (6 to 8 percent of total incomes in all the study households in the South versus 1 percent in the Center and North; see Table 13.2) came mainly from relatives in other households, many of whom, as urban residents, had more opportunities for high-income-generating activities. The other side of this phenomenon is the lesser intracommunity assistance in the two studied southern communities, as reflected in the lower percentage of interest-free loans (see Table 13.3).

The more open social landscape and the lesser intracommunity assistance in the Mekong Delta communities in the South than in Red River Delta villages in the North or central coastal communities relate systematically to the regional variation in migration into and out of those communities and the relative importance of household structure in migration.

Household Structure, Postmarital Residence, Interhousehold Networks, and Dynamics of Migration

IN-MIGRATION

Studies of rural migration tend to focus mainly on out-migration from rural communities. However, 17.7 percent of the 1,457 people still considered members of the 300 households in the southern province of Long An were born outside the two studied communes (Figure 13.6). Of this percentage, male in-migrants constituted one-third (33 percent), and women, two-thirds (67 percent). In the two Quang Ngai communes, in-migrants made up only 9.1 percent of all household members (20 percent male and 80 percent female). In the northern community in Bac Ninh province, in-migrants made up 12.4 percent (11 percent male and 89 percent female). As mentioned earlier, the percentage of in-migrants was higher in Bac Ninh than in the two studied Quang Ngai communities partly because given its considerably smaller population and very tight kinship networks, many residents of this northern community were concerned about their children marrying fairly close relatives within the village. The percentage of in-migrants was highest in the two southern communities, which reflects the more open and centrifugal landscape in the Mekong Delta than in the Red River Delta and along the central coast.

In all three regions, females migrated much more into the studied communities than males due to the prevalence of patrilocal residence, although there also existed a regional gender difference in in-migration: men made up almost one-third of the in-migrants in the two studied communities in the southern province of Long An, slightly less than one-fifth of those in Quang Ngai, and only 11 percent of those in Bac Ninh. The percentage of male in-migrants was considerably lower in the Center and the North because fewer men moved to their wives' communities there and because few born-elsewhere couples moved into studied communities in the Center and the North (see Figure 13.5). In other words, the gender difference in in-migration among the three regions of Vietnamese lowlands is rooted in the Mekong Delta phenomena of

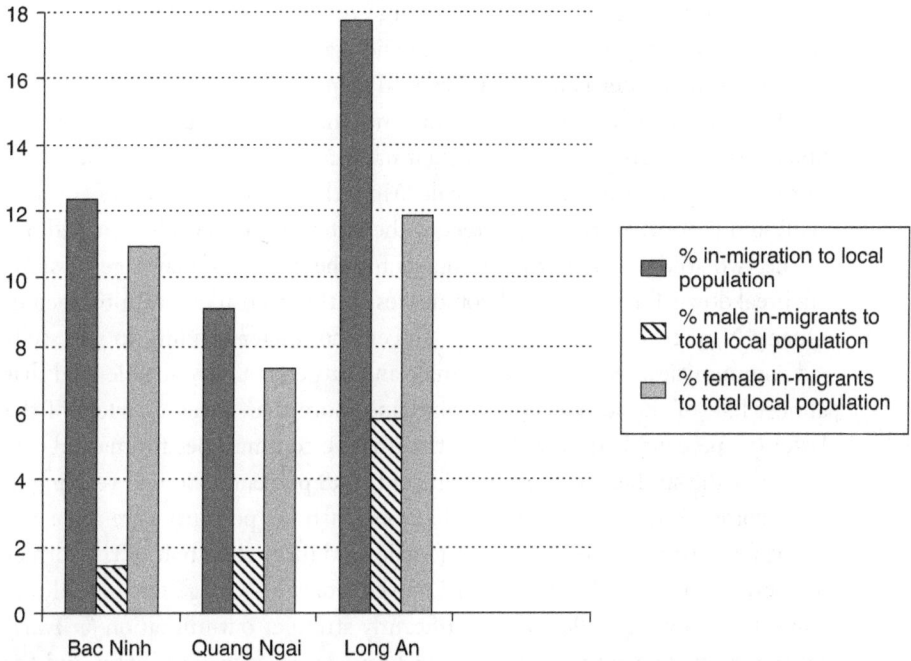

Figure 13.6 Percentages of in-migrants to total local population in three regions.

husbands moving more often into wives' communities and of both spouses moving in from elsewhere, which reflects the more open social landscape of Mekong Delta villages. In-migration clearly relates to regionally diverse sociocultural dynamics of community-mediated household formation.

OUT-MIGRATION

*Out-Migration Among Villagers Having
Moved Out of Their Natal Households*

The available data suggest a similar trend of greater out-migration of women for marital reasons, especially in the southern province of Long An. Of the 334 people in Long An, 141 people in Quang Ngai, and 260 people in Bac Ninh who had moved on a long-term basis out of the studied households in each region from 1940 to 2000, respectively 58 percent, 47 percent, and 38 percent no longer resided in their native communities.[13] I would suggest that the lower percentages of out-migration in Quang Ngai and Bac Ninh reflect the stronger trend toward community endogamy and the stronger centripetal forces in northern and central coastal communities.

Of the 58 percent of the people who, once moving out of sampled Long An households, had also moved out of their natal communities, exactly one-third were male and two-thirds were female. More than half of the former (53 percent) and more than three-quarters of the latter (80 percent) had moved out of the two studied southern communes for the reason of marriage. A similar breakdown for the studied communes in the central coastal province of Quang Ngai reveals that of the 47 percent no longer residing in the studied communities, 28 percent were male and 72 percent were female, and that almost half of the former (46 percent) and more than three-quarters of the latter (77 percent) had moved from their native communities for marital reasons. For the studied northern village, of the 38 percent no longer residing in their communities, slightly more than one-fifth (21 percent) were male and about four-fifths (79 percent) were female, and more than half of the former (63 percent) and all of the latter had moved from this village for marital reasons. Those figures reflect the significantly stronger out-migration *for marital reasons* in the southern province of Long An than in the Center and the North—and among women than among men. More specifically, of all the people having moved out of the study households, 41 percent in Long An (24 percent of the total being male and 76 percent female) had left their communities for marital reasons, while the corresponding figures for Quang Ngai and Bac Ninh are 32 percent (19 percent of the total being male and 81 percent female) and 35 percent (14 percent of the total being male and 86 percent female), respectively. The stronger tendency for out-migration for marital reasons among women than among men is underlain by the dominance of patrilocal residential patterns among Vietnamese. And the stronger tendency for out-migration for marital reasons in Long An reflects the regionally specific pattern of stronger community exogamy in the Mekong Delta of southern Vietnam.

Out-Migration Among Villagers Still Considered Members of the Studied Households

As discussed earlier, households include the migrants who are still considered an integral part of the unit by other members and who normally contribute to the household budget through remittances. The disproportionate out-migration of women for marital reasons among *those having moved out of their*

TABLE 13.5
Out-migration among villagers still considered members of sampled households

Community	All Migrants			Migrants resettled in home villages	
	Total	Male	Female	Male	Female
Bac Ninh	202	173	29	110	15
(% of migrants)	(100%)	(86%)	(14%)	(54%)	(7%)
Quang Ngai	263	157	106	42	38
(% of migrants)	(100%)	(60%)	(40%)	(16%)	(14%)
Long An	322	188	134	56	24
(% of migrants)	(100%)	(58%)	(42%)	(17%)	(7%)
Total	787	518	269	208	77
(% of all migrants)	(100%)	(66%)	(34%)	(26%)	(10%)

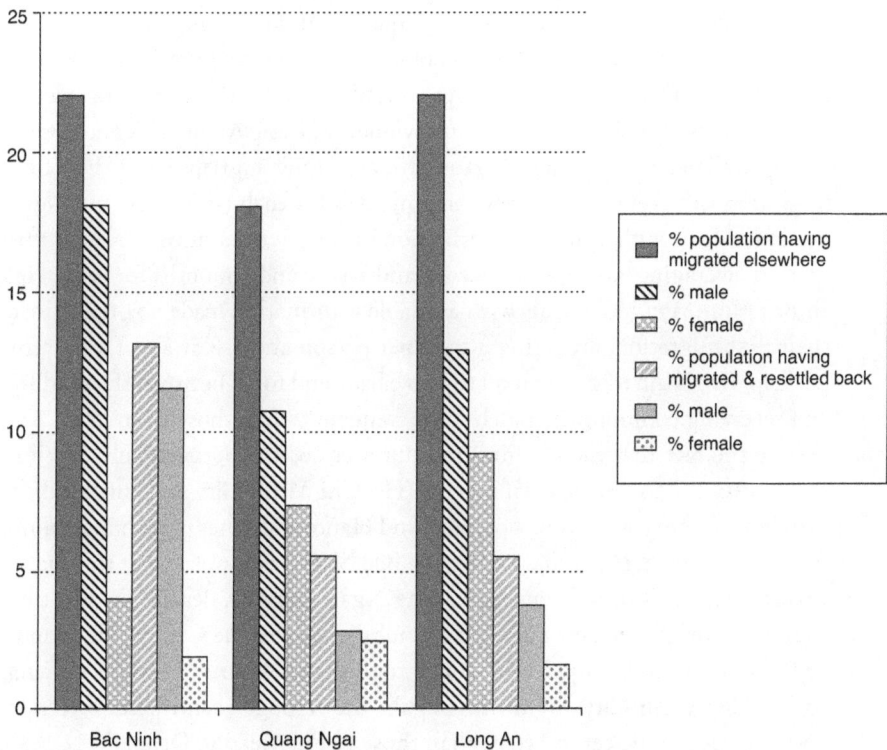

Figure 13.7 Out-migration over the years of current household members by region and gender and percentage of migrants having resettled in home communities by region and gender.

natal households is balanced by the greater out-migration of men among *people who were still considered members of the study households*, as seen in Table 13.5 and Figure 13.7. Among the people still considered members of the studied households, male preponderance in out-migration was greater in the North (86 percent) than in the Center (60 percent) and the South (58 percent).

As a reflection of the stronger centripetal forces in the North, 62 percent of the *current* household members in Bac Ninh who had ever migrated had resettled in their village by the time of the household survey in 2000. The corresponding figures for the studied communities in the central coastal province of Quang Ngai and in the southern province of Long An are 30 percent and 25 percent, respectively.

The regional difference in centripetal forces at the community level is also reflected in the duration and frequency of migration trips among migrants in the three regions (Figure 13.8). Migrants from Quang Ngai and especially from Bac Ninh tended to make more frequent and shorter migration trips, indicating an overall stronger attachment to their home communities and more temporary residence in the receiving communities. Of those still considered integral parts of their families, 306 individuals in Long An on which information is available made a total of 430 trips, averaging 1.4 trips since their first migration and averaging 2 years and 7 months for each trip. In Quang Ngai, 250 individuals with available information made 417 trips since their first migration, averaging 1.6 trips per person and 1 year and 5 months for each trip. In Bac Ninh, 177 individuals with available information made 702 trips since their first migration, averaging 4 trips per person and 1 year and 1.4 months per trip. Bac Ninh migrants tend to move back and forth between the sending and receiving communities much more frequently than those from Long An, despite the fact that the sending communities are *all* approximately 30 kilometers from the main receiving areas (Ho Chi Minh City and surrounding provinces for migrants from Long An, and Hanoi and other parts of Bac Ninh for migrants from the studied village in Bac Ninh; see Appendix at the end of this chapter). It is significant that Quang Ngai migrants, despite the fact that they generally had to cover a much greater distance to the Central Highlands or to Ho Chi Minh City, made shorter trips than Long An migrants moving to Ho Chi Minh City, confirming again the stronger centripetal forces of communities in the central coast than those in the Mekong Delta.

To explain some of the differences among Long An, Quang Ngai, and Bac Ninh migrants, I suggest that we need to ground our analyses of migration in the social processes at *both* the household and the community levels. An analy-

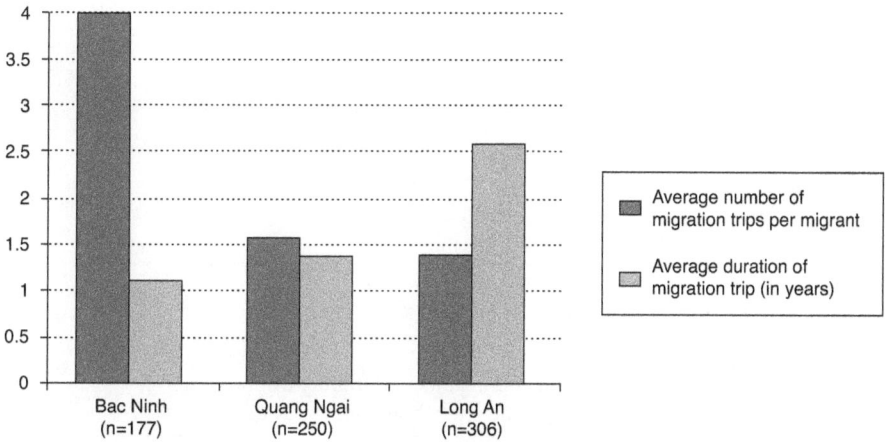

Figure 13.8   Divergent patterns of migration in three main regions of Vietnamese lowlands.

sis of the factors at work at the household level reveals significant differences between Long An, Quang Ngai, and Bac Ninh in the dynamics of migration.

Household-level regression analyses for Long An (n = 300) suggest that the two most significant independent variables are household structure (excluding physically absent migrants) and the level of household debts. As the household becomes a joint family, and the higher the level of household debts is, the larger the number of migrants that household counts. These two variables combined have a correlation coefficient of .27 to the number of migrants and account for 7 percent of the variation in the latter.

For Quang Ngai (n = 300), the three most significant variables accounting for the number of migrants in 2000 are the amount of household transfers and remittances received per capita, the amount of cultivable land per capita, and the number of migrants from the same household before 2000.[14] More specifically, the more a household received in remittances from migrating household members and in transfers from other households, the less culti-vable land per capita and the more pre-2000 migrants a household had, the more migrants that household counts in 2000. Those three variables combined have a correlation coefficient of .47 with the number of migrants in 2000, and they account for 22 percent of the variation in the latter.

For the studied village in the northern province of Bac Ninh (n = 208), the only factor that relates to the number of migrants in a household in the six months before the 2000 study is the number of migrants from the same

TABLE 13.6
Regression Analysis of Migration among Sampled Long An Households in 2000

	R	R square
Predictor: Joint household structure	.222	.049
Predictors: Joint household structure + level of debts	.272	.074

TABLE 13.7
Correlation coefficients with number of migrants
from the study household in 2000

Independent variable	Partial correlation	Level of significance
Joint household structure	.222	.000
Level of household debts	.166	.001

household before 2000. More specifically, the higher the number of migrants from the same household had been before 2000, the more likely that household would be to have more migrants in 2000. This factor alone has a correlation coefficient of .64 with the number of migrants in 2000, and accounts for 41 percent of the variation in the latter. This result is congruent with the finding from the only other multivariate analysis of data from the Red River Delta that "family migratory experiences" constitute the most important household factor influencing rural out-migration (Dang 2001, 64–66; see also Truong Huyen Chi in this volume; Tessier 2002).[15]

Statistical figures suggest, first of all, that there is more of a discernable structural pattern in the migration from the northern village in Bac Ninh than that from the two studied central coastal communities in Quang Ngai, and more from those two regions than from Long An: one variable alone has a strong correlation coefficient of .64 to the number of migrants among Bac Ninh households; three of the examined variables have a fairly strong and combined correlation of .47 to the number of migrants among Quang Ngai households; while the two most important independent variables have a combined correlation of only .27 among Long An households. More specifically, in Long An, migration in 2000 tended to take place in joint households

TABLE 13.8
Regression analysis of migration
among sampled Quang Ngai households in 2000

	R	R square
Predictor: Remittance and financial assistance received from other households	.386	.149
Predictors: Remittance and financial assistance received from other households + cultivable land per capita	.427	.182
Predictors: Remittance and financial assistance received from other households + cultivable land per capita + number of migrants from same household before 2000	.470	.221

TABLE 13.9
Correlation coefficients with number of migrants
from the study households in 2000

Independent variable	Partial correlation	Level of significance
Remittance and financial assistance received from other households	.329	.00
Cultivable land per capita	−.247	.00
Number of migrants from the same household before 2000	.217	.00

and in the context of higher levels of household debts per capita. Since Long An villagers got fewer interest-free loans and generally more debts than their Quang Ngai and Bac Ninh counterparts (Table 13.3), the debt *and* interest payments exerted a stronger pressure on prospective Long An migrants and their family members, as they faced decisions about how to improve their household welfare. Other things being equal, joint households also tended to have more household members leaving in 2000 for a number of related reasons. First, in joint families and three-generation households, the most senior member was typically in the forty-five to sixty-nine age range. Such a household typically had a few members in the fifteen to thirty-four age range (the prime age for migration), plus one or more small children. Second, considering that virtually all sampled households in Long An with members departing in 2000 owned agricultural land, and that the number of labor days invested in each hectare of land was relatively low (100 labor days per hectare), ceteris paribus, there was generally more surplus of active labor in joint family households than in nuclear families.[16] The joint family and three-generation household 273, for example, included a senior couple in the forty-five to forty-nine age range, one daughter (twenty-seven years old), one son (twenty-four years old), a daughter-in-law (twenty-two years old), and a small grandchild. In 2000, the two children migrated elsewhere for work, leaving behind the senior couple and the daughter-in-law to take care of 0.4 hectare of land and the grandchild, a situation similar to that described by Chi's ethnographic study (in this volume), though hers applied to a Red River Delta household. I suggest that the generally larger labor surplus in joint households, other things being equal, underlies the statistically significant correlation of joint household structure and the number of migrants in the two Long An villages.

However, a systematic analysis of the in-depth interviews with year 2000 migrants to Ho Chi Minh City and/or their family members in Long An indicates a powerful pattern at work that is not captured in large-scale surveys. All but one migrant relied heavily on their social network (mostly on close kinship ties) to secure employment in Ho Chi Minh City at the time when they decided to migrate (see Dang 2001, 179–192; Lomnitz 1977).

The migrants from Long An in 2000 all had good social networks in Ho Chi Minh City, partly because of the wider social networks in the South generally due to more prevalent community exogamy, and partly due to the fact that during the Vietnamese-American War, numerous villagers from the two studied Long An communities moved to Ho Chi Minh City to escape the fighting in the countryside. Many returned to their home villages in 1975, but many others stayed on in Ho Chi Minh City. The stronger tendency among southern Vietnamese villagers, in comparison to northern and central peasants, to marry people outside their home villages also widened their social networks, which in many cases included long-term residents of Ho Chi Minh City. Most interviewed migrants from Long An in 2000 had uncles, aunts, or cousins who had lived in Ho Chi Minh City for many decades. Those relatives and their acquaintances found work for the migrants, and the latter did not have to trudge the streets in search of employment. Among the interviewed migrants departing in 2000 and/or interviewed

households with such migrants, the only exception involved a migrant originally moving to Ho Chi Minh City as a student and finding employment
through newspaper advertisements upon graduation. The strong relations of
many Long An migrants to long-term residents in Ho Chi Minh City led
to their employment in a wide variety of occupations and in different parts
of the city. Since many Long An migrants also lived in their work quarters or in employers' housing compounds, and since some others lived with
their uncles, aunts, or close relatives having settled in Ho Chi Minh City
for decades, these migrants tended to disperse spatially and occupationally
throughout the city.

Statistical and interview data among year 2000 migrants from Quang
Ngai to Ho Chi Minh City and/or family members in home villages suggest
major differences from Long An in migration dynamics. I have suggested
earlier that the debt level of a household tended to exert a weaker pressure on
migration decisions in Quang Ngai and Bac Ninh than in Long An because
the practice of interest-free loans was much more widespread among Quang
Ngai and Bac Ninh villagers. Quang Ngai and Bac Ninh villagers had tighter
intravillage kinship networks due to higher rates of village endogamy. The
agricultural labor input in Quang Ngai (166–266 labor days per hectare)
was much higher than in Long An (92–111 labor days per hectare) as Quang
Ngai villagers had less land per capita. The members of households with less
agricultural land per capita tended to migrate more to improve their household welfare. The strong correlation of the number of migrants in 2000 with
remittances and financial assistance received by households as well as with
the number of pre-2000 migrants from the same households suggests that
Quang Ngai migrants tended to follow the footpaths of successful household
members, many of whom had sent remittances to their families.

Quang Ngai villagers' migration pattern was also related to their stronger
inward orientation and generally fewer ties to residents in Ho Chi Minh City
and many other parts of Vietnam than those of Long An villagers. Occupationally, migrants to Ho Chi Minh City tended to cluster in itinerant street
vending (selling chains, locks, knives, threads, lottery tickets), or in factory
work in a relatively small number of factories. One villager from Quang Ngai
1 village owned the Duc Thanh factory in Ho Chi Minh City and employed
numerous fellow villagers. The latter lived in or near the factory compound
and formed a stronger residential and occupational cluster than Long An migrants. Many of the remaining migrants worked as itinerant street vendors

who helped one another with trade information and shared rental living quarters. These factors led to a higher degree of occupational and residential clustering among Quang Ngai than among Long An migrants in Ho Chi Minh City. Data are not available at this point to determine whether a similar pattern of clustering existed among Quang Ngai migrants to the Central Highlands and the southern central coast. The greatest degree of occupational clustering took place among Bac Ninh migrants to Hanoi: about 85 percent of migrants from the northern village of Hoai Thi, most of whom were male, worked in the construction industry. This pattern of occupational clustering among Bac Ninh migrants is also found among rural migrants from other parts of the Red River Delta in Hanoi (see Truong Huyen Chi, this volume; Digregorio 1994; Li 1996). The stronger centripetal forces of northern and central coastal communities thus powerfully shaped the social and occupational clustering of their members as migrants in urban contexts.

In conclusion, on one level, household structure and postmarital residence patterns are not significantly dissimilar across the five studied rural communities in the three major regions of the Vietnamese lowlands. However, as mediated by the differences in community dynamics and specifically by the stronger centripetal forces of northern and central coastal communities, household structure relates systematically to migration flows into and out of the studied sites in the three regions. I suggest that the stronger migration into and from the studied Long An villages reflects the stronger community exogamy in the household formation process and the long-standing and more open nature of southern villages in general. I also suggest that the lesser mutual assistance among Long An villagers, as well as the wider extension of their social and kinship networks to include many Ho Chi Minh City residents, drives the migration of many villagers in debt-ridden households to Ho Chi Minh City, and Long An migrants' occupational and residential scattering throughout the city. The weaker migration to and from Quang Ngai and Bac Ninh villages reflects villagers' stronger inward orientation and more narrow networks to the outside world. With generally smaller social networks outside their home villages, Quang Ngai and Bac Ninh villagers tend to follow the lead established by a few pioneer migrants and cluster much more occupationally in the receiving areas. I suggest that the analysis of migration in Vietnam will be strengthened and enriched by greater attention to *local* sociocultural dynamics in household formation and interhousehold network characteristics.

Appendix

TABLE 13.10
Current places of residence of migrants
not yet resettled in home communities (%)

	Long An	Quang Ngai	Bac Ninh
Northern Highlands	0.0	0.0	13.0
Hanoi	0.0	0.0	60.0
Rest of Red River Delta	0.0	0.0	14.0
South central coast	0.4	23.0	1.0
Central Highlands	0.0	20.0	0.0
Ho Chi Minh City	83.0	42.0	3.0
Rest of southeast	7.0	13.0	3.0
Mekong Delta	9.0	0.0	0.0
Other	0.4	2.0	1.0
Unknown	0.0	0.0	5.0
Total	100.0	100.0	100.0
Number of households	234	181	77

Acknowledgments

Research in northern Vietnam was funded by the Social Sciences and Humanities Research Council of Canada, and that in Central and South Vietnam, by the Ford Foundation. I am also grateful to fellow research team members and the members of the five studied communities for their collaboration, and to Danièle Bélanger and Magali Barbieri for their comments on an earlier version of this chapter.

Notes

1. To minimize confusion among readers less familiar with Vietnamese names, I refer to the two Mekong Delta communities (My Le and Long Son) as Long An 1 and Long An 2, and to the two Central Vietnamese communities (Tinh Minh and Tinh Binh) as Quang Ngai 1 and Quang Ngai 2. The northern village of Hoai Thi in Bac Ninh province is referred to simply as the studied northern village or the Bac Ninh village.

2. Of the three sites, one is in the inner-city core that became urban in the nineteenth century; the second was urbanized mainly in the 1950s with the influx

of northern migrants to the South in 1954; and the third, officially a commune in 1999, was rapidly urbanizing in the 1990s. The population of this commune dramatically increased from about 13,000 in 1993 to at least 77,000 one decade later. In 2003, this "commune" was divided into three urban wards (see Luong 2005).

3. A list of Quang Ngai and Long An migrants residing in Ho Chi Minh City was compiled from the survey of three hundred households in each province. We subsequently asked their relatives at home for their contact addresses (including workplace addresses) in Ho Chi Minh City and found seventy-two of them for interviews. Relatives at home did not always have exact addresses of migrants. The search for migrants was also complicated by the chaotic address number system in rapidly urbanizing areas of Ho Chi Minh City where a large number of migrants tended to live. It was easier to find Bac Ninh migrants to Hanoi for interviews because, due to the proximity of their home village to Hanoi, virtually all of them returned home for the Vietnamese New Year.

4. The number of household members migrating before the year 2000 and household members' social networks in the possible destination areas are conceptually distinct in my model. The former includes not only household members still residing in possible destination areas, but also household members having resettled for a long term in their home communities (thus no longer in the possible destination areas). The latter includes relatives and acquaintances *other than household members* in the possible destination areas at the time of migration decision.

5. Children five years old or below and elderly eighty years old or above are weighed twice as heavy as the remaining children and elderly in the calculation of dependent care.

6. The data from Long An and Quang Ngai come from a collaborative project based at the Institute of Social Sciences in Ho Chi Minh City in which the funding for fieldwork from the Ford Foundation was channeled through this institute, and research plans were negotiated between Vietnamese and international partners. Social network data are available for all households in the northern village in Bac Ninh province because research funding was channeled through the University of Toronto, and thus I had more input into research plan formulation.

7. An extended family includes a nuclear family and one or more members who do not form another nuclear family. An example would be a nuclear family plus the husband's father. A joint family is composed of two or more related nuclear families (for example, a nuclear family, plus the husband's parents which constitute another nuclear family). The percentage of nuclear families in the studied Bac Ninh village is comparable to the figures of 70 percent and 62 percent in two northern Vietnamese communities studied by Krowolski in the 1990s (2002, 78–79).

8. Hirschman and Vu (1996, 237) lump extended and joint families into the category of extended families, but exclude from this category families with relatives other than son- or daughter-in-law or lineal ones (parent, grandparent, grand-

child). They also report a considerably higher percentage of extended families in their southern commune than in the northern one in 1991 (ibid.).

9. From a historical perspective, Mai Van Hai and Nguyen Phan Lam (2001) have suggested that at least in the case of the northern village of Dao Xa in Hai Duong province, the number of households that split up suddenly increased in 1992–93 under the impact of the anticipated land law clauses that would restrict the residential land of each household to 200 square meters and the cultivated land of each household to 3 hectares. Quite a few of those households cited that they had had larger holdings than allowed under the anticipated land law as reported in the Vietnamese press in 1992. Households with large land holdings *officially* split up, so that none would exceed the residential and/or cultivated land holding limits in the anticipated new land law. In reality, in Dao Xa, a few of the elderly who were *officially* forming single-person households and splitting off from their children's in 1992 still continued functioning as full members of their children's households. In other words, the division of many households in 1992 was simply a maneuvering on the land issue and for official purposes only. In my recalculation of Mai Van Hai and Nguyen Phan Lam's data from Dao Xa, the percentages of less-than-nuclear families, nuclear families, and extended/joint families changed from 2.4 percent, 73.6 percent, and 24 percent in 1992 to 7.6 percent, 84.7 percent, and 8.6 percent, respectively, in 1993.

However, if the same process discussed by Mai Van Hai and Nguyen Phan Lam had been operating beyond Dao Xa village in 1992–93, household division would have taken place more often in the Mekong Delta of southern Vietnam where land holdings had generally been much larger than in the Red River Delta (Dang 1995; Luong 2003). The impact of residential and agricultural land holding limits on the distribution of household forms, leading to a significant decline in extended and joint family households, would have been greater in the villages of the Mekong Delta than in those of the Red River Delta. It would not explain why the percentages of extended and joint family households were higher in the Mekong Delta than in the Red River Delta.

10. In the North and the Center, 86 percent and 89 percent, respectively, of the couples establishing their own households right after marriage settled in the studied communities, in contrast to 70 percent in the South.

11. In the studied northern population, "community" is a village (*lang* in daily discourse, or *thon* in administrative distinctions), a subunit of a commune (*xa*). Among the studied populations in the South and Center, "community" is a commune (*xa* in administrative terminology). In the studied northern population as well as in most rural localities in the Red River Delta, people identify more strongly with their villages, nucleated settlements with their distinctive ritual spaces such as communal houses and pagodas, than with communes. In the Bac Ninh commune where one village was chosen for research, each of the six villages had its own communal house,

and in most cases, its own Buddhist pagoda. At the opposite end of the spectrum, in the two studied populations in the Mekong Delta, subunits (*ap*) of communes were dispersed settlements, without their distinctive ritual spaces, and without strongly articulated identities. In Long An 1 commune, for example, eleven subunits (*ap*) shared three communal houses, six Buddhist pagodas, two Cao Dai temples, and one Catholic church, while in Long An 2 commune, six subunits (*ap*) shared two communal houses and three pagodas. In Quang Ngai 1 commune with four subunits (*thon*), there used to be one communal house and one pagoda drawing the community together. Both were destroyed in the intense warfare in this region. In Quang Ngai 2 commune with three subunits (*thon*), there used to be two communal houses, three pagodas, one Christian church, and one Cao Dai temple, most of which were heavily damaged during the same period and had not been renovated by the time of our research in 2000.

12. The difference between transfers and remittances is that the former is sent by individuals living elsewhere who, though they are often kin of the receivers, are no longer considered members of the same household while the latter is sent by migrants still considered members of the receiving households.

13. Sampled households were asked to provide the names of former household members who had moved out (normally siblings, children, but occasionally also nieces, nephews, and former spouses), as well as those members' current places of residence and relations to current household heads, among other information.

14. The fact that the number of household members migrating before 2000 significantly account for the number of migrants in a household in 2000 *only* in Bac Ninh and Quang Ngai cannot be attributed to a larger average household size in these two areas compared to Long An. Indeed, the average household size was 4.9 in Long An, 4.8 in Quang Ngai, and 4.6 in Bac Ninh at the time of the household survey. Bac Ninh and Quang Ngai households were generally not larger than Long An ones. Nor was the number of migrants per household before the year 2000 larger in Bac Ninh and Quang Ngai than in Long An.

15. Dang Nguyen Anh (2001) and colleagues present their analysis at the national level. However, the rural localities chosen for their analysis of factors influencing rural out-migration are all from the Red River Delta of northern Vietnam (Dang 2001, 44–47).

16. The number of labor days per hectare was 212 in Quang Ngai, and 394 for the two annual rice crops alone in Bac Ninh. My finding on the impact of household structure here is congruent with that from the only other systematic analysis of out-migration from Mekong delta localities (specifically also from Long An province) that suggests a fairly strong correlation between migration from a household and the number of household members (Tran and Cu 2003, 128).

References

Bélanger, D. 1997. Rapport intergenerationel et rapport hommes-femmes dans la transition demographique au Vietnam de 1930 a 1990. Unpublished doctoral dissertation in demography, Université de Montreal.

Dang Phong. 1995. Aspects of agricultural economy and rural life in 1993. In *Vietnam's rural transformation*, edited by B. J. K. Kerkvliet and D. Porter, 165–184. Boulder, CO: Westview.

Dang Nguyen Anh, ed. 2001. *Migration in Vietnam: Theoretical approaches and evidence from a survey*. Hanoi: Transport Publishing House.

Digregorio, M. R. 1994. *Urban harvest: Recycling as a peasant industry in northern Vietnam*. Honolulu: East-West Center.

Do Thai Dong. 1991. Gia dinh truyen thong va nhung bien thai o Nam bo Viet Nam (Traditional family and its transformation in southern Vietnam). In *Nhung nghien cuu xa hoi hoc ve gia dinh Viet Nam* (Sociological studies on Vietnamese family), edited by R. Liljestrom and Tuong L., 71–84. Hanoi: Nha xuat ban Khoa hoc xa hoi.

Haines, D. W. 1984. Reflections of kinship and society under Vietnam's Le Dynasty. *Journal of Southeast Asian Studies*, 15: 307–314.

Hickey, G. 1958. The problems of social change in Vietnam. *Bulletin de la Société des Études Indochinoises*, 33(4): 407–418. (new series.)

Hirschman, C., and Nguyen H. M. 2002. Tradition and change in Vietnamese family structure in the Red River Delta. *Journal of Marriage and Family*, 65: 1063–1079.

Hirschman, C., and Vu M. L. 1996. Family and household structure in Vietnam: Some glimpses from a recent survey. *Pacific Affairs*, 69: 229–249.

Krowolski, N. 2002. Village households in the Red River Delta: The case of Ta Thanh Oai, on the outskirts of the capital city, Hanoi. In *Gender, household, state: Doi Moi in Vietnam*, edited by J. Werner and D. Bélanger, 73–88. Ithaca, NY: Southeast Asia Program, Cornell University.

Li, T. 1996. *Peasants on the move: Rural-urban migration in the Hanoi region*. Singapore: Institute of Southeast Asian Studies.

Lomnitz, L. 1977. *Networks and marginality: Life in a Mexican shantytown*. New York: Academic Press.

Luong, Hy Van. 1989. Vietnamese kinship: Structural principles and the socialist transformation in twentieth-century Vietnam. *Journal of Asian Studies*, 48: 741–756.

Luong, Hy Van. 2003. Wealth, power, and inequality: Global market, the state, and local socio-cultural dynamics. In *Postwar Vietnam: Dynamics of a transforming society*, edited by H. V. Luong, 81–106. Boulder, CO: Rowman & Littlefield.

Luong, Hy Van. 2005. Thanh pho Ho Chi Minh: Van de tang truong kinh te,
di dan, va do thi hoa. (Ho Chi Minh City: Economic growth, migration, and
urbanization). In *Do thi hoa va van de giam ngheo o Thanh pho Ho Chi Minh: ly
luan va thuc tien* (Urbanization and poverty reduction in Ho Chi Minh City:
Theory and reality), edited by Nguyen The Nghia, Mac D., and Nguyen Q. V.,
165–200. Hanoi: Nha xuat ban Khoa hoc xa hoi.

Mai Van Hai. 2004. Tim hieu van hoa lang Viet vung chau tho song Hong qua su
bien doi duong ban kinh ket hon nua the ky qua. (Understanding Vietnamese
village culture in the Red River Delta through the change in the radius of
marital relations in the past half century). *Tap chi Xa hoi hoc*, 2004(1): 51–59.

Mai Van Hai and Nguyen, P. L. 2001. Luat dat dai va tac dong ban dau toi co cau
gia dinh o mot lang chau tho song Hong. (Land law and its initial impact on
family structure in a Red River Delta village). *Tap chi Xa hoi hoc*, 2001(1): 40–45.

Nguyen Huu Minh. 1998. Tradition and change in the Vietnamese marriage patterns in the Red River Delta. Unpublished Ph.D. dissertation in Sociology,
University of Washington.

Nguyen Quang Vinh, Phan V. D., Nguyen T. S., and Nguyen Q. 2005. "Kinh
nghiem van dung cac phuong phap nghien cuu khoa hoc xa hoi trong tiep can
lien nganh ve ngheo do thi" (Experiences in the use of social science methods in
an interdisciplinary approach to urban poverty). In *Do thi hoa va van de giam ngheo
o Thanh pho Ho Chi Minh: ly luan va thuc tien* (Urbanization and poverty reduction in Ho Chi Minh City: Theory and reality), edited by Nguyen The Nghia,
Mac D., and Nguyen Q. V., 201–232. Hanoi: Nha xuat ban Khoa hoc xa hoi.

Population and Housing Census Steering Committee. 2000. *Dan so Thanh pho Ho
Chi Minh: Ket qua tong dieu tra ngay 01-04-1999.* Ho Chi Minh City: Population
and Housing Census Steering Committee.

Tessier, O. 2002. Ra di de cai thien cuoc song va tinh cam gan bo voi lang que
(Departure for better life and attachment to the village). In *Lang o vung chau
tho song Hong: Van de con bo ngo* (The village in Red River Delta: Open questions), edited by P. Papin and O. Tessier, 619–661. Hanoi: Trung tam khoa hoc
xa hoi va nhan van quoc gia & École française d'Extrême-Orient.

Tran Thi Thanh Thuy and Cu D. T. 2003. Nhung tac nhan anh huong den
viec roi khoi Can Giuoc (Factors influencing departures from Can Giuoc).
In *Nhung con duong ve thanh pho: Di dan den thanh pho Ho Chi Minh tu mot vung
Dong bang song Cuu Long* (City-bound roads: Migration to Ho Chi Minh City
from a region in the Mekong Delta), edited by Vu T. H., P. Gubry, and Le
V. T., pp. 125–129. Ho Chi Minh City: Nha xuat ban thanh pho Ho Chi Minh.

Afterword

MAGALI BARBIERI AND DANIÈLE BÉLANGER

Our purpose in this volume was to document and analyze family dynamics in Vietnam in the particular context of the socialism-to-market transition. This collection underscores the relations between macrolevel economic and political changes on the one hand, and microlevel adaptations and strategies on the other. It more particularly focuses on the links between institutional, economic, and family changes in socialist societies undergoing major restructuring. Indeed, by contrast with other rapidly developing populations, such societies have experienced under communist rule several decades of policies specifically designed to "modernize" families. Collectivization of industries and agriculture, the rapid expansion of public services for education, health, and housing in particular, as well as a series of laws and regulations specifically designed to erode parental authority and to improve women's social position have weakened the previous structure and basis of family power. In these countries, families have been transformed as much, if not more, as some would argue (Davis and Harrell 1993, 6), by state authority than by economic modernization and urbanization from the 1950s to the 1970s. This situation has given rise to a debate regarding the respective roles of "tradition-restoring" and "modernizing" forces in explaining current family change (Whyte 1992). The chapters in this volume have sought to move beyond this debate by investigating interactions between deeply grounded cultural forces, muted during the socialist era and revived in a context of social opening, and rational adaptation strategies to the new social and economic order. Through a process of selective revival, families have looked into their toolbox of traditional practices to choose the mechanisms most deemed to facilitate their integration into the market system and to mediate the sometimes harmful effects of the reforms. Though they widely differ in terms of the questions raised and the methods implemented to answer them, the chapters in this book combine into what we hope is a convincing argument for the profound impact of economic transition on family life. Together, the chapters underline the centrality of family strategies as a key approach to understanding social change in Vietnam. Though the overall picture they provide remains incomplete, these chapters have laid the groundwork for further research by pointing out promising avenues and identifying the remaining ambiguities of family transformations in a rapidly changing society. On the basis of their collective results, a few generalizations can be made. Many of these generalizations reiterate those made about China,[1] though marked differences exist. The comparison is particularly compelling, considering how much Vietnam has in common with its giant neighbor. Not only do both countries share a geographic border and a partly similar cultural heritage, but the Deng reforms in China and *Doi Moi* in Vietnam have restored the family basic production and welfare functions through a very similar process of economic and social reforms, after decades of communist rule and without implementing any major change in their political system.

Echoing the results of research conducted in China, the evidence gathered in this volume collectively points to the fundamental and all-encompassing transformation of Vietnamese families through an ongoing process of adjustment. In both countries, the reforms have led to a reconfiguration of the relations between the state and other public agents, on the one hand, and the family, on the other. At the same time, and quite paradoxically, government control over one particularly private area of family life, namely reproduction, has been reinforced with the one-or-two-child fertility policy (see Scornet's chapter). The new contract has resulted in a reorientation of family livelihood strategies and a shift in the distribution of power between individuals within families and between all social institutions. The chapters by Oudin and by Luong show how, in order to maximize resources and minimize risks in an economic context of growing opportunities and increasing uncertainty, families are diversifying their sources of income and the life-course trajectories of their members, especially in rural areas where everyone in the household is asked to contribute, be it women or men, children or older adults. The psychological cost of this strategy is high, as indicated by Chi's chapter as well as by that of Bélanger and Pendakis who focus on the contradictions experienced by women, men, the young, and the old in their family relations and their difficulties in reconciling economic expectations with moral obligations.

Extended family ties and kinship networks have been reinvigorated by the transition, with an increasing reliance on distant relatives living at home or abroad as well as on current or former village acquaintances to serve as matchmakers (see Thai's chapter), to provide start-up capital for household businesses, to secure access to work and lodging for migrants (see Luong's chapter), or to share the burden of increasing schooling or medical expenses (see Deolalikar's chapter and de Loenzien's).[2]

Many of the transformations reported in this volume appear to support classic modernization theories of family change: parental control over children's occupational trajectories as well as courtship and mate selection is weakening,[3] a sign of which is the continuous increase in the age at first marriage (see Jayakody and Huy's chapter and Xenos et al.'s); young adults leave home ever earlier to seize new economic opportunities ever farther away from their immediate families (see Xenos et al.'s chapter and Barbieri's); women are becoming more assertive and their economic contributions to the household income are increasing, particularly in urban areas[4] (see Bélanger and Pendakis's chapter and Teerawichitchainan's).

However, one would do well not to overlook other signs pointing to the resilience of the family institution in these countries. Feelings of moral obligation toward one's parents, children, and mates remain strong, even when the lure of new economic opportunities entails prolonged separation of family members. Single young women employed in the cities' mushrooming factories send remittances to their parents (see Bélanger and Pendakis's chapter).[5] Young adults in general continue to seek out parental approval before they marry or make other major life decisions (see Jayakody and Huy's chapter),[6] partly out of moral obligation but probably also, as has been demonstrated in urban China (Unger 1993, 38), because they need help from their parents to set up a new home. As indicated by the very high proportion of elderly people living with their adult children's families and the intense flow of goods and exchanges of services, very few Vietnamese challenge the traditional support they are expected to provide to their ageing parents (see Barbieri's chapter),[7] a behavior that cannot be explained by expected inheritance, given the still limited extent of private land and housing ownership. More generally, increasing economic uncertainty and the disintegration of the public welfare system have resulted in a growing reliance on the family in situations of hardship (see Deolalikar's chapter and de Loenzien's).[8]

There are some indications of instructive differences between China and Vietnam in the family realm. A significant one is a seemingly stronger and continuous preference for sons in China. Son preference was exacerbated in the early postreform period, in part due to the only-daughter exception, which allowed parents whose first child was female to have a second child (Davis 1993). Recent evidence on China, however, points to a juxtaposition of a strong desire for sons, as indicated by the sex-selection of children resulting in a deficit of girls (Attané and Guilmoto 2007), and the relatively high status of singleton daughters (Fong 2004) and of daughters in sonless families (Greenhalgh and Winckler 2005; Xu 2006). In Vietnam, evidence of son preference exists (Bélanger 2002), but the phenomenon is, so far, weaker than in China and only recently have sex ratios at birth started indicating that some girls are missing. These phenomena suggest a lower status of women in China than in Vietnam.

Another sign of the higher status of women in Vietnam compared with China is the diverging trend in the female age at first marriage between the two countries. In China, the female age at first marriage declined immediately following the reforms, which has been interpreted as reflecting a strengthening of parents' control over their daughters (Whyte 1993), while in Vietnam, the female age at first marriage has increased continuously and significantly in a similar socioeconomic context (see Jayakody and Huy's chapter and Xenos et al.'s; as compared with Selden 1993 for China). Also, a higher proportion of older adults live with a daughter rather than a son in Vietnam, even when children of both sexes are available (see Barbieri's chapter), a more unusual situation in China when a son is alive (Xie and Zhu 2006). Another sign is the relative degree of power single Vietnamese women have over their wages compared with Chinese single women (Harrell 1993). For instance, in Bélanger and Pendakis's study, none of the single young women moving to the cities to seek work in textile factories have been pressured to do so by their parents (for partial evidence of the contrary in China, see Lee 1998). The very low fertility achieved in Vietnam in spite of a much less coercive family planning program than in China (see Scornet's chapter) also suggests that the prospect of an only daughter is insufficient to preclude couples from implementing a reproductive strategy designed to improve investment in children and increase their chances of upward social and economic mobility. These observations reinforce the idea that the Vietnamese "versions" of the Confucian family differ from the Chinese "versions." The chapters of this book, set against the backdrop of research on Chinese families, remind us that the Confucian family has many facets and cannot be approached as one universal and monolithic set of norms, rules, and relationships. Power between genders and generations exists in various combinations and degrees that indicate both the commonalities and important differences not only between families of the two countries but also within them.

Given the findings of this volume and the literature on other transitional societies, how are Vietnamese families likely to evolve in the near future? What, for instance, will be the long-term effect of current demographic trends, with a level of fertility now below replacement and an increasing proportion of older adults living longer lives? Will shrinking family size result in stronger son preference, as is apparently the case in parts of China, or will it improve women's circumstances and the reliance on daughters, as suggested by current research in Vietnam? What will be the consequences of accelerating migration trends? Will the independence gained by young adults separated from their immediate family lead them to contest parental supervision and to default on their responsibilities toward ageing parents, or will the increasing needs of the elderly and the lack of public institutions only reinforce the intergenerational contract, with children honoring their moral obligations toward their ageing parents? Will further socioeconomic growth and fertility decline sustain the high labor force participation of women in Vietnam, or will they reduce the need for women's work and result in a return of women to the household with the expectation that they will perform all household chores and care for the young and the old, as in the more developed countries of East Asia and parts of China (Entwisle et al. 1995)? All of these are possible. A large part will depend on two major factors, namely the continuing success of economic development and future government policies regarding the provision of services and benefits, with respect to social security and elderly care in particular. The one assertion that we feel confident to make is that the open-door policy initiated twenty years ago has so successfully propelled families to the forefront of the economic and social stages that we are convinced that this adaptation process is irreversible and that further changes, or the acceleration of current transformations, are only to be expected from the rapid economic, social, and cultural modernization under way in Vietnam. The changes have swept through all parts of Vietnam, from the North, to the Center, and to the South, and in rural and urban areas alike. Some of the research presented here (see Luong's chapter in particular) underlines the role of local circumstances in shaping Vietnam's new families. It emphasizes the need for further investigation of the diversity of family forms and organizations across regions and among ethnic and social groups within the country. What the contributions to this volume collectively suggest is that, first, we should expect a diversification of families in Vietnam and, second, no unilineal trend is to be counted upon. The increasing availability of large survey datasets and the growing opportunities to conduct social science research, including ethnographic fieldwork, for Vietnamese and foreign researchers should facilitate future studies of Vietnamese families in relation to social and economic change and help explore some of the avenues opened by this volume.

Notes

1. Due to the sheer size of the country, generalizations about Chinese families are necessarily somewhat exaggerated, all the more so because of the lack of a recent overview specifically identifying common features and regional variations within China. We are fully aware that every statement we make about Chinese family change can be countered by the opposite statement based on one of the many small-scale studies published during the past couple of decades. However, we do believe that an examination of the literature has enabled us to make a number of relevant parallels between China and Vietnam with regard to their family transformations in this era of economic reforms.

2. Johnson 1993, for China.

3. Unger 1993, 37, and Whyte 1992, 318, for China.

4. Whyte 1992, 318, for China.

5. Whyte 1992, 321, for China.

6. Johnson 1993, 118, for China.

7. Unger 1993, 40–42, and Logan, Bian, and Bian 1998, for China.

8. For China, see Croll 1999.

References

Attané, I., and C. Z. Guilmoto. 2007. *Watering the neighbour's garden : The growing demographic female deficit in Asia.* Paris : Cicred.

Bélanger, D. 2002. Son preference in a rural village in North Vietnam. *Studies in Family Planning*, 33(4): 321–334.

Croll, E. J. 1999. Social welfare reform: Trends and tensions. *The China Quarterly*, 159: 684–699.

Davis, D. 1993. Urban households: Supplicants to a socialist state. In *Chinese families in the post-Mao era*, edited by D. Davis and S. Harrell, 50–76. Berkeley: The University of California Press.

Davis, D., and S. Harrell. 1993. Introduction: The impact of post-Mao reforms on family life. In *Chinese families in the post-Mao era*, edited by D. Davis and S. Harrell: 1–22. Berkeley: The University of California Press.

Entwisle, B., G. E. Henderson, S. E. Short, J. Bouma, and Z. Fengying. 1995. Gender and family businesses in rural China. *American Sociological Review*, 60(1): 36–57.

Fong, V. 2004. *Only hope: Coming of age under China's one-child policy.* Stanford, CA: Stanford University Press.

Greenhalgh, S., and E. A. Winckler. 2005. *Governing China's population. from Leninist to neoliberal biopolitics.* Stanford, CA: Stanford University Press.

Harrell, S. 1993. Geography, demography, and family composition in three southwestern villages. In *Chinese families in the post-Mao era*, edited by D. Davis and S. Harrell, 77–102. Berkeley: The University of California Press.

Johnson, G. E. 1993. Family strategies and economic transformation in rural China: Some evidence from the Pearl River delta. In *Chinese families in the post-Mao era*, edited by D. Davis and S. Harrell, 103–136. Berkeley: The University of California Press.

Lee, C. K. 1998. *Gender and the South China miracle: Two worlds of factory women.* Berkeley: The University of California Press.

Logan, J. R., F. Bian, and Y. Bian. 1998. Tradition and change in the urban Chinese family: The case of living arrangements. *Social Forces*, 76(3): 851–882.

Selden, M. 1993. Family strategies and structures in rural North China. In *Chinese families in the post-Mao era*, edited by D. Davis and S. Harrell, 139–164. Berkeley: The University of California Press.

Unger, J. 1993. Urban families in the eighties: An analysis of Chinese surveys. In *Chinese families in the post-Mao era*, edited by D. Davis and S. Harrell, 25–49. Berkeley: The University of California Press.

Whyte, M. K. 1992. Introduction: Rural economic reforms and Chinese family patterns. *The China Quarterly*, 130: 317–322.

Whyte, M. K. 1993. Wedding behavior and family strategies in Chengdu. In *Chinese families in the post-Mao era*, edited by D. Davis and S. Harrell, 189–216. Berkeley: The University of California Press.

Xie, Y., and H. Zhu. 2006. *Do sons or daughters give more money to parents? Gender and Intergenerational Support in Contemporary Urban China*. Research Report 06-607, Population Studies Center. Ann Arbor: The University of Michigan.

Xu L. 2006. *Intra-family gender relations, women's well-being, and access to resources: The case of a northern Chinese village*. Unpublished Ph.D. dissertation. Department of Sociology, The University of Western Ontario, Canada.

INDEX

Index

Wage differentials, 30, 247
Wage labor, 19, 32, 33, 266–67, 270–71,
290, 293, 303–5, 318–19, 356, 372–73,
385, 387
Wages, 30, 31, 239, 240, 243, 246–48,
250–56, 265, 270–71, 277, 281, 283,
285, 287, 316, 319, 369–73, 382, 386,
387, 424. *See also* Economy, wage
sector; Low-wage workers, and
transpacific marriage market; Wage
differentials; Wage labor
War: against Cambodia, 1, 334; elderly's
surviving children in relation to, 145,
147; family structure and, 18; female
household headship and, 334–35,
353–54; health care and, 76, 78; male
mortality in, 238, 334–35; significance
of, 1; women's employment and, 18, 31
Wealth and prosperity, 24, 59, 158, 303,
396, 398; flows, 133; household, 22,
155, 156, 158, 394
Weber, Max, 255
Weddings, 271. *See also* Rituals, wedding
Welfare state, 18, 23–24, 26–27, 336–37.
See also Solidarity
Werner, J., 18, 21–22
WHO. *See* World Health Organization
Whyte, M. K., 15
Widowhood, 137, 144, 147, 176, 340, 342
Wiegersma, N., 14
Wilder, W. D., 268–69
Withdrawal, as birth control method, 64
Wolf, D., 270–71
Women: agency of, 274–75; bodies of,
274–75; family role of, 11–12, 31–34;
as household heads, 34, 329–58;
independence, 32, 280–82, 285, 287,
292–93, 315; roles of, 12, 31, 267, 269,
282, 291–93, 300, 317, 320, 323, 334,
338, 340, 347, 349; socialism and the
status of, 335–36; social role of, 19;
status of, 335–36, 424–25; typical life
course of, 284; working, 19, 31–33,

315–20, 323, 335–36, 377–78. *See also*
Autonomy, of women; Empowerment,
of women; Factory daughters; Girls
Work: changing patterns of, in the
renovation, 365; children and, 309–15;
decision to work, 371–72, 383; in
Dong Vang village, 304–23; elderly
and, 304–9; household types and,
380*f*, 381, 382*f*, 384–85, 385*f*, 386*f*;
security of employment, 372–73,
387; solidarity systems and, 365–87;
types of employment, 384–85, 385*f*,
386*f*; women and, 19, 31–33, 315–20,
323, 335–36, 377–78; youth and, 182*t*,
190, 193. *See also* Factory daughters;
Livelihood strategies
World Bank, 81, 103, 141
World Health Organization (WHO),
81, 103

Xenos, Peter, 29–30, 90, 209, 239

Youth, 169–95; change and stability in
lives of, 170; contemporary situation
of, 169–70; density of new experiences
for, 176, 183, 184*f*, 185*f*; in *Dong
Vang* village, 309–15; economic
liberalization and, 176, 178; education
of, 174–75, 175*f*; events experienced at
home by, 187–92, 188*t*; events in life
of, 178–87, 179*t*; independence, 28,
32, 178, 309, 312; and "independence"
events, 192–94, 194*t*; institutions, 170;
mortality rates for, 173; population,
187, 197; research study concerning,
178–82, 196–98; risk behaviors, 171,
195–96; typology of events in life of,
183–87, 186*f*; urban, 221, 378. *See also*
Autonomy, of young people; Children;
Communist, Youth Union; Dating;
Home leaving; Smoking

Zhou, M., 237

East-West Center Series on

CONTEMPORARY ISSUES IN ASIA AND THE PACIFIC

Rise of the Red Engineers:
The Cultural Revolution and the Origins of China's New Class
By Joel Andreas
2009

Southeast Asia in Political Science: Theory, Region, and Qualitative Analysis
Edited by Erik Martinez Kuhonta, Dan Slater, and Tuong Vu
2008

Rising China and Asian Democratization: Socialization to "Global Culture"
in the Political Transformations of Thailand, China, and Taiwan
By Daniel C. Lynch
2006

Japan's Dual Civil Society: Members Without Advocates
By Robert Pekkanen
2006

The Fourth Circle: A Political Ecology of Sumatra's Rainforest Frontier
By John F. McCarthy
2006

Protest and Possibilities: Civil Society and Coalitions
for Political Change in Malaysia
By Meredith L. Weiss
2005

Opposing Suharto: Compromise, Resistance, and Regime Change in Indonesia
By Edward Aspinall
2005